THE

UNITY OF LAW;

AS EXHIBITED IN THE

RELATIONS OF PHYSICAL, SOCIAL, MENTAL, AND MORAL SCIENCE.

BY

H. C. CAREY.

"Variety in unity is perfection."
Old Proverb.

PHILADELPHIA:
HENRY CAREY BAIRD,
INDUSTRIAL PUBLISHER,
406 WALNUT STREET.
1872.

COLLINS, PRINTER,
705 JAYNE STREET.

TO

PROFESSOR EUGENE DÜHRING—

WORTHY SUCCESSOR OF

FREDERIC LIST

IN THE

GREAT WORK OF PROVING TO THE GERMANIC NATION

THAT

DOMESTIC INTERDEPENDENCE, NATIONAL INDEPENDENCE,

PUBLIC PEACE, AND PRIVATE HAPPINESS,

TEND ALWAYS TO MARCH HAND IN HAND TOGETHER—

This Volume

IS DEDICATED IN TOKEN OF ITS AUTHOR'S HIGH RESPECT.

Professor Dühring's field of action is that of the University of Berlin. Of his many works none have yet been reproduced in the English language, and therefore does the author deem it well to call to the attention of the reader the two most recent, as follows:—

First of these is, "A Critical History of Political Economy and Social Science" (Berlin, 1871); a work remarkable for its critical acumen, and as furnishing a more thorough exhibit of the course of sociological science, from its earliest days, than any that, until now, has been given to the world. It is much to be desired that it should be here translated.

Second. "A Critical History of the General Principles of Mechanical Science from the days of Galileo to the present time." This work, not yet published, was prepared in response to a public invitation from the University of Göttingen, and was honored, March, 1872, by an award of the highest prize that had been offered; that award, too, accompanied by a report, in which the faculty of that renowned institution state, that "not only are the essential points discussed in a manner evincing a thorough mastery of the subject, and an extraordinary amount of accurate literary knowledge," but that thereto had been added sundry dissertations on others less important; the whole bearing witness to the "great love and care" given to the work. In conclusion, they congratulate themselves on having called into existence "a beautiful performance;" one far surpassing any anticipation they could have formed when adopting the measures that had led to its production.

It is rare to find such varied knowledge combined with such extraordinary industry as has been exhibited by Professor Dühring throughout the last decade.

CONTENTS.

APPENDIX.

PREFACE.

DESIRING FULLY to understand and properly to appreciate the men around us, we study their antecedents, thereby in some measure qualifying ourselves for predicting their probable future. So, too, is it with nations. That we may understand the direction in which they are moving, whether toward civilization, wealth, and power, or toward barbarism, poverty, and weakness, it is needed that we compare their present with their past, and satisfy ourselves as to whether their course of action has tended in the direction of developing the qualities which constitute the real MAN, the being made in the image of his Creator, fitted for becoming master of nature and an example worthy to be followed by those around him; or those alone which he holds in common with the beasts of the field, and which fit him for place among men whose rule of conduct exhibits itself in the robber chieftain's motto, "that they may take who have the power, and those may keep who can." That it is proposed now to do; but preparatory thereto, the author asks the reader's attention to a brief exhibit of the very gradual steps by which, and almost insensibly, he has been led to arrive at the idea of an UNITY OF LAW, necessary complement as it is of that great idea so recently developed, but already so universally accepted, that of UNITY OF FORCE.

So far as regards Societary Science — the link connecting physical with mental science—the first step ever made in that direction consisted in furnishing *a theory of* *value* so simple that, in the words of one of the highest authorities in economical science, "there could arise no case in which a man should determine to make an exchange in which it would not be found to apply." Here, as every where, simplicity and breadth marched hand in hand together; the law embracing every commodity or thing in reference to which the idea of value could be predicated, and thus contributing largely toward demonstration of the universality of natural laws; the value of land having been ascribed by all previous economists to causes widely different from those which gave value to its products.*

Till then, amid the many suggestions as to the "nature, measure, and causes of value," there had been none, to quote again from the same high authority, that had not proved itself "liable to perpetual exceptions." The law then furnished was that of *the labor saved;* the limit of

* "Carey, and after him Bastiat, have introduced a formula *à posteriori*, that I believe destined to be universally adopted; and it is greatly to be regretted that the latter should have limited himself to occasional indications of it, instead of giving to it the importance so justly given by the former. In estimating the equilibrium between the cost to one's self and the utility to others, a thousand circumstances may intervene; and it is desirable to know if there be not among men a law, a principle of universal application. Supply and demand, rarity, abundance, etc., are all insufficient, and liable to perpetual exceptions. Carey has remarked, and with great sagacity, that this law is the labor saved, *the cost of reproduction*—an idea that is, as I think, most felicitous. It appears to me that there cannot arise a case in which a man shall determine to make an exchange, in which this law will not be found to apply. I will not regard it as equivalent, unless I see that it will come to me at less cost of labor than would be necessary for its reproduction. I regard this formula as most felicitous; because while on one side it retains the idea of cost which is constantly referred to in the mind; on the other it avoids the absurdity to which we are led by the theory which pretends to see everywhere a value equivalent to the cost of production; and, finally, it shows more perfectly the essential justice that governs us in our exchanges."—FERRARA: *Biblioteca dell' Économista*, vol. xii. p. 117.

value being found in *the cost of reproduction*.* Subsequently adopted by an eminent French economist,† it has been made known to tens of thousands who had never seen, or even heard of, the work in which it first appeared.

Consequent upon this, was the discovery of a general *law of distribution*, embracing all the products of labor; whether that applied to cultivation or conversion—to change of place or change of form. According to the theories then most generally received, the profit of one was always attended with loss to another—rents rising, as labor became less productive, and profits advancing, as wages retrograded; a doctrine said to come as natural consequence of a great law instituted by the Deity for man's government; but which, if true, tended to the production of universal discord.‡

Directly the reverse of this, however, was the law that was then announced, and now is reproduced;§ proving, as it did, that both capitalist and laborer profited by every measure tending to render labor more productive, while losing by every one that tended to render it less so—and thus establishing a perfect harmony of interests.

Likewise adopted by M. Bastiat, and characterized by him as "the great, admirable, consoling, necessary, and

* CAREY. Principles of Political Economy, vol. i. Philad., 1837.

† BASTIAT. Harmonies Economiques, Paris, 1850.

‡ "Low wages, as a consequence of competition for the sale of labor, reduce the prices of the things to the production of which that labor is applied; and it is the consumers of those products, the whole society, that reap the profit. If, then, as a consequence of low wages, the latter find themselves obliged to contribute to the support of the poor workman, they are indemnified therefor by the reduced prices at which they obtain his products."—J. B. SAY; *Traité d'Économie Politique*, t. ii., p. 292.

It is here supposed that society profits by a state of things that impoverishes the workman, and sends him to the hospital. The real and permanent interests of the employer and his workmen being one and the same, such a state of things can not exist.

§ See Appendix A. See also pp. 66, 67.

inflexible law of capital,"* it constituted a second step in the direction of proving that in each department of the social relations there was perfect unity; and, that the whole were as much subjected to law, absolute and inflexible, as were those of inorganic matter.

Thoroughly convinced of the truth of the laws then presented for consideration, the author felt not less certain that the really fundamental principle remained yet to be discovered; and, that until it could be brought to light many societary phenomena must continue unexplained. In what direction, however, to seek it, he could not tell. He had already satisfied himself that the theory presented for consideration by Mr. Ricardo, not being universally true, had no claim to be so considered; but, it was not until ten years later he was led to remark the fact, that it was universally false. The real law, as he then was led to see, was directly the reverse of that which had been propounded; the work of cultivation having, and that invariably, been commenced on the poorer soils, and having passed to those more rich as wealth had grown and population had increased. Here was the great fundamental truth of which he before had thought; the one, too, that was needed for perfect demonstration of the truth of those he previously had exhibited. Here, too, was further proof of the universality of natural laws—the course of man, in reference to the earth at large, being thus shown to have been the same that we see it now to be in reference to all the instruments into which he fashions parts of the great machine itself. Always commencing with the poorest axes, he proceeds onward to those of steel; always commencing with the poorer soils, he proceeds onward toward those capable of yielding larger returns to labor; increase of numbers being thus

* Harmonies Economiques, Paris, 1850.

proved to be essential to increase in the supply of food. Here was a unity of law leading to perfect harmony of all real and permanent human interests, and directly opposed to the discords taught by Mr. Malthus.*

This great law was first announced nearly a quarter of a century since.† While engaged in its demonstration, the author found himself constantly impelled to the use of physical facts in illustration of social phenomena, and hence was led to remark the close affinity of physical and social laws. Reflecting upon this, he soon was brought to expression of the belief, that closer examination would

* Adam Smith having assumed that the work of cultivation commenced always with the richest soils, Mr. Malthus adopted the idea as basis for a law of population requiring that large numbers of men, women, and children should "regularly die of want." Mr. Ricardo next perfected the system, furnishing a theory of rent by means of which he sought to establish that precisely as it became necessary to cultivate the poorer soils, and as labor became less and less productive, the landlord's share of the products increased, leaving steadily less and less for the unfortunate laborer; the tendency toward absolute enslavement of the latter becoming necessarily greater with each successive hour. From that time forward, all the distress, all the pauperism, of England, was treated as natural result of a necessity for cultivating the "inferior soils." So far indeed was this idea carried out, that it was not unfrequently suggested that the remedy for existing difficulties would be found in throwing out of cultivation all such soils.

The time arriving, however, when the theory was shown to be wholly without foundation, it came then to be discovered, that this *fundamental* question—*as important in furnishing a stand point in Social Science as had been that of Copernicus in the astronomical one*—was wholly unimportant, and might be left entirely unconsidered; the essence of the Ricardo-Malthusian doctrine being, however, still retained in that assumption which constitutes the basis of the existing system, to wit: that the return to agricultural labor, when population and wealth increase, is a constantly diminishing one (see *post* pp. 17, 18); than which no assertion could by any possibility have less of even the appearance of support from facts. That the reader may judge for himself of this, as well as of the accuracy of the views now presented, the history of the earth's occupation is here reproduced in appendix B.

† The Past, the Present, and the Future, Philad., 1848.

lead to development of the great fact, that there existed but a single system of laws; those instituted for the government of inorganic matter proving to be the same by which that matter was governed when it took the form of man, or of communities of men.

In the work then published, the discoveries of modern science proving the indestructibility of matter were, for the first time, rendered available to social science — the difference between agriculture and all other of the pursuits of man having been there exhibited in the fact, that the farmer was always employed in *making* a machine whose powers increased from year to year; whereas, the shipmaster, and the wagoner, were always *using* machines whose powers as regularly diminished. The whole business of the former, as there was shown, consisted in making and improving soils; his powers for improvement growing with the growth of wealth and population. To fully develop the law of the perpetuity of matter, in its bearing upon the law of population, was, however, reserved for the author's friend, Mr. E. Peshine Smith, an important passage from one of whose works will be found at page 150 of the present volume.*

Further reflection having confirmed him in the belief that the laws thus far exhibited were but parts of a perfectly harmonious system instituted for the government of matter in all its forms, whether those of coal or iron, fish or birds, clay, corn, oxen, or men; that the Creator of the Universe had not been obliged to institute different laws for government of the same matter; that the physical and social laws must, therefore, be in harmony with each other; and, that the idea of *unity of law* must be as clearly susceptible of proof as was that of *unity of force;* he availed himself in a further work,† of the familiar pheno-

* See also *Manual of Political Economy*, New York, 1853.

† *Principles of Social Science*, 3 vols. Philad., 1857–59.

mena of heat, motion, and their effective forces in the physical world, for illustration of corresponding facts and forces in the societary one; the result having been that of showing that, with societies as with individual men, physical and mental development, health, and life, had always grown with growth in the rapidity of circulation and declined as the circulation had been arrested or destroyed.

Since then, there have been many and important scientific discoveries, chief among which are those by means of which it has been definitively established that—

"Power or energy, like matter, can neither be created nor destroyed: though ever changing in form, its total quantity in the universe remains constant and unalterable. Every manifestation of force must have come from a preëxisting equivalent force, and must give rise to a subsequent and equal amount of some other force. When, therefore, a force or effect appears, we are not at liberty to assume that it was self-originated, or came from nothing; when it disappears we are forbidden to conclude that it is annihilated: we must search and find whence it came and whither it has gone; that is, what produced it and what effect it has itself produced. These relations among the modes of energy are currently known by the phrases *Correlation* and *Conservation* of Force." *

The law thus exhibited might, as we are assured—

"Well have been proclaimed the highest law of *all* science—the most far-reaching principle that adventuring reason has discovered in the universe. Its stupendous reach spans all orders of existence. Not only does it govern the movements of the heavenly bodies, but it presides over the genesis of the constellations; not only does it control those radiant floods of power which fill the eternal spaces, bathing, warming, illumining and vivifying our planet, but it rules the actions and relations of men, and regulates the march of terrestrial affairs. Nor is its dominion limited to physical phenomena; it prevails equally in the world of mind, controlling all the faculties and processes of thought and feeling. The star-suns of the remoter galaxies dart their radiations across the universe; and although the

* Youmans. *Correlation and Conservation of Forces*, p. xiii.

distances are so profound that hundreds of centuries may have been required to traverse them, the impulses of force enter the eye, and impressing an atomic change upon the nerve, give origin to the sense of sight. Star and nerve-tissue are parts of the same system—stellar and nervous forces are correlated. Nay more; sensation awakens thought and kindles emotion, so that this wondrous dynamic chain binds into living unity the realms of matter and mind through measureless amplitudes of space and time."*

Spanning, as we are here assured it does, "all orders of existence" the paramount law thus exhibited must, of course, embrace within its field of operation that force which enters into man's composition, and by so doing gradually fits him for that elevated position for which, from the first, he had been intended. That it is so embraced, will become obvious to the reader after consideration of the following facts:—

From the days of Cæsar to the present time, a period of almost 2000 years, there has been but slight, if indeed any, increase in the numbers of mankind.† Nevertheless, the quantity of human force has so much increased, that single individuals now accomplish service that before had required hundreds; and, that even the weaker sex has so far grown in power as to be largely aiding in maintaining throughout the world an interchange of ideas which but half a century since could not have been maintained by the united efforts of all mankind. Whence, now, has come the wonderful force that we see to be thus exerted? For answer to this question we have the certainty that, as "force can be neither created nor destroyed;" as "every manifestation of force must come from a pre-existing equivalent force;" human force, whether physical, mental, or moral, results necessarily from conversion to human use of forces that have existed from all time; and, that there is, in this respect, no difference between man and

* Ibid. p. xli.

† See note to page 407.

the trees which adorn our parks; the cotton-plant which furnishes the material of our clothing; or the shrub from which we derive our fruits.

Throughout the inorganic world the variety in the manifestations of force is but very small indeed, great as is its power in whatsoever shape it comes to be presented. When, however it enters into organized forms it finds them each and all to have been so constructed as to give occasion to that almost infinite variety in the modes of manifestation which exhibits itself in both the vegetable and animal world, from the bramble to the oak, and from the ascidian to the horse, the dog, and the almost-speaking elephant.

Thus far, differences have been generic or specific only; individuals of a species being little more than a reproduction each of every other. Man, however, now coming on the stage of life, we find individual differences almost as numerous as are those of the human countenance; there being scarcely any two members of the human family precisely alike in their capacities for absorbing and converting the force that everywhere awaits demand. In one, the power of absorption is of a character tending to fit him for practice of the law, while around are others whose organs fit them for becoming farmers, merchants, physicians, chemists, traders, and so on throughout the thousand other pursuits of life. It is in variety there is unity, and the more that each and every of these men is enabled to absorb and convert the force supplied, the greater is the tendency toward that association in whose absence the being known as MAN can have no existence whatsoever.

Looking now to the early man, as he is being exhibited to us by geologists, we see him to have been almost wholly powerless in face of the wonderful forces in whose presence he had been placed. Tracing him thence onward, we find him gradually obtaining power for their direction, until at length he is enabled to compel light and heat, steam and electricity, to perform labors that would have required the united efforts of hundreds, if not even thousands, of millions of unassisted men. At each and every stage of progress the force thus converted to his use becomes part and parcel of himself; his various faculties absorbing their several portions, and the man of power coming gradually on the stage prepared to direct the already acquired force to further development of the yet latent powers of the earth, and further conversion thereof to his own use and service.* As numbers increase, men are more and more enabled to combine together, and at each such stage their faculties become more and more strengthened for absorption of further aliment; the process here being precisely the same with that observed as consequent upon steady exercise of the physical powers with which the human animal has been endowed.

* A dozen hours from the delivery of a presidential message its contents have been made known throughout the civilized world. Whence had come the force by whose means this wonderful work had been accomplished? From the types, the paper, the poles, or the wires, that had been employed? Certainly not, all these having been perfectly quiescent.—The forces of the pistol, the engine, and the telegraph, are in the men who control and direct them, and *not* in the machines by which the work is done.—A horse's force is said to be the equivalent of that of nine average men. The man who subjugates him adds that force to his own, doing now ten times his original work.—The force of the banker's millions, of the essayist's pen, and of the astronomer's telescope, is in those who direct them, and not in the instruments directed.—That of the orator, or actor, who moves multitudes to action, or to tears, differs only in its modes of manifestation from that of the engineer who explodes the charge, and sends other multitudes to their last account.—Aided by his sling, David felled Goliath to the ground. Altogether unaided, Samson levelled the pillars of the temple.—One man levels his opponent with a blow of his fist. Another does the same by aid of a club. A third accomplishes the same object by means of a well-contrived trap. The force thus used is always the same; and so it is in those larger operations which involve the use of the monster cannon, the ocean steamer, or the fast-flying locomotive.—The soldier's knapsack doubles his carrying power. Is the new force in him, or in the machine?

Side by side with the forces thus converted travels always the first of the great laws above referred to, providing, as it does, that growth of force shall be accompanied by changes in the *distribution* of labor's products; present mental and moral force claiming a constantly increased proportion as compared with that appropriated to the merely material force resulting from accumulations of the past; labor thus tending to an equality with capital, and man becoming from hour to hour more free. In the whole range of law there is nothing more beautiful than this; nothing furnishing more thorough proof that that High Intelligence to which man stands indebted for the wonderful mechanism of each and every part of his physical form, had not failed to provide for the societary body laws fully fitted to prepare him for becoming master of nature, master of himself, and prompt to unite with his fellow-men in all measures tending to thorough development of the highest faculties with which he and they had been endowed.

Looking around, however, we see that throughout by very far the largest portion of the earth there exists little but poverty and wretchedness among the millions, selfishness, extravagance, and waste among those by whom their movements are directed; the rich becoming richer, and the poor poorer, from year to year. As a consequence of this, the world at large presents for observation little beyond a constant series of wars, rebellions, and revolutions, with terrific waste of mental and physical force; of property and of life. Seeking now to understand the cause of a state of things so sad and so destructive, the inquirer looks naturally for information to the works of leaders of opinion in that country which claims to follow in the footsteps of Adam Smith; there to find, however, little beyond the assertions, that their science is limited to the consideration of material wealth alone, to the entire exclusion of mind and morals, skill and taste; that buying and selling constitute the chief end and aim of life; that "to enable capital to obtain proper remuneration, labor must be kept down;"* that carrying goods back and

* Huskisson.—For present confirmation of the idea that was then presented, the reader may take the following passages from two of the most respected of British journals, and one of the most eminent of British authors.

"The English land system, as it exists at present, necessitates over the greater part of England the misery of the peasant. Just as the events of the period which is comprised within the outbreak of the Continental war and the abolition of the corn laws, were based on the starvation of the people, so if the present mode of letting and hiring land is to remain in force, it is necessary that the agricultural laborer should be underpaid, underfed, miserably housed, and so immovable as to secure to the tenant farmer a constant supply of cheap labor."—British Quarterly Review, July, 1872; Article: "*Agricultural Labor's Strike.*"

"From these classes we hear already a protest against emigration. Keep our people at home, they say, we shall want them when trade revives. There may be no work for them at present. Their wives and little ones may be starving with cold and hunger. They may be roaming the streets in vagrancy, crowding the casual wards, or besieging the doors of the poor-houses; but still keep them,—all will be well by and by. Meantime let the poor-rate rise; let the small householder in Whitechapel, himself struggling manfully for independence on the verge of beggary, pay six shillings in the pound to feed his neighbor who has sunk below the line. The tide will turn; labor will soon be in demand again. Our profits will come back to us, and the Whitechapel householder may console himself with the certainty that his six shillings will sink again to three."—*Froude. Short Studies on Great Subjects*, London, 1872, p. 164.

"The kindly feeling, as they call it, in the counties—that is, the half contemptuous pity on one side and reverential deference on the other which has for centuries marked the semi-feudal relations of village labor—has already died away, and the farmers are determined that the men shall know what 'contract' is like. They will not take the Bishop of Gloucester's advice, and duck the lecturers, because the laborers being ten to one, and being told by a bishop that physical violence is a proper weapon to employ, might duck the farmers. . . . They will endeavor this winter to put the unions down, and we shall have all over the country villages in which ten or fifteen farmers, angry, unreasonable, and well fed, will stand face to face with a hundred or a hundred and fifty laborers, angry, unreasonable, and without food. The unionists will be locked out in heaps, and

forth is beneficial because it makes demand for ships; and that, to the end of increasing such demand, it is right and proper to employ the physical force at their command to prevent elsewhere the growth of that domestic commerce so highly valued by the great founder of their science; *that* commerce by means of which alone can man be enabled to convert to his use the great forces so infinitely abounding, and waiting but his demand to grant the aid of which he stands so much in need.

Need we now wonder that a system so thoroughly materialistic should have given rise to a school from which we learn, that "survival of the fittest," and crushing out of those less "fitted," constitute the bases of all natural arrangements for promoting advance in civilization; and, that it is in clear defiance of nature's laws to interfere in any manner, whether by vaccination, by succoring of

when they apply to the parish will be told by the guardians that, as they can have work at will, by 'merely' giving up the union, they must take the work. . . . The man has been, so to speak, morally whipped for six months. He has found no friend anywhere, except in a press he can neither read nor understand. The duke has deprived him of his allotment; the bishop has recommended that his instructor should be ducked; the squire has threatened him with dismissal in winter; the magistrate has fined him for quitting work, which is just, and scolded him for listening to lectures, which is tyranny; the mayor at Evesham has prohibited him from meeting on the green—and the lawyer—witness a recent case near Chelmsford—has told him that any one who advises and helps him to emigrate is a hopeless rascal. He has been denied the most ordinary privileges of freemen—the right of listening to lectures he approves, the right of emigrating from county to county, the right of combining to improve his condition; and this by men who, as he sees, listen to every lecture on their own side, who emigrate whenever they please, to the ends of the earth, and who form open and strict combinations to keep him in his place."—*Spectator*, August 24, 1872.

The reader who may desire to see for himself how far the tendency in regard to skilled labor has been in accordance with the policy announced by Mr. Huskisson, and with that above exhibited in reference to agricultural labor, will find himself enabled so to do by turning to page 408 of the present volume.

the maimed, or by aid of those who are deformed, to prevent, or even to arrest, that "process of elimination" by means of which the strong of body, and the rich in purse, are to be enabled to rid the world of those who are weak, poor, and incapable of self defence?* Assuredly not. From the days of Malthus such has been the tendency of the teachings of the British school, and we have but arrived at the goal toward which they have always been directed—that of *self-creation* and *self-worship;* this latter more and more exhibiting itself as the former idea becomes more and more established. At what other, by aid of such instructors, would it be possible that we *should* arrive? As the Giver of all good, man has been accustomed to venerate the Creator of the Universe. Assured now, however, that in accordance with His laws it is required that millions shall "regularly die of want;"† that floods and famines, wars and revolutions, are but parts of the machinery by means of which He works; that, to the end that His laws may be fully carried out, it is needed to refrain from acts which, beyond all others, tend toward developing the best and highest feelings of the heart,

* "With savages, the weak in body or mind are soon eliminated; and those that survive commonly exhibit a vigorous state of health. We civilized men, on the other hand, do our utmost to check the process of elimination; we build asylums for the imbecile, the maimed, and the sick; we institute poor-laws; and our medical men exert their utmost skill to save the life of every one to the last moment. There is reason to believe that vaccination has preserved thousands, who from a weak constitution would formerly have succumbed to smallpox. Thus the weak members of civilized societies propagate their kind. No one who has attended to the breeding of domestic animals will doubt that this must be highly injurious to the race of man. It is surprising how soon a want of care, or care wrongly directed, leads to the degeneration of a domestic race; but excepting in the case of man himself, hardly any one is so ignorant as to allow his worst animals to breed." Darwin, *Descent of Man*, vol. 1, p. 161.

† James Mill. *Elements of Political Economy*, p. 42

assured, we say, of all these things, can he be otherwise than led to doubt, if not even to deny, the existence of a Being all of whose laws, as now generally exhibited, tend toward reducing the millions to a condition of mere hewers of wood and drawers of water for those few who are encouraged to eat, drink, and make merry, while providing measures for securing, at the earliest moment, the "elimination" of those who, being poor and uninstructed, are incapable of self-protection? Most certainly not!

Such having been the sad results of a persistent use of the *à priori* method of reasoning in reference to the most important of all the sciences, it may now, we think, be hoped, that at no distant day it will come to be admitted that, in common with all other organized bodies, science develops from within and never from without; that the tree of science grows from the roots upward;* and, that its various branches are all co-operating for accomplishment of one great object, to wit: that of giving to man increased power for control of the great natural forces, and for development of those faculties, mental and moral, whose germs have been incorporated into the system of every individual of the race. When it shall have come, the world will cease to be mystified by economic "assumptions" that are wholly without a base on which to stand; and so little comprehended by even their very teachers, that these latter fail totally when seeking to make them comprehensible by those who would be taught.

* See p. 47, *post.*

NOTE.

As this sheet is passing through the press, the author has received the inaugural Address of the new President of the British Association, Dr. Carpenter, and finds therein such coincidence in the views above expressed, that he is led to place the closing paragraphs before his readers, as follows:—

"Thus we are led to the culminating point of man's intellectual interpretation of Nature—his recognition of the unity of the power, of which her phenomena are the diversified manifestations. Towards this point all scientific inquiry now tends. The convertibility of the physical forces, the correlation of these with the vital, and the intimacy of that *nexus* between mental and bodily activity, which, explain it as we may, cannot be denied, all lead upward towards one and the same conclusion; and the pyramid of which that philosophical conclusion is the apex, has its foundation in the primitive instincts of humanity.

"By our own progenitors, as by the untutored savage of the present day, every change in which human agency was not apparent, was referred to a particular animating intelligence. And thus they attributed not only the movements of the heavenly bodies, but all the phenomena of Nature, each to its own deity. These deities were invested with more than human power; but they were also supposed capable of human passions, and subject to human capriciousness. As the uniformities of Nature came to be more distinctly recognized, some of these deities were invested with a dominant control, while others were supposed to be their subordinate ministers. A serene majesty was attributed to the greater gods who sit above the clouds, whilst their inferiors might 'come down to earth in the likeness of men.' With the growth of the scientific study of Nature, the conception of its harmony and unity gained ever-increasing strength. And so among the most enlightened of the Greek and Roman philosophers, we find a distinct recognition of the idea of the unity of the directing mind from which the order of Nature proceeds, for they obviously believed that, as our modern poet has expressed it—

> All are but parts of one stupendous whole,
> Whose body Nature is, and God the Soul.

"The science of modern times, however, has taken a more special direction. (Fixing its attention exclusively on the *order* of Nature, it has separated itself wholly from theology, whose function it is to seek after its *cause*.) In this, science is fully justified, alike by the entire independence of its objects, and by the historical fact that it has been continually hampered and impeded in its search for the truth as it is in Nature, by the restraints which theologians have attempted to impose upon its inquiries. But when science, passing beyond its limits, assumes to take the place of theology, and sets up its own conception of the *order* of Nature as a sufficient account of its *cause*, it is invading a province of thought to which it has no claim, and not unreasonably provokes the hostility of those who ought to be its best friends.

"For whilst the deep-seated instincts of humanity and the profoundest researches of philosophy alike point to mind as the one and only source of power, it is the high prerogative of science to demonstrate the *unity* of the power which is operating through the limitless extent and variety of the universe, and to trace its *continuity* through the vast series of ages that have been occupied in its evolution."

PHILADELPHIA, OCTOBER, 1872.

THE UNITY OF LAW.

CHAPTER I.

A SCIENCE BASED UPON ASSUMPTIONS.*

§ 1. DISCOURSING of the wealth of nations, Adam Smith clearly showed his high appreciation of the importance of the moral and mental elements. Rejecting the views thus presented, his Ricardo-Malthusian successors have assured their readers that their—so called—science limited itself, and necessarily, to an exhibition of causes affecting the production, distribution, and consumption of *material wealth alone*, the economist allowing "neither sympathy with indigence, nor disgust at profusion or avarice—neither reverence for existing institutions, nor detestation of existing abuses—to deter him from stating what he believed to be the facts, or from drawing from them what appeared to him to be the legitimate conclusions." Narrow and contracted as was the *science* thus described

* "Political economy is a science based upon assumptions."—*Saturday Review.*

Political economy "necessarily reasons from assumptions, and not from facts."—*J. S. Mill.*

more than thirty years since by Mr. Senior, one of the then most eminent of British economists, the tendency from that time to the present has been toward further contraction, until at length it has come to be generally understood that it concerns itself little, if at all, with any societary operations outside of those of the mere trader—things that cannot be bought and sold being thus wholly excluded from consideration. Moving onward in that direction, Mr. J. S. Mill advises his readers that "the greater part in value of the wealth now existing in England," farmhouses, factories, a few ships and machines, being, as he says, the only exceptions, "has been produced by human hands within the past twelve months;" thus excluding from consideration not only the moral and mental elements, but also nearly all the accumulations of ages now existing in the form of farms, parks, roads, canals, viaducts, bridges, streets, mines, galleries, museums, buildings public and private, the money value of these counting by thousands of millions of pounds. Following closely in his footsteps, journalists—foreign and domestic—fondly speak of raisers of corn and cotton, miners of coal and smelters of ores, spinners and weavers, tailors, shoemakers, and the like, as being the sole "wealth producers;" thus wholly rejecting the claims to consideration of men like Watt and Stephenson, Morse and Henry, Liebig, Faraday, and thousands of others to whom the world stands most of all indebted for the wonderful growth of wealth and power that marks the period in which we live.*

Of all economic terms there is none that is just now more frequently both used and abused than is the apparently very simple one to which the reader's attention has here been called. Of all, there is none of greater real breadth; yet, of all, there is none that has been so much narrowed and belittled; that, too, having been done by men who, while claiming to be disciples in his school, have carefully repudiated the most essential portion of the teachings of Adam Smith.

Of what, now, does wealth really consist? Let us see!

Crusoe having made a bow, had thus acquired wealth; that wealth exhibiting itself in the power obtained over certain natural properties of wood and muscular fibre, thereby enabling him to secure increased supplies of food with greatly diminished expenditure of labor. Having made a canoe, he found his wealth much increased, his new machine enabling him to obtain still further increase of food, and of the raw materials of clothing, at still decreased cost of personal effort. Erecting a pole on his canoe, he now commands the services of wind, and with each and every step in this direction finds himself

* "Scientific wealth," says Sir William Thomson in his recent address as President of the British Association, "tends to accumulate according to the law of compound interest." Further even than this, it carries with a higher *rate* of interest than any other kind of property; yet is it wholly excluded from consideration by economists of the modern trading school.

advancing, with constantly accelerated rapidity, toward becoming master of nature, and a being of real wealth and power.

The picture here presented of the doings of an isolated individual is being now reproduced on a scale of wonderful magnificence by men engaged in erecting the poles, and stretching the wires, by means of which the thousand millions of the world's people are being enabled on the instant to communicate with each other, time and distance being in this manner almost annihilated. We have here a growth of wealth and power the value, moral and material, of which is almost beyond calculation; yet, according to the teachings of Mr. Mill and his fellow-economists of the British school, no wealth has been thus created except so far as is made manifest in certain poles and wires distributed over the earth's surface, or in certain other wires submerged beneath the ocean.

But recently a British army was saved from ruin by the fortunate presence of a little machine of American invention, by means of which the services of water, then greatly needed, had been almost at once obtained. Here, as a consequence of growing power over nature, we have wealth of almost inestimable money value; yet does it find no place in the eyes of British economists beyond the mere commercial estimate of the little machine itself. Still further, the great men to whose successive discoveries we have been indebted for knowledge that has led to the production of such a machine, must, according to Mr. Mill, be classed as *non-producers of wealth*, for the reason that, however beneficial their labors, an "increase of material products forms no part of that benefit."*

The landholder sinks a shaft upon his property by means of which there are brought to light large deposits of that material a single ton of which, during the period of its combustion, does the work of thousands of men. Having thus obtained control of a vast reservoir of force, he parcels it out among his neighbors, claiming of them a royalty utterly trivial when compared with the labor that by his aid is now economized, thereby adding largely to the wealth of all. Furnaces and mills next taking their places in the neighborhood of the fuel thus developed, other natural forces are brought to the aid of man, and now the farmer more and more obtains power for diversifying his cultivation, substituting green crops, which yield so largely and pay so well, for the exhaustive white ones by means of which his land

* Discoursing of mind and matter, Mr. Mill defines the latter as being a "perpetual possibility of sensation"—sensitive power being thus placed in the chairs on which we sit, and not in those who occupy them. Precisely the same erroneous transposition here again occurs—matter in the form of a machine being, as we are assured, to be regarded as wealth, wholly without reference to the knowledge how to use it. To the man who roams over South American pampas there is, nevertheless, more wealth in the possession of a single lasso than he could find in ownership of a thousand locomotives. In all these cases sensation is to be sought in the man who controls the matter, and not in the matter that is controlled.

had been so much impoverished. Released thus from all dependence on distant markets, his emancipation from the tax of transportation exhibits itself in growing power to subdue to cultivation the richer soils, and in great increase of the exchangeable value of the land itself; and here it is we find the most important element of that rapidly growing wealth which now exhibits itself in a duplication of the money value of our material property in the last decade. How such power of accumulation as is thus exhibited can be made to accord with the assertion of Mr. Mill, that nearly all the wealth of such a country as Britain had been "the product of human hands in the last twelve months," it is for that gentleman, or his disciples among ourselves, to explain.

The extent to which time and labor have been economized by the use of steam employed in transferring, by land and water, both men and things, can scarcely here be estimated; yet does the growth of wealth thus exhibited find no recognition at the hands of British economists, except so far as represented by the mere machinery by means of which the saving is effected.

§ 2. *Wealth consists in the power to command the always gratuitous services of the great forces of nature.* That power grows as men are more and more enabled to combine their efforts for nature's subjugation. That such combination may be effected, there must be that diversification in the demands for human power which results from variety in the modes of employment. The more thorough this becomes, the greater is the tendency toward production of men like Fulton, Morse, Davy, Faraday, Bessemer, Scott, and Dickens, greatest of all the "wealth producers," although wholly excluded from consideration by men who restrict the domain of economic science to material wealth alone.

The object of protection to domestic industry is that of bringing about the diversification of employment above described. Without it, men cannot combine together. Without it, they must remain slaves to nature, and the societies of which they are parts must exhibit the same weakness now so clearly obvious in all those communities which, like Ireland, India, Portugal, Turkey, and Carolina, find themselves limited to the work of exhausting the soil in raising rice, corn, and cotton, for the supply of foreign markets. With it, there must be daily increasing economy of muscular force, attended with growing development of that brain power to which we stand now indebted for the fact that each individual in these Northern States may claim to command the services of several willing slaves engaged in supplying him with food, clothing, and shelter, while consuming nothing whatsoever beyond a trivial portion of the fuel that they themselves had brought to light. Southern men, throughout the war, could, on the contrary, command little beyond the services of negro slaves for whose maintenance there was required a large proportion of the things produced; and hence the weakness that throughout the South was manifested.

The more thoroughly the great natural forces are subjected to human control, and the more numerous those unconsuming slaves, the greater becomes the power of production, and the greater the tendency toward that accumulation of wealth which manifests itself in the physical, mental, moral, and political improvement of a people.

Such, very briefly stated, is sociological science as derived from careful study of facts presented throughout the world for consideration. What is the nature of that other *science* which has "assumptions" only for its base, and which so entirely rejects the enlarged and liberal views given to the world by the illustrious author of the "Wealth of Nations," it is proposed now to show, placing before the reader a brief view of its actual condition, and thus enabling him to judge for himself what are its claims to be admitted to a place side by side with the sciences cultivated abroad by Grove, Helmholz, and Carpenter, and among ourselves by such men as Henry, Agassiz, Pierce, and Lesley.

§ 3. First among the requisites of any and every branch of science is a clear understanding among its teachers of the precise value of the terms in use; the indispensable preliminary to making others comprehend them being that they themselves comprehend each other. That such has been the course of proceeding elsewhere is proved by the fact that the vocabulary of Hipparchus and Ptolemy now makes part of that of Herschel and Le Verrier, as that of Dalton and Lavoisier is embraced in those of Huxley, Tyndall, and their associates. The language of physics is one and the same for France and England, Germany, Russia, and these United States, perfect exactness being its essential characteristic.

Precisely the reverse of this is what we see to be the case with regard to that so-called science to which the reader's attention has now been called, its professors having never yet determined the real value of any single one of all its terms. That this is so, was shown by the late Archbishop Whately, one among the most eminent of its professors, when telling his readers that "the great defect of Adam Smith, and of our economists in general, is the want of definitions," proof of this being given in the numerous and widely different significations attached by the most distinguished teachers to the highly important terms, Value, Wealth, Labor, Capital, Rent, Wages, and Profits; then showing that for want of clear conceptions the same word is used by the same writer at one time in a manner totally inconsistent with that in which he uses it at another. To that list he might, as he most truly says, add many others "which are often used without any more explanation, or any more suspicion of their requiring it, than the words 'triangle' or 'twenty'" —as a consequence of which it is that words of the highest importance are used by distinguished writers as being entirely synonymous, when really expressing not only different, but directly opposite, ideas.

Since the publication of the Archbishop's work many years have elapsed, very many additions having meanwhile been made to British economic literature; but, as yet, scarcely even an attempt has been made at correction of the error he there had indicated. In a very recent work intended for use in one of the chief English colleges, and highly lauded, we find not even a suggestion of definition. The fundamental question of value, the *pons asinorum* of the science, has been by one eminent writer recently discussed at length, with the result of enabling him to assure his readers that "the value of a thing means the quantity of some other things, or of things in general, which it exchanges for." By a second, we are told that "labor is the cause of value;" a third, equally eminent, meantime assuring his readers that "labor, in no case whatever, is a cause of value;" and, that the idea of value, even, can have no existence except when commodities or things are bought and sold.

Mr. Mill tells his readers that "the question of value is fundamental;" that "there is nothing in its laws which remains for the present or any future writer to clear up;" that "the theory of the subject is complete;" and then leaves this "fundamental question" precisely where it had stood at the date at which Dr. Whately gave to the world the perfectly accurate view of economical deficiencies above referred to. Professor Jevons holds that in so saying Mr. Mill had been "rash," value in his own belief depending "entirely on utility;" this conclusion having been arrived at in face of the greatest of the facts of our age, to wit: that as the *utility* of electricity has been more and more developed, its *value* has so steadily declined as to have already brought its services within reach of the common laborer desirous of communicating with his absent wife and children.

Other varieties of opinion and expression might here be furnished, all tending to prove the entire accuracy of one of the writers above referred to, when speaking with his readers of "the utter confusion of opinion, and inconsistency of conception of the very nature of the subject, which prevails among writers;" his own work, meanwhile, furnishing no reply whatsoever to the simple but fundamental questions—Whence comes the idea of value? Of what does value itself consist? (See McLeod, *Elements of Political Economy*, p. 8.)

So long as those questions shall remain unanswered economists must continue to occupy a position closely analogous to that occupied by astronomers throughout the Ptolemaic regime, having no standpoint from which to make their observations; and so long must the "confusion and inconsistency" above described continue to exist. That such a point may be obtained, they need to seek their old friend Crusoe, standing alone on his desert island, asking *his* views on this important question. Doing this, they will learn that so high had been the value attached by him to the idea of moving on the water, that he had expended many months in the effort to obtain a mere canoe; that to other things he had more or less attached the idea of value in the precise ratio of his estimate of the obstacles standing in the way of their production or reproduction;* that values greatly declined so soon as he and Friday had come together, and had been enabled to exchange with each other services and their products; that their experience furnished proof conclusive that exchanges tended to diminish, and not, as now constantly assumed, to increase the value of such products. Turning their eyes now homeward with a view to test the accuracy of this idea, our inquirers would find that when, a few centuries since, the English people numbered less than three millions, and when exchanges had but slight existence, labor had so little value that two hundred and twelve persons stand recorded as having been hired for a day to cut and bind fourteen acres of wheat; that food had then so high a value as to cause deaths from famine closely comparing with those so recently

* Value is the measure of the obstacles above described, of the power of nature over man; as wealth consists in the power to compel nature to do man's work. Mr. McLeod (p. 9) assures us that by reason of the fact that all their exchanges were made among themselves, "no such idea as *value* could enter the minds" of the Highlanders of olden times. Nevertheless, those people so highly *valued* the cattle of their lowland neighbors as to be always willing to peril liberty and even life in their efforts to obtain possession of them. That idea came into the world with the first man, and Eve gave proof of its existence when she attached to the possession of an apple so high a *value* as to dispose her to give the joys of paradise in exchange therefor.

observed in Ireland; that with a population of 20,000,000, and rapidity of exchange, agricultural labor had become so much more productive that half a dozen persons did the work that before had required hundreds; that famines, such as had occurred even so late as the sixteenth century, had wholly disappeared; that home experience thus furnished perfect proof of the accuracy of Crusoe's views; and, finally, that all experience, home and foreign, combined to prove that the greatest foe to value, as this latter exhibits itself in its relations to labor, is to be found in the rapidity of exchange which always accompanies that diversity in the demands for human service to which the civilized people of our age stand indebted for such development of their various faculties as has, more or less, made them masters of those great physical forces by which their predecessors had been so entirely enslaved; wealth and power growing always with most rapidity as the commodities and things needed for man's use tend more and more to decline in value, and to become as gratuitous as is the air we breathe.

To enter upon the inquiry here indicated would, however, require reasoning upward from facts to principles, a course of proceeding most distasteful to those who so long have held, with Mr. Mill, that the *a priori* method of reasoning downward from "assumptions" to facts, "is the only certain or scientific method of investigation.

§ 4. As a necessary result of the total absence above described of a recognized economic language, it is, that the economic world presents to view a mass of confusion, each and every of its members wishing to be heard, and scarcely any two of them using precisely the same terms when desiring to present the same ideas.

Of all those in the common use the broadest and most expressive is that of COMMERCE, embracing, as it does, exchanges of ideas, personally or by letter; exchanges of services or commodities; exchanges in the family or the state; in fine, the whole range of human relations. Of all, perhaps the narrowest and most contracted is that which brings before us the mere TRADER, the man of one idea, always intent on buying cheap and selling dear, and quite too often overreaching both those of whom he buys and those to whom he sells. The more frequent the vicissitudes of trade, the more numerous, as he knows, are his chances for accumulating fortune. The farmer, the planter, and the miner, on the contrary, desire steadiness, needing, as they do, to make their arrangements for years ahead. The cotton mill requires much time for its construction, and for the collection and organization of the people required for work therein. The preparation of the mine, the furnace, or the rolling-mill, demands long periods of exertion and large expenditure before their owners can begin to reap reward. The trader, on the contrary, buys and sells from hour to hour; and the greater his power to produce changes in the prices of wheat, cloth, and iron, the greater is the probability that he will ultimately enter upon possession of the land of the farmer, the mill of the manufacturer, the furnace of the maker of railroad bars, or the road of the man who has invested his fortune in a great improvement; and at half the cost at which the machinery had been constructed. Trade and commerce thus look always in opposite directions, the one desiring, and producing, frequent and rapid changes, the other seeking and promoting regularity of movement. Of all the terms in use among men there are no two representing more opposite ideas; yet are they, without exception, used by economists as being entirely synonymous, and rightfully interchangeable with each other.

Having thus provided for the world's use a *science* without a recognized language; one whose professors cannot understand each other; one that, being merely "abstract or hypothetical," demands, as we are assured, that we "reason from assumptions, and not from facts"—the next step, as will now be shown, has been that of assuming the existence of a being in human form, but deprived, as far as possible, of all human qualities, the modern political economy requiring that we—

"Do not treat of the whole of man's nature as modified by the social state, nor of the whole conduct of man in society. It is concerned with him solely as a being who desires to acquire wealth, and who is capable of judging of the comparative efficiency of means for obtaining that end. It predicts only such of the phenomena of the social state as take place in consequence of the pursuit of wealth. It makes entire abstraction of every other passion or motive; except those which may be regarded as perpetually antagonizing principles to the desire of wealth, namely—aversion to labor, and desire of the present enjoyment of costly indulgences. These it takes, to a certain extent, into its calculations, because these do not merely, like other desires, occasionally conflict with the pursuit of wealth, but accompany it always as a drag or impediment, and therefore inseparably mixed up in the consideration of it. Political economy considers mankind as occupied solely in acquiring and consuming wealth, and aims at showing what is the course of action into which mankind, living in a state of society, would be impelled, if that motive, except in the degree in which it is checked by the two perpetual counter-motives above adverted to, were absolute ruler of all their actions."—*J. S. Mill.*

Happily for mankind, the animal here exhibited is as fanciful as is the Giant Despair of the "Pilgrim's Progress," its existence, according to Mr. Mill himself, being an assumed and not a real one.*

§ 5. Ptolemy having assumed that the sun revolved around the earth, his disciples at a later date furnished a planetarium, or instrument by which, as they then asserted, the movements of all the celestial bodies could, in perfect harmony with their master's great idea, readily be explained. Mr. Malthus having, in like manner, assumed that man had always commenced the work of cultivation on the richest soils, and that with increase of numbers it had been, and always must be, necessary to have recourse to those of an inferior description, with steadily diminishing returns to labor, Mr. Ricardo followed the theory up by assuming that constantly

* "Not that any political economist was ever so absurd as to suppose that mankind is really so constituted, but because this is the mode in which science must necessarily proceed."—*J. S. Mill, Essays on Some Unsettled Questions in Political Economy*, p. 139.

diminishing production had been, and must be, attended with power on the landlord's part to take to himself a constantly increasing share of the diminished product, leaving to the poor laborer a steadily diminishing share of a constantly declining quantity; the growing inequality of the people of England being thus proved to be the result of a great law established by the Creator for government of the human race. A tendency towards subjection of the masses, or, in other words, towards slavery, having been thus established as a necessary result of divine institutions, Mr. Mill certainly did not err when telling his readers that the law of the constantly decreasing productiveness of agricultural labor whose existence had been thus assumed, was "the most important proposition in political economy;" and that, "were the law different, nearly all the phenomena of the production and distribution of wealth would be different." So far he was entirely right. When, however, the baselessness of the Malthusian assumption had been distinctly shown; when it had been proved that the work of cultivation had in all ages and countries necessarily commenced on the poorer soils, passing steadily, as numbers, wealth, power, and civilization grew, towards those more rich, with constantly increasing facility in obtaining supplies of food and other products of the soil; when it had been shown that such proceeding had been in full accordance with the law in virtue of which poor and scattered men find themselves, in every department of occupation, compelled to commence with poor machinery, passing thence to that which is better; when these things had all been proved by means of facts occurring at every age and in every part of the world, it is certainly somewhat remarkable that a philosopher like Mr. Mill should have contented himself with simply denying the existence of any "invariable law," and demanding proof that "the return to labor from the land, when population and wealth increase, agricultural skill and science remaining the same, is not a diminishing one."

How to treat such a suggestion as this it is difficult to determine, it being—and in so saying, it is earnestly desired to avoid disrespect to its author—simply absurd; more so, even, than his celebrated "wages fund" theory, now abandoned. As well might he claim of an opponent to prove that had mining skill and science remained the same from the days of the Plantagenets, the return to mining labor would not have been a steadily diminishing one. Both cases being alike impossible of occurrence, both are equally unworthy of place in a work which professes to furnish scientific information. Growing wealth involves necessarily development of "skill and science," and the philosophy of the attempt to separate them in the manner here proposed is strictly on a par with one whose aim should be that of dissolving the connection between the appearance of light and the presence of the sun.

Discussing further the question of the order of cultivation, Mr. Mill demands that his opponent show "that in any old country the uncultivated lands are those which would pay best for cultivation," Dartmoor and Shap Fell being, as he tells his readers, thereby proved "to be really the most fertile lands in England." The assumption here is, that "the uncultivated lands" referred to had always remained in a state of nature; and yet no one better than its author knows that from Land's End to John o'Groat's Britain abounds in evidence that large portions of those very lands had been the chosen seats of early cultivation; that in many cases they had been abandoned even before the historic period; that the lower and richer lands had been but very slowly, and at a comparatively recent date, reduced to cultivation; and that the now richest soils of the kingdom had been, but a century or two since, entirely unoccupied.*

* The picture of the occupation of the Scottish isles and highlands furnished by the Duke of Argyll in his little volume recently published, and now here given, applies with equal force to the whole of Britain, and her attendant islands:—

"At a time when artificial drainage was unknown, and in a rainy climate, the flats and hollows which in the Highlands are now generally most valuable portions of the land, were occupied by swamps and moss. On the steep slopes alone, which afforded natural drainage, was it possible to raise cereal crops. And this is one source of that curious error which strangers so often make in visiting and in writing on the Highlands. They see marks of the plough high up upon the mountains, where the land is now very wisely abandoned to the pasturage of sheep or cattle; and, seeing this, they conclude that tillage has decreased, and they wail over the diminished industry of man. But when those high banks and braes were cultivated, the richer levels below were the haunts of the otter and the fishing places of the heron. Those ancient ploughmarks are the sure indications of a rude and ignorant husbandry. In the eastern slopes of Iona, Columba and his companions found one tract of

Proof having been furnished that land obeys invariably the same law that we see to be true in reference to all other commodities and things, its value, like theirs, being limited within, and greatly within, what would be its cost of reproduction; that London itself, with all its advantages of situation, formed no exception to the rule; and that the value, whether in money or in labor, of all England is not even a tithe of what would be required for restoring it to its present condition, were it to be now restored to its original state; Mr. Mill assumes the possibility of a convulsion of nature whose effect should be that of at once doubling the size of the island, asking then, triumphantly, if that additional land could be supposed to have no value, for the reason that no labor had been expended on it? Had he reflected more carefully, he would have arrived at the conclusion that no such assumption could be needed, each successive year presenting cases of addition quite as fortuitous as the one he had here deemed it proper to suggest. Studying the real facts in regard to such additions, he would have been led inevitably to the conclusion that an aerolite, however large and however fully charged with gold, falling among the sands of Africa, could

land which was as admirably adapted for the growth of corn as the remainder of it was suited to the support of flocks and herds. On the northeastern side of the island, between the rocky pasturage and the shore, there is a long, natural declivity of arable soil, steep enough to be naturally dry, and protected by the hill from the western blast.

"And so here Colomba's tent was pitched, and his Bible opened, and his banner raised for the conversion of the heathen."—*Iona*, pp. 81–3.

have no money value whatsoever; whereas, falling among British workshops, its price would be very large. So, too, with a discovery of coal or ore in any one of thousands of places in these United States, as compared with similar discoveries in Germany or France. So, again, with the land whose sudden appearance he has here assumed. Added to England, it would, like the coal or ore above referred to, participate with all existing land in the advantages resulting from close proximity to markets. Added to countries where no such markets existed, it could have no value whatsoever.

The facts assumed by Mr. Mill, in preference to real facts that had been always within his reach, having been thus disposed of, it is proposed now to look for a moment to his own arguments, given to the world as being those of his opponents.

§ 6. In the sixth and last edition of his "Principles," Mr. Mill admits that what Malthus and his followers had assumed as having been universally true, had not really been so when applied to "soil cultivated in a newly settled country. It is not," as he continues, "pretended that the law of diminishing return was operative from the very beginning of society;" yet does it, as he further says, "begin quite early enough to support the conclusions they founded on it." This, be it observed, is asserted by an author residing in a country whose earliest cultivation we see to have been of lands so poor that they long since had been abandoned to give place to an agriculture like that of Lancashire, where the labors of a single individual furnish a larger yield than could have been obtained in return to those of almost a regiment of men in the days when the centre of British population, wealth, and power was found in the long since abandoned neighborhood of Tintagel, when King Arthur there held his court; and when its Celtic inhabitants were engaged "in rendering the British islands for the first time fit for the habitation of man."*

Rejecting all facts like these, Mr. Mill persists in the assertion of diminishing returns to agricultural labor, this time summoning his opponent into court, to become witness in his favor, his call being made in the following terms, to wit:—

> "Mr. Carey unconsciously bears the strongest testimony to the reality of the law he contends against; for one of the propositions most strenuously maintained by him is, that the raw products of the soil, in an advancing community, tend steadily to rise in price. Now, the most elementary truths of political economy show that this could not happen unless the cost of production, measured in labor, of those products, tended to rise."†

In this there is a confusion of money and labor values somewhat remarkable as coming from so eminent a logician. Allowing it, however, to pass, and at once admitting entire ignorance of the existence of any such "elementary truths," the reader's attention is now invited to the fact that Mr. Mill here entirely misrepresents the author he has pro-

* Müller, *Chips from a German Workshop.* Article, *Cornish Antiquities.*

† Principles, sixth ed., vol. i. p. 228.

fessed to cite, the words "raw products of the soil" not having been used, and the tendency to rise in price having been shown to be common not only to all such products, but also, *and most especially*, to land and labor, both of which have been here suppressed. That this may be clearly seen and understood, the whole passage here apparently referred to is given below, as follows:—

The power of a commodity to command money in exchange is called its PRICE. Prices fluctuate; much food and wool being sometimes, or at some places, given for little money, while at others much money is given for little of either wool or food. What are the circumstances which tend to affect prices generally we may now consider.

A thousand tons of rags, or wool, at the Rocky Mountains would not exchange for the smallest piece of money; whereas a quire of paper would command, perhaps, an ounce of silver. Passing eastward to the plains of Kansas, their relative values would have so much changed that the price of the rags would pay for many reams of paper. Coming to St. Louis, a further change would be experienced, rags having again risen, and paper again fallen. So, too, at every stage of the progress eastward, until in Massachusetts three pounds of rags would command more silver than would purchase a pound of paper. The accompanying diagram exhibits these changes.

The price of raw materials tends to rise as we approach those places at which men are most enabled to combine for obtaining power to command the services of the great forces of nature. That of finished commodities moves in an opposite direction, both tending thus to more close approximation. Cotton is low on the plantation, but high in Manchester or Lowell. Corn in Illinois is often so cheap that a bushel does not pay even for a yard of coarse cotton cloth, whereas in Manchester it pays for a dozen yards.

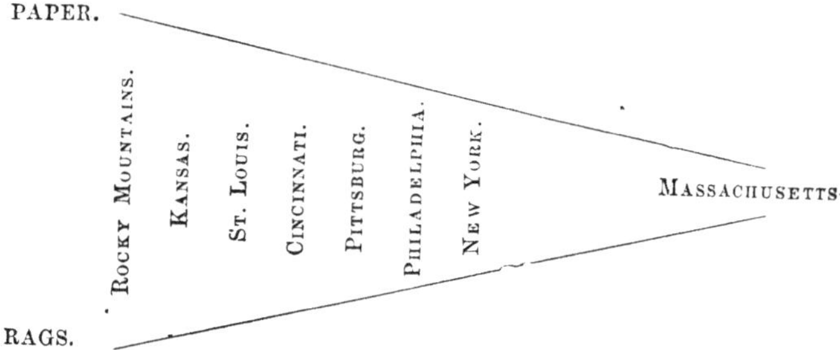

Raw material tends to rise in price with the progress of men in wealth and civilization. What, however, *is* raw material? In answer to this question, we may say, that all the products of the earth are in turn, finished commodity and raw material. Coal and ore are the finished commodity of the miner, but the raw material of pig-iron. The latter is the finished commodity of the smelter, yet only the raw material of the puddler, and of him who rolls the bar. The bar is again the raw material of sheet-iron, that, in turn, becoming the raw material of the nail and the spike. These, in time, become the raw material of the house, in the diminished cost of which are concentrated all the changes in the various stages of passage from the crude ore lying useless in the earth, to the nail and spike, the hammer and saw, used in the construction of a dwelling.

In the early and barbarous ages of society land and labor are very low in price, and the richest deposits of coal and ore are worthless. Houses are then obtained with such exceeding difficulty that men are forced to depend for shelter against wind and rain upon holes and caves they find existing in the earth. In time they are enabled to combine their efforts, and with every step in the course of progress land and labor acquire power to command money in exchange, while houses lose it. As the services of fuel are more readily commanded, pig-iron is more easily obtained. Both, in turn, facilitate the making of bars and sheets, nails and spikes, all of these in turn facilitating the creation of boats, ships, and houses; each and every of these improvements tending to augment the prices of the original raw materials—land and labor. At no period in the history of the world has the general price of these latter been so high as in the present one; at none would the same quantity of money have purchased so staunch a boat, so fleet a ship, or so comfortable a house.

The more finished a commodity, the greater is the tendency to a fall of price; and for the same reason, that all the economies of labor of the earlier processes are accumulated together in the later ones. Houses thus profit by all improvements in the making of bricks, in the quarrying of stone, in the conversion of lumber, and in the working of the metals. So, too, is it with articles of clothing—every improvement in the various processes of spinning, weaving, and dyeing, and in the conversion of clothing into garments, being found gathered together in the coat. The more numerous those improvements the lower will be its price, while *the higher will be that of the land and labor to which the wool is due.**—*Manual of Social Science*, pp. 285–6.

Reasoning "from assumptions, and not from facts," Mr. Mill rejects all of these latter here presented, except the single one that seemed to suit his purpose; even then, as has been shown, substituting the comparatively narrow expression "raw products of the soil" for the far more comprehensive "raw material," covering, as does this latter, not only land and labor, but also that from which we obtain the plough, the ship, and the dwelling. In so doing, he has certainly made a sad mistake. The best evidence men can furnish of confidence in the accuracy of their own belief consists in frankly and honestly presenting the arguments of their opponents.

* Views similar to these in effect occur necessarily in other portions of the work; but, as it is believed, in no case so presented as to afford even the slightest warrant for the use here made of them by Mr. Mill. On the contrary, land, labor, and the rude products of both are throughout most intimately connected.

§ 7. Adam Smith laid the foundation of a science far grander and more magnificent than any of those whose cultivation has brought such fame and honor to Murchison and Lyell, Tyndall and Huxley, Grove and Faraday, Morse and Henry of our own time, and to Franklin, Dalton, Fourcroy, and Berzelius in the past. Looking to the future while teaching the lessons of the past, he did not fail to caution his countrymen against the dangers, moral, mental, and physical, to which they must find themselves exposed should they continue onward in pursuit of a policy looking to the conversion of the island into a mere shop, and themselves into a "nation of shopkeepers." His immortal work was first published in 1776, its essential object having been that of enforcing upon the author's countrymen the great truth, that *trade and manufacture were useful only so far as they contributed to the development of the treasures of the earth, and to the promotion of commerce.* He saw that the colonial system, looking exclusively to trade, tended unnaturally to increase the proportion of the British population employed in the work of exchange and transportation, thereby raising up "a nation of mere shopkeepers," and forcing industry to run principally in one great channel, instead of in a number of smaller ones; and he warned his countrymen of the dangers they thus incurred. Great, however, as were even then those dangers, England had yet but entered on the effort to reduce the world at large under the system so long imposed upon her colonial dependents.* The interdiction of the emigration of artisans dated then back but a single decade, and the battle of Plassey, by which the British power in India had been established, was then not twenty years old. Five years later came the prohibition of the export of silk and woollen machinery; and before the close of the century the policy had been perfected by the extension of this prohibition to all other descriptions of machinery, to artisans by whom it might be made, and to colliers.

* How tyrannical and oppressive were those restrictions on colonial domestic commerce which were denounced by Smith as not only in themselves immoral, but as tending to the deterioration of his own countrymen, is shown in the facts here given, as follows:—

In 1699, Parliament declared "that no wool, yarn, or woollen manufactures of their American plantations, *should be shipped there, or even laden, in order to be transported from thence to any place whatever.*"

In 1719, the House of Commons declared "that the erecting of manufactories in the Colonies tended to *lessen the dependence on Great Britain.*"

In order to protect British hatters from competition in America, Parliament passed an act in 1732, prohibiting hats from being *laden upon a horse, cart, or other carriage in the Colonies*, with an intent to be exported to any other plantation, or to any place whatsoever, under a penalty of forfeiture of the hats so laden, and a fine of five hundred pounds! The same act prohibited the employment of *blacks* or *negroes* in the Colonies, in the business of making hats; and also prohibited any person from engaging in the manufacture who had not served as an apprentice in the business for *seven years!*

In 1750, Parliament passed an act *prohibiting* the erection or continuance of any mill or other engine in the Colonies, for slitting or rolling iron, or any plating forge to work with a tilt hammer, or any furnace for making steel in the Colonies, *under a penalty of two hundred pounds.* And every such mill, engine, plating forge, and furnace in the Colonies was declared a *common nuisance*, and the Governors of the Colonies, on the information of two witnesses, were directed to cause the same *to be abated within thirty days*, or to forfeit the sum of five hundred pounds!

Of all tyrannies the most debasing *to both master and man* is that of the mere trader, as then and now exercised by Britain.

From that hour to the present the British policy has been in direct opposition to all the teachings of the author of the *Wealth of Nations*, and in as direct accordance with those of Messrs. Hume and Brougham, the great object of whose desires, as expressed in Parliament, was that, at any cost, "foreign manufactures should be stifled in the cradle," and that the nations of the world might be thus compelled to make all their exchanges in the British shop. From that hour, all that was really great and good in political economy has more and more tended to disappear, man being with each successive day more and more treated as a mere machine, and "the labor market" being more and more regarded as subject to the same laws which govern those other markets in which horses, oxen, and human cattle are elsewhere bought and sold. Side by side with this system the *science* here discussed has gradually been perfected, giving to the world divine laws in virtue of which all power tends naturally toward the hands of those already rich and strong, all responsibility being thrown on the shoulders of those who are poor and weak. If the latter *will* marry and *will* have children, why should they not be allowed to starve, as have already done so many millions of Irish people? Gradually accommodating itself to the policy denounced by the great Father of political economy, the science of which he had laid the foundations has become, to use the words of more than one eminent authority, "the science which treats of buying and selling;" one almost equally eminent meanwhile cautioning the British public against "advocating the rights of labor," lest they find themselves to have been "digging a grave for free trade;" a third cautioning French authorities against admitting the truth of the idea that the work of cultivation had commenced on the poorer soils, for the reason that "it led inevitably to protection."*

Such is the politico-economical *science* whose foundations have now been placed in the grocer's shop and the peddler's wallet; whose every suggestion is opposed to that which common sense and common humanity teach the British people should of right be done;† whose one idea is found in the words

* *Journal des Economistes*, Dec. 1851, p. 297.

† "Proposals for legislative interference with a view to arrest some of the most frightful evils of society are still constantly opposed not by careful analysis of their tendency, but by general assertions of Natural Law as opposed to all legislation of the kind. 'You cannot make men moral by Act of Parliament'—such is a common enunciation of Principle, which, like many others of the same kind, is in one sense a truism, and in every other sense a fallacy. It is true that neither wealth, nor health, nor knowledge, nor morality can be given by Act of Parliament. But it is also true that the acquisition of one and of all these can be impeded and prevented by bad laws, as well as aided and encouraged by wise and appropriate legislation."—*Duke of Argyll, Reign of Law*, p. 404.

When a few years since it had been shown that in the bleaching establishments of both England and Scotland men, women, and children were required to work for sixteen to twenty hours per day under such a temperature that their feet frequently became blistered by reason of the heating of the nails in the floor, and that because of the waste of life therein they had attained the name of "wasting shops:" when these things had been officially certified to, Parliament rejected a bill providing for putting them under the same restrictions as to hours of labor as had already been established for cotton mills; so doing avowedly on the ground that such measures were opposed to true political economy as well as injurious to trade.

Mr. Herbert Spencer objects most positively to all such measures for "free trade;" whose terms are so undefined that it may safely be said of it, as has been said of metaphysics, that its language was that of one who did not understand himself, addressed to another who did not understand him; whose tendencies were well described by the elder Napoleon when he said that, carried into practical effect, "they would grind to powder the most powerful empires;" whose result, thus far, has been that of giving to England an ever-rising tide of pauperism, and a rural population with, according to *Edinburgh Reviewers*, no future but the poorhouse; and whose professors yet claim to be disciples in the school of Adam Smith, the man who, were he now alive, would stand before the world as chief opponent of the *science* that has nothing but baseless "assumptions" on which to stand.*

§ 8. The following passages from an excellent article on *The Method of Political Economy*, in a recent British journal, are, in conclusion, here reproduced for the reader's consideration:—

"So far we have considered political economy only as a mental science, because economists will insist on treating the subject

---

protecting the poor and weak against the rich and powerful, on the ground that it is the duty of government "to see that the liberty of each man to pursue the object of his desires is unrestricted." In support of this view he cites the late Mr. Cobden, but he might equally have cited the whole slaveholding body of America, opposed, as it had been, to the adoption of any course of action tending to prevent its members from "doing as they liked with their own," whether as regarded negro slaves or bales of cotton.

* The reader who may desire to see a more full examination of some of the details of the modern *science* will do well to consult an article on "Economic Fallacies" in the *London Quarterly Review* for July, 1871.

exclusively from a mental point of view. But political economy is quite as much a physical science as a mental one. Wealth is a material and tangible object, which is not to be secured by wishing for it, but by acting in strict accordance with the physical conditions of its existence. The production of the simplest commodity involves the operation of numerous laws of matter. There is a perpetual action and reaction going on of mind on matter and matter on mind. An effect which may appear as the result of one cause, may in reality be the result of a whole series of causes. To explain the effect, therefore, we must take into account, not one, but every cause that might in the remotest degree have had any influence in producing it. It so happens that in political economy the effects are more accessible than the causes, and this points to the inductive method as the proper one for an investigation of this kind. Treated by the inductive method, political economy is a science of the highest practical value; treated *a priori*, it is not a science at all, but only a scientific artifice, a mere theory of human action in one particular direction, and which has not even the merit of being approximately correct.

* * * * * * *

"Political economy has not yet even arrived at the first or preparatory period. We have not yet begun to collect and arrange our facts. Political economy is in the same state to-day that geology was before the days of Hutton and William Smith, or as the science of language was when comparative philology was unknown, and Hebrew was supposed to be the one primeval language of the human race.

* * * * * * *

"The charges brought against the science by Comte were not altogether uncalled for. Political economy exhibits no sign of progressiveness. Instead of discoveries, of which we have had none of any consequence since Adam Smith's time, we have had endless disputation and setting up of dogmas. It was so in Comte's day, and so it is in ours. Whatever progress may have been made in other sciences during the last century, there has been none in this. The most elementary principles are still matters of dispute. The doctrine of free trade, for instance, which is looked upon as the crowning triumph of political economy, is still very far from being universally recognized. Even in England, after twenty years' trial under most favorable circumstances, free trade has been put upon its defence. We make no progress, and from the very nature of our method of investigation, we can make none. The political economist observes phenomena with a foregone conclusion as to their cause. His method, in fact, is the method of the savage. The phenomena of nature, the thunder, the lightning, or the earthquake, strike the savage with awe and wonder; but he only looks within himself for an explanation of these phenomena. To him, therefore, the forces of nature are only the efforts of beings like himself—great and powerful no doubt, but with good and evil propensities and subject to every human caprice. Like the political economist, he works within the vicious circle of his own feelings, and he cannot comprehend any more than the savage how he can discover the laws which regulate the phenomena which he sees around him. The savage would reduce the Divine mind to the dimensions of the human; the political economist would reduce the human mind to the dimensions of his ideal.

"Our conclusion is that the inductive method is alone applicable to the investigation of economic science, and that we shall never be able to make any solid progress so long as we continue to follow the *a priori* method—method which has not aided, but clogged and fettered us in the pursuit of truth, and which is utterly alien to the spirit of modern scientific inquiry."—*Westminster Review*, July, 1871.

That the views thus presented are correct is beyond question. Political Economy, as now taught, is in a position closely correspondent with that occupied by Astronomy before the days of Copernicus, Kepler, and Galileo. There, too, must it remain until its professors shall qualify themselves for furnishing answers to the simple questions—Whence comes the idea of value? Of what does value consist?

CHAPTER II.

OF SCIENCE AND ITS METHODS.

§ 1. The first man, when he had day after day even for a single week witnessed the rising and setting of the sun, the former having invariably been accompanied by the presence of light, while the latter had as invariably been followed by its absence, had thus acquired the first rude elements of positive knowledge, or science. The cause—the sun's rising—being given, it would have been beyond his power to conceive that the effect should not follow. With further observation he learned to remark that at certain seasons of the year the luminary appeared to traverse particular portions of the heavens, that then it was always warm, and the trees put forth leaves, to be followed by fruit; whereas, at others, it appeared to occupy other portions of the heavens, the fruit then disappearing and the leaves falling, as a prelude to the winter's cold. Here was a further addition to his stock of knowledge, bringing with it foresight, and a feeling of the necessity for action. If he would live during the season of cold, he could do so only by preparing for it during the season of heat, a principle as thoroughly understood by the wandering Esquimaux of the shores of the Arctic Ocean as by the most enlightened and eminent philosopher of Europe or America.*

Earliest among the ideas of such a man would be those of space, quantity, and form. The sun was obviously very remote, while of the trees some were distant and others were close at hand. The moon was single, while the stars were countless. The tree was tall, while the shrub was short. The hills were high, and tending towards a point, the plains being low and flat. We have here the most abstract, simple, and obvious of all conceptions. The idea of space is the same, whether we regard the distance between the sun and the stars by which he is surrounded, or that between the mountains and ourselves. So, too, with number and form, which apply

* "These facts, that science and the positive knowledge of the uncultured cannot be separated in nature, and that the one is but a perfected and extended form of the other, must necessarily underlie the whole theory of science, its progress, and the relations of its parts to each other. There must be serious incompleteness in any history of the sciences which, leaving out of view the first steps of their genesis, commences with them only when they assume definite forms. There must be grave defects, if not a general untruth, in a philosophy of the sciences considered in their interdependence and development, which neglects the inquiry how they came to be distinct sciences, and how they were severally evolved out of the chaos of primitive ideas. * * * Is not science a growth? Has not science, too, its embryology? And must not the neglect of its embryology lead to a misunderstanding of the principles of its evolution and of its existing organization? There are *a priori* reasons, therefore, for doubting the truth of all philosophies of the sciences which tacitly proceed upon the common notion that scientific knowledge and ordinary knowledge are separate; instead of commencing, as they should, by affiliating the one upon the other, and showing how it gradually came to be distinguishable from the other. We may expect to find their generalizations essentially artificial, and we shall not be deceived."—*Herbert Spencer, Genesis of Science.*

to the sands of the sea-shore as readily as to the gigantic trees of the forest, or to the various bodies seen to be moving through the heavens.

Next in order would come the desire, or the necessity, for comparing distances, numbers, and magnitudes, the means for this being at hand in machinery supplied by nature, and always at his command. His finger or his arm would supply a measure of magnitudes, his pace doing the same by distance; and the standard with which he would compare the weights would be found in some one among the most ordinary commodities by which he was surrounded. In numerous cases, however, distances, velocities, or dimensions proving to be beyond the reach of direct measurement, there is thus produced a necessity for devising means of comparing distant and unknown quantities with those that, being near, can be ascertained, and hence arises mathematics, or The Science—so denominated by the Greeks, because to its aid was due nearly all the positive knowledge of which they were possessed.

The multiplication table enables the ploughman to determine the number of days contained in a given number of weeks, and the merchant to calculate the number of pounds contained in his cargo of cotton. By help of his rule, the carpenter determines the distance between the ends of the plank on which he works. The sounding-line enables the sailor to ascertain the depth of water around his ship, and by aid of the barometer the traveller determines the height of the mountain on which he stands.

All these are *instruments* for facilitating the acquisition of knowledge; such, too, being the formulæ of mathematics by help of which the philosopher determines the magnitude and weight of bodies distant from him millions of millions of miles, and is thus enabled to solve innumerable questions of the highest interest to man. They are the key to science, but are not to be confounded with science itself, although often included in the list of sciences, and even so recently as in M. Comte's well-known work. That such should ever have been the case has been due to the fact that so much of what is really physics is discussed under the head of mathematics; as is the case with the great laws for whose discovery we are indebted to Kepler, Galileo, and Newton. That a body impelled by a single force will move in a right line and with a velocity that is invariable, and that action and reaction are equal and opposite, are facts at the knowledge of which we have arrived in consequence of pursuing a certain mode of investigation; but, when obtained, they are purely physical facts, obtained by help of the instrument to which we apply the term mathematics—and which is, to use the words of M. Comte, simply "an immense extension of natural logic to a certain order of deductions."*

Logic is itself, however, but another of the instruments devised by man for enabling him to obtain a knowledge of nature's laws. To his eyes the earth

* *Positive Philosophy*, Martineau's Translation, vol. i. 33.

appears to be a plane, yet does he see the sun rising daily in the east and setting as regularly in the west, from which he might infer that it would always continue so to do; but of this he can feel no certainty until he has satisfied himself why it is that it does so rise and set. At one time seeing the sun to be eclipsed, while at another the moon ceases to give light, he desires to know why such things are—what is the law governing the movements of those bodies; having obtained which, he is enabled to predict when they will again cease to give light, and to determine when they must have done so in times that are past. At one moment ice or salt melts; at another, gas explodes; at a third, walls are shattered and cities are hurled to the ground; and he seeks to know why these things are—what is the relation of cause and effect? In the effort to obtain answers to all these questions, he observes and records facts, then arranging them with a view to determining the laws by virtue of which they occur—and he invents barometers, thermometers, and other instruments to aid him in his observations, but the ultimate object of all is that of obtaining an answer to the questions: Why are all these things? Why is it that dew falls on one day and not on another? Why is it that corn grows abundantly in this field and fails altogether in that one? Why is it that coal burns and granite will not? What, in a word, are the laws instituted by the Creator for the government of matter? The answers to these questions constitute science—and mathematics, logic, and all other of the machinery in use, are but instruments used by him for the purpose of obtaining them.

Discussing the subject of rational mechanics under the head of mathematics, M. Comte informs his readers that we here "encounter a perpetual confusion between the abstract and the concrete points of view; between the logical and the physical; between the artificial conceptions necessary to help us to general laws of equilibrium and motion, and the natural facts furnished by observation, which must form the basis of the science."* This, however, is only saying that as "the natural facts," furnished by observation, increase in number, there arises a necessity for endeavoring to perfect the machinery by help of which they are to be studied; and that such is the case in the instance here referred to is shown in M. Comte's admission that the science of which he treats is "founded on some general facts, furnished by observation, of which we can give no explanation whatever."† Passing from gate to gate of science, we pass from simple to compound locks, requiring additional wards in the keys by which they are to be opened; but the key still remains a key, and can never become a lock, even though the wards become fifty-fold more numerous than those of any yet constructed by Bramah, Chubb, or Hobbs, and require years of study for acquiring its proper management. There arises then what may

* *Positive Philosophy*, Martineau's Translation, vol. i. p. 107.
† Ibid.

be called the science of the key, but it constitutes no part of natural science. When D'Alembert made, to use the words of Comte, "a discovery, by help of which all investigation of the motion of any body or system might be converted at once into a question of equilibrium," he merely opened a new ward in the key by which we were to unlock the cabinet of nature, and thus enlarge the boundaries of that department of knowledge which treats of the properties of matter and the laws by which it is governed, and known as physical science.

§ 2. Abstract mathematics necessarily took precedence of the more concrete physics, because they were the sole product of logic, and dependent upon those first principles which are in their elements so nearly intuitive that when a boy commences the study of geometry he finds that he had already acquired a knowledge of much that is now being given to him as science. Hence, too, it was that moral science, poetry, the fine arts, and metaphysics were so far advanced in Greece, while mechanical science had scarcely an existence.

In default of observation, men of speculative habits looked inwards to their own minds and invented theories that were given to the world as laws, but, as has well been said, "Man can *invent* nothing in science or religion but falsehood, and all the truths that he *discovers* are but facts or laws that have emanated from the Creator." The men of the Middle Ages—the philosophers of the schools—taught the theories that had been invented by their

Grecian predecessors, leaving it for Bacon to teach the philosophy that leads to the search for truth among the facts of nature and not among the speculations of men. From his day to the present there has been a perpetual tendency towards the substitution of careful observation and induction for the dreams of theorists, and as the Cartesian doctrine of Vortices gave way to the discovery of gravitation, so the imaginary phlogiston of Stahl, and the Plutonian and Neptunian cosmogonies, have yielded to the discoveries of modern science. The former was early displaced by the oxygen of Lavoisier, while the latter held their ground until disproved by the observations of geologists, whose branch of science dates its existence but little beyond the present century.

In physics, the more abstract and general has in its development tended to take precedence of that which is concrete and special, both, however, moving gradually onward, each aiding and aided by the other. Astronomy, the science of the laws governing bodies exterior to our own planet, was studied at an early period, the shepherds of Chaldea having carefully noted the movements of the celestial bodies, and Babylonians having calculated eclipses thousands of years before the commencement of the Christian era. From a well in Syene Eratosthenes obtained the observations required for determining the terrestial meridian; and many centuries before Copernicus, Archimedes taught the double motion of the earth around its axis and around the sun.

The precise length of the solar year was determined by Hipparchus, corresponding within ten minutes with the figures obtained by both Mexican and Etrurian observations.

The motions of the celestial bodies were thus early studied and comprehended, yet was it left to Newton to discover the reason why the apple falls to the earth; to Franklin to discover the identity of lightning and electricity; to Cavendish to discover the composition of the air we breathe; and to philosophers of our own day to discover the laws in virtue of which we see and hear. Laplace's great work of Celestial Mechanics was the product of the same period that witnessed the birth of a new science having for its object to determine the composition of the globe on which we live and move, and from which we derive our daily bread. It is thus, as we approach nearer to man, his uses and purposes, we find the greatest retardation of that positive knowledge so early attained in reference to the method to be pursued in the effort for its attainment. The study of the history of science leads inevitably to an agreement with Buffon in the opinion that "however great may be our interest in knowing ourselves," we probably "understand better all that is not ourselves"—and with Rousseau in the belief that "much philosophy is required for observing the facts that are very near to us."

Passing from the more abstract and general laws governing the movements of distant bodies towards those determining the composition of the matter by which we are immediately surrounded, we find new laws, but all in harmony with those first obtained. Chemistry, following physics which deals with masses, deals with the elements of which they are composed, giving us atoms as obedient to the law of gravitation as are the earth, the satellites of Jupiter, and Jupiter himself. "The distinction between physics and chemistry," says M. Comte, "is much less easy to establish" than between chemistry and astronomy, and, as he continues, "it is one more difficult to pronounce upon from day to day as new discoveries bring to light closer relations between them."* That such is the case will readily be seen by the reader who reflects how much of the present great development of physical knowledge has been due to the labors of Cavendish, Priestley, Black, Davy, Lavoisier, Fourcroy, Gay-Lussac, and other eminent chemists.

On another occasion M. Comte thus shows the intimate relation between physics on one side of chemistry, and physiology on the other:—

> "By the important series of electro-chemical phenomena chemistry becomes, as it were, a prolongation of physics: and at its other extremity, it lays the foundation of physiology by its research into organic combinations. These relations are so real that it has sometimes happened that chemists, untrained in the philosophy of science, have been uncertain whether a particular subject lay within their department, or ought to be referred either to physics or to physiology."†

---

* *Positive Philosophy*, Martineau's Translation, vol. i. p. 216.

† Ibid., vol. i. p. 298.

As yet, he is of opinion that "the direct dependence of chemistry on astronomy" is very slight, but

"When the time shall come for the development of concrete chemistry, that is, the methodical application of chemical knowledge to the natural history of the globe, astronomical considerations will no doubt enter in where now there seems no point of contact between the two sciences. Geology, immature as it is, hints to us such a future necessity, some vague instinct of which was probably in the minds of philosophers in the theological age, when they were fancifully and yet obstinately bent on uniting astrology and alchemy. It is, in fact, impossible to conceive of the great intestinal operations of the globe as radically independent of its planetary conditions."*

Passing thus from the masses of physics through the atoms into which they are resolved by chemistry, we next find those atoms arranging themselves in organized and living forms, and constituting the still more special subjects of vegetable, animal, and human physiology, whose connection with chemistry is thus described:—

"Physiology depends upon chemistry both as a point of departure and as a principal means of investigation. If we separate the phenomena of life, properly so called, from those of animality, it is clear that the first, in the double intestinal movement which characterizes them, are essentially chemical. The processes which result from organization have peculiar characteristics; but apart from such modifications, they are necessarily subjected to the general laws of chemical effects. Even in studying living bodies under a simply statical point of view, chemistry is of indispensable use in enabling us to distinguish with precision the different anatomical elements of any organism."†

Again, in treating of biology, he says:—

* *Positive Philosophy*, Martineau's Translation, vol. i. p. 299.

† Ibid., vol. i. p. 300.

"It is to chemistry that biology is by its nature most directly and completely subordinated. In analyzing the phenomena of life, we saw that the fundamental acts which, by their perpetuity, characterize that state, consist of a series of compositions and decompositions; and they are therefore of a chemical nature. Though in the most imperfect organisms vital reactions are widely separated from common chemical effects, it is not the less true that all the functions of the proper organic life are necessarily controlled by those fundamental laws of composition and decomposition which constitute the subject of chemical science. * * * Chemistry must clearly furnish the starting-point of every rational theory of nutrition, secretion, and, in short, all the functions of the vegetative life considered separately; each of which is controlled by the influence of chemical laws, except for the special modifications belonging to organic conditions."*

It is not, however, with chemistry alone that physiology is connected. Remote from astronomy as that department of knowledge appears to be, the relation between them "is more important," says M. Comte, "than is usually supposed. I mean," continues he—

"Something more than the impossibility of understanding the theory of weight, and its effects upon the organism, apart from the consideration of general gravitation. I mean, besides, and more especially, that it is impossible to form a scientific conception of the conditions of vital existence without taking into the account the aggregate astronomical elements that characterize the planet which is the home of that vital existence. * * *

"It may at first appear anomalous, and a breach of the encyclopedical arrangement of the sciences, that astronomy and biology should be thus immediately and eminently connected, while two other sciences lie between. But indispensable as are physics and chemistry, astronomy and biology are by their nature the two principal branches of natural philosophy. They,

---

* *Positive Philosophy*, Martineau's Translation, vol i. p. 379.

the complements of each other, include in their rational harmony the general system of our fundamental conceptions. The solar system and Man are the extreme terms within which our ideas will forever be included. The system first, and then Man, according to the positive course of our speculative reason: and the reverse in the active process: the laws of the system determining those of Man, and remaining unaffected by them. Between these two poles of natural philosophy the laws of physics interpose, as a kind of complement of the astronomical laws; and again, those of chemistry, as an immediate preliminary of the biological. Such being the rational and indissoluble constitution of these sciences, it becomes apparent why I insisted on the subordination of the study of Man to that of the system, as the primary philosophical characteristic of positive biology."

Passing now toward the more concrete and special department of knowledge treating of the relation of man with his fellow-man, and with the earth from which he derives his means of support, we find chemistry laying the foundation for it when "abolishing the idea of destruction and creation,"* and thus establishing the facts that the consumption of food is but a necessary step towards its reproduction; that in all the processes of agriculture man is but making a machine which supports him while engaged in making it; that the more time and mind he devotes to the development of the powers of the earth, the greater must be his power of production; and that the more rapidly the consumption of food follows its production, the more prompt will be the reproduction of the elements required for new supplies thereof. These views of the effect of the principle thus established had not occurred to M.

* *Positive Philosophy*, Martineau's Translation, p. 305.

Comte, but he shows clearly the direct connection of chemical and social science when telling his readers that—

> "Before anything was known of gaseous materials and products, many striking appearances must inevitably have inspired the idea of the real annihilation or production of matter in the general system of nature. These ideas could not yield to the true conception of decomposition and composition till we had decomposed air and water, and then analyzed vegetable and animal substances, and then finished with the analysis of alkalies and earths, thus exhibiting the fundamental principle of the indefinite perpetuity of matter. In vital phenomena, the chemical examination of not only the substances of living bodies, but their functions—imperfect as it yet is—must cast a strong light upon the economy of vital nature by showing that no organic matter radically heterogeneous to inorganic matter can exist, and that vital transformations are subject like all others to the universal laws of chemical phenomena."

The exhibit thus made by M. Comte of the close relation of the various departments of science has been not only confirmed but extended at every stage of progress since he wrote. In his recent address, delivered before the British Association, its President, Sir William Thomson, told its members, that "the earnest naturalists of the present day," not appalled by difficulties, were "struggling boldly and laboriously to pass out of the mere natural history stage of their study, and bring zoology within the range of natural philosophy." The course of things is thus upward and onward, chemistry aiding in the development of physics, the researches of physiologists meanwhile making new demands upon, and thereby promoting the growth of, chemical science. Each helps and is helped by the other.

The root, the stem, the branches, the leaves, and the blossoms of the tree are obedient to the same system of laws. Colored water applied to the root changes the color of the blossom, and stoppage of nourishment to the root destroys the tree. It is still but a single tree, and so is it with the tree of science, whose root is found in physics, its stem branching into those divisions which are based upon observation and experiment, leaving us to find the leaves, the blossoms, and the fruit in the less demonstrable departments of knowledge.

That this is true as regards the more abstract and general portions of science to which reference has here been made, can scarcely now be doubted. Wherefore, then, should we doubt that it would be found equally so in relation to those more concrete and special which treat of man in his relation with the material world—of man in his relations with his fellow-man—of man as a being capable of acquiring power over the various natural forces provided for his use, and responsible to his fellow-men, and to his Creator for the proper use of the faculties with which he has been so wonderfully endowed? If the root, the stem, and the branches obey the same laws, should we not find the blossoms and the fruit of the tree of science equally obedient to them, and will not the diagram opposite represent with considerable accuracy the relation of the various departments of knowledge and—having always regard to the fact that each has aided, as it has been aided by, each and every other—the order of their march toward becoming perfect and exact science?

§ 3. "The distributions and partitions of knowledge," says Lord Bacon in his *Novum Organum*, "are not like several lines that meet in one angle, and *touch but in a point;* but are like branches of a tree that meet in a stem, which hath a dimension and quantity of entireness and continuance before it comes to discontinuance and break itself into arms and boughs; therefore," as he continues, "it is good, before we enter into the former distribution, to create and constitute one universal science by the name of Philosophia Prima, or Summary Philosophy, as the main or common way, before we come where the ways part and divide themselves."

Concerned as he was with the order and division of the sciences, and pledged as he was in the introduction to his work to furnish it, he failed to do so, "the first part of the Introduction which comprehends the division of the sciences" being, says his editor, "wanting." A study, so far as the idea of the text appears to require elucidation, rather than an attempt to supply the deficiency, is submitted in its stead.

The several *branches* of natural science are commonly spoken of, but the figure has a larger parallelism with the subject—a tree having not only branches but also roots. These latter are properly underground branches, constituting the structural support and furnishing the vital subsistence of the

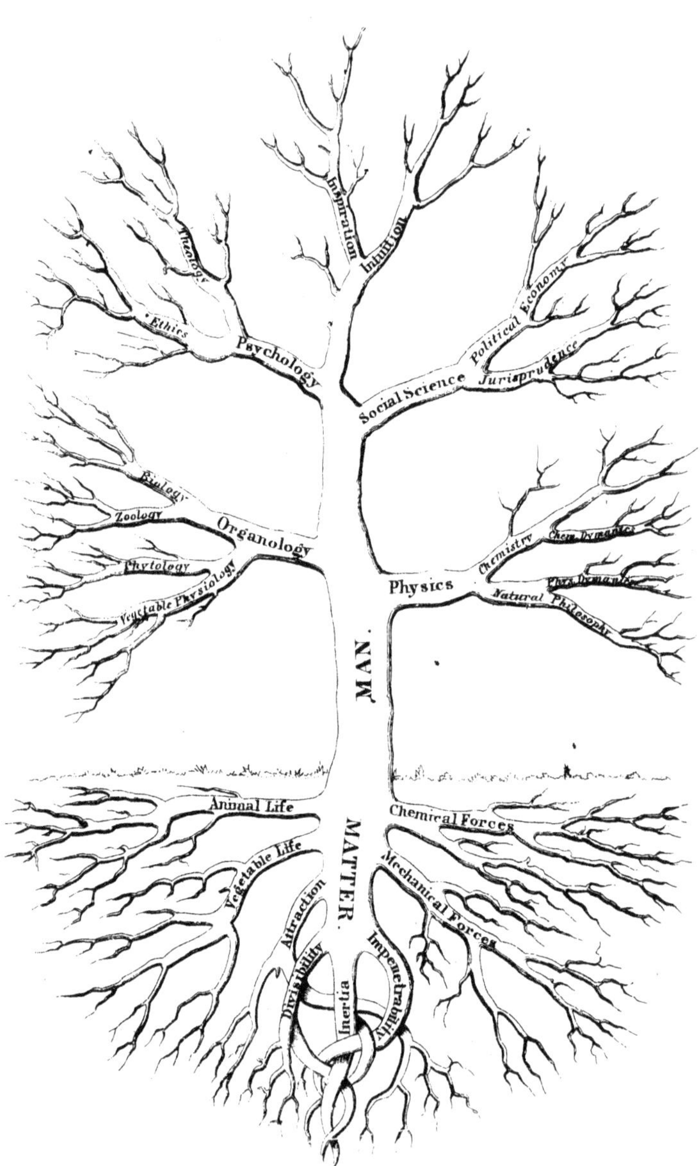
Inspiration
Intuition
Theology
Ethics
Psychology
Political Economy
Jurisprudence
Social Science
Biology
Zoology
Organology
Phytology
Vegetable Physiology
Chemistry
Chem. Dynamics
Phys. Dynamics
Physics
Natural Philosophy
MAN.
Animal Life
Vegetable Life
Chemical Forces
Mechanical Forces
MATTER.
Attraction
Divisibility
Inertia
Impenetrability

tree, which grows from its roots and with them. Its stem, branches, flowers, and fruits, being converted aliment supplied by and through the roots, the allusions of the figure are in good keeping with the natural history of the subject intended to be illustrated.

The central or tap root, as the reader sees, represents matter with its essential properties of inertia, impenetrability, divisibility, and attraction. The lateral ones stand on one side for mechanical and chemical forces, and on the other, for vegetable and animal ones; and from these substantive roots of being rises the stem, man, so composed as to his natural constitution. The soul, being the occult life of the structure, is incapable of representation, though manifested by its proper evidence in the flowers and fruits, the emotions and thoughts of his faculties.

We have now the stem—the man—"having dimension and quantity of entireness and continuance before it came to discontinue and break itself," branching off into his diverse activities. These branches are his functions, ramifying into all their specific differences of application. The first branch on the material side is Physics, as represented in the diagram. Its ramifications are into natural philosophy and chemistry—masses and atoms—and the shoots from these are mechanics and chemical dynamics; the one being the action of masses, and the other that of atoms.

The main branch on the vital side of the tree,

rising a little above Physics, must necessarily be Organology, branching first into the science of vegetable beings, Phytology, then sending off the shoot, Vegetable Physiology; and second, into that of animal beings, Zoology, leading to Biology, or the science of life.

Following the stem in the natural order of rank and successive development, it is seen next giving off Sociology, which divides itself into Jurisprudence and Political Economy, while on the corresponding side of the main branch, Psychology ramifies itself into Ethics and Theology—the tree finally topping out with Intuition as the material branch and Inspiration as the vital one. These highest and last named are rightly the source of the other science or sciences to which Bacon alludes as standing above Metaphysics, when he says that, "as for the vertical point, the summary law of nature, we know not whether man's inquiry can attain unto it;" that is, so as to order and methodize its teachings.

In this scheme of the sciences of things there is no place for either Logic or Mathematics, the respective regulative sciences of mind and matter. Neither of these belongs to Natural History, being both alike mere instruments to be used in the study of nature.

Historically, the top branches of the tree of knowledge, as of all other trees, are first produced, and the branches next below are soon put forth, but mature later, the instincts of religion and reason appearing in their vigor in the childhood of the race. Social science necessarily, and metaphysics spontaneously, extend themselves as early as societies take form, and speculation is awakened—bringing quickly forth the flowers and fruits of music, poetry, the fine arts, logic, mathematics, and those generalities of speculative truth which are the products of imagination and reflection.* The correspondence between the figure chosen and the facts to be illustrated would seem to be complete.

In time, the branches nearer to the earth, more material in their substance and more dependent upon observation, obtain development in their larger diversity of use. The sciences of substance, of natural objects, grow and ramify themselves almost indefinitely—physical philosophy and organology, in their dependencies, shooting out in every direction of observation and experiment, at first overshadowed by the speculative branches above them, but always vivified by them; while in their turn repaying this service by affording substantive strength and corrective modification as they grow into maturity.

Such is the history of science, and such the illustration of its orderly divisions, succession, and co-ordination; it represents the compound nature

* Xenophon urged upon his Athenian countrymen that in default of the domestic market for food that would have resulted from proper development of the mineral treasures with which their soil abounded, agriculture had become impossible; many having been forced to abandon it, becoming usurers or brokers. See *Journal des Economistes*, Sept. 1871, p. 365. This is probably the earliest exhibit on record of the dependence of agriculture on the mining and manufacturing industries.

of man, the sources of his powers, and the order of their development.

§ 4. Seeking to obtain power over matter, man desires to obtain a knowledge of the laws instituted for its government. To become the subject of law, it is required that there be a regular and uniform succession of causes and effects, the nature of which may be expressed in distinct propositions—so that when we observe the former we may be enabled to predict the latter; or that when the latter are observed, we may safely assume the former to have pre-existed.

In the early ages of society theories abound, and for the reason that, in default of knowledge, almost every occurrence is regarded as accidental, or is attributed to the direct interposition of mythological powers whose qualities are so vaguely conceived as to make the idea of the events depending upon their action scarcely one remove from that of its being absolutely fortuitous and irreducible to order and rule. The Greeks of the days of Homer solicited the aid of imaginary deities, themselves moved to action by the same feelings and passions that influenced their worshippers; precisely as does now the poor African who makes his oblations of corn or oil, palm-wine or rum, to the stock or stone, the alligator, or the bundle of rags, he has chosen for his idol. With time, however, the regular succession of effects and causes comes to be understood, and at every stage of progress theory tends to pass away, yielding place to knowledge; this latter bringing with it power to direct the forces of nature to man's service. At each such stage he obtains new evidence of the universality of natural laws—new proof that where exceptions appear to exist they are but appearances, and will, when carefully analyzed and fully understood, but prove the rule; as does the smoke when rising in apparent opposition to the great law in virtue of which all the matter of which the earth is composed tends towards its centre.*

To prove the universality of law, thereby establishing the unity of science, seemed at first to be the intention of M. Comte, from whose work preliminary to, and intended as the basis of, the one that was to be specially devoted to social science, the preceding extracts have been made. The promised work subsequently appeared, but in it, as before when treating of man and his operations, he intentionally ignored that mathematical method to which the earlier and more developed departments of science had so largely been indebted. That he should so have done would seem to have been a consequence of regarding mathematics as a science, and not as a mere instrument for the acquisition of scientific knowledge. Thus, in treating of chemistry, he tells us that "every attempt to refer chemical

* "We ought to conceive the study of nature as destined to furnish the true rational basis of the action of man upon nature; because the knowledge of the laws of phenomena, of which the invariable result is foresight, and that alone, can conduct us in active life to modify the one by the other to our advantage. In short, SCIENCE WHENCE FORESIGHT, FORESIGHT WHENCE ACTION, such is the simple formula which expresses the general relation of Science and Art."—*Comte.*

questions to mathematical doctrines must be considered, now and always, profoundly irrational, as being contrary to the nature of the phenomena."* What, however, are those doctrines? Are they anything beyond simple formulæ adapted to the peculiar circumstances of the case under consideration? Certainly not. The geometer tells us that every whole is equal to all its parts, and that things which are halves of the same thing are equal, axioms of universal application, and equally true in relation to all bodies, whether those treated by the chemist, the sociologist, or the measurer of land, but involving no question of doctrine whatsoever.

Occasionally M. Comte speaks of mathematics as what it clearly is, an "instrument of admirable efficacy," but being an instrument it can no more be a science than can a key become a lock. That instrument, the mathematical method, is always applicable, whatever may be the subject of investigation. That method is analysis—the study of each separate cause tending to produce a given effect. To it we owe all the discoveries of Copernicus, Kepler, Newton, and their successors; such, too, being the method of the chemist, who commences by ascertaining the separate force of each of his various ingredients, and ends by deducing the law of the effect. When engaged in the study of the skeleton, the physiologist uses the formulæ of the physicist; but when studying the composition of the blood, he resorts necessarily to those of the chemist, in which

* *Positive Philosophy*, Martineau's Translation, vol. i. p. 299.

is embodied all the knowledge derived from the observation of the philosophers by whom he had been preceded. This method, however, is discarded by M. Comte in treating of social science, as will be seen by the following passage:—

"There can be no scientific study of society, either in its conditions or its movements, if it is separated into portions, and its divisions are studied apart. I have already remarked upon this in regard to what is called political economy. Materials may be furnished by the observation of different departments; and such observation may be necessary for that object; but it cannot be called science. The methodical division of studies which takes place in the simple inorganic sciences is thoroughly irrational in the recent and complex science of society, and can produce no results. The day may come when some sort of subdivision may be practicable and desirable; but it is impossible for us now to anticipate what the principle of distribution may be; for the principle itself must arise from the development of the science; and that development can take place no otherwise than by our formation of the science as a whole."

"In the organic sciences, the elements are much better known to us than the whole which they constitute; so that in that case we must proceed from the simple to the compound. But the reverse method is necessary in the study of man and of society; man and society as a whole being better known to us, and more accessible subjects of study, than the parts which constitute them."*

To pursue the course thus indicated would be to go back to what M. Comte was accustomed to denominate the metaphysical stage of science. The philosopher of old would, in like manner, have said: "These masses of granite are better known to us than the parts of which they are composed, and

* *Positive Philosophy*, Martineau's Translation, vol. ii. p. 81.

therefore we will limit our inquiries to the questions as to how they came to have their existing form and occupy their present position." Without the analysis of the chemist it would have been as impossible that we should be enabled to "penetrate into the details" of the piece of stone, and thus to acquire a knowledge of the composition of the distant mountain from which it had been taken, as it would now be for us to penetrate into those of the communities that have passed away, were we not in the midst of living ones, composed of men endowed with the same gifts and animated by the same feelings and passions observed to have existed among those of ancient times; and were we not, too, possessors of the numerous facts accumulated during the many centuries that since have intervened. It is the details of life around us that we need to study, commencing by analysis and proceeding to synthesis, as does the chemist when he resolves the piece of granite into atoms, and thus acquires the secret of the composition of the mass. Having ascertained that it is composed of quartz, feldspar, and mica, and having fully satisfied himself of the circumstances under which it appears in the country near to him, he feels entire confidence that wherever else it may be found, its composition and its position in the order of formation will be the same. He is constantly going from the near and the known which he can analyze and examine, to the distant and the unknown which he cannot; studying the latter by means of formulæ obtained by analysis of the former.

Thus it was that by study of the deposits of Siberia and California, the geologist was enabled to predict that gold would be found among the mountains of Australia.

Seeking now to understand the history of man in past ages or in distant lands, we must commence by studying him in the present, and having mastered him in the past and present, we may then be enabled to predict the future. To do this, it is required that we do with society as the chemist does with the piece of granite, resolving it into its several parts and studying each part separately, ascertaining how it would act were it left to itself; then comparing what *would be* its independent action with that we see *to be* its societary action. That done, by help of the same law of which the mathematician, the physicist, the chemist, and the physiologist avail themselves—that of the composition of forces—we may perhaps arrive at the law of the effect. So to do would not, however, be to adopt the course of M. Comte, who gives us the distant and the unknown—the societies of past ages—as a means of understanding the movements of the men by whom we are surrounded, and of predicting what will be those of future men. To us it seems that as well might the teacher furnish his students with a telescope by which to study the mountains of the moon, that he might be thus enabled to understand the movements of the laboratory.

The necessary consequence of this inverse and erroneous method is that he is led to arrive at conclusions directly the reverse of those to which men's natural instincts lead them; directly opposed, too, to the tendencies of thought and action in all the times of advancing civilization, whether in the ancient or modern world; the result being that he leaves his readers as much at a loss to understand the causes of disturbance that now exist, or the remedy needed to be applied, as would a physician who should limit the study of his patient to an examination of the body in a mass, omitting all inquiry into the state of the lungs, the stomach, or the brain. His system of sociology does not explain the past, and cannot therefore be used to direct the present; the reason why it neither does nor can do so being that he has declined to use the method of physics, that philosophy which studies the near and the known for the purpose of obtaining power to comprehend the distant and the unknown; which studies the present to obtain knowledge by aid of which to understand the causes of events in the past, and to predict those which are bound to flow from similar causes in the future.

§ 5. Turning from France to Britain, we find ourselves in the home of Adam Smith, whose most essential doctrines have, however, been wholly repudiated by his successors of that modern school which had its origin in the teachings of Messrs. Malthus and Ricardo. "Social Science," as the world is there taught by one of its most distinguished teachers, "is a deductive science; not, indeed," as he continues, "after the model of geometry, but after that of the highest physical sciences. It infers the law of each effect from the laws of causation upon which the effect depends; not, however, from the law merely of one cause, as in the geometrical method, but by considering all the causes which conjointly influence the effect, and compounding those laws with one another."*

Such is the theory. The practice under it consists in providing for the use of science a politico-economical man, or monster, on one hand influenced solely by the thirst for wealth, and on the other so entirely under the control of the sexual passion as to be at all times ready to indulge it, however greatly such indulgence may tend to prevent the growth of wealth.†

What, however, is this thing in the quest for which he is so assiduously engaged? What is wealth? To this question political economy furnishes no reply, it having never yet been settled in what it is that wealth consists. Were it suggested that land constituted any part thereof, the answer would at once be made, that, by reason of a great law of nature, the more of it brought into use, and the larger the quantity of labor given to its improvement, the less must be the return to human effort, the poorer must the community become, and the greater must be the tendency toward poverty and death; the law of constantly diminishing returns to labor applied to cultivation being, as Mr. Mill

* J. S. Mill. *System of Logic*, Book vi. ch. 8.

† See *ante*, p. 15.

assures us, the most important one in the whole range of economic science. Were it next assumed that wealth might be found in development of the individual faculties, proof apparent could be furnished that not only would search in that direction be vain, but that it would result in establishment of the fact that increase in the number of teachers must be attended with diminution of the quantity of wealth at the community's command.* Foiled thus in all his efforts, the inquirer, after having studied carefully all the books, would still be found repeating the question—What is wealth?

Turning next to the being so sedulously engaged in the pursuit of an undefined something that seems to embrace so much, and that yet excludes so large a proportion of the things usually regarded as wealth, he would desire to satisfy himself if the subject of political economy were really the being known as man. He might perhaps be led to ask, has man no other qualities than those here attributed to him? Is he, like the beasts of the field, solely given to the search for food, and shelter for his body? Does he, like them, beget children for the sole gratification of his passions, and does he, like them, leave his offspring to feed and shelter themselves as they may? Has he no feelings or affections to be influenced by the care of wife and children? Has he no judgment to aid him in the decision as to what is likely to benefit or to injure him? That he did possess such qualities would be admitted,

* See Mill, *Principles*, 6th edition, vol. i. p. 61.

but the economist would maintain that his science was that of material wealth alone, to the entire exclusion of that wealth of affection and intellect held by Adam Smith in such high esteem; and thus would he, at the close of all his search, discover that the subject of political economy was not really a man, but an imaginary being moved to action by the blindest passion, and giving all his energies to the pursuit of a thing in its nature so undefinable that all the books would be vainly searched for a definition that would be admitted by a jury of economists as embracing all that should be included, and excluding all that should not.

The law of the composition of forces requires that we study *all* the causes tending to produce a given effect. That effect is MAN—the man of the past and the present; and the social philosopher who excludes from consideration his feelings and affections, and the intellect with which he has been endowed, makes precisely the same mistake that would be made by the physical one who should look exclusively to gravitation, forgetting heat; and should thence conclude that at no distant day the whole material of which the earth is composed would become a solid mass, plants, animals, and men having disappeared. Such is the error of modern political economy, its effects exhibiting themselves in the fact that it presents for our consideration a mere brute animal to find a name for which it desecrates the word "man," recognized by Adam Smith as expressing the idea of a being made in the likeness of its Creator.

It was well asked by Goethe—"What is all intercourse with nature, if by the analytical method we merely occupy ourselves with individual material parts, and do not feel the breath of the spirit which prescribes to every part its direction, and orders or sanctions every deviation by means of an inherent law?" And what, we may ask, is the value of an analytical process that selects only the "material parts" of man—those which are common to himself and the beast—carefully excluding those common to the angels and himself? Such is the course of modern political economy, which not only does not "feel the breath of the spirit," but even ignores the existence of the spirit itself, and is therefore found defining what it is pleased to call the natural rate of wages as being "that price which is necessary to enable the laborers, one with another, to subsist and perpetuate their race, without either increase or diminution;"* that is to say, such price as will enable some to grow rich and increase their race, while others perish of hunger, thirst, and exposure. Such are the teachings of a system that has fairly earned the title of the "dismal science"—that one the study of which led M. Sismondi to the inquiry: "What, then, is wealth everything, and is man absolutely nothing?" In the eyes of modern political economy he *is* nothing, and can be nothing for the reason that it takes no note of the qualities by which

* Ricardo.

he is distinguished from the brute, led thus inevitably to regarding him as a mere instrument to be used by capital for enabling its owner to obtain compensation for its use. "Some economists," said a distinguished French economist, shocked at the material character of the so-called science, "speak as if they believed that men were made for products, not products for men;"* and at that conclusion must all arrive who commence by the method of analysis, and close with exclusion of all the higher and distinctive qualities of man.

§ 6. In the progress of knowledge we find ourselves gradually passing from the compound to the simple; from that which is abstruse and difficult to that which is plain and easily learned. That simplicity and truth travel generally together is proved by the beautiful simplicity and wonderful breadth of propositions in science--themselves the result of a long induction—leading to the knowledge of great truths not at first perceptible, but when announced so conclusive as to close, almost at once and forever, all discussion in reference thereto. The falling of the apple led Newton to the law of gravitation, and to the discovery of that law we owe the astonishing perfection of modern astronomy. The establishment of the identity of lightning and electricity laid the foundation of a science by help of which we have been enabled to command the services of a great power in nature that has to a great extent superseded the contrivances of man. Kepler and Galileo, New-

* Droz. *Economie Politique.*

ton and Franklin, would have failed in all their efforts to extend the domain of science, had they pursued the method of M. Comte in his attempt to establish a system of social science.

Does this method, however, supersede entirely the *à priori* one? Because we pursue the method of analysis, are we necessarily precluded from that of synthesis? By no means. Each in turn makes preparation for the other. It was by the careful observation of particular facts that Le Verrier was led to the grand generalization that a new and unobserved planet was bound to exist, and in a certain part of the heavens, and there it was almost at once discovered. To careful analyses of various earths it was due that Davy was led to the announcement of the great fact that all earths have metallic bases—one of the grandest generalizations on record, and one whose truth is being every day more and more established. The two methods were well described by Goethe, when he said that synthesis and analysis were "the systole and diastole of human thought," and that they were to him "like a second breathing process—never separated, ever pulsating."

"The vice of the *à priori* method," says the writer from whom this passage is taken, "when it wanders from the right path, is *not* that it *goes before* the facts, and anticipates the tardy conclusions of experience, but that it rests contented with its own verdicts, or seeking only a partial, hasty confrontation with facts —what Bacon calls '*notiones* temerè à rebus abstractas.'"*

* *Westminster Review*, Oct. 1852: Article, *Goethe as a Man of Science.*

Science being one and indivisible, so must the method of study be. That this is so with regard to all the departments of knowledge that underlie social science—physics, chemistry, and physiology—cannot now be doubted, yet is it but recently that there has been reason to believe in any such connection. With each new discovery the approximation becomes more close, and with each we see how intimately are the facts of all the earlier and more abstract departments of knowledge connected with the progress of man toward that state of high development for which he seems to have been intended. From hour to hour, as he acquires further control over the various forces existing in nature, he is enabled to live in closer connection with his fellow-man—to obtain larger supplies of food and clothing—to improve his own modes of thought and action, and to furnish better instruction to the generation destined to succeed him. The knowledge that leads to such results is but the foundation upon which we are required to build when undertaking to construct that higher department denominated social science, and the instrument that has been so successfully used in laying the foundation cannot but be found equally useful in the construction of the edifice itself.

Mathematics must there be used, as it is now in every other branch of inquiry, and the more it is used the more must sociology take the form of real science, and the more intimate become its relations with other departments of knowledge. The

Malthusian law was the first instance of its application, and had it proved a true one, it would have given a precision to political economy of which before it had been utterly incapable, making the progress of man directly dependent upon numbers on one hand and the powers of the soil on the other. So, too, with Mr. Ricardo's celebrated theory of rent, by which was established what he deemed to be the natural division of labor's products among those who labored and those who owned the land on which they were raised. The *method* of both these great laws was right, and the fact of their having adopted it has properly placed their authors in the front rank of economists, giving to their works an amount of influence never before exercised by any writers on economical science. That they fell into the error above described, of "seeking only a partial, hasty confrontation with facts," and, therefore, furnished the world with theories directly the reverse of true, does not prevent us from seeing of what infinite advantage to the progress of science it would have been to have the facts brought under these relations, if true, nor of how great importance it must be to have the real facts brought under such relations whenever possible.

Let us, for example, take the following proposition:—

In the early period of society, when land is abundant and people are few in number, labor is unproductive, and of the small product, the landowner or other capitalist takes a large *proportion*, leaving to the laborer a small one. The large proportion yields, however, but a small amount, and both laborer and capitalist are poor—the former so poor that he is everywhere seen to have been slave to the latter. Population and wealth, however, increasing, and labor becoming more productive, the land-owner's share diminishes in its *proportion*, but increases in its *amount*. The laborer's share increases not only in its amount, but also in its proportion, and the more rapid the increase in the productiveness of his labor the greater is the *proportion* of the augmented quantity retained by him; and thus, while the interests of both are in perfect harmony with each other, there is a constant tendency towards the establishment of an equality of condition—the slave of the early period becoming the free man of the later one.

Admitting this to be true—and if so it establishes directly the reverse of what was propounded by Messrs. Malthus and Ricardo—we have here the distinct expression of a mathematical relation between the concomitant variations of power of man and matter—of the man representing only his own faculties, and of the man representing the accumulated results of human faculties exerted upon matter and its forces. The problem of social science, and the one attempted to be solved, is: "What are the relations of man and the outside material world?" They change, as we see, men becoming, in some countries, from year to year more and more the masters, and in others, the slaves of nature. In what manner is it that changes in one tend to produce further changes in itself, or to effect changes in the other? To this question we need a mathematical answer, and until it be furnished—as it is believed to be in the above very simple proposition —political economy can bear only the same relation to social science that the observations of the Chaldean shepherds bear to modern astronomy.

Social science can scarcely be said to have an existence. That it might exist it was essential to possess the physical, chemical, and physiological knowledge required for enabling us to observe how it is that man is enabled to obtain command over the various forces provided for his use, and to pass from being the slave, to becoming the master of nature "Man," says Goethe, "only knows himself in as far as he knows external nature," and it was needed that the more abstract and general departments of knowledge should acquire a state of high development before we could advantageously enter upon the study of the highly concrete and special, and infinitely variable, science of the laws by which he is governed in his relations with the external world, and with his fellow-man. Chemistry and physiology are both, however, of recent date. A century since, men knew nothing of the composition of the air they breathed, and it is within that period that Haller laid the foundation of the physiological science that now exists. In physics, even, the Aristotelian doctrine of the four elements had yet possession of many of the schools, and still probably remains in some of those on the outer borders of civilization. In this state of things there could be but little progress toward attainment of the knowledge how far it was in the power of man to compel the earth to yield the supplies required for a steadily increasing population; and without that knowledge there could be no such thing as social science.

Science requires laws, and laws are but universal truths—truths to which no exceptions can be found. Those obtained, harmony and order take the place of chaos, and we are led in every department of knowledge as much to recognize effects as having been the natural results of certain definite causes, and to look for the reappearance of similar effects when like causes shall again occur, as did the first man when he had definitely connected the presence and absence of light with the rising and setting of the sun.

Where, however, is there in social science a proposition whose truth is universally admitted? There is not even a single one. A century since, the strength of a nation was regarded as tending to increase with augmentation of its numbers, but now we are taught that growth of numbers brings with it weakness instead of strength. From year to year we have new theories of the laws of population, and new modifications of the old one; and the question of the laws governing the distribution of the proceeds of labor between the owner and occupier of land, is now discussed as vigorously as it was half a century since. Of the disciples of Messieurs Malthus and Ricardo, scarcely any two are agreed as to what it was that they had really meant to teach. On one day we are told that the Ricardo-Malthusian doctrine is dead, and on the next we learn that it is an evidence of want of knowledge to doubt its truth; and yet the parties to whom we are indebted for all this knowledge belong to the same politico-economical school.* The strongest advocates for the removal of all restrictions on trade in cloth are found among the fiercest opponents of freedom of the trade in money; and among the most enthusiastic friends of competition for the sale of merchandise, are to be found the most decided opponents of competition for the purchase of the laborer's time and talents. Teachers who rejoice in everything tending to increase the prices of cloth and iron, as leading to improvement in man's condition, are found among the foremost of those who deprecate advance in the price of the laborer's services, as tending to diminution of power for the maintenance of trade. Others who teach non-interference by government when it looks to the diffusion of knowledge among the people, are among the most

* "We believe it (the Ricardo principle of rent) dominates in the long run, and is the main cause of the decline of nations. * * We believe the law of population to which Malthus first directed public attention, to be founded in fact."—*London Spectator.*

"Nobody, except a few mere writers, now troubles himself about Malthus on population, or Ricardo on rent. Their error may yet indeed linger in the universities, the appropriate depositories of what is obsolete."—*London Economist,* same date.

decided as to the propriety of such interference when it looks to measures leading to war and waste. All being therefore confusion, nothing is settled; as a necessary consequence of which the world looks quietly on, waiting the time when the teachers shall arrive at some understanding among themselves as to that first of all conditions incident to the existence of any branch of science, to wit: the real value of the terms in use. As has been already shown (see p. 10, *ante*), toward this first stage no approach whatsoever has yet been made.

§ 7. The causes of the existence of this state of things are readily explained. Of all, societary science is the most concrete and special; the most dependent on the earlier and more abstract departments of science; the one in which the facts are most difficult of collection and analysis; and, therefore, very late in making its appearance on the stage. Of all, too, it is the only one that affects the interests of men, their feelings, passions, prejudices, profits, and, therefore, the one in which it is most difficult to find men collating facts with the sole view to deduce from them the knowledge they are calculated to afford. Treating, as it does, of the relations between man and man, it has everywhere to meet the objection of those who seek the enjoyment of power and privilege at the cost of their fellow-men. The sovereign holds in small respect the science that would teach his subjects to doubt the propriety of his exercise of power by the grace of God. The soldier cannot believe in one that looks to the annihilation of his trade, nor can the monopolist readily be made to believe in the advantages of competition. The politician, living by managing the affairs of others, has small desire to see the people taught the proper management of their own concerns. All these profiting by teaching falsehood they therefore frown upon those who seek to teach the truth. The landlord believes in one doctrine and his tenant in another, the payer of wages, meantime, looking at all questions from a point of sight directly the opposite of the one occupied by him to whom the wages are paid.

We here meet a difficulty with which, as has been already said, no other science has needed to contend. Astronomy has wrought its way to its present prodigious height with but temporary opposition from the schools, because no one was personally interested in continuing to teach the revolution of the sun around the earth. For a time the teachers, secular and spiritual, were disposed to deny the movement of the latter, but the fact was proved and opposition ceased. Such, too, was the case when geology began to teach that the earth had had a longer existence than previously had been believed. The schools that represented by-gone days did then as they had done in the days of Copernicus and Galileo, denouncing as heretics all who doubted the accuracy of the received chronology, but short as is the time that has since elapsed the opposition has already disappeared. Franklin, Dalton, Wollaston, and Berzelius prosecuted their inquiries without fear of opposition, their discoveries being unlikely to affect injuriously the pockets of land-owners, merchants, or politicians. Social science is, however, still to a great extent in the hands of the schoolmen, backed everywhere by those who profit by the ignorance and weakness of the people.

The occupants of academic chairs in Austria or Russia may not teach what is unfavorable to the divine rights of kings, or favorable to increase in the powers of the people. The doctrines of the schools of France vary from time to time as despotism yields to the people, or the people yield to it. The landed aristocracy of England was gratified when Mr. Malthus satisfied it that the poverty and misery of the people resulted necessarily from a great law emanating from an all-wise and all-benevolent Creator; and the manufacturing one is equally so when it sees, as it thinks, the fact established, that the general interests of the country are to be promoted by measures looking to the production of an abundant supply of cheap, or badly paid, labor.

Social science, as taught in most of the colleges of this country and of Europe, is now on a level with the chemical science of the early part of the last century; and there it will remain so long as its teachers shall continue to look inwards to their own minds and *invent* theories, instead of looking outward to the great laboratory of the world for the collection of facts with the view to the *discovery* of laws. In default of such laws they are constantly repeating phrases that have no real meaning, and that tend, as Goethe most truly says, to "ossify the organs of intelligence" of their hearers and themselves.*

The state in which it now exists is what M. Comte is accustomed to denominate the metaphysical one, and there it must continue to remain until its teachers shall waken to the fact, that there is but one system of laws for the government of all matter, whether existing in the form of a piece of coal, a tree, a horse, or a man,—and but one mode of study for all departments of it. "The leaf," says a recent writer, "is to the plant what the microcosm is to the macrocosm—it is the plant in miniature; a common law governs the two, and, therefore, whatever disposition we find in the parts of the leaf, we may expect to find in the parts of the plant, and *vice versa.*" So it is with the tree of science and its many branches, what is true of its root cannot be otherwise than true of the leaves and the fruit. The laws of physical science are equally those of social science, and in every effort to discover the former we are but paving the way for the discovery of the

* "The pagan, the idolater, the ignorant even of the Catholic church worship their stocks and stones; and, instead of regarding these as signs only shadowing forth what in its intellectual state the human mind cannot otherwise express of its religious sentiments, takes the signs for the things they represent, and worships them as facts. We, too, worship our signs—our words. Let any man set himself to the task of examining the state of his knowledge on the most important subjects, divine or human, and he will find himself a mere word-worshipper; he will find words without ideas or meaning in his mind venerated, made idols of—idols different from those carved in wood or stone only by being stamped with printer's ink on white paper."—Laing, *Chronicle of the Sea Kings, Introd. Dissertation* chap. ii.

latter. "The entire succession of men," said Pascal, "through the whole course of ages, must be regarded as one man, always living and incessantly learning;" and among the men who have most largely contributed toward the foundation of a true social science are to be ranked the eminent teachers to whose labors we have been so largely indebted for the great development of physical, chemical, and physiological science in the last and present centuries.

The later man is, therefore, the one possessing the most of that knowledge of societary operations required for comprehending the causes of the various effects recorded in the historic page, and for predicting those which must result in future from causes now existing. The early man possessed little of science but the instrument required for its acquisition, and what of it he did acquire was purely physical in its character and most limited in its extent. The existing one is in possession not only of physical science to an extent that is wonderful compared with what existed a century since, but to this has added the chemical and physiological sciences then scarcely known, and has proved the existence throughout of a harmony that before had been unimagined. If, then, there is truth in Pascal's suggestion, may it not be that the laws of all the earlier and more abstract departments of science will be found to be equally true in reference to that highly concrete and special one which embraces the relations of man in society; and that, therefore, all science will prove to be but one, its parts differing as do the colors of the spectrum, but producing, as does the sun's ray, undecomposed, one white and bright light? To show that such is the case is the object of the present work.*

Turning again to the figure, the reader will remark that the branch of science of which it is proposed to treat finds its place between those of material and mental life, organology and psychology, and that it is through it that both must look for their development. That the mind may be active and vigorous, the body must be properly cared for. Social Science looks to the care of both. It treats of the relations of man with the physical world over which it is given to him to rule, and with that social one in which it is given to him to perform a part. Upon the nature of those relations depends the stimulation into activity of those qualities which constitute the real MAN—those by which he stands distinguished from other animals. What they are it is proposed now to show.

* "The view propounded in this work allows, however, a greater and more important part to the share of external influences, it being believed by the author, however, that these external influences equally with the internal ones are the results of one harmonious action underlying the whole of Nature, organic and inorganic, cosmical, physical, chemical, terrestrial, vital, and social."—Mivart, *Genesis of Species*, London, 1871.

"All science is but the partial reflection, in the reason of man, of the great all pervading reason of the universe. And thus the unity of science is the reflection of the unity of nature, and of the unity of that supreme reason and intelligence which pervades and rules over Nature, and from whence all reason and all science is derived."—Rev. Baden Powell.

CHAPTER III.

OF MAN—THE SUBJECT OF SOCIAL SCIENCE.

§ 1. MAN, the molecule of society, is the subject of social science. In common with all other animals he must eat, drink, and sleep, but his greatest need is that of ASSOCIATION with his fellow-men. Born the weakest and most dependent of animals, he requires the largest care in infancy and to be clothed by others, whereas to birds and beasts clothing is supplied by nature. Capable of acquiring the highest degree of knowledge, he appears in the world destitute even of that instinct which teaches the bee, the spider, the bird, and the beaver to construct their habitations, and to supply themselves with food. Dependent upon the experience of himself and others for all his knowledge, he requires language to enable him either to record the results of his own observation, or to profit by those of others; and of language there can be none without association. Created in the image of his Maker, he should participate in His intelligence; but without language there can be no ideas—no power of thought. Without it, therefore, he must remain in ignorance of the existence of powers granted to him in lieu of the strength of the ox, the speed of the hare, the sagacity of the elephant, and must remain below the level of the brute creation. To have language there must be association and combination of men with their fellow-men, and it is on this condition only that man can be man; on this alone that we can conceive of the being to which we attach the idea of man. "It is not good," said God, "that man should live alone," nor do we ever find him doing so—the earliest records of the world exhibiting to us beings living together in society, and using words for the expression of their ideas. Whence came those words? Whence came language? With the same propriety might we ask—Why does fire burn? Why does man see, feel, hear, or walk? Language escapes from him at the touch of nature herself, the power of using words being his essential faculty, enabling him to maintain commerce with his fellow-men, and fitting him for that association without which language cannot exist. The words society and language convey to the mind separate and distinct ideas, and yet by no effort of the mind can we conceive of the existence of the one without the other.*

* "Ever since the time of Wilhelm von Humboldt, all who have seriously grappled with the highest problem of the science of Language have come to the conviction that thought and language are inseparable—that language is as impossible without thought as thought is without language; and that they stand to each other like soul and body, like power and function, like substance and form. The objections which have been raised against this view arise generally from a mere misunderstanding. If we speak of language as the outward realization of thought, we do not mean language as deposited in a dictionary or sketched in a grammar; we mean language as an act, language as being

The subject of social science then is man—the being to whom have been given reason and the faculty of individualizing sounds so as to give expression to every variety of idea; and who has been placed in a position to exercise that faculty. Isolate him, and with the loss of the power of speech, he loses the power to reason, and with it the distinctive quality of man. Restore him to society, and with the return of the power of speech he becomes again the reasoning man.

We have here the great law of molecular gravitation as the *indispensable* condition of the existence of the being known as man. The particles of matter having each an independent existence, the atom of oxygen or of hydrogen is as perfect and complete as it could be were it in connection with millions of others like itself. The grain of sand is perfect whether flying alone before the wind or resting with its fellows on the shores of the broad Atlantic. The tree and the shrub, brought from distant lands and standing alone in the conservatory, produce the same fruits and yield the same odors as when they stood in the groves from which they had been transplanted. The individual dog, cat, and

spoken, language as living and dying with every word that is uttered. We might perhaps call this speech, as distinguished from language."—Professor Müller in the *Contemporary Review*, December, 1871.

"We imagine we are altogether free and independent, and are not aware that our thoughts are manacled and fettered by language; and that, without knowing or perceiving it, we have to keep pace with those who walked before us thousands and thousands of years ago."—Ibid. *Chips from a German Workshop*, Article, *Cornish Antiquities.*

rabbit possess all their powers in a state of entire isolation. Such, however, is not the case with man. The wild and isolated man, wherever found, has always proved to be not only destitute of the reasoning faculty, but destitute also of that instinct which in other animals takes the place of reason—and, therefore, the most helpless of beings.

Man tends of necessity to gravitate towards his fellow-man. Of all animals, he is the most gregarious, and the greater the number collected in a given space the greater is the attractive force there exerted, as is seen to have been the case with the great cities of the past, Athens and Rome, Nineveh and Babylon; and as now is seen in regard to those of both the Eastern and Western Continents. Attraction is here, as everywhere else in the material world, in the direct ratio of the mass, and in the inverse one of the distance.

Such being the case, why is it that all the members of the human family do not tend to come together on a single spot of earth? Because of the existence of that same simple and universal law by means of which is maintained the beautiful order of the system of which our planet forms a part. We are surrounded by bodies of various sizes, each having its local centre of attraction by means of which its parts are held together. Were it possible that that attractive force could be annihilated, the rings of Saturn, the moons of our earth and of Jupiter, would crumble to pieces and fall inward upon the bodies they now attend, a mass of ruins. So, too, with the planets themselves. Small as are the asteroids, each has within itself a centre of attraction enabling it to preserve its form and substance, despite the superior attraction of the larger bodies by which it is everywhere surrounded.

So it is throughout our world. Look where we may, we see local centres toward which men gravitate, some exercising less influence, others more. London and Paris are now the rival suns of our system, each exercising a strong attractive force, and were it not for the counter attraction of Prague and Munich, Vienna and Berlin, Florence and Naples, Madrid and Lisbon, Brussels and Amsterdam, Copenhagen, Stockholm, and St. Petersburg, Europe would present to view one great centralized system, the population of which was always tending toward those two cities, there to make all their exchanges, and thence to receive their laws. So, too, in this country. It is seen by all how strong is even now the tendency toward New York, despite the existence of local centres of attraction in the cities of Boston, Philadelphia, Baltimore, Washington, Pittsburg, Cincinnati, St. Louis, New Orleans, Augusta, Savannah, Charleston, and the numerous capitals of the several States. Obliterating these centres, and placing a centralized government like that of England, France, or Russia, in New York city, not only would this latter grow to the size of London, but soon would far exceed it, with an effect similar to that which would be produced in the astronomical world by a like course of operation. The local governments falling to pieces, all the atoms of which they had been composed would tend at once towards the new centre that had been thus produced. Local and voluntary association for the various purposes of life, throughout what would then be the provinces of a great centralized State, would be at an end, but in its place would be found the forced association of dependents on one hand, and masters on the other. Every neighborhood that required to have a road or a bridge, to establish a bank, or to obtain a redress of grievances, would be required to make its application therefor at the great city, distant many hundreds of miles, and to pay innumerable officers before it could obtain the desired permission, as is now the case in France. Every community that found itself suffering from heavy taxes, or from other oppressions from which it desired to be relieved, would be found seeking to make itself heard, but its voice would be drowned by those of the men who profited by such abuses, as is now the case with complaints to the British Parliament of Ireland and India.*

* "Indian questions do not excite so much interest in the House of Commons as the squabble about the cost of a road through St. James's Park; and all this is taking place while the finances of India are getting into inextricable confusion, debt rapidly accumulating, expenditure steadily increasing, and taxation becoming so burdensome that far and wide the seeds of disaffection are sown."—*Fortnightly Review*, Oct. 1871.

In the last ten years the salt tax, already most oppressive, has been five times increased; a heavy income tax has been imposed, and taxes on feasts and marriages have been proposed; two and a quarter millions of people have died of famine; the debt, including guarantees of badly

Instead of going, as now, to the capital of the State close at hand, and obtaining at little cost the required laws, they would find themselves compelled to employ agents for the negotiation of their business, those agents then, as now in England, accumulating enormous fortunes at the cost of poor and distant suitors. Much of this is already seen at Washington, yet how trivial is it compared with what it would be were all the various business transacted by State Legislatures, and by County Boards, brought within the sphere of Congress, as to so great an extent it now is within that of the British Parliament.

The centralizing tendency of State capitals is, in its turn, greatly neutralized by the existence of opposing centres of attraction at the various county seats, and in the numerous towns and cities of the Union, each managing its own affairs, and each presenting places at which the people of the various districts, and of the whole country itself, are brought into connection with each other for exchange of the products of physical or mental affort. Obliterate these—centralize the powers of towns and counties in State Legislatures—and the power of local association within the States would be almost altogether annihilated. The State capital, or that of the Union, would grow rapidly, as would

constructed and expensive railroads, has grown to nearly $1,000,000,000; the sole reliance for payment of interest thereon being now found in continued maintenance of the power to poison the Chinese people with the produce of Indian opium fields.

the sun were the local attractions of the celestial bodies to disappear. The splendor of both might be much increased, but in the space now traversed by the planets motion would cease to exist, as would be the case throughout this country were it made dependent on a single centre; and without motion there could be neither association, force, nor progress.

Further, with the growth of centralization there would be seen a diminution in the counteracting force by which families are held together, despite attractions of the capital. Whatever tends to the establishment of decentralization, and to the production of local employment for time and talent, tends to give value to land, to promote its division, and to enable parents and children to remain in closer connection with each other; and the stronger the ties that bind together the various families of which the community is composed, the more perfect must be the attraction within the bosom of the communities which constitute the State. Whatever tends, on the contrary, to the diminution of local employment tends to the consolidation of land, the breaking up of families, and the building up of great cities at the expense of the country, as has been the case in Italy, France, India, and Britain; and as even here is seen in the rapid growth of cities, accompanied, as it always is, by the expulsion of our people to new territories, with diminution of the power of association and combination.

The pages of history furnish throughout evidence

that the tendency towards association—without which the human animal cannot become the being to which we apply the denomination of man—has everywhere grown with increase in the number and strength of local centres, declining, on the contrary, with their diminution. Such centres were found in nearly all the Grecian Islands, Laconia and Attica, Bœotia and Argos, Arcadia and Elis, Megara and Corinth, meanwhile, each rejoicing in its own. Local association existed there to an extent that had until then been unequalled in the world, yet the tendency towards general association was exhibited in the foundation of the Isthmian and Nemean and the yet more celebrated Olympic games, which drew together all that were distinguished for physical or intellectual power, not only in the States and cities of Greece itself, but in the distant Italy and Asia. In the Amphictyonic league we find further evidence of the tendency to general as a consequence of local association; but here, unhappily, the idea was not fully carried out. The attractive force of this sun of the system was not sufficient for the maintenance of order in the movements of the planets, which frequently, therefore, shot madly from their spheres and jostled against each other.

To the equal action of opposing forces it is due that the celestial world is enabled to exhibit such wonderful harmony and such unceasing motion. In the application of this principle to the societary movement the people of Greece had all this yet to learn, the consequences being found in frequent wars among themselves, resulting in the establishment of a highly centralized government controlling the disbursements of a treasury filled by the contributions of a thousand subject cities. Thenceforward the subject peoples lost the power of association for determination of their own respective rights, and had to seek for justice among themselves in the courts of Athens. To that city resorted all who had money to pay to, or receive from, the State; all who had causes to try; all who sought places of power or profit; all who found themselves unable to obtain a living at home; and all who preferred the work of plunder to that of labor; centralization growing with every step in this direction, until at length Athens and Sparta, Samos and Mitylene, and all the other states and cities, became involved in one common ruin; Attica herself becoming, to a great extent, the property of a single individual surrounded by hosts of slaves, the disposition for voluntary association, and the power to exercise it, having wholly passed away.

Looking to Italy, we see a similar course of things. In its early days Etruria and the Campagna, Magna Græcia and the Samnite Hills, presented to view numerous cities, each the centre of a district throughout which existed in a high degree the habit of local and voluntary association. With time, however, we see it gradually disappearing, and first among the people of Rome itself, perpetually engaged in disturbing their peaceful neighbors. The central city growing by help of plunder, the local centres gradually diminished in importance, with constantly growing necessity for resorting to the arbitration of Rome itself. As power thus centralized itself within her walls her people became more and more dependent on the public treasury, and the power of voluntary association gradually disappeared; Italy throughout, meanwhile, presenting the spectacle of great landlords occupying palaces, and surrounded by troops of slaves. So long as the opposing forces were in equal balance she furnished the world with men; but with her decline she is seen more and more to have presented it with slaves, sometimes attired in the beggar's rags, at others in the imperial purple.

Studying the history of the Republic and the Empire, we see that their long duration is to be attributed to the fact that to so great an extent the people of the provinces were left to govern themselves, subject only to the performance of certain duties to the central power. Local association for almost every purpose was for centuries left untouched, towns and cities imposing their own taxes, determining their own laws, and selecting the magistrates by whom they were to be carried into effect.*

Modern Italy, from the days of the Lombards, presented during many centuries striking evidences

* The extraordinary extent to which this system of localization was carried, and its wonderful results, have been recently admirably exhibited by M. le Comte de Champagny, an account of whose works will be found in the *British Quarterly Review* for July, 1870.

of the connection between local attraction and the power of voluntary association. Milan, Genoa, Venice, Florence, Rome, Naples, Pisa, Sienna, Padua, and Verona, were each centres such as had existed once in Greece, but in default of a sun with attractive force sufficient to maintain the harmony of the system they were perpetually warring with each other, until at length the habit of association entirely disappeared.

India had numerous centres of attraction. Besides its several capitals, each little village presented a self-governing community in which existed the power of association to an extent scarcely elsewhere equalled; but with the growth of central power the habit and the power of exercising it have almost altogether disappeared.

Spain had numerous local centres. Association there existed to a great extent not only among the enlightened Moors but among the people of Castile and Arragon, Biscay and Leon. The discovery of this continent, of which the government became the absentee landlord, greatly increased the central power, with corresponding decline in local activity and association, the result exhibiting itself in the depopulation and weakness that have since ensued.

In Germany we find the home of the decentralization of Europe—of jealousy of central power—and of the maintenance of local rights—as a consequence of which the tendency towards association has always been strong among her people, bringing with it in our own time a commercial union that has proved itself the foundation of the present magnificent and powerful Empire. Like Greece, Germany has been until now deficient as regards the sun around which the numerous planets might peacefully revolve; and, as in Greece, powers exterior to her system have been enabled to use one community against another to an extent that has greatly retarded the progress of her own civilization, although as as rule she has elsewhere interfered little with its progress.* Strong for defence she has, therefore, been weak for offence, and has exhibited no tendency to wars for conquest, or toward the levying of contributions upon her poorer neighbors, as has been so much the case with her highly centralized neighbor, France.† Abounding always in local centres it has been found impossible to create a great central city to direct the modes of thought and action, and to that it is due that Germany is now so rapidly taking the position of the great intellectual centre, not only of Europe, but of the world at large.

Among the German States there is none whose policy has so much tended to the maintenance of local centres of action, as promotive of the best interests of both the people and the state, as Prussia.

* Austria is a compound of numerous bodies, a large portion of which is entirely exterior to Germany. Her wars in Italy have been Austrian and not Germanic.

† The occurrences of the last few years might seem to be in contradiction of this, but when properly examined such will not prove to be the case. The object of both of the recent wars was the establishment of German independence.

All the ancient divisions, from the communes to the provinces, have been carefully preserved, and their constitutions as carefully respected; as a consequence of which it is that we here find the people advancing towards freedom with great rapidity, the State itself meanwhile rapidly advancing in wealth and power. Long before the recent wars the peaceful effects of decentralization had here fully exhibited themselves in the fact that, under the lead of Prussia, Northern Germany had been brought under a great federal system, by help of which internal commerce had been placed on a footing almost precisely corresponding with that of these United States.*

Nowhere in Europe had decentralization more existed, and nowhere had the tendency to peaceful association, or the strength of resistance to attacks from without consequent upon union, been more fully exhibited than in Switzerland, notwithstanding the existence of the widest religious differences.

The French Revolution annihilated, when it should have strengthened, the local governments—centralization being thus increased when it should have been diminished, the consequences being seen in a perpetual succession of wars and revolutions. Much was done towards decentralization when the lands of absentee nobles and of the church were divided among the people, and to the counteracting effect of this measure it is due that France so long continued to grow in strength notwithstanding the extraordinary centralization of her system.

Belgium and Holland present remarkable instances of the tendency of local action to produce habits of association. In both, towns and cities are numerous, and the effect of combined action is seen in the wonderful productiveness of what was originally one of the poorest countries of Europe.

In no part of Europe was the division of land so complete, or its possession so secure, as in Norway, at and before the date of the Norman conquest of England; and in none, consequently, was the power of local attraction so fully exhibited. The habit of association, therefore, existed to an extent then unknown in France and Germany, developing itself in the establishment of "a literature in their own language, and living in the common tongue and minds of the people."* Elsewhere, the languages of the educated and uneducated classes have differed so widely as to render the literature used by the former entirely inaccessible to the latter; and, as a necessary consequence, there has been "a want of that circulation of the same mind and intelligence through all classes of the social body, differing only in degree, not in kind, in the most educated and most ignorant; and of that circulation and interchange of impressions, through a language and literature common to all, which alone can animate a

* *Chronicle of the Sea-Kings of Norway.* Introductory chapter by S. Laing, p. 33.

population into a nation."* They were in advance of other nations, too, in the fact that employments were diversified, affording further proof of the existence of the habit of association and combination. "Iron," continues Mr. Laing, "is the mother of all the useful arts; and a people who could smelt it from the ore, and work it into all that is required for ships of considerable size, from a nail to an anchor, could not have been in a state of such utter barbarism as they have been represented to us. They had a literature of their own, and laws, institutions, social arrangements, a spirit and character, very analogous to the English, if not the source from which the English flowed; and were in advance of all Christian nations in one branch of the useful arts, in which great combinations of men are required—the building, fitting out, and navigating large vessels."† The same habit of local association has ever since existed, accompanied by a tendency to union whose effects were fully exhibited in the establishment, half a century since, of a system of government in which the centralizing and decentralizing forces were balanced to an extent not exceeded in the world.

The attraction of local centres throughout the British islands, formerly so great, has, for a long time past, tended steadily to diminish. Edinburgh, once the metropolis of a kingdom, has become a

* *Chronicle of the Sea-Kings of Norway.* Introductory chapter by S. Laing, p. 36.

† Ibid., p. 146.

mere provincial city; and Dublin, once the seat of an independent Parliament, has so greatly declined that were it not for the fact that it is the place at which a representive of majesty holds his occasional levées, it would scarcely at all be heard of. Throughout the United Kingdom there is exhibited a constantly growing tendency towards centralization, accompanied by diminution in the strength of local attraction, increase of absentee proprietorship keeping steady pace with the growth of emigration from its shores. With every step in that direction we see a steady increase in the necessity for involuntary association, manifested by the growth of fleets and armies, and of the contributions required for their support.

The Northern States of the American Union present, as has been already shown, a combination of the centralizing and decentralizing forces to an extent that has never been elsewhere equalled,.and here accordingly we find existing in a high degree the tendency to local action for the creation of schools and school-houses, the making of roads, and the formation of associations for almost every imaginable purpose. The system of laws that maintains harmony throughout the Universe is here closely imitated, each State constituting a body perfect in itself, with local attraction tending to maintain its form, despite the gravitating tendency towards that centre around which it and its sister States are required to revolve.

Looking to the Southern States the reverse of

the picture has hitherto been presented to our view. Masters there owned men who were altogether deprived of the power of voluntary association, and might not even sell their own labor, or exchange its product for that of the labor of others. This was centralization, and hence it is that throughout the South there has been exhibited so strong a tendency toward disturbance elsewhere of the power of association. All the wars of the Union have here had their origin.

Barbarism is a necessary consequence of the absence of association. Deprived of this, man loses the essential qualities of man, and ceases to be the subject of social science.

§ 2. The next distinctive quality of man is INDIVIDUALITY. Each rat or robin, fox or wolf, is the type of his species wherever found, possessing habits and instincts in common with all his race. Not such is the case with man, in whom we find differences of tastes, feelings, and capacities almost as numerous as those observed in the human countenance. That such differences may be developed it is indispensable that he be brought into association with his fellow-men; and where that has failed to be the case the individuality can no more be found than it would be were we seeking it among the foxes or the wolves. The wild men of Germany and those of India, *Caspar Hauser* being the type of all, differ so little that in reading the description of the one we might readily suppose we were studying that of the other. Passing from these to the lower forms of association, such as exist among savage tribes, we meet a growing tendency to development of the varieties of individual character; but to find it in its highest degree we must seek it in those places in which there exists the greatest demand for intellectual effort; those in which there is the greatest variety of employment; those in which, therefore, the power of association most perfectly exists, in towns and cities. That this should be the case, is perfectly in accordance with what throughout nature is everywhere else observed.

"The more imperfect a being is," says Goethe, "the more do its individual parts resemble each other, and the more do the parts resemble the whole. The more perfect a being, the more dissimilar are the parts. In the former case, the parts are more or less a repetition of the whole; in the latter case they are totally unlike the whole. The more the parts resemble each other, the less subordination is there of one to the other; subordination of parts indicates a high grade of organization."*

This is as true of societies as it is of the plants and animals in reference to which it was written. The more imperfect they are—the less the variety of employments, and the less, consequently, the

* "The differences are the condition of development; the mutual exchanges, which are the consequences of these differences, waken and manifest life. The greater the diversity of organs, the more active and superior is the life of the individual. The greater the variety of individualities and relations in a society of individuals, the greater also is the sum of life, the more universal is the development of life, the more complete, and of a more elevated order. But it is necessary, not only that life should unfold itself in all its richness by diversity, but that it exhibit itself in its utility, in its beauty, in its goodness, by harmony. Thus we recognize the proof of the old proverb, 'Variety in unity is perfection.' "—Guyot. *Earth and Man*, p. 80.

development of intellect—the more do the parts resemble each other, as may readily be seen by any one who will study man in the purely agricultural countries of the earth. The greater the variety of employments—the greater the demand for intellectual effort—the more dissimilar become the parts and the more perfect becomes the whole, as may readily be seen on comparing any purely agricultural district with another in which agriculture, manufactures, and commerce are happily combined. Difference is essential to association. The farmer does not need to associate with his brother farmer, but he does need to do so with the carpenter, the blacksmith, and the miller. The mill operative has little occasion to exchange with his brother workman, but he does require so to do with the builder of houses, or the seller of food; and the more numerous the shades of difference in the society of which he is a part, the greater will be the facility for, and the tendency to, that combination of effort required for developing the various faculties of its several members. All history, past and present, furnishes evidence as to the extraordinary extent to which, when a demand arises, peculiar qualities are found whose existence had before been unsuspected. Here, as everywhere else, it is demand that creates supply. Thus, in our own revolution blacksmiths and lawyers proved themselves distinguished soldiers; and that of France brought to light the military abilities of thousands of men that otherwise might have passed their lives at the tail of the plough. It is the occasion that makes the man. In every society there exists a vast amount of latent capacity waiting but the opportunity to show itself, and thus it is that in communities in which there is no diversity of employment the intellectual power is so largely wasted, producing no result. Life has been defined as being a "mutual exchange of relations," and where difference does not exist there can be no exchange.

So it is everywhere throughout nature. To excite galvanic electricity, two metals need to be brought into combination; but even then their latent capacities are made active only by help of a third body differing totally from both. That accomplished, what was before dull and inert becomes active and full of life, and capable at once of entering into new combinations. So, too, with the lump of coal. Breaking it up into pieces, however small, and scattering them in the ground, there they will remain, still fragments of coal. Let its atoms, however, under the favoring influences of heat, be solicited by oxygen atoms to enter into combination with them, and at once a new substance is formed having other powers, and capable of entering into new combinations, forming parts of the trunks, branches, leaves, or blossoms of trees; or the bones, muscles, or brain of man. The wheat yielded to the farmer's labors might remain, as we know it to have remained for numerous centuries, undecomposed and uncombined with any other matter. Let it, however, pass through the stomach, and it becomes resolved into its original elements, parts becoming bones, blood, or fat; parts again passing off in the form of perspiration; others meanwhile being ejected in the form of excrement, ready to enter instantly into the composition of new vegetable forms. The power of association thus exists everywhere throughout the material world in the ratio of individualization. So, too, has it everywhere been with man—the development of individuality, at all times and in all countries, having been in the ratio of his power to act in obedience to that prime law of his nature which imposes upon him a necessity for association with his fellow-men.

That power, as has been already seen, has always existed in the ratio of the equal action of the centralizing and decentralizing forces, and where such action has most been found we should most find individuality, as certainly has been the case. In no country of the world had it ever so much existed as in Greece immediately anterior to the Persian invasion, and then and there it is that we find the highest development. To the men produced in that period it is that the age of Pericles owes its illustration. The destruction caused by Persian armies brought with it the conversion of citizens into soldiers, with steady tendency to increase of centralization and decline of the power of voluntary association and of individuality, until the slave alone was found cultivating the lands of Attica; the free citizens of the earlier period having entirely disappeared.—So, likewise, was it in Italy, where the highest individuality was found when the Campagna was filled with cities. Following their decline the great city grows, filled with paupers, the capital of a land cultivated by slaves.—So it is now throughout the East, where society is divided into two great parts—the men who toil and slave on one side, and, on the other, those who profit by the labors of the slave. Between two such masses there can be no association, and with the members there can be but little; there being among them none of that *difference* of pursuits which is required for producing exchanges of relations. The chain of society being there deficient in the connecting links there is no motion among the parts; and in the absence of motion there can be no more development of individuality of character than could be found in the pebble-stone before it had been subjected to the action of the blow-pipe.

The numerous towns and cities of Italy of the Middle Ages were remarkable for their activity, and for the development of individuality. So, likewise, was it in Belgium, and in Spain prior to the centralization which followed close upon the expulsion of the Moors, and the discovery of the gold and silver deposits of this continent.—Such was the case, too, in each of the kingdoms now composing the united kingdom of Great Britain and Ireland. Taking Ireland separately we find her at the close of the last century giving to the world such men as Burke, Flood, Grattan, Sheridan, and Wellington; but since then, centralization having greatly grown, individuality has passed away. So, likewise, has it been in Scotland since the Union. A century since that country presented to view a body of men occupying positions as distinguished as any in Europe, but her local institutions have decayed and there are now, as we are told, "fewer individual thinkers" in that country than at any period "since the early part of the last century."* The mind of its whole youth, as the same journal tells us, is required to be "cast in the mould of English universities," which exercise upon it "an influence unfavorable to originality and power of thought."

In England herself centralization has made great progress with consequent increase of pauperism, a condition of things wholly adverse to individual development. The little landed proprietors have gradually disappeared to make way for the farmer and his hired laborers, and for the great manufacturer with hosts of operatives—of whose names even he has no knowledge; the power of voluntary association diminishing with every step in this direction. London grows to an enormous size at the cost of the country at large, centralization thus producing the disease of over-population, to be cured by a colonization tending at every step further to diminish the power of association.

Looking to France, we may see the steady decline of individuality attending the growth of centralization. In the highly centralized days of Louis XIV. almost the whole land of the kingdom was in

* North British Review, Aug. 1853.

the hands of a few great proprietors and of dignataries of the chureh—mere courtiers whose faces but reflected the expression apparent on that of the sovereign they were bound to worship. The right to labor was then held to be a privilege to be exercised at the pleasure of the monarch, and men were forbidden, on pain of death, to worship God according to their consciences, or even to fly the kingdom.

Passing homeward, we find in these Northern States individuality developed to an extent elsewhere entirely unknown, and for the reason that centralization exists in a very limited degree, while decentralization facilitates the rapid growth of associative power. All the links of the chain are here found, and as every man feels that he can rise if he will there is the strongest inducement to strive for intellectual development. In the Southern States power centralized itself in the hands of the few, association among slaves was prohibited, and as a consequence, but little individuality has been developed.

It is in variety there is unity, this being quite as true of the social as it is of the material world. Let the reader watch the movements of a city and study the facility with which men so various in their qualities combine their movements for the production of a penny newspaper, a ship, a house, or an opera; then comparing it with the difficulty experienced throughout the purely agricultural portions of the country of combining for even the most simple purposes, and he will see that it is difference that leads to association. The more perfect the societary organization, and the greater the variety of demands for exercise of the physical and intellectual powers, the higher will be the elevation of man as a whole, and the stronger will be the contrasts among men.

Individuality thus grows with the growth of the power of association, preparing the way for further and more perfect combination of action.

The more perfectly the local attraction tends to counterbalance that of the centre—the more society tends to conform itself to the laws we see to govern our system of worlds—the more harmonious must be the action of all the parts, and the greater must be the tendency toward voluntary association, and to the maintenance of peace abroad and at home.

§ 3. Association and individuality growing thus together, each aiding and aided by the other, with correspondent increase in the rapidity of the societary motion, and in the growth of societary force, man is thus gradually enabled to assume the position for which he had been from the first intended—that of controller of the great natural forces by which he is everywhere surrounded, and to which he had at first been so entirely enslaved; the growing power for direction thus exhibited being accompanied by corresponding development of that POWER FOR SELF-DIRECTION which, when obtained, constitutes the most important of all the faculties by which the human animal is distinguished from the brute.

Being so, it waits on others for its own development, at each and every stage of progress, however, aiding as aided by those other faculties to which the reader's attention has above been called.

The law here is thus precisely the same that elsewhere is observed; the most productive soils, the most useful of the metals, the strongest of the fuels, the most pervading and most powerful of the natural forces, having, in their subjection to human use, invariably followed long after those of less utility and still less power. In the effort at this subjection of matter to mind the various human faculties are at each and every step more and more stimulated into action, the self-directing force growing with every stage of progress toward more full and complete power for direction. From infancy to age, from isolation to association, from poverty to wealth, that faculty stands always present and waiting to be called into vigorous and active life, the condition precedent thereto being that the societary action tend toward stimulating into greater activity the subordinate human faculties above referred to; the social heat and force consequent on rapid motion being here as much required as is physical heat in the case of the fig-tree and the orange. With every step in that direction the circulation increases in its rapidity, each and every stage of advance being accompanied by diminution in the value of all commodities and things required for man's use, and corresponding increase in the value of man himself; the real MAN, capable of acquiring power for both direction and self-direction, from day to day more and more exhibiting himself on the stage of life.

That in the physical world the more rapid the circulation the greater is the force is a truth that becomes more obvious to the common mind as the telegraph from day to day tends to annihilate both time and space, and as it more and more comes to understand that the power which has thus been subjugated is that of chief control throughout the universe. That so it is, and so must be, throughout the societary world, will be equally obvious to those who compare the rapidity of movement in, and the force exercised by, great cities, with those of the agricultural bodies of which they are the centres; or who compare for themselves the power exercised by a single great community in which, as a consequence of producers and consumers being enabled to act in concert with each other, agriculture, manufactures, and commerce have been happily united, with that exercised by all the exclusively agricultural communities of the earth combined; thereby satisfying themselves that these latter, with their hundreds of millions of population, are but mere hewers of wood and drawers of water for the more powerful of the earth; and that not only do they exercise no power for self-direction, but that nothing short of the most vigorous resistance will enable them to obtain even a shadow of independence.

The more thorough the diversification in the demands for human service the greater becomes the power of association, the more complete the development of the various human faculties, and the greater the tendency toward development of that crowning human faculty, the power for self-direction; human freedom, whether as regards thought, speech, or action, keeping steady pace with that growing power over nature which everywhere exhibits itself as a consequence of that increased development of heat and force which throughout both the physical and social world results from increased rapidity of circulation.

Reasoning thus upward from facts to principles, the inquirer finds the highest of human faculties waiting everywhere to be developed; thereafter to constitute a force as susceptible of being weighed and measured as are any of the properties of mere brute matter.*

In that direction it is we are to look for obtaining such really voluntary action as makes of man a being responsible before his Creator and his fellow-men for all his actions.

Reasoning, on the contrary, from assumed premises downward, metaphysicians encounter that

* In his recent address to the British Association, President Thomson speaks "of the grand conception of Lucretius, who," as he says, "admits no subtle ethers, no variety of elements with fiery or watery, or light and heavy principles; nor supposes light to be one thing, fire another, electricity a fluid, magnetism a vital principle; but treats all phenomena as mere properties or accidents of simple matter."

To study men and things by means of occurrences passing daily before his eyes was more agreeable to the Roman philosopher than to do so by means of the invention of a being as fanciful as were any of those of the heathen mythology, and facts that had no existence but in the minds of those by whom they had been suggested. (See *ante*, note to page 16.)

pons asinorum to which they have attached the name of WILL—a thing so fanciful that although thousands and tens of thousands have essayed at explaining its nature and extent, the world remains as ignorant in regard to both as it had been at the commencement of the Christian era. Utterly incapable of being either weighed or measured, it finds no place in science.

In both the moral and the civil law intelligence is held to be an indispensable condition of exercise of *will*. That such intelligence may exist there must, however, have been such previous exercise of the power of association as had led to such development of the peculiar faculties of the individual man as has enabled him to acquire power for self-direction. The views above presented would seem, therefore, to be in full accordance with those to which common sense has led mankind in general, however opposed to those who hold that the power of WILL, and its accompanying responsibilities, attach themselves at birth to every aggregate of material atoms that assumes the human form, whether as earth-eating Digger Indians, or as pauper occupants, from birth to death, of an English almshouse.*

* "If *Will* is changed into *Volition* it becomes an innocent word which may receive any force that any particular teacher likes to give it; which will fit without resistance into any corner of a system that is not otherwise occupied. Retaining its old name, it has proved a most disturbing force in the universe. What is it? Why *will* it appear when all things could be arranged so comfortably if it were not there? These are questions which philosophers have been obliged to ask them-

§ 4. Next among the qualities by which man is distinguished from all other animals, is that of RESPONSIBILITY before his fellow-man, and before his Creator, for his actions.

The slave is not a responsible being, for he but obeys his master. The soldier, exercising no power of self-direction, is not responsible for the murders he commits, being but an instrument in the hands of his superior officer, he in turn but obeying the irresponsible chief of the State. The pauper is an irresponsible being, though often held by man to be responsible. Responsibility grows with the growth of individuality and self-directing force, both of these latter growing, as we have seen, with increasing power of association.

The savage slays and robs his fellow-men, then proudly exhibiting their scalps, or the plunder he has acquired, as evidence of his cunning or his courage. The soldier boasts of his prowess in the field, gladly enumerating the men who have fallen by his arm; this, too, in a community whose laws award fine and imprisonment as the punishment for even the smallest violation of personal rights. The warlike nation prides itself upon the glory

selves, because common men are asking them; because they are sure that a *will* is in them if it is ever so impotent; that they are rattling their chains if they are ever so much in bondage."—Professor Maurice, in the *Contemporary Review*, Jan. 1872.—These men *desire* that their "chains" may be removed, but cannot *will* it to be done. The exercise of "volition" comes with growth of power for self-direction, that itself coming as a consequence of power to control the forces by which we are surrounded.

acquired in the field at the cost of hundreds of thousands of lives, and decorates its galleries with pictures plundered from their rightful owners, generals and admirals meanwhile living in affluence upon their respective shares of the spoils of war. With growing individuality men learn to denominate such acts by their true and only legitimate titles—robbery and murder.

The savage is not responsible for his children, nor is the slave, who regards them as only his master's property. With every step toward perfect individuality—always the result of increase in the power of voluntary association—men learn more and more to appreciate their severe responsibility toward society at large, and toward their Creator, for careful preparation of their children for the performance of their various duties. To that feeling, more than to any other, are due the vigorous efforts made for acquiring that mastery over the forces of nature by which the associated man is distinguished from the isolated one; each distinguishing characteristic of man thus aiding, and being aided by, each and every of the others. The savage being indolent, destroys his female children. The farmer extends his cultivation that he may provide more fully for the moral and physical training of his sons, and so fit them better than he himself had been for the performance of their duties to their fellow-men. The artisan improves his machinery that he may call to his aid the power of electricity or of steam, each and every step in this direction tending more fully to develop his own peculiar powers. He thus becomes more individualized with great increase in the feeling of responsibility for both his children and himself, and in the disposition for combination of his efforts with those of his fellow-men—whether for increasing the productiveness of their common labor, or for administering the affairs of the community of which he is a part.

Here again we find a development of the essential human qualities in the ratio of the equal action of the centralizing and decentralizing forces. Permitting no responsibility for children the Spartans endeavored to prevent the growth of wealth, while surrounding themselves with slaves to whom all individuality was denied. The helot had no will of his own. In Attica, on the contrary, although slaves were numerous labor was held in high respect, diversity of employment causing great demand for intellectual effort. There, consequently, the rights of parents were respected, while those of the child were fully cared for under the Solonian laws.

In the East, and in Africa, where individuality has no existence, parents kill their children, these latter in turn exposing parents when unable to support themselves. In the highly centralized France, foundling hospitals abound, and it is but quite recently that any effort has been made to diffuse the blessings of education among the masses of the people. The growth of centralization in the United

Kingdom has been accompanied by growing disregard for the rights of children, child-murder now occupying the place that in France is filled by the foundling hospital. Until now there has been not even an attempt at provision for general education of the people, as a consequence of which pauperism and crime have kept steady pace with that decline of individuality which has attended consolidation of the land, and the substitution of day laborers for small proprietors.

In decentralized Germany, on the contrary, there has for half a century past been a steady increase in the provision for education.* It is, however, in the highly decentralized Northern States of our Union that we find the earliest and most persistent manifestation of a feeling of responsibility in this regard. The system of universal education commenced in Massachusetts by her earliest settlers has made its way gradually through New England, New York, Pennsylvania, and all the Western States, aided throughout by grants of land from the general government expressly devoted to this object.

* "The Prussian nation is the most enlightened in Europe, owing to the education so thoroughly distributed among every class of society. * * * Large schools abound in great numbers, and while in France the seats of learning and intellectual development are confined to a few great cities, Germany is covered with such institutions, and to enumerate them it would be necessary to include towns and cities of the third or fourth order. * * * It is important that it should be known in France that here unceasing efforts are made to bring every detail of any institution, civil or military, to the greatest possible state of perfection."—*Report of Baron Stoffel, French Military Attaché at Berlin*, 1868. One of the first acts of the government after the great war of 1866 was that of largely increasing the expenditures for educational purposes.

Directly the reverse of this, the highly centralized States of the South have stood almost alone in the fact that instruction of the laboring population has been by law prohibited. As a natural consequence of this, schools of any kind are few, and the proportion of uninstructed even among the white population is extremely great.

Responsibility, individuality, and association grow thus together, each helping and helped by the other; each and all aiding man in his efforts to obtain a full and perfect power of self-direction.

§ 5. Lastly, man is distinguished from all other animals by his CAPACITY FOR PROGRESS. The hare, the wolf, the ox, and the camel are the same as those that existed in the days of Homer, or in those of Egyptian monarchs who left behind them, in the pyramids, evidence of the absence of individuality among their subjects. Man alone records what he has seen and learned, and man alone profits by the labors of his predecessors. To do this he requires language, and to that end he must be enabled to associate and combine with his fellow-men.

That there may be progress, there must be motion. Motion is itself a result of the incessant decomposition and recomposition of matter, and the work of association is but the incessant decomposition and recomposition of the various human forces. In a heap of penny newspapers we find portions of the labor of thousands of persons, from the miners of ores and coal and the collectors of rags, to the makers of types and paper, the engine-makers and engineer, the compositor, pressman, writer, editor, and proprietor, and finally the boys by whom they are distributed; this exchange of services going on from day to day throughout the year, each contributor to the work receiving his share of the pay, and each reader of the paper receiving his share of the work.

To have motion there must be heat, and the greater the latter the more rapid will be the former, as is seen in the rapidity with which, in the tropical regions, water is decomposed and returned again in the form of rain; and in the rapid growth and development of their vegetable products. Vital heat is the result of chemical action, the fuel being food, and the solvent some of those juices which result from its consumption. The more rapid the process of digestion the more healthful and perfect is the motion of the machine. Social heat results from combination, and that the latter may be produced there must be *difference*. "Everywhere," says a writer heretofore referred to, "a simple difference, be it of matter, be it of condition, be it of position, excites a manifestation of vital forces, a mutual exchange of relations between the bodies, each giving to the other what the other does not possess*—the picture thus presented of the movements of the material world being just as true in reference to the social one.

The more instantly the consumption of either ma-

* Guyot. *Earth and Man*, p. 74.

terial or intellectual food follows its production the greater will be the heat that must result, and the more rapid the increase of power to replace the quantity consumed. That consumption may so follow there must be association, and that there cannot be without variety in the modes of employment. That such is the fact will be obvious to all who see how rapid is the spread of ideas in those countries in which agriculture, manufactures, and commerce are combined, compared with that observed in those which are purely agricultural—Ireland, India, the West Indies, Turkey, Portugal, Brazil, and others. Nowhere, however, is the difference more strongly marked than in the Northern States of the Union as compared with those of the South. In the one there is great heat and corresponding motion, and the more motion the greater is the force. In the other there is little heat, but little motion, and very little force.

Progress requires motion. Motion comes with heat, and heat results from association. Association brings with it individuality, freedom, and responsibility, each aiding in the development of the other while profiting by the help received from them.

§ 6. The laws here given are those which govern matter in all its forms, whether of coal, clay, iron, pebble stones, trees, oxen, horses, or men. If true of communities they must be equally so of each and every of its members, as are those relating to the atmosphere at large in reference to all the atoms of which it is composed. That they are so will be ob-

8

vious to every reader who reflects to how great an extent he profits, physically and intellectually, by association with his fellow-men; and that the severest of all punishments is universally recognized as being deprivation of the intercourse he is accustomed to obtain by means of that association. Further reflection will satisfy him that the more perfect his individuality—the greater his material or intellectual wealth — the more perfect is his power to determine for himself what shall be the extent of his association with his neighbor men. Again, he will see that his responsibility for his actions increases in the ratio of the increase of power to determine for himself what shall be his course in life; that if he be poor and perishing far want of food he cannot be held to the same rigid responsibility that might with propriety be exacted were he in affluent circumstances. Lastly, he will be satisfied that his power of progress is in the direct ratio of his ability to combine his efforts with those of his fellow-men; and that, materially and intellectually, the power of production tends to increase with every increase in that demand for either commodities or ideas which results necessarily from an increased ability of others to furnish commodities or ideas in exchange therefor.

Were the reader now to ask himself to what it was that he had been indebted for being the man he is, his answer would be that it had been to his power of association with his fellow-men of the present, and with those of the past who had left behind the records of their experience. Extending his inquiry with a view to determine what it was of which he would least desire to be deprived, he would find that it was the power of association. Next, and only second to that, he would desire perfect power of self-direction, determining when, how, and with whom he would labor, and what disposition he should make of the product. Deprived of that, he would feel himself an irresponsible being. With it, knowing that it depended upon himself what should be his future, he would feel responsible for the proper use of the advantages that he possessed, and would have every inducement so to strengthen his faculties as to qualify himself for rising in the world and for providing for his wife and children; and every step in this direction would be but the preparation for further progress.

Social science treats of man in his efforts for the maintenance and improvement of his condition, and may now be defined as being *the science of the laws which govern man in his efforts to secure for himself the highest individuality, and the greatest power of association with his fellow-men.*

CHAPTER IV.

OF THE PHYSICAL AND SOCIAL LAWS.

§ 1. In the decade just now completed the accumulated contributions of leading physicists have gone so far toward demonstration of the doctrine of the correlation and conservation of the forces known in their several distinctive manifestations as heat, light, electricity, magnetism, and chemical affinity, that it may now be regarded as entirely established. The new philosophy resolves all these subtle agencies into modes of motion, asserting that they are all capable of mutual conversion; that they are one and the same force, differing only in its manifestations and effects; that their various mutations are rigidly subjected to the laws of quantity; that the force of the form assumed is the precise equivalent of that which disappears; and, therefore, that every manifestation of force must come from some pre-existing equivalent force, and must give rise to some subsequent and equal amount of force in another form. Originating with Count Rumford and Sir Humphrey Davy, this grand idea was left to be rounded into its present fulness and symmetry by a host of men of the present day, among whom may here be mentioned Grove, Helmholtz, Meyer, Faraday, Liebig, Henry, and Carpenter.*

The identity and convertibility of these subtlest of forces have abundantly justified the analogies which had thus far been assumed between the heat and motion of matter and the forces of societary life, but the choice of electricity, as the preferable analogue would give us now a greatly larger and happier application of the correspondence.† Retaining all the persistency of the heat into which it is convertible, it presents a far more striking resemblance to the brain-power which is its correspondent in the societary life. So striking indeed is it that when we need to express the idea of rapid action of the societary thought and will we find ourselves compelled to look to the physical world for the terms to be employed, availing ourselves of those of electricity and magnetism.

So universal is this force that all the combinations and decompositions, all the processes of dissolution and reconstruction, are effected through its agency. In organic structures, vegetable and animal, that agency is intimate, pervading, and essential. Between it and the nerve force physiologists scarcely find a trace of difference, except that

* The works of several of these writers on this subject have been collected and published by Professor Youmans, with an introductory preface to which the author here acknowledges his obligations.

† "THE SOUL OF INDUCTION," says the Rev. Baden Powell, "IS ANALOGY; and higher, more efficacious, and more enduring, as the analogies adopted are more strictly accordant with the harmonies of nature."—*Unity of Worlds*, p. 19.

of absence of subjection to the human will. Ever present, it serves to vitalize the globe, and in its most obviously manifest movements, as in those which as yet are most inscrutable, it stands for the best correspondent to mental and moral action that imagination could devise.

Franklin, assuming that the fluid was simple, or uncompounded, gave the names positive and negative to its modes of manifestation. Other philosophers have preferred the names vitreous and resinous, thereby suggesting the idea of a compound nature in the fluid, and all the analogies seem to favor this presentation of the case. A mere disturbance of electrical equilibrium might perhaps explain the movements of lightning in the atmosphere, but certainly does not at all account for electric affinities of the positive and negative manifested in the various processes of chemistry.

Rubbing and rubbed bodies acquire opposite electricities, the contact and interaction requiring the sort of co-relation which subsists between an acid and an alkali. That contact is combination, not mere aggregration—distinctive individuality being here, as in every department of societary life, the condition of perfect association.

Substances assume vitreous or resinous electricity in adjustment to the conditions or capacities acting or acted upon. Woollen cloth is strongly vitreous with zinc, but with gold or iron it is resinous. Such mutations occur in all electric bodies, varying in their intensities, also, under the influence of diversely related substances. Here again do we find a beautiful correspondence with the law of societary association—an infinitely varying adaptation to, and influence upon, the infinitely varied individualities required for giving rapidity to the societary circulation.

This force of immeasurable and resistless energy flows silently, gently, imperceptibly, through perfect conductors, supplying its currents of vitality to the whole organic world. Disturbed, resisted, or misdirected, it blasts and crushes, on the contrary, every obstacle encountered in its course; and here, again, do we find a perfect correspondence to the social force. The actual relation of each and every member of a community, as giver and receiver, teacher and learner, producer and consumer, is possitive and negative by turns and relatively to every difference of function and force in his associates, the whole mass constituting a great electric battery to which each individual contributes his pair of plates. Perfect circulation being established as a consequence of perfect development of all the various individualities, the economic force flows smoothly through every member of the body politic, general happiness and prosperity, improved mental and moral action; following in its train. When, however, by reason of failure on the part of those charged with exercise of the co-ordinating power of the State, the circulation is obstructed, capital misused, and labor abused, the gentle vital force is converted into thunderbolts whose existence is made manifest by the presence of consuming fires. The broken balance rushes by a pathway of ruin to regain its equilibrium, the war of elements thus presented being the correspondent of the strife engendered by resistance to the laws of human life.

The production of electricity, or its excitation for use, requires order and relations that are full of suggestiveness to those who desire fully to understand the conditions upon which alone there can be a prosperous and permanent societary life. Zinc and copper plates promiscuously piled are mere rubbish, powerless as the fragments of any other waste. Let them, however, be connected in orderly alternation, and the range may continue indefinitely with increase of latent force, ready upon the instant when the circuit shall be completed to gather together at one extremity the whole accumulated negative, and at the other the whole accumulated positive, and thus present an active force sufficient to bind and unbind the elements of matter; to penetrate to the innermost parts of their constitutions; to subdue their resistance to its will; to shatter to atoms the largest masses; or to enable man to hold instant converse with his fellow-men throughout the earth.

Turning now to the societary organization we find the precise parallel to this, poverty and weakness being the lot of all those communities in which, as in Turkey and in Ireland, the human plates are promiscuously piled, and in which, as a necessary consequence, there is little or no circulation—wealth and power, on the contrary, growing everywhere in the ratio in which each and every pair of plates is placed in proper relation with each and every other; the vitalized circuit being thus established throughout the entire mass and made to bear, with the concentrated energy of the whole, upon every object of general interest. For the establishment of such order and consequent production of such action, it is that men, as is now being shown in all the new communities of the world, are of their own motion led to grant to certain individuals exercise of the power of co-ordination, a course of proceeding directly opposed to the doctrine of *laisser faire*. The more this power is exercised in the direction of promoting rapid circulation among the plates of which the great battery is composed, the greater is the tendency to development of an inspiration and an energy closely resembling the service of the lightning of heaven subdued to human use. The more the reader shall make himself familiar with the wonderful force of which, even yet, so little is known, the more certainly must he be struck with its extraordinary correspondence with the life forces that govern the destinies of the race; and the more must he be led to arrive at the conclusion that the author had not erred in taking it as the force required for illustrating social action, and for aiding in the study of social science.

§ 2. "To Nature," says Professor Tyndall,*

* Heat considered as a Mode of Motion.

"nothing can be added; from Nature nothing can be taken away; the sum of her energies is constant, and the utmost man can do in the pursuit of physical truth, or in the applications of physical knowledge, is to shift the constituents of the never-varying total, and out of one of them to form another. The law of conservation rigidly excludes both creation and annihilation. Waves may change to ripples, and ripples to waves—magnitude may be substituted for number, and number for magnitude—asteroids may aggregate to suns, suns may resolve themselves into floræ and faunæ, and floræ and faunæ melt in air—the flux of power is eternally the same. It rolls in music through the ages, and all terrestrial energy—the manifestations of life, as well as the display of phenomena, are but the modulations of its rhythm."

We have here, according to Dr. Faraday, "the highest law in physical science which our faculties permit us to perceive, that of the conservation of forces.' But recently discovered, it seems now to have become the crown of the edifice of that great system of law by means of which harmony is secured throughout the whole range of matter, from coral insects which build up islands destined to form the nuclei of continents, to the innumerable suns, with their attendant planets, of which the universe is composed.

By unity of force, and *unity* and *universality of law*, is here intended that persistency of impulse and constancy of action in the multiform substances and subjects of natural law, which is above described; and which is found to follow them through all mutations of form and modifications of office, exhibiting an infinite variety of phenomena, yet without any change of essence or of intrinsic qualities and necessary tendencies in action. The cohesive attraction which produces and maintains the forms of material things, though apparently controlling, cannot be regarded as the abolition, or even the temporary suspension of, that law of gravity which governs all masses of matter at all distances; for it is not so destroyed or suspended. It clings to every atom as persistently and permanently as the existence of the atom itself, for it is a condition of its existence. The disintegrating force of gravitation abides, and is as active in the integrity of the resistant forms of things as it is when displayed in their decomposition. Nay, cohesive attraction, thus exhibiting an apparent opposition to, or difference from, the attraction of the planet, is probably the very same force acting with greater effect by virtue of the greater proximity of the atoms in the defiant form; just as an underground water-current descends from its source in one hill, and ascends from beneath the intervening valley to the crest of the neighboring height, pressed upward to its point of issue by the very same force which carried it downwards from its spring-head. In a multitude of familiar instances, we in like manner learn to find unity and even identity where, in appearance, we seem to see diversity and opposition.

It is certain that every atom of matter must carry with it, through all changes of form and action, the entirety of the properties which make it what it is; else the earth and the universe would have no constitution, and could not be the subject of any law.

This doctrine is not fate, but fact; not materialism, but order, organism, law, government. In its extension to all its subjects it trenches neither upon life, liberty, will, morals, religion, nor responsibility; it affirms only that matter in the human form, as in the rest of the universe, is subject to positive, permanent, and universal rules of action, and that all of his functions which involve material agencies and relations, fall under the laws which arise out of their constitution. If by the terms mind, spirit, or immateriality, *nothingness* is meant, all inquiry, and with it all discussion, is at an end, for of nothing we know nothing: but if mind is a something, a substance, an entity, it too must have a constitution and laws, and neither its will nor liberty is lawless. Surely, therefore, we are safe in saying, that, if mind bears any relation to matter or substance, however transient in duration, it cannot be even conceived of as totally exempt from, or unfurnished with, such answering or correlative powers and properties as are necessarily required to qualify it for such co-ordinated existence and reciprocal action.

The unity of which we speak, as in all other instances in which the idea is used among men, is not identity or sameness, but the harmony of correspondence—unity by relation, fitness, or co-operation, effected by such continuity of character and force of all substances through all spheres of being, and all adaptations of use, as alone can constitute a *universe* of the atoms and individualities which it embraces —of that one entire system " whose body nature is, and God the soul."

Physiologists exhibit the functions of human life as divided into individual or vegetable on the one hand, and relative on the other; the organs of the first of these classes being uniformly single, while those of the latter are as uniformly double and symmetrical. There are two kinds of blood to be circulated, and for each there is a heart, the two being joined together as by a party wall, but not in any sense, as with the eyes and ears, a pair, of which each performs the same office. The life of relative functions consists in their connection with, and their action upon, the physical and societary world; and it is by means of that action that the real MAN is gradually developed.* Deprived of these there would remain nothing proper to the man, and he could have no existence beyond that of a mere vegetable life—such an one as would be that of a solitary individual placed in the heart of the rich prairies of this Western continent. Of power for self-direction he could have none whatsoever, nature being there all-powerful, and he himself being weakness per-

* Mr. Herbert Spencer regards psychology as the necessary predecessor to sociology. The real MAN, capable of acquiring the power of self-direction, being, however, begotten in the societary womb, his study should follow, and not precede, that of the societary body.

sonified. Let him have a companion, and at once his proper human life is awakened; the opposing electric states of consumers and producers, givers and receivers, teachers and learners, having been induced, as air awakens the quiescent lungs, and as light kindles and informs the eye; the real MAN then coming into existence, just as, by reason of association with his fellow-man, he is enabled to feel that he really has begun to acquire that power, and has ceased to be the absolute slave of nature.

The closer and more intimate the contact of these men, and the more rapid the circulation of ideas and services, the greater is the tendency toward development of the faculties peculiar to each, and toward further combination with accelerated rapidity of circulation. Other men, their wives and children, now arriving, the phenomena are with each and every step in this direction repeated and intensified, human force steadily growing at the cost of Nature, and man obtaining by slow degrees that self-direction so entirely at first denied. Population steadily increasing, there arises that diversification in the demand for human force which leads to new developments of the various faculties of each and every member of the association, but in order to such development there must be that orderly arrangement which we see to be required in a galvanic battery, producers and consumers—the electric poles—being brought in close relation with each other. The closer those relations the more rapid becomes the motion, and the more the power of self-government. The greater that power the more rapid is the growth of man's ability to compel Nature to yield in full abundance all the things required for maintenance and enjoyment of life, and for further development of human force; and the more rapid the growth of that feeling of responsibility which has so slight existence in the barbarian, the slave, or the pauper of civilized life. The more these great questions shall be studied the more will it become obvious that man—the real MAN, capable of self-direction, and responsible for his actions—holds his existence in virtue of laws of universal force and effect; and that the teacher who fails to familiarize himself with them, and with their bearing on societary and Christian life, fails in the performance of his duty to his Creator and to his fellow-men.

§ 3. The close relation of physical and social laws is so well exhibited in a passage from an unpublished work by one of the author's friends,* that he deems it well to place it before his readers, as follows:—

"From the indestructibility of matter, as the physical premise, it obviously follows that what we term production and consumption are mere transformations of substance. Whether fossil coal is converted into heat, smoke, and ashes, corn into hogs' flesh, turnips into mutton; corn, pork, turnips, and mutton into human muscle and brain; the uniform phenomenon is alteration of matter in its quality merely, without increase or diminution of its quantity.

"In every transition of matter from one condition to another,

* Hon. E. Peshine Smith, author of a "Manual of Political Economy," and now occupying a high position in the Japanese administration.

force is employed, or, as we say, *consumed*, and force is also evolved or *produced*. When we regard any commodity as an object, the forces necessary for its production are summed up and measured by value. When we regard it as an instrument, the forces capable of being generated—set free would be the more accurate expression—by its consumption are summed up and measured by utility. Electricity, positive and negative, magnetism, exhibiting the same force as attractive and repellant at opposite poles of the same object, afford analogies which may serve to illustrate the subject. If we look to mechanics for an analogy, we may find the equivalent of value in inertia, and that of utility in momentum. The consumption of a product is nothing else than its passage from a state of inertness to one of activity, as from the inorganic or mineral region to the vegetable or vital. It is only through this transition, and at the moment of its occurrence, that a commodity becomes the *pabulum* to production, and that its utility, which was before latent and potential only, becomes manifest and efficient.

"The amount of muscular energy resulting from the human consumption of a certain quantity of food is an instance of the convertibility of the terms force and utility, as the quantum of human activity required to reproduce that food is, conversely, of the same fact in respect to value. The forms of language, the repository and interpreter of common sense, that is, of the general deductions from universal experience, are such that we always predicate value of a thing in reference to its production, and utility in regard to its consumption. The sum of the forces necessary to elevate a ton of coal from its bed at the bottom of the mine equals its value; the quantity of force which, under the boiler of a steam engine, it is capable of generating, equals its utility; are only the formulæ which express, after the method of physical science, a truth which every spoken language implicitly recognizes.

"Between the production of any commodity whatsoever, and its consumption, the interval, long or short, is one of inertness. It stands the monument of human power and natural forces which, having expended themselves in bringing it into shape, slumber in suspended animation, communicating no impulse to the incessant activity which, from the vegetable to the social order, is the essential characteristic of vitality, but is itself a clog and obstruction involving a draft upon the vital force to put it in motion. It is like an inorganic body contained in and afflicting an organism. The space to overcome and the time to intervene before it evolves utility by its consumption, becoming then an instrument and a FORCE, are co-efficients of its value, neutralizing in the same proportion the power of the community in which it rests paralyzed. The growth of wealth, therefore, depends upon the rapidity of circulation; not the rapidity with which products are transported in space, nor the frequency of mere changes of ownership, but the continuity of transformations through the immediate succession of actual consumption to production. This involves the concentration and interfusion of producers and consumers, the growth of population and diversification of industry. The spontaneous social tendencies are in this direction, but they may be promoted, retarded or reversed, according as a community adapts its intelligent and active arrangements to co-operate with them, or suffers them to be thwarted by the artificial arrangements of other communities. The use of science is to give us the power of forecast with a view to action. That is but idle disquisition which ends in abjuring all determinate intervention of the collective sagacity of a nation through its legislative organs—in *laissez aller*, *laissez faire*—the sum of the philosophy of the free-trade economist."

The more these facts are studied, and the more the reader shall be led to appreciate the close intimacy of the physical and social laws, the more, it is believed, will he be led to agree with the illustrious Oersted in the belief expressed in his "Soul in Nature," that "the laws of nature are laws of reason;" that they altogether form "an endless unity of reason;" and that they are "one and the same throughout the universe."

To what extent the views above presented have been, or are being, carried into practical effect in past or present societary organizations will next be shown.

CHAPTER V.

OF THE SOCIETARY ORGANIZATION.

§ 1. THROUGHOUT nature the rank and perfection of organisms are in direct proportion to the number and dissimilarity of the parts, proof of this being found at every stage of progress from the simplest composition of organic matter up to the structure of MAN, in whom are reproduced all the forms and faculties of being over which, for the service of his needs, it has been given to him to rule. This law not only marks the relative rank of classes of creatures, but it serves, also, to measure the respective positions of the individuals of whom the several classes are composed—the nearest approach to perfection being found in those men in whom the distinctive human qualities are found most active and most developed. Following out the rule, those communities in which are found the largest variety of differences, and their most effective development into action, should present the nearest approach to perfection of societary organization. Seeking these, we find them where the demands for human powers are most diversified; where the orderly arrangement of societary positives and negatives is most complete, enabling men most fully to combine their efforts; rapid societary motion there stimulating into activity all the power that thus far had remained latent, and facilitating the passage of their members from the brutifying labors of transportation, through those of the workshop, to those of a scientific agriculture.

Subordination of specialties to a general intention—diversity of functions or uses, so combined as to produce a perfect harmony of related action—is at once the mark and test of organization. The individual man is healthy and efficient within himself in proportion to the vigor and exactness with which the bodily instruments of his will obey the governing brain; those charged with carrying on his automatic life meanwhile furnishing full support to his voluntary powers. Absolute subordination in the parts of a machine to the moving force is the constant characteristic of inanimate organizations. In a watch, steam engine, mill, or ship, all the parts are in prompt and complete obedience, their perfection being measured by the exactness of their subordination.

In societary organizations we have the same law modified, but not repealed, by that power of self-direction which, more or less, accompanies human life, bringing with it responsibility to both God and man. The crew of a ship—the hands in a factory—the thousands of human positives and negatives of which an army is composed—are organized and subordinated, that they may accomplish the work for whose performance they have been brought together. So, too, is it in civil government—subordination of the subjects being essential to the well-being and the progress of the community, and to those very individual liberties which it limits, as well as to the national order for whose security it has been designed; the most remarkable case of societary organization on record being that under which the Hebrews sojourned in the desert, during the long period that intervened between the passage of the Red Sea and their entrance into the promised land.

Throughout nature, the more perfect the organization, and the more absolute the subordination, the more harmonious and beautiful is the interdependence of the parts. A rock or lump of coal being broken, each and every portion remains as perfect as it had been before. Dividing a polypus into a dozen parts the vital force is found existing in each and all, and to such extent that each becomes again a perfect animal. Doing the same by man, he speedily passes into dust. So, too, is it with societies—the mutuality of interdependence growing with every stage of progress, from that simplest of societary forms presented to view in the history of Crusoe and his man Friday, toward that high state of organization in which tens of thousands of human positives and negatives combine to satisfy the public want for a single newspaper; hundreds of thousands then profiting by its perusal at a cost so small as scarcely to admit of calculation.

Throughout nature, the more complete the subordination, and the more perfect the interdependence of the parts, the greater is the individuality of the whole, and the more absolute the power of self-direction. The rock is chained to earth, obeying but a single force; the bird, at will, rises in the air, or skims across the lake. The dog obeys his master; the master has power to direct himself and nature too. The man in perfect health, with all the parts moving in perfect subjection to the directing brain, determines for himself if he will go abroad or stay at home; the invalid, on the contrary, being compelled to keep his chamber. So, too, must it be with society—independence growing with the growth of interdependence among its various parts, and the latter becoming developed as the organization becomes more perfect, and the subordination more complete.

Organization and subordination, association and individuality, responsibility and the power of self-direction, travel thus together throughout the social world.

§ 2. In man, the brain holds the office of co-ordinator of the whole system, the existence of a necessity for co-ordination on one hand involving the duty of subordination on the other.

The more perfect the co-ordination of the whole the greater is the development of each and every part, the co-ordinating power itself included. Failing to direct to the stomach a proper supply of food the arms and legs lose their power, and the eyes become affected; the brain in turn participating in the loss of strength until at length life ceases to exist.

The more perfect the development of the various portions of the MAN, and the more numerous and marked the differences of the qualities thus developed, the greater must be the power to maintain commerce within himself, and with the exterior world; rapidity of the circulation being an essential characteristic of the highest organization.—So, too, must it be with society—the more numerous the differences and the greater the power of association, the more complete being the subordination, and the more absolute that respect for the rights of others, in which consists the most perfect freedom. That this is so is shown by the following diagram representing the American Union as it stood thirty years since.

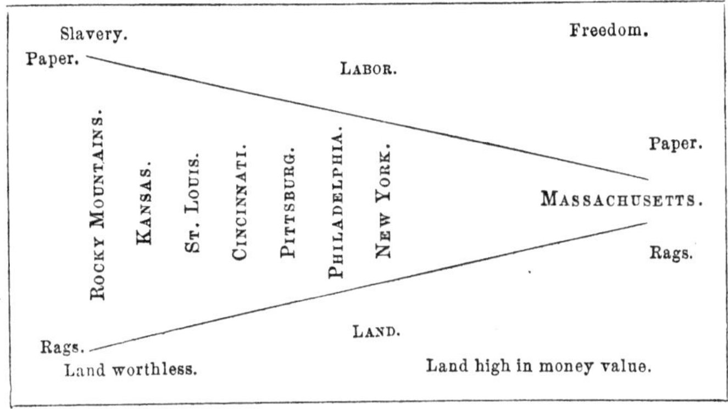

On the left, there are few differences. Societary organization having, therefore, no existence, force furnishes the only law, the laborer is enslaved, and land has no money value. On the right, differences being numerous, society has become organized, co-ordination and subordination growing thus together, and man becoming more free—exercising from day to day more and more of the power of self-direction.

Looking to early Attica we see, in the many little communities by which the small and barren territory had been occupied, the first rude efforts at societary organization. The demand for human powers being very limited differences were few in number—each and every man uniting in himself the various characters of sailor, trader, soldier, and mechanic. Interdependence among men had but very little existence, and, as a necessary consequence, there was little among the communities of which they were a part—each and every of them being ready at any moment to invade the territory, and annihilate the rights of person and of property, in each and every other.—Tracing them thence onward, we find differences increasing as society becomes more developed—the positives and negatives, producers and consumers, coming now together; co-ordination and subordination keeping steady pace with the growth of wealth and population, until, at length, the well-formed societary body, with Athens for its head, appears upon the stage with Solon exercising the power of co-ordination in giving to the people a constitution in which freedom on one hand, and subordination on the other, are provided for in a degree never before equalled in the world.

As a consequence of this approach to order is it

that Athens now occupies in history a position more distinguished than has, even yet, been assigned to any community of either ancient or modern times.—The step thus made should, however, have been only preliminary to another in virtue of which the interdependence of the various little communities of Greece at large would have been promoted, and the subordination of each and all to a central power well established. Failing to carry out the idea here so well begun Greece became a scene of perpetual war, and differences disappeared; the once free communities becoming resolved into masses of traders and soldiers on the one hand, and slaves on the other.

Comparing now the policies of Solon and Lycurgus, we find the tendency of the former to have been in the direction of the development of human faculties, the *production* of differences, and the bringing together of the societary positives and negatives; whereas the latter looked to the limitation of human pursuits, the *prevention* of differences, and the wider separation of the human plates. In the first, the interdependence of the various portions of society, for almost a century after Solon, was a constantly augmenting force—stimulating all to effort, and producing that high development of which Athens was the scene. In the other, the system tended in reverse direction, annihilating all desire for distinction other than that to be obtained by force or fraud, and closing by the reduction of society to two great classes, the great landholder on the one hand, and the slave on the other. In the one, subordination became, for a time, from year to year more perfect. In the other, it declined as the small proprietors diminished in number, until at length they wholly disappeared.

Crossing the Adriatic, we obtain a reproduction of Sparta, and not of Athens—fraud and force, and not a growing interdependence, being the foundations of Roman power Those who would open for themselves the road to fortune, must use the sword, and that alone; and hence it is that while early Italy presents for our examination numerous and prosperous cities, placed among fields that were owned by the men who tilled them, imperial Italy exhibits so little beyond a single city, filled with paupers, traders, and bankers, and owned by great proprietors whose distant lands were tilled by slaves; the human plates becoming from day to day more widely separated. Seeking the cause of this, we find in Roman history, from the days of the Tarquins to those of Marius and Sylla, Antony and Octavius, but a record of growing brutality and insubordination on one hand, and of declining power of co-ordination on the other—the directing brain becoming weaker as the land becomes consolidated, and the people more enslaved. Examine that history where we may, we find a growing tendency toward separation of positives and negatives—consumers and producers; toward augmentation of the proportion of the class of middlemen; toward diminution in the demand for any of the human faculties, that one excepted which man exerts in common with the beasts of the field—mere brute force. The result is seen in the fact, that extended as was her empire Rome contributes but little to the general fund of art or literature, while the little Attica constitutes the great treasury to which all resort who delight in either.

With the downfall of the empire, and the general ruin of towns and cities, the artisan and the mechanic almost entirely disappear—society becoming resolved into its original elements; insubordination becoming universal, and anarchy taking the place of the little order which had before existed Later, we find Charlemagne engaged in the effort at co-ordination and seeking to command subordination; calling together assemblies composed of various portions of the people, and instituting laws which all, both great and small, were required to respect. At his death, the power of combination suddenly disappears, anarchy and insubordination taking its place; the feudal system, as it existed in both France and Germany, recognizing fully the power of the master to command his slave, while *practically* denying the necessity of subordination on the part of the master himself. Here, again, we have a resolution of society into its elements, accompanied by further and more complete disappearance of differences among its various portions—slaves and nobles abounding, and physical force furnishing the law in obedience to which all are required to bend.* Following French history downward, we find a perpetual effort at the establishment of subordination, followed by repeated failures consequent upon the omission, until the days of the great Colbert, of attempt at bringing together in orderly arrangement the societary positives and negatives, and thereby so diversifying the employments of the people as to make demand for the qualities by whose possession the real MAN is distinguished from the brute.

§ 3. Turning now to other portions of Europe, we meet with insubordination in the ratio of the absence of those differences without which society cannot assume its natural form, nor can men acquire the power of self-direction—striking evidence of this being presented by England in the days of the Plantagenets—Scotland, in those of the Stuarts—Denmark, in the period anterior to Frederic III.—and Poland, down to the day of its partition.

Tracing history onward, any and everywhere, we obtain evidence that in every case of advancing civilization, as the latent human faculties have become more and more developed; as the power of association has grown into strength; as man has become more master of nature and of himself; as society has tended to take its natural form; as competition for the *purchase* of labor has grown; sub-

* The insurrection of the *Jacquerie*, A. D. 1351, with its accompanying horrors, was a necessary consequence of the total disappearance of subordination from among the nobles of France, during the English war.—See SISMONDI: *Histoire de France*, vol. x. p. 530.

ordination has become more complete, while all have risen in the scale of being, and the man who labors has more and more acquired the power of self-direction. Examining, next, the movement of declining countries, we find the reverse of this—uniformity taking place of difference—anarchy and insubordination replacing order—and the laborer becoming re-enslaved.—Looking now around us, we find that men have become more free in all the countries that have followed in the lead of Colbert, seeking earnestly to bring about an orderly arrangement of human positives and negatives, producers and consumers; land having become more divided, and the laborer having become more master of nature and of himself, in France, and in all the countries of Northern and Central Europe, with constantly growing tendency toward development of that respect for the rights of others without which there can be no real power of self-direction.

Turning next toward those which follow in the lead of, or in the direction indicated by, professors of that science which finds its base in mere "assumptions," we meet, in Ireland, an insubordination resulting in destruction of life, property, and happiness, to an extent that has rarely been exceeded; in Jamaica, an unceasing state of warfare between the slave and his master, that has since resulted in the ruin of both;* in Turkey, an almost entire disappearance of the societary organization;

* See DALLAS: *History of the Maroons*, London, 1805.

in Mexico, a great community that is being rapidly resolved into its original elements; in Spanish America generally, a constant series of wars, having for their object the determination of the question as to who shall control the societary movement; in India, famines and rebellions, the last of which has just now closed with the firing off, from the mouths of cannon, of numerous prisoners.*

* "For years and years," wrote an Indian official, at the date of the last great rebellion, "we have been acting as if we were under no moral responsibility whatsoever—as if India were a thing made expressly for our mere worldly advantage, and for nothing else—*the natives of the soil no better than the wild beasts of the jungles, or, of being more helpless, only fit to be made hewers of wood and drawers of water, the slaves of the white man*—that any pretence on their part to a share of the inheritance God had assigned them was rank treason—that opinions, customs, and usages, as old as these hills, and as fondly cherished as an Englishman's liberty, were to be given up, and cast aside, with as much ease as you would throw aside an old bonnet, if they did not square with John Bull's notions, or stood in the way of his selfishness and cupidity. This is exactly what we have been doing for the last twenty years—we have attempted many things which even the boldest and most daring of their own native princes would never have had the madness to venture on. *That cursed itch to annex; the vile and abominable corruptions, bribery, and extortion, practised in our civil courts, and by the police; the dislike of the natives to our system of land tenure,* which, however fine and specious in theory, and to write on, or to make a speech on in Parliament, was most distasteful to the native cultivators, and left them entirely at the mercy of merchants and money lenders, and was simply ruin to the poor ryot. * * * All alike ignored their cries, and treated them with contempt, till at last they had recourse to the only mode of redress left to them—mutiny, insurrection, and rebellion! And I do say, for all the horrors, and sad calamities which followed, England is responsible." What were those "horrors" is shown in the following passage from an article in the *Westminster Review* for January, 1867:—

"A historian of some promise has said that he knows nothing in early English history, except William's devastation of the North, that approaches the horrors that our troops have committed in putting down the Indian revolt, a judgment that appears to be confirmed by Captain

Coming now to England herself, we find a constant war of classes; one holding with Mr. Huskisson that "to enable capital to obtain a fair remuneration, labor must be kept down;" the other meanwhile protesting against that doctrine as leading to enslavement of their children and themselves. As a consequence of this, "strikes," attended with immense loss to the community, and ending generally in defeat of the laborer, are of constant occurrence; the result being seen in the facts, that the land becomes more and more consolidated; that the little landowner and the little manufacturer gradually disappear from the stage of action; that the power of association declines; and that the direction of the

Trotter's statement, p. 284, when, speaking of Lord Canning's clemency, he says:—

"'When the gallows, the cat, the torch, were threatening to blot out the last distinctions between guilt and innocence, to turn whole districts into grave-yards, deserts, haunts of beggared or fear-stricken outcasts, it was time for some voice of power to cry out upon the folly, the savage meanness, of overdone revenge. In thirteen days alone of June and July, one commissioner had sent to the gibbet forty-two wretches guilty, all save one murderer, of nothing worse than robbery, rioting, or rebellion. Some of them paid with their lives for having goods or money—even bags of copper half-pice—about which they failed to give any plausible account. In less than six weeks up to the 1st of August, some hundred and twenty men, of whom none were Sepoys, and only a few were of higher rank than villagers, servants, policemen, had been hanged by the civil commissioners of one county alone. Of course, in many cases, the evidence against the prisoners seemed strong only to minds that saw all objects through a film of blood. *Of the numbers arrested, not one in ten appears to have escaped some form of punishment, not two to have escaped the gallows.*'

"This is the way in which Englishmen sometimes recommend their civilization and illustrate their Christianity in British dependencies, not without sympathetic applause from excitable compatriots at home."

societary machine becomes more difficult with each successive year.*

Turning next to central Europe we find Prussia from the days of the great Frederick, with occasional enforced intervals, to have been engaged in an effort to lead consumers and producers, capitalists and laborers, to take their places by each other's sides, thereby bringing into orderly arrangement the positives and negatives of that wonderful battery whose plates now count by tens of millions, and by whose extraordinary performances the world has recently been so much astonished.† Creating thus an attractive force such as has been but rarely equalled, the great empire that has thence resulted stands now a monument to the memory of the men who had seen that wealth and power had gone always with growth of the power of association; with development of the various individualities of a people; with increase in that power for self-direction which it is given to men to seek, and which comes as a necessary consequence of growth in power to compel the great natural forces to become the slaves and cease to be the masters of mankind.

Looking now to the American Union, we find the diverse conditions above described, the South

* "We level the poor to the dust by our general policy, and take infinite credit to ourselves for raising them up with the grace of charity." FONBLANQUE.

† "Such an achievement as the restoration of the germs of order and prosperity which Frederick so rapidly brought about after the appalling ruin which seven years of disastrous war had effected, is unmatched in the history of human government."—*Fortnightly Review*, Oct. 1871.

having sought the maintenance of an exclusive agriculture, and the prevention of that great commerce whose growth is so wholly dependent on the coming together of producers and consumers, societary positives and negatives. As a consequence of this, the power of association there declined and individualities remained undeveloped, with steady diminution of the power for self-direction of both masters and slaves, employers and employed. Throughout the North, on the contrary, all was directly the reverse; the general result of their strictly opposite policies having recently most strikingly manifested itself in the poverty and weakness of the one, and wealth and strength of the other. Look where we may, we find these latter growing in the direct ratio of the exercise of that co-ordinative power on the part of governments by means of which their people are to be enabled most freely to combine together for establishing that control over the great natural forces to which alone can they look for obtaining for themselves a perfect power for self-direction.

All the facts of history may now be cited in evidence of the proposition, that the societary organization becomes more complete, subordination more perfect, and man more free, in the direct ratio of the approach of the consumer to the producer, the development of a scientific agriculture, and consequent approximation of the prices of the rude products of the earth to those of the finished commodities into which they are converted.

§ 4. The more thorough the development of differences among men, and the more perfect the power of self-direction, the more complete becomes their interdependence; the greater the harmony in the societary relations; the larger the production; the more rapid the circulation; the more equitable the distribution; the more absolute the subordination; and the greater the tendency toward growth in the power of self-direction, whether among individuals or in the communities of which they are parts. The less, however, is the tendency towards the production of those "positive checks" to population relied upon by Mr. Malthus, and known to the world as war, pestilence, and famine.

That this is so, must be obvious to all who see in the individual man the type of that grand man to which we apply the term *society*, and who appreciate the fact, that this great law governs matter in all its forms, whether in that of systems of mountains or communities of men. Throughout our solar system, harmony of movement—interdependence, is a result of that local attraction which preserves a perfect independence. So, too, is it with nations, the tendency toward general peace and harmony being in the ratio of their interdependence; that, in its turn, being in the direct ratio of their independence. As among individuals, the power of association grows with the development of individuality, and as this latter grows with the growth of the habit of combination, so does the tendency towards peaceful action among communities grow with the growth of local centres, and with that of self-dependence; subordination to the laws of right and justice among nations growing with the growth of the power of self-direction and protection. Here, as everywhere throughout nature, action and reaction are equal and contrary, harmony being the result of the perfect balance of these opposing forces.

The reverse of this, however, is what we are told in English books. From them we learn that universal peace is to follow in the train of a system that seeks to establish centralization of the manufacturing power of the world; thereby separating societary positives and negatives, and thus depriving the various nations of all ability to develop the latent powers of either earth or man; limiting the latter to the work of scratching out the soil and selling it in distant markets, thus preventing the growth of agriculture Under that system, interdependence in the bosom of the society dies away, dependence meantime growing, with corresponding tendency to the development of insubordination, and toward production of the "positive checks" of the "assumptions" school. The effort now being made toward the establishment of trading centralization—that system which now is advocated by the men who teach that political economy relates exclusively to commodities that may be bought and sold—tends to the general production of a state of things similar to that exhibited in France, in the days of the Jacquerie; in Germany, in those of John of Leyden and his Anabaptists; in England, in those of Henry VIII., when criminals by tens of thousands were hanged in a single reign;

in Scotland, in the days of Fletcher; in Ireland, throughout the present century; in China and South America at the present hour; that state of things in which insubordination comes as the companion of a division of society into two great forces—the very rich and the very poor, the master and the slave. Hence it is that it has given rise to the doctrine of over-population, which is simply that of slavery, anarchy, and societary ruin, as the ultimate condition of mankind; that, too, coming as a consequence of laws emanating from an all-wise and all-powerful Being who could, if He would, have instituted laws in virtue of which freedom, order, peace, and happiness, would have been the lot of man.

That these latter *have been* instituted—that the scheme of creation is not a failure; that it is marred by no such errors as those assumed by Mr. Malthus; is proved by all the facts presented for consideration by the advancing communities of the world—the habit of peace, among both individuals and nations, growing with growth of numbers, and increase in power for self-direction. The more perfect that power, the greater is the tendency towards increased control of mind over matter; the wretched slave to nature gradually yielding place to the MASTER OF NATURE, in whom the feeling of responsibility to his family, his country, his Creator, and himself, grows with the growth of power to guide and direct the vast and various forces placed at his command. This last grows in all those countries in which the societary energies, represented by their co-ordinating centres, are most directed to the removal of obstacles to association and combination, and, therefore, most in accordance with the great laws instituted by the Creator of the universe for government of matter in all its forms, whether in that of myriads of suns, or of communities of men.

CHAPTER VI.

OF MATTER AND MIND.

§ 1. "THE laws of mind and laws of matter," says Mr. Mill—

"Are so dissimilar in their nature, that it would be contrary to all principles of rational arrangement to mix them up as parts of the same study. In all scientific methods, therefore, they are placed apart. Any compound effect or phenomenon which depends both on the properties of matter and on those of mind, may thus become the subject of two completely distinct sciences, or branches of science; one treating of the phenomenon in so far as it depends upon the laws of matter only, the other treating of in so far as it depends upon the laws of mind.

"The physical sciences are those which treat of the laws of matter, and of all complex phenomena in so far as dependent upon the laws of matter. The mental or moral sciences are those which treat of the laws of mind, and of all complex phenomena in so far as dependent upon the laws of mind."*

"Political Economy, therefore, presupposes all the physical sciences; it takes for granted all such of the truths of those sciences as are concerned in the production of the objects demanded by the wants of mankind; or, at least, it takes for

* Unsettled Questions on Political Economy, p. 130.

granted that the physical part of the process takes place somehow. It then inquires what are the phenomena of *mind* which are concerned in the production and distribution of those same objects ; it borrows from the pure science of mind the laws of those phenomena, and inquires what effects follow from these mental laws, acting in concurrence with those physical ones.

"The physical laws of the production of useful objects are all equally presupposed by the science of Political Economy; most of them, however, it presupposes in the gross, seeming to say nothing about them. A few (such, for instance, as the decreasing ratio in which the produce of the soil is increased by an increased application of labor) it is obliged particularly to specify, and thus seems to borrow those truths from the physical sciences to which they properly belong, and include them among its own."*

The laws of two sciences having been separately studied "seeming to say nothing" of the physical portion thereof, the results are then to be combined—the general result thus obtained being the politico-economical *science* of our age and generation. How far such separation and combination would be possible the reader may determine for himself after consideration of the facts already placed before him relating to the occupation and cultivation of the earth. Referring thereto, he will see that to accord with the doctrines of Mr. Mill and his disciples matter must steadily obtain increased power over mind, the control of the few over the constantly diminishing product of labor steadily increasing, and that of the many as steadily diminishing; the tendency towards slavery thus established coming as necessary consequence of a great law assumed to have been insti-

* Unsettled Questions on Political Economy, p. 133.

tuted by a wise and beneficent Creator for government of the human race. Were that different, "all the other phenomena of the production and distribution of wealth would," as Mr. Mill assures us, "also be different," labor then becoming more and more productive, mind then becoming more and more master over matter, and man then becoming with each successive day more and more qualified to exercise that power of self-direction by which he is, or should be, distinguished from all other portions of the animal creation.

We have here that which is confessedly the most important of all the questions which connect themselves with the movements of the societary world. Looking always on one side of the shield Mr. Mill assumes that, in obedience to his great law of constantly diminishing returns to agricultural labor, all must eventually become dark as midnight. His opponents, on the contrary, recognizing the fact that there is "a silver side to every cloud," assert that however intense the darkness the bright side tends, with each and every stage in the growth of wealth and population, more and more to present itself to view.

Which of these is right? That answers may be obtained to any or all such questions Mr. Mill requires us to assume that the "physical part of the process takes place somehow," studying the remainder by aid of a science—

"Which presupposes the whole science of the nature of the individual mind; since all the laws of which the latter science takes cognizance are brought into play in a state of society, and the truths of the social science are but statements of the manner in which those simple laws take effect in complicated circumstances. Pure mental philosophy, therefore, is an essential part, or preliminary, of political philosophy."*

What, however, is there in this all-important question that needs for its proper comprehension the aid of this "science of the nature of the individual mind;" this latter itself so incomprehensible that it is yet, in all its parts, as much open for discussion as it was in the days of Socrates and Plato? Is it the fact, that soils differ in their qualities in the manner heretofore described? Or the fact, that some are high and dry while others are low and wet? Or the fact, that the early and isolated settler is a poor man, with an almost unaided hand, about to commence his contest with an all-powerful nature? Or the fact, that, poor and weak as he is, the high and dry land presents the only soil from which he can hope to obtain any supplies whatsoever? Or the fact, that, as numbers increase and as wealth more and more abounds, he and his neighbors are enabled to subjugate those richer lands upon which he must in the earlier days, had he undertaken their cultivation, have perished of famine? Nothing of the kind, whatsoever! These facts no more need for their examination "the whole science of the nature of the individual mind" than do those other facts which relate to movements of the heavenly bodies. Like to these latter they demand

* Unsettled Questions on Political Economy, p. 136.

to be carefully studied with a view to ascertaining what is the real law of the case, thereby enabling us to determine whether or not the Creator had on the one hand willed that with the growth of wealth and population food and other raw material should become from year to year more difficult of attainment; that with each successive year the rich should grow richer, and the poor poorer, these latter becoming as regularly more and more slaves to the caprices and the passions of their masters: or, on the other, that food and raw material should become more abundant; that the poor and the weak should gradually come to take their places side by side and on an equality with their heretofore rich and powerful neighbors; and finally, that every stage of progress in this latter direction should be accompanied by new development of that power of self-direction in whose absence there can be none of that real freedom of thought, or action, without which man cannot be held responsible for errors to whose commission he has been forced by means of action on the part of others over whom he exercises no control whatsoever.

Taking next the "fundamental question" of value, we may here inquire to what extent "the science of the individual mind" is required for enabling us to determine the real cause of the existence of that idea. Of that "science" Eve certainly knew nothing; yet did she furnish a reply when giving so high a price for a single apple. Since then, of all her descendants there has been not even one who has not on every day of his life proved that he valued commodities of every kind more or less in the ratio of the difficulty or the facility with which they might be obtained. The poor Digger Indian attaches so high a value to the wretched food on which he so much depends that he gives his whole time to the search therefor. The schoolboy values the apple so highly that he risks his life in the effort to climb the tree on which it hangs. The trader attaches more or less value to commodities as the obstacles to their reproduction diminish or increase. How much of the "science of the individual mind" is required by these persons for determining a question that so greatly puzzles teachers of economic science? Is there one among these latter who would not obtain an answer thereto by merely looking around his library and satisfying himself that the value he attaches to its various books is greater, or less, in the precise ratio of the obstacles that would stand in the way of their replacement in case of loss? Might he not then profit by studying facts rather than by exploring the recesses of his "individual mind"? Would not such study result in convincing him that values declined as mind obtained power over matter, and increased as this latter grew in strength? Assuredly it would.

When John Smith first robbed a hen-roost he did so for the reason that he attached to the eggs a higher value than he was disposed to attribute to the possible flogging that was to be their price. Here we meet at once that "positive knowledge of the uncultured," which, according to Mr. Spencer, constitutes the foundation of all real science; and it is in its utter neglect by economists we are to find the causes of those "artificial generalizations" to which, as he tells his readers, such a course of action must inevitably lead. See p. 34, *ante.*

Reasoning from "assumptions," Mr. Mill denies that such is the true method of this "abstract and hypothetical" science. Laws having been *invented*, facts must be made to sustain them. Hence it is, that what in the hands of Adam Smith was the commencement of the simplest and most beautiful of all the sciences, has become now so complicated and repulsive that every student rejoices when he can throw his books aside, fully determined, as he generally is, to forget forthwith all the economical *science* with which his tutor had so sedulously sought to cram him.

The life of man is a constant combat with nature, matter sometimes triumphing over mind, but the latter more frequently triumphing over the former, and always using the power thus acquired as a means of obtaining further triumphs. Throughout, matter, mind, and the laws of both, are so closely interwoven that any attempt at separate study thereof, such as is above suggested, must prove, as thus far it has proved, an utter failure. How, indeed, would it be possible even to enter upon such study of the value of the eggs on one hand, and the possible flogging on the other, above referred to?

§ 2. There being but two sets of laws, those of

mind and those of matter, and political economy finding no place under the latter, it must, of necessity, according to Mr. Mill, be ranked among the former, the material portion of the societary process being assumed "somehow" to have "taken place." Lines of separation so sharp as the one here indicated are, however, of so rare occurrence as to warrant doubt of the view thus presented. Nowhere does the idea seem to have suggested itself to him that a place might possibly be found intermediate between the two; one in which matter and mind themselves were being brought face to face with each other contending for the mastery—action and reaction becoming more instant as the heat of the fight becomes more and more intense—the former backed by all the resisting power of the natural forces; the latter standing at first alone, the very type of weakness, but gradually obtaining more and more control, each successive step in that direction being accompanied by new development of its own latent powers, thus enabling it to pass from one triumph to another, each succeeding one more important than that by which it had been preceded. That such a place does exist; that there such conflict rages; and that the development of mind is in the direct ratio of the fierceness with which it is maintained: it is proposed now to show.

Throughout the whole range of organized life the passage from lower to higher forms and structures is, with rare exceptions, so exceedingly gentle as in many cases to be almost imperceptible, making it at times difficult to decide if the individual find its proper place in the animal or the vegetable kingdom. Recent discoveries having tended steadily toward bringing more nearly together than they before had seemed to be, not only the several kingdoms but also their divisions and subdivisions, the world has now been furnished with a theory of the "Descent of Man," in which to the minute Ascidian is assigned the honorable position of remote ancestor to all vertebrated animals of both sea and land.*

* The foundation on which the Darwinian theory rests exhibits itself in the assertion that there is and has ever been a "survival of the fittest;" those least fitted for maintenance of a perpetual strife for life having been steadily and necessarily trampled out of existence. This, however, is but a new application of the politico-economical *laissez faire;* the one denying all intelligent interference from above precisely as the other insists that no such interference here below can be allowed. With both, progress lies necessarily in the direction of that increased power of matter over mind so well described by the Rev. Mr. Kingsley, in his recent charming volume, as here given :—

"Throughout the great republic of the forest, the motto of the majority is—as it is and always has been with human beings—'Every one for himself and the devil take the hindmost.' Selfish competition, overreaching tyranny, the temper which fawns and clings as long as it is down, and when it has risen, kicks over the stool by which it climbed—these and the other 'works of the flesh' are the works of the average plant as far as it can practise them. So by the time the bamboo-vine makes up its mind it will have discovered by the experience of many generations, the value of the proverb, 'Never do for yourself what you can get another to do for you,' and will have developed into a true high climber, selfish and insolent, choking and strangling like yonder beautiful green pest, of which beware—namely: a tangle of razor-grass."—*Christmas in the West Indies.*

In all decaying communities—those whose members are being more and more compelled to depend upon the rude labors of the field—the course of things is precisely that here described, the soil fittest for giving abundant supplies of food being the first abandoned; the plants best fitted for man's purposes becoming the prey of useless or noxious

P.157.

Inspiration
Intuition
Theology
Ethics
Psychology
Social Science
Political Economy
Jurisprudence
Biology
Zoology
Organology
Phytology
Vegetable Physiology
Chemistry
Chem. Dynamics
Physics
Phys. Dynamics
Natural Philosophy
MAN
Animal Life
Chemical Forces
Vegetable Life
MATTER
Mechanical Forces
Attraction
Divisibility
Inertia
Impenetrability

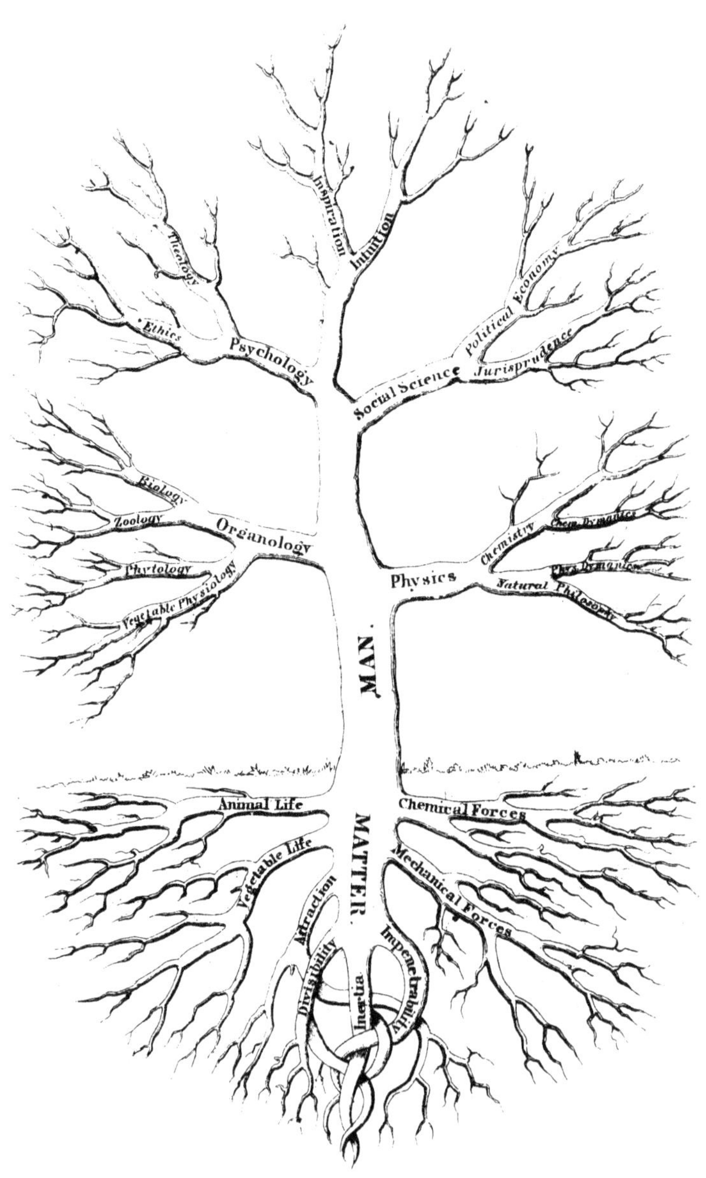

Whether the view thus presented be true or false—whether it come to be finally accepted or rejected—does not now concern us, its only importance here being found in the picture thus presented of the passage of the same particles of matter from the lowest to the highest forms and structures, each individual atom carrying with it, through all changes, the entirety of the properties which make it what it is; and remaining, therefore, always subject to the same laws by which it had at first been governed. That the reader may trace this upward movement his attention is here again invited to the figure opposite, having studied which he can determine for himself at what point, if any, the great physical laws could, by possibility, have been suspended in favor of the few atoms entering into the composition of the human frame.

With the appearance on the stage of life of new forms and more complex structures new laws present themselves, always, however, coöperating harmoniously with those previously observed. Here, too, we mark the same gradual and quiet movement

weeds; the animals fittest for man's service disappearing before the beasts of the forest; the faculties fittest for enabling man to become master of nature becoming once again latent and unemployed; matter thus resuming its control over mind. In all advancing communities, on the contrary, those in which diversified employment gives power for reducing to cultivation the richest soils—the strife for life declines, and the weak are daily more and more brought to a level with the rich and strong, as is proved by the daily increasing influence of the gentler sex. Look where we may, societary life, ancient or modern, furnishes no facts favorable to permanent adoption of the materialistic theories—philosophic or economic—now so much in vogue.

that had attended changes of form and structure, organology following physics, and the instinct of the coral insect and the oyster slowly expanding itself into that of the beaver, the bird, the horse, and the dog, the approach toward reason becoming now so marked as to lead to hesitation in regard to classing these latter with merely instinctive animals.* Thus far, however, matter and its laws have continued paramount, the slight mental activity above referred to having been little more than had been needed as preparation for approach to the stage of action above described—that one on which matter and mind were to be brought face to face with each other, contending for mastery of the world; the former armed with powers so prodigious that words scarcely suffice for their enumeration and description; the latter at first so weak as to be deficient in many of the qualities by means of which even the lowest animals had been

* "Whether this neurosis is accompanied by such psychosis as ours, it is impossible to say; but those who deny that the nervous changes which, in the dog, correspond with those which underlie thought in a man, are accompanied by consciousness, are equally bound to maintain that those nervous changes in the dog which correspond with those which underlie sensation in a man, are also unaccompanied by consciousness. In other words, if there is no ground for believing that a dog thinks, neither is there any for believing that he feels. * * * For even supposing that in man, and in man only, psychosis is superadded to neurosis—the neurosis which is common to both man and animal gives their reasoning processes a fundamental unity."—Prof. Huxley in the *Contemporary Review*, December, 1871.

The dog, seeking help for his wounded master, passes back and forth until he has gained the attention of those to whom he looks to grant it, a mode of speech in full accord with the limited power of thought of the animal by whom it is used. See note to p. 78, *ante*.

fitted for self-preservation. A contest more unequal could scarcely be imagined; and yet, step by step, mind is seen gaining on its opponent, seizing his outworks and on the instant turning upon him the captured guns, each forward movement proving thus but simple preparation for a new and greater one. That such has been the case in the past, and must be in the future, is proved by the fact that the subjugation of matter to mind in the last thirty years has been greater than that of the previous century, wonderfully great as even that had been.

Where matter is, there must the laws of matter be. Where mind is, there must be found the laws of mind. Looking once again at the figure the reader will see both moving steadily upwards, the former at first exercising supreme control, yet gradually yielding place and power to the latter; this latter, too, slowly obtaining more and more development, with corresponding increase of force, until at length we have THE MAN of the present armed on one hand with power for direction such as even half a century since could not have been imagined; and on the other, exercising a self-directing power which, though yet far more limited than could be wished, is greater far than till now had been ever known.

§ 3. Is it, however, the reader asks, possible that while thus mastering the great physical forces he should himself have remained subject to the same laws by which they themselves are governed and directed? Walking, talking, riding, swimming, at his pleasure; exercising, apparently, perfect freedom of will, can it be that he still remains as completely subject to those laws as do the sands of the shore or the clouds of the heavens? Has he not, indeed, been placed above the law, having eaten of the fruit of the tree of knowledge, and thus qualified himself for the exercise of perfect volition?

Postponing for a moment answers to these important questions, the person here interrogated might, and with some propriety, ask—if it could be deemed possible that Infinite Wisdom had found it needful, in regard to the few and insignificant atoms which temporarily enter into the human frame, to suspend the action of great laws then in full activity throughout this wonderful universe, with its millions of suns and their attendant planets? To the moment that such atoms had taken that direction their subjection had been complete. From the moment the body of which they are parts becomes resolved into dust, subjection becomes once again complete. Can it then be doubted that such subjection had existed in the period that had intervened? Is it not far more difficult to suppose it otherwise than it can by any possibility be to arrive at the belief in the unity and universality of divine laws?

The objection, nevertheless, is plausible, and needs to be considered, bearing, however, always in mind that the apparently true and the really false most generally walk hand in hand together throughout the world. So plausible, thus, seemed to be the assumption—then made with confidence as perfect as that now manifested by Mr. Mill and his disciples—that the sun revolved around the earth, that centuries have been required for effacing it from the mind of Europe alone; that the work even there is not yet one-half accomplished; and that of the earth's whole population four-fifths are yet believers in the Ptolemaic doctrine, proved to Jews and Christians as it has seemed to be by the words of Scripture itself. Equally plausible appears now the objection that thus is made, and yet, as it is proposed to show, it has certainly no foundation whatever on which to stand.

First, however, it is proper to remind the reader that the science to which his attention has here been called treats only of the *relations* between mind and matter, having to do with mind or morals themselves only in so far as is required for showing how they are liable to be affected, favorably or unfavorably, by societary action, and how the latter is, in turn, liable to be affected by them. Increase in the power of association, and in that of self-direction, tends towards mental and moral improvement; that improvement meantime tending toward more complete association, and further increase in the power for self-direction—mind, morals, tastes, feelings, and affections, however, being, as shown by the figure, subject to laws higher than those here discussed; laws that cannot be studied with advantage until the science of the relations between mind and matter shall first have been fully mastered. By their study it is that we are to be enabled to understand *the process* by means of which it had been provided that the higher human attributes should be stimulated into action, the real MAN, capable of commanding respect for his own rights, while fully respecting those of others, now presenting himself on the stage of life. That it has now, and for the first time, become possible advantageously to enter on this important study, is due to the fact that both physical and biological science have attained such full development. They it is that constitute the foundation on which societary science now must rest; this latter destined, in its turn, to furnish the foundation on which the apex of the edifice may at no distant period be at length constructed. For many centuries men have been laboring to that end, puzzling themselves and their hearers with metaphysical discussions whose latest result exhibits itself in the grave assertions that matter is itself only "a permanent possibility of sensation;" and that the laws of the relations between that "possibility" and the mind by which it is governed, have no foundation other than that of crude "assumptions" on which to rest.* Organology could no more have

* "Matter, then, may be defined a Permanent Possibility of Sensation." —*Mill's Examination of Hamilton*, p. 196.

"When I think of matter as a Potentiality of Sensation, I mean that I think of it as having the power to awake sensations in me. I do not think of it as having itself the capability of experiencing sensations. Mr. Mill is confounding the active agent with the passive subject. There is a well-known story of a country Scotchman, who, when he was asked by a dentist to open his mouth, replied with characteristic caution: 'Naa, maybe ye'll bite me.' This Scotchman, like Mr. Mill, was think-

been constructed in advance of physics than metaphysics can now be profitably studied in advance of sociology. These things premised, the questions above propounded may be now considered.

§ 4. In the whole range of physics there is no proposition whose truth more instantly commends itself to the common mind than does that one from which we learn that the strength and durability of any body of matter is in the direct ratio of the base to the elevation, a pyramid being of all the forms that one which gives most assurance of its power of resistance to the attraction of gravitation, to the force of the elements, and to the ravages of time. That it is the most natural of all the forms must have been clearly obvious to all who had ever seen a heap of rubbish, a load of coal or stone, discharged, and left to determine for itself the disposition of its several portions.

A bird's-eye glance at the earth brings before us thousands of pyramids great and small, those of the Eastern hemisphere finding their apex in the Himalaya, and those of the Western one in the Peaks of Chimborazo. Looking seaward, we see such pyramids in process of erection, "the pigmies of

ing of tooth as a Potentiality of Sensation, but he forgot also, like Mr. Mill, that the potentiality to cause that sensation lay in the man that had the mouth in a position to bite, and not in the man who had the finger in a position to be bitten. When will metaphysicians understand that a short phrase does not always mean a simple idea? When will they understand that they do not succeed in analyzing thought by simply ignoring some essential part of it?"—DUKE OF ARGYLL. "Hibernicisms in Philosophy," in *Contemporary Review*, January, 1872.

creation, the true world makers," being everywhere engaged in enlarging the foundation of great islands destined in time to be united into continents of which as yet, however, the navigator has little knowledge beyond that arising out of the presence of the dangerous coral reef. Returning to the land we find beavers providing for themselves conical habitations; the African termites, meanwhile, erecting great sugar loaves a dozen feet in height and strong enough to bear the weight of the heaviest cattle.

In all these cases the law above referred to is blindly obeyed, there existing on the part of all those animals no power for self-direction. Man, on the contrary, may, if he will, set it at defiance, giving to his edifice, financial or architectural, the form of an inverted pyramid, and doing this with full knowledge that he thus exposes himself to utter ruin. That very many do so is proved on every occasion of commercial crisis, great houses then toppling over and burying in their ruins not only their own honor but the fortunes and the hopes of all connected with them, thus furnishing proof that the minute atoms had carried up with them the great physical law by which they had before been governed, and that its operation in the societary world was as complete as it before had been in that of matter.

"Admitting all this," says the advocate of the "assumptions" doctrine, "are we at once to throw out of view the fact that, while some of the parties thus affected have been prompted to action by avarice others have been misled by ambition, and yet a third class, dazzled by the idea of advantage to result from great display and large expenditure on the part of wives and children? For this, as they continue, there is, and can be, no law whatsoever. How, then, is it possible that we should admit the presence of physical laws controlling the movements of societary life?" Would, however—it may in reply be asked—would such views be urged in reference to other laws to which, as we certainly know, man has been and is subjected? Let us inquire.

Of all the moral laws, there is no single one whose violation excites so general detestation as does that of parricide, or matricide. Whatever doubt may exist in regard to any other there is, and can be, none in reference to the one that is here presented. Nevertheless, the crime occurs, and at times under circumstances so atrocious as almost to warrant the summary application of Judge Lynch's law. Does that in any manner tend to prove the non-existence of the law? Is it needed that we inquire into the motives of the criminal before admitting existence of the decree by which such conduct had been made a crime? Scarcely so; yet would there appear to be quite as much reason for so doing as for pausing to study the motives which had led to the wrong construction of an edifice, preparatory to determination of the question as to whether there had existed any law in virtue of which greater security might be obtained by means of the adoption of another form.

Again, first among the hygienic laws is that by which it is provided that temperance, health, and duration of life tend strongly to march together. The horse and the ox yield obedience thereto; carefully avoiding, too, plants that would be hurtful. Man, on the contrary, indulges in excesses of every kind, at one time overfeeding himself and at another filling his stomach with poisons carefully prepared to suit his tastes, the general result being that of frequent disease and early death. Need we here inquire into the motives by which he is influenced to such excess, preparatory to recognition of the existence of the great law above referred to?

Further, governing the relations between man and his mother earth there is a law by which is provided that raw products of the soil are but lent, and *not given;* that when the farmer honestly pays the debt contracted, returning always the refuse of what had been supplied and thus establishing his credit at the great bank, his land shall become more productive from year to year. When, on the contrary, he declines to pay his debts, sending to a distance all the soil extracted from his land, the loans diminish from year to year and he himself is finally expelled. That such law exists is proved by the experience of all communities, past and present. That it is perpetually violated, and that punishment follows commission of the crime, are as fully proved. Do we, then, need to know the motives by which men are led to its commission, before acknowledging the existence of this great law determining the relations between land and man?

Yet further, the pyramidal form, as has been shown, is that of greatest strength and permanence, the law applying to each and every form of edifice, as well to the societary one whose figure is here presented, as to those of stone or brick. That a community may go steadily forward in the direction of thorough development of its people and of the land given for their use, the foundation must be broad and deep, a great domestic commerce being built upon a scientific agriculture. The deeper the foundation the higher may the edifice be carried, production and consumption growing steadily together and making demand for the productions of other climes while providing means by which their producers may be paid, the harmony of all permanent human interests being perfect. Looking, however, throughout the world, ancient and modern, we see that from the days of Tyre and Carthage communities have been everywhere doing precisely that against which Adam Smith so strongly cautioned his countrymen, to wit, struggling and fighting for transportation and a distant foreign trade the extent of which can never be otherwise than limited; and sacrificing at its shrine that domestic commerce whose every tendency is toward improving both mind and morals, and toward bringing into direct communication with each other all the positives and negatives of which a society is composed. Failure, as a consequence of constantly growing dependence on trade, has been the uniform result, Venice and Genoa, Portugal, and Holland* having followed in the wake of the great cities before referred to, and both France and England being now in train to furnish additional proof of the fact that no stability can result from the creation of an inverted pyramid. Must we then conclude that no physical law exists by compliance with which such failures might be averted?

Does not, on the contrary, every page of history furnish evidence that the more thorough the conformity of human action to those great laws by which are governed all the atoms which enter into the human frame, the greater is the force by which men are stimulated to act together; the greater their power to compel the natural forces to do their work; and the greater the tendency toward that development of the peculiar faculties of each societary atom to which alone we are to look for attainment of the power of self-direction; strict obedience on the one hand, keeping steady pace with growing power on the other?

§ 5. Governments institute laws, then providing

* The decline of Holland in naval power and importance has been remarkable and furnishes an interesting subject to the student. Within little more than two hundred years, she was the first naval power of Europe. Dutch ships sailed up the Thames and threatened to burn London, and Dutch admirals triumphed over the combined fleets of England and France. Since that time her decline has been slow but sure, until now the time seems not far distant when England will have deprived her of all her colonial possession and thus of all her naval importance.

houses of correction, hospitals, or prisons, for those who fail to yield obedience to them. In this they do but follow the example set by nature in providing punishment for those who fail to obey the laws which accompany matter in its passage from the lowest to the highest forms and structures. Go where man may—let him do what he may—those laws pass side by side with him, and with the community of which he forms a part, offering rewards for obedience, and threatening punishment in all cases of disobedience.* How is it, then, that these latter are so numerous, seeing as we do that punishment so constantly follows in their wake; that individuals, states, and nations so severely suffer when a contrary course of conduct would certainly have been attended with results so very different? Let us inquire.

That all these people, and all communities, exercise perfect freedom of will—mind thus controlling matter—is assumed by those who interest themselves in providing punishment, here or hereafter, for the

* "Side by side, but not *in* him; only in the atoms of his corporeal frame, which is not *himself*." Such having been the remark of an enlightened and friendly critic, and such being likely to be that of others, it is deemed proper here to say, that the physical laws above referred to no more enter *into* the composition of atoms than do human laws enter that of the physical frame. As the planetary bodies are controlled by laws in virtue of which their masses gravitate toward, and their atoms from, the great centre of our system, so does man travel side by side with laws in virtue of which he is attracted outward toward the society of which he is a part, and inward toward the family of which he is the head. The more complete the balance of these opposing forces the greater is the tendency toward production of the "himself" here referred to—the real MAN, master of nature and fully capable of self-direction.

crime that comes to be committed; yet where do we find individual men, or societies, exercising, with any approach whatsoever to completeness, that power of self-direction without which there can be no voluntary action whatsoever? Man, as we see him, is a product of the societary womb, and if the food assimilated throughout the period of gestation be not calculated for development of that power, it is little likely at any time thereafter to spring into existence. "Just as the twig is bent, the tree," as we are told, "will be inclined," and that such is the case throughout the societary world we have daily evidence.

Let the reader, for instance, take the child who early finds his place among the denizens of Glasgow wynds or East London parishes, tracing him thence, his wits becoming gradually sharpened to fit him for association with the Fagins and the Dodgers so well described by Dickens, and then determine if the poor animal has ever exercised, to even one-half the extent of that exercised by the prairie dog, the power of self-direction. Mere slave to circumstances over which he could exercise no control, and having mixed all his life with drunkards, he himself becomes contributor to that internal revenue which owes its existence to the dram shop, and upon whose growing extent the British finance minister is accustomed to congratulate himself as furnishing evidence of the increasing prosperity of the working classes of England. Let him now look to the millions of whole or half pauperized English people, remarking the treatment they receive at the hands of well fed and well paid officers, and then determine how much self-direction is exercised by them. Studying next the course of things in Lancashire throughout the last few years, finding hundreds of thousands of men, women, and children suffering, even when not perishing, for want of food and clothing; passing thence to the whole body of farm laborers, present representatives of the hundreds of thousands of small proprietors of the days of Adam Smith—having before them, as we are told by *Edinburgh Reviewers*, no future but the poor-house—let him determine as he goes to what extent they, or the tramps with whom the country so much abounds, exercise such power. Let him then look to the mass of traders, large or small, dependent wholly on the chances of peace or war, and liable to be swept from commercial existence on the occasion of financial crises such as have so steadily accompanied the growth of the mere trading movement, and see how slight is the self-directing power that can there be found. Slaves to circumstances over which they have no control whatsoever, these people are yet held responsible for crime, whether of omission or commission, precisely as if they had that free exercise of will assumed by metaphysicians to have come into existence with each and every case of assumption of the human form by material particles that had before been purely passive in the presence of great laws by which the universe is everywhere controlled.

So, too, is it with communities, and the farmers

of whom they are in part composed. In close proximity to the English people those of Ireland have never been permitted so to diversify employments as to cause Irish positives and negatives to come together in such order as was required for production of any societary force whatsoever. Directly the reverse of this, everything has been done, both without and within, to maintain disorder and to perpetuate the dominion of matter over mind; the result being seen in constantly-recurring famines, and in the expulsion of millions of men, women, and children who, had they been allowed the power of self-direction would before this time have constituted a nation of high intelligence, and great productive power. Have they at any time since the days of Henry II. been capable of any real exercise of will?

So, too, has it been with Portugal, Turkey, India, Mexico, and other States, all of which have been mere puppets in the hands of traders whose duty to their country and themselves required them, as they supposed, to prevent by all the means in their power the establishment of order among the many millions of human positives and negatives of which those communities are composed; thereby compelling them to violate that law by which it is established that the earth is a mere lender, and that those who constantly withdraw from her the materials of food, returning nothing back, shall in due season suffer for want of food.

With whom now rests the responsibility for the

maintenance of material power thus exhibited, and for the evils thus described? Is it with the poor boy, who has been sent from the societary womb educated to become a forger or a thief? Is it with the wretched pauper, who may all his life have striven, but in vain, to obtain an honorable living for wife and children? Is it with the poor Irishman, part of a community that at times "starves by millions," thus enabling a British statesman (Mr. Disraeli) to congratulate his fellow-citizens on the great famine "as having done more for the Irish people than a long succession of statesmen had been able to do?" Is it with the poor Turk, compelled as he is to stand idle while surrounded by all the material elements required for diffusing the highest prosperity among a population tenfold greater than that which now occupies the territories of the Turkish Empire? Is it with the poor Hindoo, compelled to send his cotton half round the world to be spun and woven, he himself meanwhile remaining unemployed? Is it with the poor Chinese, forced to become an opium-eating drunkard that he may be thus compelled to contribute toward the maintenance of British power in India? Is it with the poor white of our Southern States, who has been now so severely punished for allowing himself to be controlled and directed by those whose every effort had been given toward preventing that diversification of employment by means of which societary positives and negatives would long since have been brought in contact with each other, thus generating a social force which would peaceably have brought freedom to the negro, and prosperity to the white, whether laborer or planter? Is it not, on the contrary, with the great and powerful whose various modes of perpetuating and extending the dominion of matter over mind will be now described?

CHAPTER VII.

OF MATTER AND MIND.—(*Continued.*

IN a perfect power of self-direction, bringing with it absolute responsibility before both God and man, we find the highest of human attributes. That man may be enabled even to hope for its attainment it is needed that, as a consequence of that diversified demand for the various human faculties which results necessarily from diversification of employments, he be enabled freely to associate and combine with his fellow-men, whether for commanding recognition of his rights or for enabling him more fully and completely to perform his duties, these latter growing always in importance as the former become more perfectly assured. At each and every stage of progress the societary positives and negatives become more intimately connected; mind acquires new power over matter; mere brute force tends to yield place to law; the power and the habit of association become more and more confirmed; exchanges become more rapid;

values decline as utilities become developed; production increases as consumption follows more instantly on its path;* each societary atom more and more readily finds the place for which it had been fitted—that in which it can best promote its own true interests and those of the community of which it is a part; an enlightened feeling of self-respect gradually supersedes that blind selfishness which so generally characterizes ignorant and isolated men; morals, tastes, feelings, and affections become developed; and men become from day to day more and more enabled, with advantage to themselves and all around them, to claim the exercise of that perfect freedom of speech, thought, and action which so well befits the being that has acquired power to control and direct those wonderful natural forces by which we are everywhere surrounded.

Directly the reverse of this, the warrior, representing mere material force, seeks to prevent all voluntary exercise of the power of association; to prevent the growth of that feeling of security for person or for property in whose absence employments can never become diversified; to make of men mere machines, and thus prevent development of any feeling of individuality; to concentrate within himself all power for direction, thereby preventing growth of power for self-direction; and thus creating an inverted pyramid. As a consequence of this it is, that the great empires of the world from

* See *ante*, pp. 127–29.

the days of Semiramis to those of Charles V., exhibit so almost total an absence of cohesive force; that their existence has generally been so very brief; that but little more than a century since matter reigned so supreme over mind throughout the whole of continental Europe; and that so little else than ignorance, pauperism, and crime could be found among the various peoples; selfishness and weakness meanwhile exhibiting themselves as chief characteristics of those by whom tax-payers were being tortured for the purpose of maintaining their own subjection.*

Look now where we may among the communities of the past we see little else than collections of inverted pyramids tottering to their fall, the magnificence of the few having been in the direct ratio of

* The anarchy prevailing throughout Germany in the days of Charles V., and the consequent wretchedness of the people, pass almost beyond conception. A century later came the Thirty Years' War of which Wallenstein was the most conspicuous figure. Of this latter Baron Bunsen said, some thirty years since, that such had been the ruin of which it had been the cause that Germany had not even yet recovered from it.—Looking to France after more than half a century of wars abroad and *dragonnades* at home, we find, in 1739, one of the king's ministers thus describing the condition of the people: "At the moment when I write, in the month of February, in the midst of peace, with appearances promising a harvest, if not abundant at least passable, men die around us like flies, and are reduced by poverty to eat grass." He ascribes their condition to excessive taxation, declaring that the kingdom was treated like an enemy's country laid under military contribution. The Duke of Orleans, to bring the condition of his people to the knowledge of the sovereign, finally carried a loaf of *fern* bread to the meeting of the king's council, and at the opening of the session laid it before his Majesty, saying, "See, Sire, what your subjects live upon."

the poverty and wretchedness of those by whom they were surrounded; all this resulting necessarily from the fact, that blind and ignorant selfishness in the former had prevented them from seeing that the road toward wealth, strength, and power led in a direction tending toward giving mind control over matter, and not in that which tended to the maintenance, if not even increase, of the proportions of mere material force.

Coming down to recent times, we find the first Napoleon to have been engaged in creating, by means of mere brute force, an inverted pyramid of which at the date of his deposition the ruins alone remained. Looking now on France, the chief memorials extant of his reign are those which present themselves in a codification of the laws that has given to legal proceedings throughout the empire an uniformity that previously had not existed; in a highly developed industry; and in a sugar manufacture that has proved itself the most important of all the contributions of science toward the creation of a real agriculture.*

* The general result of the protective policy in regard to sugar may briefly thus be stated. Thirty years since the production was less than 30,000 tons. Before the late unhappy war it had reached 300,000, and although the consumption of foreign and domestic products had been doubled, there had arrived a necessity for finding exterior markets to which to send the surplus. Agriculture meanwhile had so much benefited that cattle in the sugar districts counted by thousands where before had been but hundreds. Seeking elsewhere evidence of the advantages to mankind at large that have resulted from this most beneficient measure of protection, we find in Germany mind triumphing over matter to such extent that the sugar product has already reached

Simple and quiet as have been all these latter operations, they have furnished great and permanent results; and for the reason that their tendency has been that of removing obstacles which before had stood in the way of association; of promoting development of the various individualities of the French people; of bringing into orderly arrangement the societary positives and negatives; and of giving to all the members of the societary body a power for self-direction that previously had had no existence whatsoever; or, to sum up all in a single brief expression, of giving to mind that power over matter which France had before so greatly needed.

Looking to the younger Napoleon we find him to have been steadily engaged in destroying the power of home association by means of constantly increasing demand for men to be employed in maintaining wars abroad; by stimulating his people to huge investments in a distant canal, in foreign railroads, and in loans to Mexico and other States; the canals of France herself remaining in a condition disgraceful to both the people and the State; her farmers and manufacturers to a great extent deprived of the advantages that would have resulted

250,000 tons, having nearly doubled in the last decade; that its contributions for the support of Government have reached $10,000,000; and that the consumption per head is now twice what it was thirty years since. Throughout much of Europe similar results have been obtained, making it now quite safe to say that the grandest and most enduring monument to the Napoleonic memory—that by which a century hence he will best be known—is that of which he laid the corner-stone when ordaining the naturalization of the sugar culture.

from rapid railroad intercourse;* her population becoming almost stationary; her agriculture suffering for want of hands to do the work; her people remaining ignorant to a supreme degree, millions on millions being meanwhile spent on places of amusement;† and the whole system exhibiting in its highest perfection the idea denounced by Mirabeau when cautioning his countrymen against centraliza-

* Belgium and France together constitute the great highway of the world; yet has the latter, with its 38,000,000 of people, fewer miles of railroad than are possessed by the three States of New York, New Jersey, and Pennsylvania, with less than a fourth of the population.

† "Who does not know the immense sacrifices that Germany has made for the advancement and diffusion of knowledge; spending, for instance, twenty thousand pounds sterling at Bonn in a chemical laboratory, forty thousand at Heidelberg in a physical laboratory? Little Wurtemberg devoted more money to superior instruction than big France. A thing unheard of, France made the very fees of the university students a source of revenue. She gave, without counting it, more than a couple of millions of pounds sterling (between fifty and sixty million francs) for the new Opera, and she refused forty thousand pounds for school buildings. Last year on the deck of the steamer which was conveying us to the inauguration of the Suez Canal, M. Duruy, the one man of merit who ever served under the imperial government, told me the tale of his griefs in the ministry of public instruction. He wanted to introduce compulsory education; the Emperor supported him; he had all the other ministers against him. He had organized fifteen thousand night schools for adults; it was with difficulty that he succeeded in carrying off forty thousand pounds against the fatuous resistance of the Council of State. There was the whole system of public instruction to reorganize, and he could get nothing. They preferred to employ the gold of the country in maintaining the ladies of the ballet, in building barracks and palaces, in gilding monuments, the dome of the Invalides, the roof of the Sainte Chapelle. It was in vain that men like Jules Simon, Pelletan, Duruy, Jules Favre, cried out year after year, 'There must be millions for education, or France is lost.' The Government was deaf. It denied nothing to pleasure, to luxury, to ostentation. It denied everything to education."—M. de Laveleye in the *Fortnightly Review*, Dec. 1870.

tion, and telling them that "when the head grows too large the body becomes apoplectic and wastes away," losing power to perform its necessary work. Of all this the result is seen in the fact that the legacy bequeathed by the second empire to its posterity consists in an almost ruined State; in a population that in point of numbers has almost ceased to grow; in a magnificent capital abounding in unoccupied houses; and in a taxation so severe as to make it doubtful if the country that had been thus misgoverned and demoralized can ever resume the position it so long had occupied among the powers of the world. The price at which all this ruin has been accomplished is found in the fact that the national debt has grown in less than twenty years from $1,200,000,000 to $5,500,000,000; this, too, notwithstanding a great increase in the amount of public contributions.*

That the policy of the merchant princes of the earth has in like manner been exhaustive has been already shown.†

Dealing, as they did, in slaves and other merchandise they discouraged combination among their subjects, and, as a necessary consequence, left behind them little beyond the ruins by means of which we

* Five years since, the author, in a "Review of the Decade" then published, showed that the Napoleonic policy was exhaustive in its character, and that without a radical change France would soon cease to be counted among the great powers of the earth. The result thus predicted has since come dangerously near to being realized.

† See pages 167–8 *ante*.

are now enabled to see that they had once existed. That "curses, like young chickens, always come home to roost," is a Hindoo proverb, evidence of whose truth is found in the history of all communities whose rulers have looked to the establishment of permanent power by means of measures tending towards giving to matter increased control over mind —to capital increased control over labor.

§ 3. To another mode of warfare the reader's attention will be now invited, to wit: that modern one by means of which like results have been sought to be obtained by means of laws prohibiting that combination among societary positives and negatives by aid of which alone mental force could be developed; thereby *compelling* the employment of ships, wagons, and other machines in carrying rude products of the earth to distant countries, to be there so changed in form as to be fitted for consumption and thence returned to the place of production, reduced by this circuitous operation to a fifth, if to even more than a tenth, of the quantity that had been first supplied.

How destructive must be the effects of such a "warfare" will at once be obvious to all who reflect that it is by means of combination such as is here prohibited, and by that alone, that labor can be economized; that the infinitely various human faculties can be developed; that power to control the great natural forces can be obtained; or, that man can attain that power of self-direction which manifests itself in freedom of thought, speech, or action.

To England is due the honor of having first invented a course of action so obviously tending to retain man in the condition of slave to nature, and the weaker portion of mankind in that of slaves to their fellow-men. First commenced in Ireland, and there continued under various forms—with the exception only of the period of Irish legislative independence from 1782 to 1800—to the present time, its effects exhibit themselves in a subjection of mind to matter without parallel in any country claiming to be civilized; men, women, and children perishing at times by millions; and poverty, wretchedness, and slavery far worse than that of the well-fed American negro, having been the normal condition of the Irish people.

Transplanted to distant countries, this colonial system proved so oppressive in what are now the States of the American Union, as to compel that resistance whose final result was seen in the establishment of independence at the close of a seven years' war in 1783.*

* See note to page 27, *ante*. How destructive was the system thus established is shown by the fact that while thus debarred from all power to diversify their employments the taxes for the profit of middlemen of all descriptions, and for the public uses, were so severe that Virginia planters hesitated to send their crops to England, fearing that they might thereby be really brought in debt to their distant agents. So was it, and so did it continue, in the sugar producing colonies to the date of emancipation; the effect exhibiting itself in a destruction of life wholly without precedent, except in the case of actual war. Of almost 2,000,000 of slaves that had been imported, nearly two-thirds had dis-

Theoretically, this system has been since abandoned; how, practically, it is now enforced is shown in a Report to Parliament made some dozen years since, an extract from which is here submitted, as follows:—

"The laboring classes generally in the manufacturing districts of the kingdom, and especially in the iron and coal districts, are very little aware of the extent to which they are often indebted for their being employed at all to the immense losses which their employers voluntarily incur in bad times, in order to destroy foreign competition, and to gain and keep possession of foreign markets. Authentic instances are well known of employers having in such times carried on their works at a loss amounting in the aggregate to £300,000 or £400,000 in the course of three or four years. If the efforts of those who encourage the combinations to restrict the amount of labor and to produce strikes were to be successful for any length of time, the great accumulations of capital could no longer be made which enable a few of the most wealthy capitalists to overwhelm all foreign competition in times of great depression, and thus to clear the way for the whole trade to step in when prices revive, and to carry a great business *before foreign capital can again accumulate* to such an extent as to be able to establish a competition in prices with any chance of success. *The large capitals of this country are the great instruments of warfare against the competing capitals of foreign countries*, and are *the most essential instruments now remaining by which our manufacturing supremacy can be maintained;* the other elements—cheap labor, abundance of raw materials, means of communication, and skilled labor—being rapidly in process of being equalized."

---

appeared, leaving behind no children to furnish proof that they ever had existed. Contrary to the Darwinian theory, the "fittest" had rebelled, and had perished in the fastnesses to which they had retired, leaving those least fitted for the strife for life to carry on the work of procreation.

What now is the object of the "warfare" here so accurately described? Does it look to development throughout the world of man's peculiar faculties? Does it look to that economy of human force which results from combination?* Does it look to promotion of that habit of association so essential to development of the various individualities of the thousand millions of the world's people? Does it look to enabling those toiling millions to obtain that control over the great natural forces in whose default they can never hope to arrive at that power for self-direction which manifests itself in perfect freedom of thought, word, and action? Does it look to bringing about that orderly arrangement of societary positives and negatives so necessary to the

* Of all commodities or things the only one that disappears on the instant of its production is labor power, or human force, mental or material. If not instantly utilized it passes away, lost forever. The more prompt the utilization the greater of course is the economy of force, the larger is production, and the greater the laborer's share of the increased product. See *ante*, pp. 66, 127. How diversification of employments tends to bring about such result is shown below in a passage from a recent article on "wages" by a member of the Ricardian school who certainly has not fully appreciated the fact, that what is here described as so beneficially occurring in an English county is precisely that which England herself is seeking elsewhere *to prevent*, and which other nations are seeking by means of protection against her system to obtain for themselves, to wit: that rapidity of circulation in whose absence there can be neither economy of labor power, nor growth of societary force.

"The manufacturing industry of the county offers a ready explanation of these greater facilities [for raising food], since it enables the farmer to obtain better instruments at the same, or a lower, price, to obtain more easily a supply of manure, and by scattering towns more thickly through the country places brings the markets within easier reach." —Shadwell in *Westminster Review*, Jan. 1872, article *Theory of Wages*.

development of force? Does it look to giving to the minds of those millions increased control over matter, thereby placing those who are physically weak more and more on a level with those who are physically strong? Does it look to the creation of local centres whose attractive powers shall tend to counterbalance the attraction of the great central sun of the trading system? Does it look to relieving the world's people from that most oppressive of all their burdens, the tax of transportation? Does it look to enabling them not only to maintain but to further develop the powers of their land? *Does it not*, on the contrary, look to prevention of association; to preventing positives and negatives from taking their places by each other's side; to preventing development of individuality; to preventing anywhere the growth of power for self-direction, whether in individuals or in the communities of which they are parts; to increasing the burthen of transportation, and thus more and more subjecting mind to matter; to maintaining, even when not increasing, the barbarism that now exists?

For answer to this question let the reader look to India, Portugal, Turkey, Mexico, Jamaica; to Ireland with its continually recurring famines; to China devastated as it has been by rebellions that have had their origin in opium wars; to the world at large, studying there the question as to whether there now exists a single community that by reason of its poverty, ignorance, or weakness has continued subject to the tyranny of this monstrous system, and that yet has made any essential advance in the direction of giving to mind that increased control over matter in which consists a real civilization.*

§ 4. Appreciating fully the destructive character of the policy above described, Prussia commenced as early as 1819 an organized resistance thereto, seeking to promote association within her own borders and with her immediate neighbors, while preventing interference from abroad on the part of those whose potent instrument of warfare is above described. For many years progress was very slow, her every effort having been met with resistance on the part of Hanover, then German representative of the foreign *trading influence.* Step by step, however, she grew in attractive force, that of the foreigner meantime declining, until at length and at the close of sixteen years of effort, nearly the whole German nation became united for maintenance of the resistance that had been so well com-

* The people of Australia having found that under the system of *laissez faire* the country was rapidly becoming "a huge sheep-walk;" that "their farmers could no longer struggle in the face of discouragement and disaster;" that "their youth were growing up in a state of semi-barbarism, without education, without employment, and without hope for the future;" that "their manufactories were falling into decay, their capital was idle, and the whole body in the saddest state;" have now adopted measures for bringing together the societary positives and negatives—producers and consumers; a course of action in which they naturally find themselves opposed by all those who heretofore have profited by means of buying wool cheap and selling dear the cloth the shepherds needed. Canada tends now in the same direction, the necessity therefor becoming from day to day more clearly obvious as emigration to the protected country south of the lakes tends more and more to arrest the growth of population.

menced. From and after that date progress became more rapid from year to year, mind daily obtaining increased power over matter, and to such extent that more than a dozen years since the present author was led to express the opinion that Germany, whose "national sin for the last two centuries," according to Chevalier Bunsen, "had been poverty, the condition of all classes with few exceptions;" Germany which but thirty years before had been held to be so greatly overpopulated as to warrant suggestion of a resort to infibulation as the only remedy:* then already stood "first in Europe in point of intellectual development," and was "advancing in the physical and moral condition of her people with a rapidity exceeding that of any other portion of the Eastern hemisphere."†

Since then, an empire has been created embracing a population little short of 40,000,000, among whom education is universal; with an admirable and rapidly-growing system of internal railroad communications; with a commerce as perfectly organized as any in the world, and growing from day to day with extraordinary rapidity; with a market on the land for nearly all its products, and, as a necessary consequence, with an agricultural popu-

* Weinhold. *Von der Uebervolkerung in Mittel Europa.* Halle, 1829. —He proposed that *infibulation* should be established by law, and accomplished by means of soldering up all males at their 14th year, and so retaining them until they could prove that they had the means required for supporting a family.

† Principles of Social Science. Chap. xxiv. § 11.

lation that grows daily in both intelligence and power; with a public treasury so well provided that not only have the expenditures of recent wars been readily provided for, but that large additions have been made to the provision for public education; and with private treasuries so well supplied as to enable her people not only to build their own furnaces and factories and construct their own roads, but also to furnish hundreds of millions to the improvident people of America, to be by them applied to the making of roads in a country the abundance of whose natural resources should long since have placed it in the position of money lender, rather than that now occupied of general money borrower.

How rapid has been, and now is, progress in those mechanic arts in whose absence there can be no economy of labor, no increase in the power of self-direction, will be seen on an examination of the following facts in regard to iron, that one commodity in whose greater or less consumption we find the most conclusive evidence of advancing or declining civilization. In 1850, the product of steel was valued at $350,000. Since then, having meantime endowed the world with the great gift of the Bessemer process, it has grown to $17,000,000. In 1850, the total product of pig and wrought iron was but $15,000,000; whereas, in 1869, it was considerably in excess of $100,000,000, the growth becoming more rapid from year to year.

From year to year the tendency to combination, as exhibited in the creation or enlargement of industrial, co-operative, and educational associations, becomes more and more fully developed; and it is as a necessary consequence of this that the whole community has in the recent war manifested a power so terrific. From year to year mind obtains increased power over matter; the land becomes more and more divided;* and the people more and more obtain that power for self-direction which follows always in the wake of increase of power to control and direct the great forces of nature to man's service.†

* "In Prussia, by the law of 1850, the smallest occupier of peasant's land acquires the proprietorship at twenty years' purchase, the amount being paid to the landlord, not in money, but in rent debentures issued by the authority of the State, and bearing four per cent. interest; and gradually redeemable by means of the one per cent. difference, which at compound interest extinguishes the principal in a little over forty-one years. The Prussian peasant has, however, two other options: he may pay less by one-tenth to the State bank than the rent he formerly paid to his landlord, in which case the purchase debentures take fifty-six years to redeem; or he may, if he can raise the cash, compel his landlord to accept eighteen years' purchase-money to the annual rent. By this means nearly 100,000 peasant proprietors have been created in Prussia. Rent debentures to the extent of many millions have been issued to the landowners, and in less than eighteen years more than one-eighth of the debentures issued have been entirely redeemed and extinguished."

† The extraordinary growth of the associative force, its influence in developing the various individualities, and its tendency toward development of power for self-direction, are all well exhibited in the following paragraph, giving particulars of the practical operations of the largest co-operative German bank, in Silesia. "It is a loan bank, the loans being advanced to the members on easy terms of payment, secured by mortgages which it but rarely forecloses, encouraging members by aid and counsel when they are in difficulties. It deals with laboring people; fines and forfeitures are not imposed for delinquencies. A weaver, for instance, having learned his trade, pays his initiation fee, subscribes for shares in the bank to the amount of the loan he expects to need,

Out of the shattered fragments which half a century since were marked on the map as Germany, there has now been created the most powerful empire of the Eastern world; one in which the power for self-direction, whether on the part of the people or their government, is a constantly increasing force; and one that promises to do more for the final emancipation of mind from the control of matter than any the world until now has seen.

To what, however, has this all been due? To the quiet and simple operation of the protective features of the system of the Zoll-Verein, long regarded by

and in the course of a month or two the bank enables him to purchase directly the yarn that he proposes to weave, the loom that he will weave it upon, perhaps the house which will contain the loom and in which he and his family will reside. A dozen weavers clubbing together, similarly helped, may start a cloth factory. In general the bank endeavors to enable its members to be the merchants and managers of their own labor. Co-operative stores for provisions receive its assistance, in all cases dispensing with intermediate dealers. The aid that it supplies to farmers and to students in difficulties, is comparable only in its beneficence to the highest form of benevolence, since it sustains the recipient without degrading him. It has no dealings with the wealthy. Not only in Breslau itself, but also in the towns around it, co-operative stores and small factories spring up; some of them have already paid back their loans and are returning dividends to their stockholders. The bank has 3500 members who clear 9½ per cent. on their money, besides a percentage of benefit funds. Its cash capital, made up of small initiation fees and instalments on shares, is upward of $1,000,000, and its profits last year exceeded $100,000. This bank is one of a confederacy of 1500 banks, having 300,000 members, 100,000,000 money on hand, making loans last year of not less than 139,000,000 thalers, and a common centre in the Genossenschafts Bank in Berlin, which itself assists in turn these banks, and aids in preserving the financial equilibrium of this vast system from its own resources, which include 16,000,000 thalers circulating, and nearly 40,000,000 permanent capital."

the author as the most important measure of the century, and among the most important ever adopted in Europe. Under it, as in France under the system of Colbert, internal commerce was free, the laborer meanwhile being protected against the destructive system of warfare invented by England, and above described. Under it labor was everywhere economized. Under it, the positives and negatives of a whole nation were brought into communication with each other, and thus has been created a great battery of 40,000,000 pairs of plates throughout which there is a rapidity of circulation scarcely elsewhere on so large a scale exceeded; and destined ultimately, in all probability, to produce effects throughout the Eastern continent fully equal to any that may, by even the most sanguine, be hoped for in this Western one.

The lion and the tiger—the Cæsar and Napoleon of the animal world—leave behind no evidences of their ever having existed. The little coral insect creates islands that endure forever. So is it like to be with that great monument just now erected to the memory of Frederic List and his associates, the humble laborers to whom the world at large stands indebted for the formation of the Zoll-Verein.

§ 5. The "Continental System" of the first Napoleon gave to Russian manufactures a temporary impulse, but at the close of the great war, in 1815, resistance to the system of trading "warfare" above described was altogether abandoned; the results speedily exhibiting themselves in the closing of manufacturing establishments; in paralysis of the domestic commerce; in bankruptcy of the public treasury; and in the daily increasing poverty and wretchedness of all who needed to sell their services. Foreign bankers, manufacturers, and traders, meanwhile grew rich as matter thus increased in its power over mind, and as the power of association and combination among the Russian people more and more tended to disappear.

There, however, as everywhere has been the case, but few years of such sad experience were required for teaching the Emperor Alexander, theoretical free-trader as he was, that further abstinence from an intelligent exercise of the co-ordinative power could end in nothing short of absolute and entire ruin to both his people and himself. Therefore was it, that almost simultaneously with the Prussian movement above described, and the American one to be hereafter noticed, a policy of resistance to trading "warfare" was entered on, the results whereof are exhibited in a work by an English gentleman whose position as head of one of the most extensive industrial enterprises of the empire, and whose extensive travels, have enabled him to bring before the world a large collection of highly interesting facts, to some few of which we here give place, as follows:—

"The manufacturing industry of Russia increases rapidly, whilst it is curious to observe that, although a Russian workman is capable of imitating everything that is shown to him, his power of initiation is generally *nil*. Still there are manufactures in which Russians excel. The printed cloths, for instance, are unique, well-made, and of good designs: well known in the Eastern markets, throughout Central Asia and China.

"In the manufacture of woollen goods they also have made some progress, and a very respectable kind of cloth is now produced in Russia, which has superseded the manufacture of our own country in many Oriental markets. China, Afghanistan, Persia, and the northwest borders of India are now supplied with the produce of Russian looms, which, if not so good in quality, is as well liked by the Eastern people as English cloth, and is considerably cheaper.

"Her manufactures in the precious metals are celebrated throughout the world for elegance and beauty. Her productions in leather are unrivalled, and the versatility of her manufacturing genius is so unbounded that it would be difficult to name an article of modern invention that is not made somewhere in her empire.

"And with all this it must be remembered that the manufacturing industry of Russia is not yet fifty years old. It required nursing under a system of protection, but is now so far developed as to admit a great deal of competition, and the gradual introduction of a liberal policy.

"The great annual fairs, Nijny-Novgorod and Isbit, are now crowded with Russian manufactures. In the former alone the turnover exceeds 17,000,000 pounds.

"Everything now is done to stimulate trade. Every inducement held out to encourage manufacture. * * * Fabrics are now springing up fitted with native-made machinery. Branches of industry are started which before were thought to be impossible for Russian ingenuity to master, and trade flourishes as it never flourished before. Ever since the Crimean war the amount of interchange of commodities has been increasing; this in the face of a tariff that was the worst in Europe* must show what a power this empire has in herself.

"For one article of manufacture, that of sugar from beet-root, Russia possesses more establishments than any other country in the world.

* That is, the most protective.

"See what they have done in cotton spinning. There are now upwards of three hundred establishments in which this staple is prepared, and where something like 400,000 bales are worked up annually. The import of raw cotton last year was one-quarter more than in 1868. * * * The prints are capital in quality and beautiful in design. I think, take the same quality, the designs are far prettier and neater than our own; and from experience the Russian prints wear as well as ours.

"The manufacture of silk has attained considerable proportions, and in Moscow and the neighborhood are some two hundred establishments where this industry is developing itself."*

As a necessary consequence of the great movement thus described, there has been an increase of the domestic commerce without a parallel in the Eastern hemisphere to have been so speedily brought about. Steam vessels now abound, all built at home; from year to year new river routes are opened; locomotives are now of domestic manufacture; railroads have already so far grown that their extent now equals that of France; local centres increase in number and importance as consumers and producers are more nearly brought together; land increases rapidly in its money value as cultivation is extended and improved; the demand for labor so much increases that the day is held to be not far distant when Russia will make demands on central Europe for its surplus population; the government meanwhile "straining every nerve in the effort to become independent;" that is to say, to secure for itself that power for self-direction whose growth in all countries has been, and must ever be, in the

* Barry, *Russia in* 1870. London 1871.

ratio of the orderly arrangement of the human positives and negatives submitted to its direction.

Throughout the long period of forty years the efforts of the first Alexander, of his brother Nicholas, and of his nephew the present Emperor, were directed toward the substitution of a true pyramid for that inverted one which previously had existed —the results having recently exhibited themselves in a measure of emancipation the most remarkable of all that the world yet has seen; one whose success is here described as having been in all respects most complete; one that has given to the societary structure a broad base of admirably disposed, though as yet but very ignorant, body of workingmen free to sell their labors in the dearest market; and one that has proved but the precursor of other and most "important reforms," tending to enable the Empire "to move forward with a steady progress that promises in this generation to make up for much wasted time in the past."

"In no country of Europe," says Mr. Barry, "has the march of civilization and progress in modern times been more rapid, decided, and systematic than in Russia;" all this, as he continues, "having been effected by the energy and wisdom of a few master minds; and to become a matter of astonishment to future generations; proving, when fully revealed, one of the most instructive chapters of history;" proving further, as it does, the utter worthlessness of that trading policy of *laissez faire* by means of which the societary body is proposed to be denied all power of intervention for promoting association among the individuals of which it is composed.*

That the broader the base the higher may the building be carried is a truth as certain in social as it is in architectural science. Having, as above described, laid the foundation in a great and rapidly increasing domestic commerce, Russia carries steadily up the apex of her edifice; her foreign commerce having grown with the growth of power amongst her people to pay for the products of other climes, and the day being now held to be fast approaching when Moscow will be the grand centre of commerce between the various peoples of Asia and those of Europe. That such *will* be the case is highly probable, transportation throughout the empire being even now effected at a cost that is wonderfully small, and Russian transportation ranking among the best the world can furnish.

For nearly half a century Germany and Russia have been engaged in the effort at bringing into orderly arrangement their hundred millions of human positives and negatives; that effort having been maintained in absolute defiance of gentlemen who have sought to enlighten the world by means of "a science based upon assumptions;" a science by whose

* In one of his pamphlets Mr. Cobden told his countrymen that in the free trade period, 1815–24, Russia had been so entirely dependent upon foreigners that stoppage of intercourse with them would have been "to doom a portion of her people to absolute nakedness." By promoting interdependence at home the government has secured for itself independence abroad, the two marching every where together throughout the world.

present teachers they are daily taught that national prosperity and happiness must inevitably result from submission to a system of "warfare" having for its object that of enabling a few of the "most wealthy English capitalists" to annihilate foreign competition, and thus prevent every where outside of Britain the growth of that habit and those powers of association to which alone can we look for such development of human force as is required for enabling man to become controller and director of the great natural forces, and to obtain for himself full exercise of that greatest of human faculties, the power for self-direction.

The Russian statesman looks to giving mind a mastery over matter, the result exhibiting itself in the fact, as stated by our author, that "starve the peasants don't, and beg they don't." The English policy, now so generally taught, looks on the contrary to maintaining and increasing the power of matter over mind, its results exhibiting themselves, as has been already shown, in a rapidly rising tide of pauperism, and in an agricultural population having before it no future but the poor-house.

The tendencies throughout the two great empires of the eastern continent having thus been shown to be in the former direction, we may now with advantage study the course of events in these United States, constituting as they do the great empire of the West.

CHAPTER VIII.

MATTER AND MIND.—(*Continued.*)

§ 1. When Lord Chatham asserted his determination that Englishmen who had gone to countries beyond the Atlantic should not be allowed to make for themselves even so much as a "hob-nail," he merely gave to the bankers, brokers, trading and manufacturing capitalists of England assurance that they should continue to be protected in their already existing *right* to demand and receive three-fourths of the produce of American labor?* The colonists might, if they would, exhaust their soils and thus ruin themselves in the effort at furnishing the world's supply of tobacco, provided only, that their products passed outward by aid of the ships, sailors, traders, and brokers of England. They might, if they would, raise sheep, but to enable them to convert their wool into hats or coats they must ask the aid of British ships and mills, paying to their owners the accustomed tribute. They might

* "If we examine into the circumstances of the inhabitants of our plantations, and our own, it will appear that *not one-fourth of their product redounds to their own profit, for, out of all that comes here, they only carry back clothing and other accommodations for their families*, all of which is of the merchandise and manufacture of this kingdom. . . . . All these advantages we receive by the plantations, *besides the mortgages on the planters' estates and the high interest they pay us, which is very considerable.*"—*Gee on Trade*, London, 1750.

convert timber and ore into crude iron, but before they could be allowed to use it for construction of a plough, a wheel, or a house, it must twice cross the ocean. Diversity of employments was thus by law prohibited, and thus were the unfortunate colonists deprived of all exercise of that power of association to which alone could they look for such development of their various faculties as was required for enabling them to become masters and directors of the great natural forces, thereby acquiring for themselves power for self-direction.* Capital, as its owners were assured, was to remain master over labor, and matter was to be maintained in its mastery over mind, precisely as was then the case throughout the British West India Islands, and as it since has been in both India and Australia. Then, as now, the positives and negatives of society were to be everywhere prevented from so taking their places side by side together as would give occasion to any development whatsoever of mental force.

The grievous subjugation of labor to capital thus established compelled a resistance that was followed by revolution so complete that the right to independent legislation became at length secured. That it should be profitably exercised it was, however, needed that all the late provinces should be brought to act together, thereby forming "a more perfect union" than that by which their people had been carried through the troubles of the past. For ob-

* See note to p. 27, *ante*.

taining this much time was yet required, and it proved a period of the severest trial, the domestic markets having been so flooded with the produce of foreign workshops that poverty and wretchedness every where prevailed; the farmer finding no market for his products, and the workman no demand for the services he desired to render. From day to day the suffering became more intense, until at length they found themselves compelled to adoption of a Constitution, by means of which they were to be enabled to present a united front in resistance to the trading monopolists by whom they had been so long oppressed, and were then being ruined.

With the year 1789 came the so-much-desired Union, and among the earliest of the phenomena attendant on its arrival was the appearance of Washington in the halls of Congress arrayed in clothing all of which had been the produce of American fields and workshops. Following in the same direction we find Franklin exhibiting to the people the advantages to result from diversified employments; Hamilton, the Statesman of the age, whether at home or abroad, meantime urging the adoption of measures tending to the establishment of that domestic interdependence in whose absence there could be neither political nor industrial independence. Among the earliest proceedings of Congress, therefore, we find the adoption of a resolution calling on this last, then Secretary of the Treasury, for "a plan or plans," of measures looking to the "encouragement and protection of such manufactures as will tend to render the United States independent of other nations for essential, and particularly for military supplies." In the following year such measures were adopted, the axe having thus been laid at the root of that colonial dependence by means of which association had been prevented, and with it that diversification in the demands for labor, mental or physical, so essential to the development of freedom, whether of thought, speech, or action. Mind, henceforth, was to be allowed to exercise that dominion over matter which in the past had been by law prohibited.

Thenceforward, however, for nearly a quarter of a century, mere brute force was more widely triumphant than at any previous period of the world since the fall of the Roman Empire. French armies time and again ravaged and plundered the various countries of Europe; English fleets in turn ravaging and plundering on the ocean, and gradually driving therefrom every flag but that of Britain.* Of all the triumphs then secured of capital over labor, matter over mind, there was, however, none so enduring in effect as that accomplished by means of

* As the result of a single decree of Sir William Scott, then Admiralty Judge, a thousand American ships and cargoes were confiscated, to the ruin of thousands, if not even tens of thousands, of American citizens, their wives and families. Since then Lord Chancellor Campbell has told his countrymen that not only had the Orders in Council been "grievously unjust to neutrals," but also that it had come to be "generally allowed that they were contrary to the law of nations and to our own municipal law."

measures whose effects soon after exhibited themselves in the utter ruin of that wonderful cotton manufacture which had made demand for labor and skill in almost every household of Hindostan; a change attended with ruin and distress to which, as official documents testify, "no parallel can be found in the annals of commerce."* The interdependence that previously had existed was thus annihilated, an absolute dependence far worse than that of the American negro slave being established in its place.

Driven from the ocean by means of measures so discreditable that none could now be found so hardy as to utter a word in their defence, the American people resorted first to measures of protection in the form of non-intercourse laws; but at length to a war that for nearly three years closed their ports against all British products. The effect of this policy of resistance was that of so stimulating the domestic commerce that at the close of the war, in 1815, they had better reason than had ever before existed for

* The process by means of which this revolution was accomplished was a very simple one, consisting, as it did, in prohibiting the export to India of either machinery or of artisans by which it might be made; in prohibition of duties on British cottons imported into India; in the imposition of heavy duties on India cottons imported into England; and in the imposition of heavy taxes on all the poor machinery then used in India. Of all the tyrannies recorded in the historic page there is none that has proved so searching and so destructive—none that has so greatly tended to maintenance and extension of the already existing control of matter over mind—as that exhibited in British India. On this continent, and in all other of the British possessions, the end in view has been only that of *preventing* all combination of effort and therewith all growth of civilization; but in India it has been that of *annihilating* an already existing civilization.

looking to the future as promising complete emancipation of labor from the tyranny of distant capitalists, and the establishment of an interdependence at home by means of which they would be enabled to make of their political independence a reality never to be obtained pending the existence of industrial dependence. Unfortunately, however, as shortly previous had been done by both Germany and Russia, they wholly forgot the lessons of the past; levelling the barriers by which their great industries had been defended and placing themselves wholly in the power of the very men who, throughout so many years, had heaped upon them injuries that had compelled resort to war; doing this, too, in face of the fact that Mr. Brougham had from his place in Parliament just then told his countrymen that "it was well worth while to incur a loss upon the first exportation, in order by the glut to stifle in the cradle those rising manufactures in the United States which the war had forced into existence, contrary to the natural order of things."* The policy of resistance having been thus abandoned, furnaces and factories were everywhere closed; producers and consumers, societary positives and nega-

* Almost simultaneously with the delivery of this speech, Mr. Jefferson was writing to one of his friends as follows: "You tell me I am quoted by those who wish to continue our dependence on England for manufactures. There was a time when I might have been so quoted with more candor. . . . . We have since experienced what we did not then believe, that there exists both profligacy and power enough to exclude us from the field of interchange with other nations—that to be independent for the comforts of life, we must fabricate them ourselves. *We must now place the manufacturer by the side of the agriculturist.*"

tives, were separated; and the nation was thus remanded to the position of submissive dependence on the will of those same foreign bankers and traders in whose favor the "Great Commoner" had, less than half a century before, announced his determination not to permit that diversification of pursuits to which alone could it look for obtaining power for self-direction in either the people or the State. Matter was now to be reinstated in its control over mind, capital in its control over labor.

What were the results of the policy of non-resistance, now so unhappily re-inaugurated, is shown in a passage here below given from the works of an eminent statesman of that day, Senator Benton, whose persistent opposition to measures of resistance forbids the idea of exaggeration:—

"The years of 1819 and 1820 were a period of gloom and agony. No money, either gold or silver; no paper convertible into specie, no measure of, or standard of, value left remaining. The local banks (all but those of New England), after a brief resumption of specie payments, again sank into a state of suspension. The Bank of the United States, created as a remedy for all those evils, now at the head of the evil, prostrate and helpless, with no power left but that of suing its debtors and selling their property, and purchasing for itself at its own nominal price. No price for property or produce; no sales but those of the sheriff and the marshal; no purchaser at the execution sales but the creditor or some hoarder of money; no employment for industry; no demand for labor; no sale for the products of the farm; no sound of the hammer but that of the auctioneer knocking down property. Stop laws, property laws, replevin laws, stay laws, loan-office laws, the intervention of the legislature between the creditor and the debtor, this was the business of legislation in three-fourths of the States of the Union—of all south and west of New England. No medium of exchange but depreciated paper; no change even but little bits of foul paper marked so many cents, and signed by some tradesman, barber, or innkeeper; exchanges deranged to the extent of fifty or one hundred per cent. Distress, the universal cry of the people; relief, the universal demand, thundered at the door of all legislatures, States and Federal."

That the state of affairs here described was to a great extent an enduring one, and that its cause was to be found in the waste of labor, and of its rude products, that follows necessarily in the wake of measures tending towards production of an exclusive agriculture, are shown conclusively in an extract from a letter of General Jackson's of later date, here given, as follows:—

"I will ask, what is the real situation of the agriculturist? Where has the American farmer a market for his surplus products? Except for cotton, he has neither a foreign nor a home market. Does this not clearly prove, when there is no market, either at home or abroad, that there is too much labor employed in agriculture, and that the channels of labor should be multiplied? Common sense points out at once the remedy. Draw from agriculture the superabundant labor; employ it in mechanism and manufactures, thereby creating a home market for your breadstuffs, and distributing labor to a most profitable account; and benefits to the country will result. Take from agriculture in the United States six hundred thousand men, women, and children, and you at once give a home market for more breadstuffs than all Europe now furnishes us. In short, sir, we have been too long subject to the policy of British merchants. It is time we should become a little more Americanized, and instead of feeding the paupers and laborers of Europe, feed our own; or else, in a short time, by continuing our present policy, we shall all be paupers ourselves."

Like to the solvents of the electric battery the *converters* of a community—makers of cloth and iron, books, instruments, ships, houses, mills, and furnaces—constitute a body of conductors of an electric force whose action becomes more and more intense as societary positives and negatives, producers and consumers, are brought into closer relations each with every other. Withdraw the former and circulation ceases, the metallic plates becoming as inert and lifeless as had been the material of which they are composed when it still remained embosomed in the earth. Withdrawing the latter—closing mills, furnaces, and workshops—similar results are everywhere produced; the circulation ceasing; power, whether physical or mental, being wasted; and paralysis taking the place of activity and life, precisely as has been the case in Ireland, India, and all other countries that, under the control of the trading monopoly above described, have been compelled to look to a semi-barbarous agriculture for the means of life. To that end tended the policy of the Union when non-resistance had been adopted, the result here exhibited having been precisely that which might in advance have been predicted.

§ 2. Sad experience having proved that in that direction lay poverty, wretchedness, and growing subjection of mind to matter, labor to capital, we find in 1824* a return to measures of resistance,

* Prussia commenced the work of resistance in 1818, but to this date had had but little success in her effort at constructing that "Customs Union" to which she since has owed the wonderful power that now is manifested.

and with results such as are here described by Mr. Clay, another of the eminent men of that important period:—

"Eight years ago it was my painful duty to present to the other House of Congress an unexaggerated picture of the general distress pervading the whole land. We must all yet remember some of its frightful features. We all know that the people were then oppressed and bowed down by an enormous load of debt; that the value of property was at its lowest point of depression; that ruinous sales and sacrifices were everywhere made of real estate; that stop laws and relief laws and paper money were adopted to save the people from impending destruction; that a deficit in the public revenue existed which compelled Government to seize upon and divert from its legitimate object the appropriations to the sinking fund to redeem the national debt, and that our commerce and navigation were threatened with a complete paralysis. *In short, sir, if I were to select any term of seven years since the adoption of the present Constitution which exhibited a scene of the most wide-spread dismay and desolation, it would be exactly that term of seven years which immediately preceded the establishment of the tariff of* 1824.

"I have now to perform the more pleasing task of exhibiting an imperfect sketch of the existing state of the unparalleled prosperity of the country. On a general survey we behold cultivation extended, the arts flourishing, the face of the country improved, our people fully and profitably employed, and the public countenance exhibiting tranquillity, contentment, and happiness. And if we descend into particulars, we have the agreeable contemplation of a people out of debt; land rising slowly in value, but in a secure and salutary degree; a ready though not extravagant market for all the surplus production of our industry; innumerable flocks and herds browsing and gambolling on ten thousand hills, and plains covered with rich and verdant grapes; our cities expanded, and whole villages springing up as it were by en-

---

The adoption by Russia of measures of resistance was simultaneous with that of the United States, like causes having thus produced like results.

chantment; our tonnage, foreign and coastwise, swelling and fully occupied; the rivers of our interior animated by the perpetual thunder and lightning of countless steamboats; the currency sound and abundant; the public debt of two wars nearly redeemed, and, to crown all, the public treasury overflowing—embarrassing Congress not to find subjects of taxation, but to select objects which shall be liberated from the impost. *If the term of seven years were to be selected of the greatest prosperity which this people have enjoyed since the establishment of their present Constitution, it would be exactly that period of seven years which immediately followed the passage of the tariff of* 1824."

To the testimony that has thus been furnished of three eminent statesmen of that date, all differing in regard to other questions of high importance but all concurring in their exhibitions of the destructive tendency of the non-resistant policy, might here be added that of Madison, Jefferson, and many other men of high position. In proof of the perfect accuracy of Mr. Clay's exhibit of the benefits resulting from adoption of the resistant one we need but look to the fact that so abounding were the public resources that the Treasury found itself compelled to redemption, at par, of the last remaining portion of the national debt, though bearing an interest of but three per cent. To those now living who had been then familiar with the occurrences of the day it is scarcely necessary to say, that throughout the whole country there was a rapidity of the societary circulation, and a development of power for the subjugation of matter to man's control, wholly without parallel to have been accomplished in so brief a period.

§ 3. Results so brilliant, and so entirely unparalleled, would certainly have had the result of establishing resistance as the permanent policy of the nation, had it not been, most unfortunately, that by the whites of nearly one-half of the States it was held as a part of their confession of faith, that of right capital should own labor, the laborer himself having "no rights that his owner was bound to respect;" and being liable to be bought and sold in open market, with or without his wife and children, at that owner's pleasure. Directly the reverse of this, it was held throughout the other States that all had been "born equal," and that all were alike entitled to claim perfect volition in reference to speech, thought, and action. As a consequence of this essential difference, their industrial tendencies were directly the opposite of each other—those of the one looking to an exclusive agriculture; to exhaustion of the soil;* to dispersion of their popula-

* "An Alabama planter says that cotton has destroyed more than earthquakes or volcanic eruptions. Witness the red hills of Georgia and South Carolina, which have produced cotton till the last dying gasp of the soil forbade any further attempt at cultivation; and the land turned out to nature, reminds the traveller, as he views the dilapidated condition of the country, of the ruins of ancient Greece."

Dr. Daniel Lee, in his *Progress of Agriculture*, in the United States Patent Office Report for 1852, says:—

"Cotton culture presents one feature which we respectfully commend to the earnest consideration of southern statesmen and planters, and that is the constantly increasing deterioration of the soil devoted mainly to the production of this important crop. Already this evil has attained a fearful magnitude; and under the present common practice it grows a little faster than the increase of cotton bales at the South. Who can say when or where this ever augmenting exhaustion of the natural resources of the cotton-growing States is to end, short of their ruin?

"Of the land cultivated in this country, one hundred million acres are

tion; to prevention of association among the chattels as among the masters; and to consequent maintenance of material power: the other, on the contrary, looking to the creation of a scientific agriculture; to development of the powers of the soil and of the various individualities of the people; and to subjection to human control of all those great natural forces by whose aid labor and its rude products could be so much economized. The one dispersed its people and left its roads in a state of nature. The other sought to concentrate its people and to improve its roads. The one prohibited education among its toiling millions; the other, meanwhile, expending tens of millions on schools and colleges. The one favored *emigration* from the centre to the south and southwest, with constant decrease of power for either mental or material improvement. The other favored *immigration* from abroad as tending to give daily increase of power for the building of furnaces and mills, for the maintenance of roads, and for the establishment and support of schools, churches, libraries, and all other of the appliances of a constantly advancing civilization. The one desired maintenance of mere material power, and to that end sought return to that policy of non-resistance under which they but a few years previously had so severely suffered. The other desired that mind should obtain increased power over matter, and therefore

damaged to the extent of three dollars per acre per annum; or, in other words, a complete restitution of the elements of crops removed each year cannot be made short of an expense of $300,000,000."

advocated maintenance of that resistance by means of which they had now so greatly prospered. The one desired continuance of dependence on distant traders, and to them it was that it looked for material and mental aid in all political contests. The other desired the establishment of domestic interdependence as a means of securing both political and industrial independence, and therefore did it look always homeward for support. The one, in short, advocated the policy of barbarism; the other meanwhile giving all its efforts in the direction of an advancing civilization. This last as a necessary consequence grew steadily in strength, becoming from year to year more self-reliant. The other, fearing decline in its power for controlling the societary movement, found itself from day to day more and more compelled to look for help to that people whose journals most abounded in denunciations of its peculiar system.*

To the contest here exhibited between matter and mind the world stands now indebted for having witnessed the formation of an organization for the maintenance of material power differing from all that had ever before existed; and formidable to a

* As a counterbalance to denunciations of slavery in the abstract, the great advantages resulting to England from its maintenance in practice were constantly exhibited to the English people in articles of which the one here given may be taken as a specimen.

"When his (the Manchester operative's) blood boils at the indignities and cruelties heaped upon the colored race in the 'Land of the Free,' he does not always remember that to the slave States of America he owes his all—that it is for his advantage that the negro should wear his chains in peace."—*Household Words.*

degree that could scarcely have been imagined by any who had not seen how almost infinite had been the injury of which it had been the cause. Southern planters stood now side by side with poor southern whites who could neither write nor read;* the ignorance, the vice, and the intemperance of both North and South furnished an army arrayed in opposition to the resistant policy;† the trader, whether in negroes or in merchandise, made common cause with the aristocratic planter, who thought and spoke of him only with contempt; Irish immigrants combined with men who held that the laborer might righteously be both bought and sold; the extraordinary alliance thus formed being backed by British capital, at all times ready to be used for aiding in reducing to subjection those of the American

* "Whether the North Carolina 'dirt-eater,' or the South Carolina 'sand-hiller,' or the Georgia 'cracker,' is lowest in the scale of human existence would be difficult to say. The ordinary plantation negro seemed to me, when I first saw him in any numbers, at the very bottom of not only probabilities, but also possibilities, so far as they affect human relations; but these specimens of the white race must be credited with having reached a yet lower depth of squalid and beastly wretchedness."—Correspondance of the *Boston Daily Advertiser.*

† For very many years the whole majority of Virginia favorable to the non-resistant policy came from a single district—then denominated the "tenth legion"—in which reading and writing were almost as rare as in Central Africa. In like manner, the great northern centre of the submissive policy is found in a city whose population largely represents the ignorance and intemperance of foreigners; and whose officers, municipal and judicial, are now under trial for offences of the most grievous and disreputable kind. Of the regular frequenters of the grog shop throughout the Northern States, nine-tenths are men whose votes may be always counted on as adverse to that policy of resistance which finds its most ardent advocates where schools and churches most abound.

people who believed in an universal diffusion of education, and in the most full development of the various individualities of a rapidly growing population; but who, unfortunately for "wealthy capitalists" abroad, had arrived at the conclusion that it was in the direction of resistance to trading monopoly, and in that alone, that men could look for obtaining such power for direction of the great natural forces as was required for enabling them even to hope for final establishment of the equal right of each and every man before the law, and for growth in the power of self-direction in either the people or the State.

Controlled and directed by this remarkable pro-slavery combination, Congress readopted the policy of non-resistance, to begin to take effect at the close of 1835, and thenceforward, until 1860, with the exception of a single brief and brilliant period to be hereafter noticed, the country presents to view a series of industrial, financial, and agricultural crises so serious as to have been almost adequate to realization of the wish which soon thereafter came so near accomplishment; to wit: that of shattering to atoms an Union in whose formation had participated Washington, Adams, Franklin, Hamilton, Jefferson, and other eminent men, whose ante-revolutionary experience had fully satisfied them that the road toward political independence led through those same measures of resistance which have been required for the production of domestic interdependence.

Throughout the generally dreary quarter of a

century thus described the centre of American commerce more and more tended to find its place in British ports, southern planters daily more and more effecting their exchanges with northern farmers through Manchester and Birmingham workshops. Throughout, southern men were united in preventing the growth of northern manufactures, desirous to so depress the prices of agricultural products as to enable them cheaply to feed the slaves who were needed for enabling them to drive from European markets the cotton that the poor Hindoo was, in effect, prohibited from converting into cloth at home.* Throughout, domestic commerce being in effect prohibited, no roads running north and south

* "*We must prevent the increase of manufactories, force the surplus labor into agriculture, promote the cultivation of our unimproved western lands, until provisions are so multiplied and reduced in price that the slave can be fed so cheaply as to enable us to grow our sugar at three cents a pound.* Then, without protective duties, we can rival Cuba in the production of that staple, and drive her from our markets." "While then the bounds of slave labor were extending from Virginia, the Carolinas, and Georgia westward over Tennessee, Alabama, Mississippi, and Arkansas, the area of free labor was enlarging with equal rapidity in the Northwest, Ohio, Indiana, Illinois, and Michigan. Thus within these provision and cotton regions were the forests cleared away or the prairies broken up simultaneously by those two antagonistic forces. Opponents no longer, they were harmonized by the fusion of their interests, the connecting link between them being the steamboat. Thus also was a *tripartite alliance* formed, *by which the western farmer, the southern planter, and the English manufacturer became united in a common bond of interest,* the whole giving their support to the doctrine of free trade."—Elliott. *Cotton is King,* Augusta, Georgia, 1860.

Of all conspiracies on record for the maintenance of slavery and barbarism, this is the most remarkable for the heterogeneous nature of the elements of which it was composed Most innocently, the leading anti-slavery advocates, in and out of Congress, gave to it their aid, and in the most effective manner. In the absence of knowledge, enthusiasm causes mischief rather than good.

could possibly be made. At every stage of progress in this direction discord grew, the general result of more than twenty years of non-resistance being found in that rebellion whose cost has been hundreds of thousands of lives and thousands of millions of money; and in the almost entire ruin of those communities which had allowed themselves to be misled into acquiescence in that trading system which looks, both at home and abroad, to perpetuation and extension of the control of capital over labor, matter over mind.*

§ 4. As the reader has been already told, the generally dreary quarter century through which we now have passed presents to view a single brief and brilliant period, constituting an oasis on which the eye can rest with pleasure, as exhibiting an increase in the power of mental over material force that even yet, as it is believed, is without a parallel to have been so speedily, and under circumstances so adverse, accomplished. To its examination we now proceed, as follows:—

The non-resistant policy, established by the end of 1833, became first effective at the close of 1835. Thenceforward, crisis succeeded crisis with such rapidity that the year 1842 presented a state of affairs worse even than that which had characterized the same system in the period 1817–24. Then, utter as was the demoralization throughout the land, the national credit remained almost unim-

* "To enable capital to obtain its proper remuneration, labor must be kept down."—*Huskisson.*

paired, and loans, when needed, could be negotiated; this, too, notwithstanding the existence of a very considerable debt, consequent upon heavy expenditure in two great wars. Now, not a dollar could be borrowed either at home or abroad; and yet the public debt had been entirely extinguished at the date of entrance on the non-resistant system. This of course compelled a change of policy, that of resistance being now again re-inaugurated by aid of the act of August, 1842. At that date, however, everything was out of joint, producers and consumers having long been separated; skilled labor having been compelled to seek employment in the field; mills and furnaces needing to be refurnished, even when not rebuilt; the whole body of societary positives and negatives requiring rearrangement previous to the production of any force whatsoever; and the whole society presenting to view a state of weakness absolutely inconceivable as having resulted from erroneous policy throughout so brief a period.

In the year following, 1843, the resistant policy became to some slight extent effective; but it was not until 1844 that its stimulative power came to be somewhat fully felt. By law, non-resistance was re-established at the close of 1846, but it was not until the spring of 1848 that it came into effective action, giving thus five years only as the whole period of resistance.* Brief, however, as it was,

* The Irish famine made large demands in 1847 for American food, and thus gave to the farmers a prosperity whose effects were felt in an enlarged demand for products of the workshop and the mill.

the consumption of iron was carried up to nearly 1,000,000 tons, or thrice that of the closing years of the non-resistant period; thus affording conclusive proof of advancing civilization.* Mind was now obtaining control over matter, as matter under the non-resistant system had steadily grown in power. Throughout the closing years of this brilliant period there was consequently an increase in the rapidity of circulation, and in the growth of force, comparing wonderfully with the paralysis by which it had been preceded.

Most important, however, of all the changes of that great period, the domestic consumption of cotton now rose to more than half a million of bales, having been almost doubled; with a growth six times more rapid than that of population. Now, for the first time, as a consequence of the resistant policy, the spindle and the loom were being enabled to plant themselves in close neighborhood to cotton fields, and with such effect that early in 1848 it came to be predicted, and by a southern statesman of high authority, that before the lapse of another decade consumers and producers would be brought so near together as to close for all the future the export of southern land and labor's staple product in its rudest form. Had the resistant policy been

* Notwithstanding an addition to the population from 1835 to 1842 of nearly 20 per cent., neither the production nor consumption of that great commodity which constitutes the test of growing civilization had much increased. In the five years that followed, with a growth of population not exceeding 15 per cent., consumption almost trebled, and of this greatly increased quantity more than seven-eighths were made at home.

maintained, this prediction would have been largely verified, and with every step in that direction the control of capital over labor—matter over mind—would have tended downward; the slave becoming free as land more and more acquired a money value; and the master becoming more and more independent at every stage of progress toward interdependence among the societary positives and negatives by which he was surrounded.

Unhappily, however, the "great capitalists" of England had been then most busily engaged in the effort at "destroying foreign competition," with a view to "gaining and keeping possession of foreign markets." Their "large capitals," constituting the "great instrument of warfare against the competing capital of other countries," had been lavishly applied in the work of corruption, with the result of once again breaking down all resistant barriers, and once again re-inaugurating the passive policy of non-resistance. From that hour southern manufactures declined; the internal commerce more and more tended to disappear before the assaults of foreign traders; discord grew; the whole culminating in a great rebellion, all the losses consequent upon which, whether of property or of life, are chargeable against the men whose "warfare" for maintenance of material power, and for annihilation of that of mind, has been, and by their own agent, above so well described. It was a great responsibility to assume, but the war of elements now existing within the British

Islands furnishes proof conclusive that at some not distant date it must be fully met.

§ 5. With constantly declining interdependence, and as constantly growing dependence on distant traders, each and all of whom believed that his private interests, as well as those of the whole body of "great capitalists," were to be promoted by means of fanning the flames of discord, we meet in the closing years of the non-resistant period a paralysis of the body politic, an arrest of the circulation, and a waste of physical and mental force, closely corresponding with those to which the reader's attention has above been called, as having occurred in the non-resistant periods which had closed in 1824 and 1842. For the products of northern agriculture there was almost literally no demand among the manufacturing nations of Europe, the average of three years' export of food in that direction having been but $10,000,000. Corn in the west was then being used for fuel, and thus was the producer compelled to lose not only the interest upon his capital, but the very capital itself that had been invested. Labor power was in excess, and men were everywhere wandering in search of such employment as would enable them to purchase food.* Mills and furnaces

* "1860 and 1861, and from 1857 to the autumn of the latter year, was one of the darkest periods ever seen by the laboring people of America. Not one out of five of the skilled workmen of the country was steadily employed. In Philadelphia, when they wanted to build a street railroad they advertised for two hundred and fifty hands at sixty cents a day, and more than five thousand offered, a majority of whom were skilled artisans who could find no other employment. In the neighborhood of one of the estab-

stood idle, and so trivial was the domestic intercourse that the average price of railroad investments was less than fifty per cent. For years the country, under the non-resistant system, had been trying the experiment as to how large an outlay of labor could be made for the accomplishment of any given result; the effect exhibiting itself in the fact that the community was paralyzed, and so wholly destitute of force that had the government then found occasion to call upon the whole nation for a sum so small as even a single hundred millions, it could scarcely have at all been furnished. Here, as is everywhere else the case, diminished rapidity of circulation had been attended with diminution of force.

Such was the state of things when the mind of the nation—that portion of it which believed in the creation of schools; in the extension of the benefits of education to every portion of the community; in the diversification of employment and development of all the various individualities of the toiling millions; in the necessity for obtaining control over the great physical forces as the means required for securing to themselves the power for self-direction—found itself called, at a moment's notice, to a con-

lishments, the statistics of which go into this report, a rolling mill, the number of unemployed men was so great that the county authorities, to save its skilled workmen from open pauperism, determined to build a turnpike, and experienced hands from rolling-mills were employed at breaking stone and road-making at fifty cents a day rather than become paupers. For the comparatively few who had employment the wages are, I assume, honestly given in the report; but of the many who were picking up a precarious living by getting an occasional day's work at half wages or quarter wages no account is taken.—*Hon. W. D. Kelley's Speeches*, p. 257.

test with that portion of the nation which had in the past maintained that capital should own labor; that the laborer's education should be prohibited; and, that the road to civilization, wealth, and power lay in the direction of an exclusive agriculture whose results were every day being more and more exhibited in the exhaustion and abandonment of lands that under a different system would have been daily growing in productive force. A contest the most remarkable that the world ever yet has seen, it required, on an average, throughout four long years, the services of more than a million of men, or more than five per cent. of the total northern population, male and female, sick and well, young and old. Not only were those services given, but during all that time the men employed were well clothed, abundantly fed, and furnished with transportation to an extent and in a perfection till then unparalleled in the history of the world.

Whence, however, came the extraordinary force that we see to have been thus exerted? How was it that a people which just before had been so very feeble could then have made donations to the extraordinary extent of a thousand millions of dollars a year? The answer to this question is found in the fact that the conditions of national existence had wholly changed, almost perfect circulation having been established throughout a gigantic battery of 20,000,000 pairs of plates, activity and life having succeeded to paralysis, and the societary movement having become strong and vigorous to an extent that had never before been known. For the first time in the history of the world there was then presented for examination a nation in which the demand for labor and its products went ahead of the supply, enabling both farmer and planter to stop the interest upon capital that had so long been petrified in the crudest forms of agricultural production;* and, as a necessary consequence, to make demand for the products of other labor applied to development of the mineral wealth that so much abounded, and to the conversion into commodities fitted for human use of the products of hills and valleys, farms and mines. The secret of all the force that was then so well exerted is to be found in that simple principle, evidence of whose truth is found in the books of every trader, the records of every nation; embodied, as it is, in the simple words from which we learn that the power of accumulation exists in the ratio of the rapidity of circulation and of the economy of human force. To what, however, was the nation indebted for that rapid circulation which furnishes, whether in the societary or the human frame, the most conclusive evidence of health and life? To nothing other than the fact of the re-adoption by the intelligent mind of the country of the ideas, that exercise of the co-ordinating power was first among the duties of the government; that the produce of the farm ought no longer to be compelled to remain inert and losing interest while

* See *ante*, pp. 127–129.

waiting demand in distant markets; that the capital which daily took the form of labor power ought no longer be allowed to go to waste; that the fuel which underlaid the soil ought no longer to remain to be a mere support for foreign rails; that the power which lay then petrified in the form of coal ought everywhere to be brought to aid the human arm; that the vast deposits of iron ore should be made to take the forms of engines and other machinery to be used as substitutes for mere muscular force; that all their wonderful resources, material and moral, should be at once developed; and, that for the prompt accomplishment of all these objects, the policy of resistance to trading domination must be re-established. To the change then so promptly made does the world stand now indebted for the fact that the people of America, in less than five years, and at a cost of thousands of millions of dollars, were enabled to retrieve the downward steps of more than twenty years; to establish freedom throughout the land; to save from destruction a nation of more than 30,000,000 that, by long practice on the pernicious doctrine of non-resistance, had been brought so near the verge of ruin that its escape therefrom constitutes now the most remarkable event in the world's history ; and to accomplish all this in the face of constant and most vigorous effort on the part of the "great capitalists" of England for giving to an aristocracy, whose cardinal principle of action was to be found in the assertion that capital should own labor, an effectual control over the actions of those who held that the laborer should not only own himself, but that he should be in every manner aided in his efforts for obtaining for his wife, his children, and himself, a perfect power for self-direction.

To what extent, under the resistant policy above described, mind was then, and since has been, obtaining control over matter, is well exhibited in the following statement, now several years old, of the late Revenue Commissioner:—

> "Within the last five years, more cotton spindles have been put in operation, more iron furnaces erected, more iron smelted, more bars rolled, more steel made, more coal and copper mined, more lumber sawed and hewn, more houses and shops constructed, more manufactories of different kinds started, and more petroleum collected, refined and exported, than during any equal period in the history of the country; and this increase has been greater both as regards quality and quantity, and greater than the legitimate increase to be expected from the normal increase of wealth and population."

That the great movement thus exhibited has been since continued, and that labor, physical and mental, has been steadily advancing toward equality in its relations to capital, is shown by facts which will here be given connected with the recent census just now published, as follows:—

The "true value" of the real and personal property of the Union, as given by the census of 1860, was, in round numbers, $16,000,000,000.

In this, however, was included as the value of colored men who now own themselves, and are, for that reason, no longer returned as property, an amount not varying materially from $3,000,000,000.

Deducting this, we have as the value of all property, slaves excluded, $13,000,000,000.

The "true value," as now given by the census of 1870, is $30,000,000,000, giving as the *increase* of the last decade an amount greater, by 30 per cent., than the total accumulation since the first settlement of Virginia and Massachusetts.

The result thus presented is a very remarkable one, yet is it proposed now to show that it gives *less than half the truth*, as follows:—

The greater the competition for the purchase of human service, physical or mental, the more does man himself rise in value. At the date of the census of 1860, there being then no such competition, wages had so greatly fallen that the average immigration of that and the two previous years had been less than half that of 1849, the last of the years in which this important question had been beneficially affected by the resistant tariff of 1842. Of the few who then arrived thousands wandered over the country, seeking employment that was nowhere to be obtained. Now, the reward of labor has so much increased that immigration has already more than doubled, each and every man finding prompt demand for the service he is prepared to render. Adding to this the increased value resulting from increased facilities of obtaining education and from the conversion of common into skilled laborers; and the increased reward of the mental labors of merchants, manufacturers, and professional men generally; it would appear scarcely unsafe to say that the annual average value of the American people, old and young, skilled and unskilled, laborers with the head and with the hand, was $50 greater than it had been ten years since. Putting it, however, at but $30, and population in round numbers at 40,000,000, we have $1,200,000,000 as the increased annual value of labor; that sum representing a capital larger than that represented by the increased material wealth; the two combined giving, as the growth of a single decade, the wonderful amount of $37,000,000,000.

In the previous decade, 1850–60, the growth, allowance being made for that which had resulted from increase of negro population, was but $8,000,000,000. From its commencement to its close wages had so greatly fallen that the desire to bring labor here to sell had more than one-half declined. Two hundred and fifty laborers being advertised for in Philadelphia, the claimants for employment at sixty cents a day, very many of them skilled workmen, proved twenty times more than had been called for. Railroad property throughout the Union having fallen to less than half its cost there was little demand for labor, physical or mental, to be given to construction of new roads, or to enlargement of the capacities of those already in existence. To take, therefore, the annual average value, in 1860, of physical and mental service as being the precise equivalent of that which had existed in 1850 is doing it, as it is believed, the extremest justice. Admitting this, the growth of wealth in the last decade, much of it a period of war and waste, has been more than four times greater than that of the previous one, although to the latter it was that we had stood first indebted for the vast influx of California gold.

To what now are these facts due? Plainly, to readoption of that policy of resistance to the British monopoly system to which the country had been so largely indebted in the brief periods of the tariffs of 1828 and 1842—that policy which looks to giving mind increased control over matter, and to bringing the laborer more and more to a level with the capitalist.*

§ 6. That the pyramidal form is the one which tends most to quiet permanence is a truth which here and everywhere forms part of that "positive knowledge of the uncultured," to which, as has been shown, we need to look for the basis of all scientific knowledge. To the attainment of that form it is that the resistant policy is directed, a great domestic commerce being regarded as the foundation on which to rest that foreign one which constitutes the apex, rising always in its height in strict proportion to enlargement of the base. That such *was* its tendency in the two periods which found their terminations in 1835, and in 1847–8, becomes clearly obvious to those who study the peaceful and quiet extension that then occurred in American relations with the outside world. So precisely has it been

* See Appendix C. for some details of the changes above described.

throughout the last decade, and so must it be in all the future, that policy continuing to be maintained. In none of those periods have there been any crises to affect injuriously those abroad with whom exchanges have been made. All, consequently, have profited by the prosperity of each and every other. Directly the reverse of this, the non-resistant policy looks to sacrifice of the domestic commerce in the vain hope of thus establishing a great foreign one, the result being that of creating an inverted pyramid always tottering to its fall, and threatening to involve in ruin all around—laborers and capitalists; producers and consumers; positives and negatives; alike the guilty and the innocent. That such *have been* the results of its adoption is shown by the financial crises with which its periods have always closed, and most especially by that last great crisis by which the Union was threatened with ruin so complete as must, had it been accomplished, have compelled it to abdicate its position among the powers of the world. In all these cases punishment has followed commission of the crime involved in violation of a great law to which obedience so implicit is rendered by that great "world builder," the coral insect, and so rarely obeyed by man.

§ 7. Of the three countries which have been thus described, those in which mind is advancing most rapidly toward the control of matter, labor toward equality with capital, and the whole toward that point at which measures of resistance will have ceased to be required—protection of their own labor against those "wealthy capitalists" who now are so actively engaged in the "warfare" above described, having resulted in the establishment of a domestic interdependence so complete as to secure to them both industrial and political independence — the American Union is the one which most has been exposed to the assaults of those wealthy men; the one whose policy has been most vacillating; and the one, therefore, which now most needs maintenance of the resistant policy. More stable than America, but less so than Germany, Russia stands next in the necessity for such resistance. Most of all consistent and regular in its action, the German Empire seems to be the one which will soonest find itself prepared to say to the world that resistance had fully done its work; diversification of employment having resulted in such development of the various faculties of its people, and such orderly arrangement of the positives and negatives of its great battery, as had been required for enabling it to present itself in the great industrial field as fully prepared for action as it so recently had done in those of both Sedan and Sadowa. That such is likely to be the case seems proved by the following extracts from a German letter given in a recent English journal, and here received as this sheet is passing through the press:—

"Manufacturing in all its branches is extraordinarily brisk; so brisk that our railway traffic has proved insufficient. For months and months passenger trains have been suspended to give room for additional goods trains, and, in despite of that, goods have often been on the way as many weeks and months as they ought to have been days. * * * Many railroads this winter refused to take any other goods but those which were paid for at the rate of passenger trains. * * * That everything has increased in price, and that money has decreased in value, might of itself account for the advance in wages which has taken place ; but another thing which has acted, and which is acting even more powerfully in that direction, is the scarcity of hands in all branches * * The pressure of trade causes employers in competition with each other to bid higher and higher for work, and at last wages are forced up even in those few branches, and there are very few, where trade is not so very brisk. * * * Hitherto, they have always got what they asked for, and the steps they have taken have not been small. * * It was thought they might feel contented ; but, actually, these last months they have raised the new prices again, and makers are obliged to pay the fresh advance. Handle and haft makers, turners, &c., have not been behind their fellows, the grinders, in asking an advance. Their work has been paid, since last autumn, about 50 per cent. more than before. Smiths, filers, not to forget the file-cutters, have all managed to secure their share."

The more the diversification in the demand for human force the more rapid is the growth of that domestic interdependence which enables a nation to direct its blows, when such are needed, with full effect; and to acquire for itself, as for all the individuals of which it is composed, that power for self-direction which constitutes the highest of all those faculties by which the human animal is distinguished from the brute.

NOTE.

Since the above was put in type the author has found in the *Cobden Club Papers* for 1871–1872, a *Chapter in Economical History*, by the late Revenue Commissioner, Mr. D. A. Wells, differing so widely from statements of his own of earlier date, here above given, and so utterly at variance with the real facts as above presented, that he deems it well, by examination of a single case to enable his readers to determine the value of the rest; to that end submitting for their consideration the following paragraph:—

"But, notwithstanding this limitation of the sources and amount of income, the requirements of the National Government for military, naval, and civil expenditures, and the payment of the principal and interest of any debt, were so moderate, that the receipts of the Treasury continually tended to exceed its disbursements; and the difficulty which most frequently presented itself to the financial administrators was, not the customary one of how to avoid an annual deficit, but rather how to manage to escape an inconvenient and indispensable surplus. And it is a curious fact, and one perhaps altogether unprecedented in history, that, from the years 1837 to 1857, there was not a single fiscal year in which the unexpended balance in the National Treasury—derived from various sources—at the end of the year was not in excess of one-half of the total expenditure of the preceding year; while in not a few years the unexpended balance was absolutely greater than the sum of the entire expenditure of the twelve months preceding."

Before entering on the proposed examination he asks the reader's attention to the fact, that the twenty years here lumped together consist of three widely different groups, to wit, the non-resistant one of the years 1837–42; the resistant one, 1843–48; lastly, that of the Californian golden age 1849–57. This premised, we may now advantageously compare the real facts as given below,* with the impression intended to be produced on the minds of the Commissioner's readers, as follows:—

* Amount of moneys derived from loans and treasury notes, as exhibited in the published statements of the Treasury Department.

NON-RESISTANT PERIOD.	
1837	$2,992,000
1838	12,716,000
1839	3,857,000
1840	13,659,000
1841	14,809,000
1842	12,551,000
RESISTANT PERIOD.	
1843–44	$1,878,000

Of these it may safely be affirmed, that not even one has failed to be impressed with a belief that the "revenue" had throughout been all sufficient; that not one has imagined that the words "various sources" had been inserted for the purpose of covering up large receipts from loans made necessary by great deficiencies of "revenue;" that not one has supposed that the first six of these 20 years had brought with them a constant need for loans; that a nation which just before had extinguished its debt could have found itself in 1842 wholly unable, either at home or abroad, to borrow a single dollar;* that the need for loans had disappeared almost on the instant of the re-adoption of the resistant policy;† that the California discoveries had for a time adjourned the period of suffering under the then existing non-resistant one; that the *brilliant* years 1858–1860, than which,

MEXICAN WAR YEARS.	
1846–47	$28,900,000
1847–48	21,293,000
1848–49	29,075,000
1849–50	4,056,000
CALIFORNIAN PERIOD.	
1850–57	none.
NON-RESISTANT PERIOD.	
1857–58	$23,717,000
1858–59	28,259,000
1859–60	20,776,000

* "After a failure in the American market, a citizen of high character and talent was sent to Europe with no better success; and thus the mortifying spectacle has been presented of the inability of this Government to obtain a loan so small as not in the whole to amount to more than one-fourth of its ordinary income; at a time when the Governments of Europe, although involved in debt, and with their subjects heavily burdened with taxation, readily obtained loans of any amount, at a greatly reduced rate of interest."—*President's Message*, December, 1842.

† "The credit of the Government which had experienced a temporary embarrassment, has been thoroughly restored. Its coffers, which for a season were empty, have been replenished. A currency, nearly uniform in its value, has taken the place of one depreciated and almost worthless. Commerce and manufactures, which had suffered in common with almost every other interest, have once more revived; and the whole country exhibits an aspect of prosperity and happiness."—*President's Message*, December, 1844.

as they had been assured, there could be none that would afford a more happy illustration of the influence of the "non-interference," or "non-obstructive" policy of Government, had been excluded for the reason that their revenues had proved so greatly deficient as to have required loans to the extent of more than 70 millions; or, finally, that there had then arrived a state of things so desperate that money could no longer be obtained except at rates so usurious as indicated a total loss of the public credit. Nevertheless all these things were so.—*Ex pede Herculem.* From commencement to close this "Chapter" is all alike. No one could imagine from its perusal that the reward of labor had, in the decade 1860–1870, so much increased as to have caused a duplication of immigration; that the *consumption* of wool by the people of the Union had so greatly grown as now to exceed two-thirds of the whole *manufacture* of Britain, in 1864, for home consumption and for the world at large;* that the consumption of cotton had grown nearly 75 per cent., as compared with the average of the three—so-called—*prosperous* years 1858–1860;† that cotton producers were profiting of this by obtaining a large increase of price; that the *consumption* of cottons, of home or foreign manufacture, had arrived at half the British *production* for the thousand millions of the world's people, those of Britain herself included;‡ that

		POUNDS.
* Domestic wool consumed, 1870		163,000,000
Foreign wool, 1870–71		68,000,000
Imported worsteds and woollens, 1870–71		35,000,000
		266,000,000
Total British manufacture, in 1864		384,000,000
		BALES.
† Average cotton consumption of 1858–60		666,800
1871		1,153,900
		POUNDS.
‡ Total British cotton consumption, 1871		1,207,000,000
Average British consumption, 1869–71 about		1,100,000,000
American for 1871	520,000,000	
Net import, $26,000,000	30,000,000	
		550,000,000

railroad tonnage had quadrupled; that the *consumption* of iron had grown to half the *production* of Britain for herself and for the world at large; or, finally, that the growth of material wealth had been far greater than all the accumulations since the date of the Mayflower's arrival on the coast of Massachusetts.*

CHAPTER IX.

MATTER AND MIND.—(*Continued.*)

§ 1. As has been already shown, the first attempt at subjecting to cultivation the soil of England was made in the bleak and barren Cornwall, and there was found for many centuries the centre of English power. Later, in the days of the earlier Plantagenets, a population of less than two millions was thinly scattered over the higher, drier, and comparatively unproductive soils of the kingdom; Gurth and Wamba then wearing around their necks the collars by which the world was made to know that they, alike the jester and the clown, were "born thralls" of their compatriot, the Saxon Cedric.—Passing now

* On the treasury books the States of the Union stand severally charged with their shares of $28,000,000 nominally deposited with, but really given to, those States in the year 1836. This was done at a time when the effects of a non-resistant policy, then recently readopted, were exhibiting themselves in a general deluge of British merchandise, furnished on long credits, and thus stimulating a speculation that, for the moment, caused large excess of the public revenue. Counting as *money* the *figures* representing those deposits the Commissioner may, perhaps, find some justification for his statements; and yet none better than himself should appreciate the fact that they are but the *shadow* of moneys long since expended.

onward a couple of centuries, population having meantime much increased, and Edward III. having instituted measures by means of which local centres had been made to greatly grow in both number and importance, we find the descendants of Saxon churls on the field of Agincourt, freed from all outward mark of slavery and sending their cloth-yard shafts among the chivalry of France with a force and effect that since then have never been exceeded, and rarely, if even ever, equalled.* Simultaneously therewith, landlords are everywhere seen praying for protection against their so recent serfs, to be secured to them by means of laws regulating the prices at which labor should be sold, and imposing heavy penalties on any who should pay or receive more than those to be thus established.†

Passing again onward, we reach the brilliant

* Discussing the period immediately anterior to the day of Agincourt, Prof. Rogers speaks as follows:—

"In fifty years, then, the tenant farmers were able to accumulate, in order to supersede stock and land leases, not much less than treble the value of the land they occupied, and this even in despite of somewhat unfavorable times, for agricultural produce was low in the last ten or twelve years of the fourteenth century. Is it wonderful, therefore, that men who in the early part of the century had no place in the political history of the times, assert their rights with so much vigor in the latter part, embrace Lollardism, delight in 'Piers Plowman,' adopt his style, inveigh bitterly against the friars and great ecclesiastics, and crowd 'tumultuously' to county elections?"—*History of Agriculture and Prices in England*, vol. i. p. 688.

† The first Statute of Laborers bears the date of 1349.—Thenceforward throughout a whole century we have constant repetitions thereof, each and all tending to prove how futile had been the previous efforts at maintaining even qualified slavery in face of a policy looking to increased diversification in the demand for human service, and manifesting its powers by causing great increase in the societary circulation.

period when the mind of England was being illustrated by Bacon and Shakspeare, Bunyan, Hale, Hampden, and Milton; her stalwart yeomanry, under the lead of Cromwell, meanwhile advocating the cause of labor on the fields of Naseby and Marston Moor.* The change thus indicated in the relations of mind and matter, labor and capital, is one of the most remarkable phenomena of modern Europe; and is attributable to the fact, that from the day of Bosworth (1485) the country had been steadily engaged in home-development, its wars, with slight exceptions, having been of a purely defensive character. Side by side with it, however, now stands another of even greater moment, to wit: that indicated by the fact that, notwithstanding a wonderful growth of wealth and power, the relative positions of labor and capital have since then wholly changed; a *proletariat* constantly imploring protection *against its masters*, standing now in the place once occupied by those men of Agincourt protection *against whom* had been so often sought by their then recent masters at the hands of Parliament.† The

* The general character of the English people at this period stands proved by the fact that so great a revolution was accomplished at so little cost of life, or of interference with private rights. As there was then no *proletariat*, there was then no *jacquerie*. Speaking of the action of the government that was then established, Macaulay says: "Property was secure. Even the cavalier who refrained from giving disturbance to the new settlement enjoyed in peace whatever the civil troubles had left him. * * * Justice was administered with an exactness and purity not before known."

† The frequent use now made of the discreditable and humiliating word "proletaire," and the sanction just now given to its naturalization, as being one "much needed," by a leading English journal (See *Quarterly Review*,

growth of material at the cost of mental power—of capital as against labor—thus indicated, has been accompanied by a decline of physical force so complete that throughout the whole realm of England there would now be found few, if even any, capable of drawing "to their heads" those terrific shafts which down even to the day of Flodden (1513) constituted the essential instrument of English warfare.* What has been that "deteriorating influence" by means of which changes so remarkable have been brought about we may now inquire.

§ 2. Throughout the brilliant period above re-

Jan. 1872, article, "The Proletariat on a False Scent"), warrants some inquiry into its real import. Turning now to his dictionary, the reader will probably find a definition corresponding with that of *Ainsworth* in the volume now before us, as follows: "Proletarius—Of a poor, mean, condition; poor, vulgar, beggarly."—The proletaire is not a slave, for he may not be bought and sold in the open market. He is not a freeman, having no power for self-direction. His physical powers having been exhausted by overwork he may, if he will, seek refuge in the almshouse. Dying of over-exertion and want of proper sustenance, the services of the coroner are not demanded; and yet the case is often one of murder as absolute and complete as if the poor man had been shot to death. The incorporation into the language of a word so depreciatory, on the score of its being "needed" for bringing properly before us the toiling millions of the English people, is one of those "straws" which indicate clearly the direction in which the wind is blowing; one that invites for its careful consideration all those who interest themselves in the question of the future of mankind at large.

* "Why, for example, has it been found necessary at the Horse Guards to lower the standard of recruits? Because through a series of deteriorating influences, beginning at bad times, the breed of Englishmen has miserably gone down. The recruiting standard has been lowered and lowered again; and men at this moment, it is declared, 'cannot be got of the minimum height.' 'The present recruiting prospect,' it is stated, 'is short companies to the line regiments, companies of men scarcely exceeding five feet in height.'"—*Contemporary Review*, 1871, p. 549.

ferred to the richest soils of England remained uncultivated, the now so highly productive Lancashire having been then a wilderness so formidable as to have daunted the antiquary Camden even so late as the days of James I. Of the natural forces other than those required for the production of food there was but little known, and power for their direction was then so limited as to claim but slight consideration. Ships were few in number, and the aid of wind was but little called for. Gunpowder was then in its infancy, and the guns then used were difficult of proper management The use of mineral coal for smelting ores had not yet been thought of. Steam had yet to wait throughout a century before being subjected to human use. So, too, with even that poor tram-road which proved the precursor of the iron rail and the locomotive, and of thousands and tens of thousands of improvements by means of which human labor has been so greatly aided that it may with safety be asserted that Britain alone commands now the services of 500,000,000 non-consuming laborers, capable of a larger amount of work than could have been performed by the whole human race in the days when the Marquis of Worcester was experimenting on the powers of steam, and when Charles II. sat on the English throne.*

* The coal now used in the production of force is estimated as being the equivalent of 300,000,000 of men. Add to this the wind power utilized for the propelling of 5,000,000 tons of shipping; the tractive power obtained by means of the iron rail and the locomotive; the telegraph which annihilates both time and space; the utilization of human force consequent upon the invention of various machinery now in use; and the estimate will certainly be found within the mark.

Of the wonderful industrial army here exhibited, by far the greater part has been created within the last half century, the rate of progress from the days when mineral coal was first used in smelting furnaces, and when Watt first utilized the powers of steam, having been a constantly accelerated one. Equally divided among the whole population of the British Islands it might a century since perhaps have given some two or three non-consuming slaves to each, male and female, the infant and the aged, the enlightened and the ignorant. So divided now it would give nearly 80 to each and every family consisting of father, mother, and three children, or five in all.

For whose profit, however, have these most productive slaves labored in the somewhat distant past? For that of American colonists? That such was not the case stands proved by the fact, that these latter labored through seven years of great privation for the sole purpose of securing to themselves and their children power to command the services of just such non-consuming laborers. Was it in the service of the then highly civilized people of India?* That the facts were directly otherwise is shown by

* "I do not exactly know what is meant by civilizing the people of India. In the theory and practice of good government they may be deficient; but if a good system of agriculture—if unrivalled manufactures—if a capacity to produce what convenience or luxury demands—if the establishment of schools for reading and writing—if the general practice of kindness and hospitality—and above all, if a scrupulous respect and delicacy towards the female sex, are among the points that denote a civilized people, then the Hindoos are not inferior in civilization to the people of Europe."—*Sir Thomas Munro.*

Lord Macaulay in the passage here given, as follows:—

"The misgovernment of the English was carried to a point such as seemed hardly compatible with the existence of society. They forced the natives to buy dear and sell cheap. They insulted with impunity the tribunals, the police, and the fiscal authorities of the country. Enormous fortunes were thus rapidly accumulated at Calcutta, while 30,000,000 of human beings were reduced to the extremity of wretchedness. They had been accustomed to live under tyranny, but never under tyranny like this. They found the little finger of the Company thicker than Surajah Dowlah's loins. Under their old masters, they had at least one resource: when the evil became insupportable, the people rose and pulled down the government. But the English government was not to be so shaken off. That government, oppressive as the most oppressive form of barbarian despotism, was strong with all the strength of civilization. It resembled the government of evil genii, rather than the government of human tyrants."

Was it, then, in behalf of the toiling millions of the British Islands that such labors then were given? That such was not the case is clearly shown by the fact, that Mr. Malthus then was led to *invent* a law of population by means of which to relieve the rich and powerful from all responsibility for the existing state of things; giving them assurance that the poverty and wretchedness by which they were everywhere surrounded had resulted from the fact that the Creator had sent upon the earth large numbers of people for whom He had provided no table at which they might be allowed to eat, no materials by aid of which they might be clothed; thus furnishing the theory by aid of which subsequent writers have been enabled, as they supposed, to prove that, in the British Islands, man had become "a drug," and "population a nuisance."

Failing thus, at that early period of the now-existing system, to find among the working people of the British empire, whether home or foreign, the persons in whose behalf the labors of non-consuming slaves were being given, the search may be now continued by looking altogether homeward among the British and Irish people of half a century since. Doing this, we may here inquire if such labors had been in any manner given in aid of Scottish Highlanders, compelled, as they were, to relinquish their little holdings under circumstances so atrocious as to have called forth a shriek of horror both abroad and at home.* Were they then being given in aid of the millions of impoverished Irish before whom there lay but the choice between "land at any rent," on the one hand, or "starvation" on the other? In aid, perhaps, of the wretched men, women, and children, who then were laboring together, often wholly naked, in the coal mines of England? Or in that of the wretched Birmingham workmen whose condition was then so well described by Southey in his admirable Letters?† Failing in that direction,

* See Loch's work on the Clearances in Sutherlandshire, London, 1820. Mr. Loch was the agent under whom all this had been done, and he published his account thereof under the extraordinary impression that he had been thus aiding in the advancement of civilization.

† "The poor must be kept poor, or such a state of things could not continue; there must be laws to regulate their wages, not by the value of their work, but by the pleasure of their masters; laws to prevent their removal from one place to another within the kingdom, and to prohibit their emi-

may we find the masters of these non-consuming slaves in Lancashire children of the tenderest age who were being then employed in breaking down the great India cotton manufacture; and to that end, as was stated by Sir Robert Peel, were compelled to labor ninety-six hours per week; giving further six hours of Sunday to the work of cleaning the machinery, and doing all this for less than a dollar per week?

That it is not in the cause of these most wretched people that the non-consuming slaves have labored in the past seems very certain. How then is it in the present, when those slaves have become more than thrice as numerous as they had been in the days of Peel and Southey above described. Are those who profit by all the gratuitous service that now is rendered to be found among that third of the Scottish people which lives, or tries to live, in houses of but a single room? Among the very youthful, and the aged, of Ireland left behind by the lithe and active who have been driven from the homes in which their parents and themselves had

gration. They would not," he continues, "be crowded in hot task-houses by day, and herded together in damp cellars by night; they would not toil in unwholesome employments from sunrise until sunset whole days and quarters, for with twelve hours' labor the avidity of trade is not satisfied; they would not sweat night and day, keeping up this *laus perennis* of the Devil, before furnaces which are never suffered to cool, and breathing in vapors which inevitably produce disease and death;—the poor would never do these things unless they were miserably poor, unless they were in that state of abject poverty which precludes instruction, and by destroying all hope for the future, reduces man, like the brutes, to seek for nothing be-beyond the gratification of present wants."—*Espriella's Letters;* Letter xxxvii.

first seen the light?* Among the almost million surplus English and Scottish females who have been in like manner left behind, having now before them little other choice than that between hard labor at starvation wages on the one hand, and prostitution on the other?† Among the millions who can neither read nor write? Among the serfs of the loom who have now replaced the serfs of the glebe?‡ Among spinners and weavers who have so severely suffered throughout the last decade, and whose whole future is dependent on the power to compel competition among American and Indian laborers for supplying cheap cotton on which to work?§ Among farm

* Of foreigners arriving in the United States, 82 per cent. are over 5 and under 40 years of age.

† "I saw young women, with bright and intelligent faces, as bright as any of those we meet in our daily walks, who were earning but five shillings per week, and most of which they had to pay for their clothes and living. How it is possible to do this is more than I can tell. It would probably be best for poor, downtrodden, and oppressed humanity in this country not to inquire. Of course, there are others who get higher wages; but the average wages earned by the female operative in this country probably would not exceed eight shillings and sixpence to nine shillings per week. It is impossible for a person, who only has this, to pay for clothes, lodging and food, to eat meat every day, or to subsist on anything but the coarsest and most common food."—English Correspondence of *New York Tribune.*

‡ "A vassalage in manufacture and trade is succeeding the vassalage in land, and the serf of the loom is in a lower and more helpless condition than the serf of the glebe, because his condition appears to be not merely the effect of an artificial and faulty social economy, like the feudal, which may be remedied, but to be the unavoidable effect of natural causes."—Laing: *Notes of a Traveller,* p. 177.

§ "The feudalization going on in our manufacturing social economy is very conspicuous in some of the great cotton factories. The master-manufacturer in some districts, who employs eight hundred or a thousand hands, deals in reality only with fifty or sixty sub-vassals, or operative cotton-spinners, as they are technically called, who undertake the working of so

laborers, male and female, "whose sustenance," as public documents assure us, "bears no due proportion to the toil to which they are reared;"* who have before them, according to *Edinburgh Reviewers*, no future but the poor-house; and "whose condition," according to *Quarterly Reviewers*, "is growing worse from year to year?"† Among the children who work

many looms, or spinning-jennies. They hire and pay the men, women, and children, who are the real operatives, grinding their wages down to the lowest rate, and getting the highest they can out of the master-manufacturer. A strike is often the operation of these middle-men, and productive of little benefit to, and even against the will of, the actual workmen. They are, in the little imperium of the factory, the equivalent to the feudal barons."—*Ibid.*

* The *Reports on the Employment of Women and Children in Agriculture* inform us that "Beef and mutton are so rarely tasted by farm laborers and their families, that they may be said to form no part of their diet; that bacon is not partaken of more than, if so often as, once or twice a week, and not in any proportion amounting to a meal; and that bread and cheese form the main food of adults." The cheese is described to be of the worst possible quality. "The children mostly exist on bread soaked in water, or, at the best, are obliged to put up with thrice-skimmed milk. The house accommodation is of the worst possible description. But without going into details that would prove tiresome, let us take the chief features of the summing up of the report. It declares that the sustenance of the peasantry at all ages bears no due proportion to the toil to which they are reared, and the privation is sadly and needlessly aggravated by the distances which many of them have daily to walk, through the decay or actual destruction of cottages. There have been too many instances in which, before the termination of a lifetime of labor, men have, through this cause, been compelled to perform a foot penance equalling, in many a case, a journey once around the world: in some, even twice! and in some, thrice!"

† "The condition of the agricultural laborer in most districts is an opprobrium and a calamity to the nation. He ought not to be suffered to remain in it; and he cannot (unassisted) raise himself out of it. We need not describe what has been over and over again depicted and proved *usque ad nauseam*. The thing is a disgrace and a danger—and we need say no more. We are not sure that the condition is not even growing worse year by year. Certainly it is worse in many essentials than it was a century or a century

in "gangs," and under slave "overseers" throughout the eastern counties?* Among the "proletaires" of western counties, whose condition has been so well described by Canon Girdlestone?† Among the hun-

and a half ago. The wages these laborers obtain are a shame. The condition of their cottages is a shame. The general and inescapable prospect of the poor-house for their old age is a shame. Their often having no cottages at all in the parish where they work is, perhaps, the greatest shame of all."—Jan. 1872, Article, *the Proletariat on a false Scent.*

* "The gang system," as recently exhibited in Parliament, "in brief is this: In the Fen districts, covering nearly a million of acres of the richest land in England, Huntingdonshire, Cambridgeshire, Nottinghamshire, Norfolk, Suffolk, and in parts of the counties of Northampton, Bedford, and Rutland, about seven thousand children, from five years of age and upwards, besides persons of both sexes of from fifteen to eighteen years of age—are employed in gangs numbering from fifteen to twenty laborers in each gang, under a master, and in a condition differing from slavery only because it is infinitely worse. * * * *

"This exhibition, shocking as it is, is by no means the most frightful phase of the gang system. The gangs are under no moral restraint whatever. Oftentimes at night both sexes are huddled together in barns, where, among the older boys and girls, the most shameful events naturally follow. Clergymen and other respectable witnesses testified to the Commission of Inquiry that the gang laborers are 'beneath morals.' They have no consciousness of chastity, and do not know the meaning of the word. Medical directors of infirmaries state that gang girls, as young as thirteen years, have been brought to them to be confined. Their language and conduct are so depraved that dozens of parish clergymen, surgeons, and respectable laboring people, declared to the commission that the introduction of gang labor in any village extinguishes morality."—*Evening Post.*

† "Wages are low; fuel and provisions are dear; education has become a necessary of life for a family; the poor rate is so administered as to quench every feeling of independence. In the west of England an agricultural laborer had till lately only 7*s.* or 8*s.* a week, and now only 8*s.* or 9*s.* Unless he is a housekeeper or a shepherd, he has to pay out of this 1*s.* to 1*s.* 6*d.* or more a week for house rent, and provide food, clothing, medical attendance, fuel, and every other necessary for himself, wife, and family. Potato-ground he pays a high rent for, and fuel he seldom gets, except at the cost of as many hours of hard work of getting it as its full value. He has three pints or two quarts of cider a day, and has a portion of his wages often paid in

dreds of thousands who, as we are assured, "must either emigrate or die?"* Among the tens of thousands of paper-makers, printers, shipbuilders, and other skilled laborers that but recently have been described as out of work, and as "now going upon the poor rate?" Among the almost infant females who labor in English brickyards, required, as they are, to carry nine tons of clay a distance of fifty yards, and to walk twenty-two miles, for eighteen pence of

quit, which, when corn is dear, is an advantage, but otherwise a loss to him. He is often not allowed to keep a pig or poultry, for fear of stealing food for them from his master. He works nominally ten or ten and a half hours a day with an hour and a half deducted for meals. He is almost always, however, in reality kept a much longer time than this, and is seldom paid anything for overtime, except by bread and cheese in harvest time. Women get 7*d.* or 8*d.* a day for out-door work, with a quart of cider, and boys small sums in proportion. The men breakfast before they leave home on tea-kettle broth, which consists of an infusion of bread and water, with a little milk, if, which is not often the case, it can be got. For luncheon and dinner, which they take with them, they have coarse bread and hard, dry skim-milk cheese, at 3*d.* per lb. For supper, on their return home, they have potatoes or cabbage, with a very small slice of bacon, sometimes to give it a flavor. Butcher's meat they seldom see, except it is given to them."

* "*There are now above* 70,000 *souls in the east end of London who must emigrate speedily or die.* They are being shipped off as fast as charity and government can transport them to North America. Above 25,000 of these are workmen more or less skilled in engineer and shipbuilding occupations. These are not shepherds, nor are they ploughmen, nor will they ever be to any great extent one or the other. They are mechanics, and will be so go where they may. *In the vast hives of industry in Lancashire there are a greater number who must emigrate or die.* These are getting off as fast as they possibly can to Massachusetts to find full occupation in cotton. Not one is either pastoral or agricultural, and few are likely ever to be either. Irishmen and Scotchmen can be anything, but not so Englishmen; and they will not need to be anything in the world but what they have been."—Kirk: *Social Politics in Great Britain and Ireland*, page 112. London and Glasgow, 1870.

wages?* Among the tens of thousands of railroad employés compelled, as they are, to labor sixteen or twenty hours per day, and under circumstances such as almost insure loss of life as consequence of inattention or neglect?† Among the hundreds of thousands of a better class with whom "the wolf" is always "at the door?"‡ Or, finally, may they be found among the almost countless hosts of paupers, tramps, and vagrants so well described by Hoyle in his work on the "National Resources," as exhibiting "an amount of demoralization and destitution" so

* "Children are found working in brickyards at as early an age as three and a half years. What they can do at that age we are not told; but at nine years old the toil imposed on them is so severe and prolonged that nothing but the most unimpeachable evidence could render it creditable. *There is, however, no doubt whatever of the facts*, and we commend them to the reflection of the anxious parents of well-fed and tenderly-nurtured children. These unhappy little creatures, many of them girls, are engaged for thirteen hours a day in carrying on their heads lumps of clay weighing forty pounds from the clay heap to the table on which the bricks are made. * * * Boys and girls grow up together in conditions of immodest and almost animal association, until it is no exaggeration to say that 'men, women, and children are brought down to a point of degradation and suffering like the beasts of the field.'"—Smith: *Cry of the Children in the Brickyards of England.* London, 1871.

† "Many of the engineers had been kept on continuous duty for twenty-two and twenty-three hours; indeed until some of them fell exhausted on the floors of their engines. On Saturday, eighteen hours was on several roads the regular period of labor, and signal men were often found asleep in their boxes. Accidental deaths of employés exhausted by too much labor frequently happened, the overwork having rendered them incapable of taking care of themselves. The meeting was convened to devise some method of reforming this bad system."—*English Journal.*

‡ "Those who themselves are at present above want or poverty, nevertheless are still looking down at that abyss of misery and destitution beneath them, and, while congratulating themselves at their own escape, they do not, and dare not, complain of evils of a less terrible character. They are silent on that *anxiety* which besets their own position, and robs

"perfectly appalling" as to constitute "a lasting disgrace to our civilization and our Christianity?"*

That it is not among the toiling millions of the British Islands we need to look for those who profit by the altogether gratuitous services of an army of non-consuming laborers, whose numbers count by hundreds of millions, is very certain. Clear does it seem, that so far are they from benefiting by such services, their condition, physical and moral, is greatly lower than it had been at the time when the industrial utility of coal, the powers of steam, and those still more remarkable of electricity, yet re-

every household of its peace; they are silent on that perpetual contest and strife of commerce which sow the seed of hatred so abundantly through every town and village. Is not the wolf still at the door?"—*Thorndale; or, the Conflict of Opinions.*

* Referring to this subject, Mr. R. Dudley Baxter, in his work on *National Income*, speaks as follows:—

"The average number of paupers at one time in receipt of relief in 1866 was 916,000, being less than for any of the four preceding years. The total number relieved during 1866 may, on the authority of a return of 1867, given in the Appendix, be calculated at three and a half times that number, or 3,000,000. All these may be considered as belonging to the 16,000,000 of the manual labor classes, being as nearly as possible twenty per cent. on their number; but the actual cases of relief give a very imperfect idea of the loss of work and wages. A large proportion of the poor submit to great hardships, and are many weeks, and even months, out of work before they will apply to the guardians. They exhaust their savings; they try to the utmost their trade unions or benefit societies; they pawn little by little all their furniture; and are at last driven to ask relief."

"But even the figures which have been given do not by any means represent adequately the pressure of our poverty. There are a very large number of persons who are dependent upon their friends and relations; and there are a number who submit to great hardships sooner than apply for relief. If all who are thus situated be summed up, it cannot amount to less than one-third of the entire population of the manual labor class, or from fifteen to twenty per cent. of the entire population."—*Hoyle.*

mained to be developed; when hundreds of thousands of small proprietors—the yeomanry long so justly prized—could proudly boast of "their own, their native land;" and when northern and southern Britain could send forth armies such as were led to the field by Cromwell and Montrose.*

Seeking elsewhere the people who profit by the labors of these non-consuming and never-tiring slaves, may we hope to find them now in Portugal, once the most profitable of all the customers of Britain? In Jamaica, where, in defiance of all understanding to the contrary, new-born freedmen, yet disorganized, were required almost at once to compete on equal terms with armies of Brazilian negro slaves? In Turkey, where the foreign peddler has driven out the manufacturer, and where millions of men are almost starving in the sight of mineral treasures by whose development they would be enriched; the nation itself meanwhile acquiring force to assert its rights? In India, where the salt and the cotton manufactures have alike been ruined; and where millions of men stand idle waiting the return in the form of cloth of the raw cotton they had been compelled to send to Britain?† In China, where an-

* "The agricultural laborer of those times was not the overworked slave that he is now. * * * He was better treated in the last old days of a dying feudalism than he is now under the new laws of supply and demand."—*H. Kingsley.*

† "A great part of the time of the laboring population in India is," says Mr. Chapman, "spent in idleness. I," as he continues, "don't say this to blame them in the smallest degree. Without the means of exporting heavy and crude surplus agricultural produce, and with scanty means, whether of capital, science, or manual skill, for elaborating on the spot

archy prevails as a consequence of opium wars, and of perpetual interference of foreign agents whose every effort is being given toward bringing about an entire dependence on British ships and mills? In Spanish America, throughout the whole of which exists a chronic state of revolution consequent upon absence of that power of association for whose development there is required a diversity of employments whose existence it is the object of foreign traders to prevent? Is there, indeed, any part of the world's laborers, outside of those few countries which have effectually resisted this monstrous system of "warfare," to which we can safely point as now profiting, or as having profited, by the great discoveries of the past and present centuries; any that is not now suffering under the constantly reiterated attacks of the wonderful army now gathered together in Great Britain?† That none such

articles fitted to induce a higher state of enjoyment and of industry in the mass of the people, they have really no inducement to exertion beyond that which is necessary to gratify their present and very limited wishes: those wishes are unnaturally low, inasmuch as they do not afford the needful stimulus to the exercise requisite to intellectual and moral improvement; and it is obvious that there is no remedy for this but extended intercourse. Meanwhile, probably the half of the human time and energy of India runs to mere waste. Surely, we need not wonder at the poverty of the country."—Chapman: *Cotton and Commerce of India*, p. 110.

"It is calculated that there are often 10,000,000 qrs. of fine wheat rotting in the Punjab alone for want of demand, utterly useless except to feed hogs, which the prejudices of the people forbid them to breed. If science ever succeeds in banishing the weevil from wheat ships and preserving mutton for six months, the English people may yet be fed to the throat on flesh and flour at less than the cost of their present insufficient food."—*English Journal.*

† For some years Australia profited largely by that diversity of em-

can be found has been admitted by Mr. Mill, his readers having been assured that he regarded it as "questionable if all the mechanical inventions yet made had lighted the day's toil of any human being;" their only effect, in his view, having been that of enabling a greater population to live the same life of drudgery and imprisonment, and an increased number of manufacturers and others to make fortunes." Such is the sad admission of a writer who, in face of the fact that the world at large is now almost as little peopled as it had been in the days of Cæsar, proposes, as the essential remedy for all human suffering, and as preventive of a decline of wages, "a limitation of the size of families in the laboring classes;" that limitation to be brought about, not by means of moral improvement, but by conversion of the "moral obligation" not to have too many children "into a legal one;" courts and judges being authorized to punish all who contribute more than their fair share to the production of beings whose duty it had been made to "subdue the earth and occupy it;" and who have scarcely yet, after the lapse of so many centuries, fairly entered upon the performance of their appointed work.

To whom, then, may we look, hoping to find the men who really *do* profit by the labors of a body of non-consuming slaves so wonderful as that which

ployment which resulted from the gold discoveries, as Canada benefited, and now does benefit, by her close relations with protected neighbors. Both, however, are now preparing for a resistance by means of which to bring about interdependence among themselves, preparatory to claiming a place among the independent nations of the earth.

Britain has brought together? For answer, we have to say that here, as in all other wars, it is to the class embracing the marshals, generals, colonels, and other officers of this industrial army, titled and untitled; to the bankers, brokers, and other middlemen who control and direct the warlike movements above described; to those "wealthiest capitalists" whose predecessors have for centuries been engaged in preventing everywhere outside of England that growth of the habit of association, which finds its cause in development of the individual faculties, and to which alone can we look for increase in the power of mind over matter; for improvement in the relations of capitalist and laborer; for development of artistic taste and mental force; and for growth of that power of self-direction which, wheresoever found, has come as a consequence of having the positives and negatives of society—producers and consumers—brought into more intimate relations, each with every other.*

To what extent, however, do even these officers profit by the ruin of which they are the cause? To that of the hundred millions of pounds now assumed to be annually added to capital, and exhibiting itself mainly in the form of enlargement of that

* "The whole mass of human life, as seen in England at the present day, presents violent extremes of condition, huge mountains of wealth and luxury, contrasted with awful depths of poverty and wretchedness; but in respect of mental ability, we find immense flats of uniformity, dead levels of respectable talent, with scarcely any such thing as originality, freshness, or high creative genius in any department of literature, art, science, or even trade."—Johnson: *England as it is*, vol. 1, p. 217.

non-consuming army by means of which the world at large is to be kept in check; all advance in civilization being thus prevented. Outside of this trifling sum the whole labor of this vast army is WASTED in an unnecessary and relentless "warfare" on the mind and labor of the world for the profit of a trivial number of capitalists, foreign and domestic, who make their home in Britain.* How that army is directed with a view to accomplishment of the results desired it is proposed next to show.

§ 3. The more the diversity of employments, and the greater the competition for the purchase of labor, the more is the laborer enabled to negotiate on equal terms with those who need the commodity

* "As in the Tudor epoch it became an oligarchy of landlordism, now it has become an oligarchy of wealth. The new nobility in this case are the capitalists who, after a temporary antagonism caused by the Corn Laws, and a certain amount of coy resistance on social grounds, have been recognized by the land-owners, and in their turn are decking themselves with the titles of feudal barons, ordering Norman pedigrees with their equipages and liveries, doubling the crush and the deliquescence of St. James's, and thinking it a part of their rights as millionaires to make public honor and national government their family property, and to hand them down, with the other fruits of successful speculation, to their aristocratically educated sons. The great Elizabethan mansions, reared in their day among the hovels of a wretched peasantry, are the graceful monuments of Tudor land-grabbers. England is now being covered with the palaces of this new aristocracy of wealth; piles as huge as the workhouses in which labor ends its days, and filled and surrounded with such hosts of flunkeys, such paraphernalia of luxury as a man of sense and spirit would blush to see devoted to his own enjoyment, much more to create for himself. In the days of the Tudors, when the country was still wild and unprovided, the builders of such piles had at least the excuse of needing room for a body guard and a train of artisans, nor had they entirely given up the ancient custom of eating in the same hall with the crowd that lived under their roof."—Professor Goldwin Smith, in the *Fortnightly Review*, March, 1872.

he has to sell; to wit: physical or mental service. Man thus grows in freedom with every step in that direction; becoming, on the contrary, more and more enslaved with every increase of competition for the sale of service; matter then obtaining increased control over mind, capital more control over labor. So, too, is it with nations, their power for the purchase of the labor of other nations, in whatsoever form, growing with growth of their own power for production, and declining as this last declines; each and all being therefore interested in the prosperity of each and every other. At each and every stage of progress in the one direction man tends more and more to rise in the scale of being, with rapid increase in the demand for those of labor's products requiring the exercise of skill or taste, and exhibiting advance in mechanical or scientific knowledge; progress in the opposite direction, on the contrary, being attended by decline in the demand for such commodities, as well as in power for their production.

In what direction, now, tends the British system? In that of increasing competition for the purchase of labor, with growing tendency toward freedom? Or, is it in that of increasing competition for its sale, the tendency toward serfdom becoming more and more obvious at each and every stage of progress? That the reader may be enabled to answer to himself these questions, his attention is now invited to an extract from a speech of Mr. Ernest

Jones, made some years since on an election ground in Yorkshire, as follows:—

"That system is based on foreign competition. Now I assert, that under the buy-cheap-and-sell-dear principle, brought to bear on foreign competition, the ruin of the working and small trading classes must go on. Why? Labor is the creator of all wealth. A man must work before a grain is grown or a yard woven. But there is no self-employment for the working-man in this country. Labor is a hired commodity, a thing in the market that is bought and sold; consequently, as labor creates all wealth, labor is the first thing bought. 'Buy cheap! buy cheap!' Labor is bought in the cheapest market. But now comes the next: 'Sell dear! sell dear!' Sell what? Labor's produce. To whom? To the foreigner—ay! and to the laborer himself; for labor, not being self-employed, the laborer is not the partaker of the first fruits of his toil. 'Buy cheap, sell dear!' How do you like it? Buy the working-man's labor cheaply, and sell back to that very working-man the produce of his own labor dear! The principle of inherent loss is in the bargain. The employer buys the labor cheap; he sells, and on the sale he must make a profit; he sells to the working-man himself; and thus every bargain between employer and employed is a deliberate cheat on the part of the employer. Thus labor has to sink through eternal loss, that capital may rise through lasting fraud. But the system stops not here. This is brought to bear on foreign competition—which means, that we must ruin the trade of other countries, as we have ruined the labor of our own. How does it work? The high-taxed country has to undersell the low-taxed. Competition abroad is constantly increasing, consequently cheapness must increase also. Therefore, wages in England must keep constantly falling. And how do they effect the fall? By surplus labor. How do they obtain the surplus labor? By monopoly of the land, which drives more hands than are wanted into the factory. By monopoly of machinery, which drives those hands into the street; by woman-labor, which drives the man from the shuttle; by child-labor, which drives the woman from the loom. Then planting their foot upon that living base of surplus, they press its aching heart beneath their heel, and cry: 'Starvation! Who'll work? A half loaf is better than no bread at all!' and the writhing mass grasps greedily at their terms. Such is the system for the working-man. But, electors, how does it operate on you? how does it affect the home trade, the shopkeeper, poor rate, and taxation? For every increase of competition abroad, there must be an increase of cheapness at home. Every increase of cheapness of labor is based on an increase of labor surplus, and this surplus is obtained by an increase of machinery. I repeat, how does this operate on you? The Manchester liberal on my left establishes a new patent, and throws three hundred men as a surplus in the streets. Shopkeepers! three hundred customers less! Rate-payers! three hundred paupers more! But, mark me, the evil stops not here. These three hundred men operate first to bring down the wages of those who remain at work in their trade. The employer says: 'Now I reduce your wages.' The men demur. Then he adds: "Do you see those three hundred men who have just walked out? You may change places if you like; they are sighing to come in on any terms, for they're starving.' The men feel it, and are crushed. * * * But the evil stops not yet. Those men, driven from their own trade, seek employment in others, when they swell the surplus, and bring wages down."

Sad as is the picture here presented, none can doubt its accuracy who may have noted the proceedings in Parliament on every occasion when its intervention has been claimed in behalf of overworked and under-paid men, women, and children, wholly unable to protect themselves, and constantly assured of the existence of a "foreign competition" that forbids attempt at improvement of their condition.* Gloomy as it is, the same painter, were he

* Referring to the question of limitation of the hours of labor, *Quarterly Reviewers* thus speak with the "Proletariat" to which their recent article is addressed:—

yet living, might now present it far more darkly shaded—exhibiting, as he might, the Saxon weaver, the Swedish carpenter, the Belgian founder, the Spanish miner, competing with British workmen for possession of a home market steadily diminishing in its absorptive power, as the poor-house more and more becomes the goal toward which the footsteps of these latter tend.* Compared with their condition, as now constantly described in works of high authority, that of the American negro slave was an enviable one, *his* master having had a direct interest in preservation of his health and life, and

"Now, if the cost be thus increased foreign nations will produce cheaper and undersell us in the articles in which we come into competition with them, and where will our trade and the wages for our artisans be then? And who, that knows how vast a proportion of our industries are supported by foreign demand, dare face the slightest risk of such results?"

The utter helplessness here exhibited on the part of a nation recently so powerful is most suggestive. Very different would this article have been had the writer observed the fact, that the "competition" so constantly alleged to exist is precisely that of the cock-pit, where unfortunate birds are being stimulated by their masters "to pluck out each other's eyes."

* Weight and value of cleaned cotton in manufactures retained for home consumption, as given by Mr. Hoyle in his chapter *On the Falling off in Trade:*—

	Weight.	Value.
1858	lbs. 145,006,000	£ 9,306,163
1859	168,630,000	11,443,371
1860	217,973,000	14,971,330
1867	112,121,000	10,657,861
1868	107,463,000	9,332,629
1869	95,271,000	8,501,737

With a population only 20 per cent. greater than that of the United Kingdom the American Union consumes five times as much cotton. Its mere imports, mainly of the very fine descriptions, are more than two-thirds as much in value as the total British and Irish consumption. See *Ante.* p. 233.

in caring properly for his wife and children; the bleacher, on the contrary, who works his hands, old and young, male and female, a hundred hours a week in a temperature higher than blood heat, knowing well that when *his* slaves die there will be abundant others competing for the places thus rendered vacant in the terrible "dance of death" that is being now performed.*

To what, however, is all this due? How is it that a wretched "proletariat" now occupies the place that had once been filled by men *against whom* the aid of Parliament had so frequently been invoked by the powerful predecessors of those who now own the land of Britain? Let us inquire.

When the Parliament of England prohibited domestic competition for the purchase of Irish wool, and of Irish labor to be employed in its conversion into cloth, it in effect prohibited Irish competition for the purchase of English labor applied to the preparation of those commodities and things requiring the exercise of mechanical skill or artistic taste, for which a prosperous Irish people would have made a market constantly growing in its extent as producers and consumers, positives and negatives, were more nearly brought together; and as agricultural labor necessarily became more and more produc-

* "When I hear of men recommending clubs for recreation, is it possible that they mean cutlers? When is it to be, what part of the day? for there are plenty who work sixteen hours a day and can scarcely live. Why do men insult us like this? To talk to cutlers about recreation is like holding a loaf to a hungry man that is bound, and showing it to him increases his misery by mockery."—*Sheffield Daily Telegraph.* See note to p. 29.

tive. Thenceforth, so far as Ireland was concerned, the English people were to be retained in the condition of mere spinning and weaving machines employed in satisfying the lowest needs of their Irish neighbors, the two co-operating constantly for their own abasement; whereas, under other circumstances, they would have been combining with each other for promotion of the general good. With each and every step in this direction capital increased in its power over labor—matter in its power over mind—with results such as are now exhibited; the poverty and wretchedness of Lancashire weavers and spinners, and their weakness for self-protection, keeping steady pace with those of Irish laborers whose only choice in the past has been that between "land at any rent," on one hand, and "starvation" on the other.*

Later, we find American colonists in like manner to have been deprived of all power for domestic competition as regarded the purchase of wool, or of labor to be applied to its conversion into hats or coats; power for purchase of commodities of a higher order steadily diminishing as competition

* "Every man who will take the statistic spectacles off his nose, and look, may discern in town and country, that the condition of the lower multitude of English laborers approximates more and more to that of the Irish competing with them in all markets; that whatsoever labor, to which mere strength with little skill will suffice, is to be done, will be done, not at the English price, but at an approximation to the Irish price; at a price superior as yet to the Irish, that is, superior to scarcity of third-rate potatoes for thirty weeks yearly; superior—yet hourly, with the arrival of every new steamboat, sinking nearly to an equality with that."—*Carlyle.*

for the sale of wool became more intense, and as labor became more unproductive. Thenceforth Irish and American wool-growers were to be in constant contest with each other for possession of a market whose power for absorption of their product declined as Englishmen became more and more compelled to limit their labors to those required by the spindle and the loom; and more and more deprived of power for engaging in employments requiring exercise of mind and display of taste.

From that time to the present the course has been always onward, and in the same direction, the army of non-consuming laborers—growing constantly in number and force until it now counts by hundreds of millions—having been steadily employed in destroying everywhere outside of England that power of association and co-operation to which alone could English working-men look for such demand for skilled labor and its products as would tend toward full development of their various faculties, and increase of self-directive force. The more that power could be destroyed abroad, the more became the necessity for forcing textile materials on the little market, and for converting a once stalwart people into a nation of mere weavers and spinners, powerless to protect themselves, and constantly compelled to beg for protection at legislative hands. At each and every step there has been increase of competition for the sale of labor in all the countries controlled by the great non-consuming army, accompanied by that constantly diminishing power for purchasing even the ruder products of British labor to which the "proletaires" stand now indebted for that cry of "foreign competition" with which their ears are so invariably dinned when compelled to seek protection against "great capitalists" whose power for mischief grows with the growth of power to compel the earth's people to limit themselves to the rudest works of cultivation; to exhaust their soils by constant export of its products; and to compete in the limited market of England for the sale of their labor in the rude forms of cotton, wool, flax, and hemp, none of which can be made available for human use until after having been passed through mills that by those "capitalists" themselves are owned.

How the English laborer profits by this war of capital on the labor of mankind at large has well been stated by Mr. Ruskin in a paragraph that here below is given, and that is remarkable for its condensation of a great truth which demands consideration at the hands of all who desire to witness that advance in civilization, and that tendency toward peaceful action, which become so clearly manifest among nations whose positives and negatives are being brought into closer connection each with every other, to wit: those which resist with all their force that trading monopoly which controls a great non-consuming army always employed in rooting out civilization where it exists, and preventing its development in countries that have yet to wait for its first appearance.

"Though England is deafened with spinning-wheels, her people have not clothes; though she is black with digging of fuel, they die of cold; and though she has sold her soul for grain, they die of hunger."

In no portion of the world that is controlled by the great army above described does there exist any competition for the purchase of labor, and hence the lamentable state of affairs at home that Mr. Ruskin has so well described.

§ 4. The village shopkeeper rejoices in the prosperity of his customers, knowing that his own profits must increase as, materially and mentally, they grow in wealth and strength. The farmer, his neighbor, rejoices when the mason, the carpenter, and the saw-miller take their places near him; clearly seeing that, while lessening the cost of improvements he may desire to make, their presence will create demand for many of his products that now are wasted. All alike rejoice when the little woollens-mill is started to make demand for the services of women and children now unemployed; and for wool that would otherwise need to seek the distant market. At each and every step in this direction the societary circulation becomes more rapid; utilities are more and more developed; labor grows in value as compared with the commodities needed for consumption; mind gains new control over matter; exchanges become more and more numerous; and men are more and more enabled to combine together for the execution of works likely to be promotive of the common good.

We have here the simple, sound, and practical

political economy at which men are led to arrive who reason from facts to principles. Among these villagers there is probably not even one who has for an instant thought of that "science of the nature of the individual mind," which constitutes, according to Mr. Mill, so "essential" a part of "political philosophy;" and which, in his view, must certainly be mastered before we can hope to arrive at any proper comprehension of the societary movement. What, however, they *do* possess, is that "positive knowledge of the uncultured" which, says Mr. Spencer, "must necessarily underlie the whole theory of science, its progress, and the relations of its parts to each other;" and with which, therefore, we need to commence when, as now, desiring fully to comprehend what are the real and permanent interests of those larger bodies of men of which towns, cities, states, and nations are composed. Doing this, we are led inevitably to the conclusion, that as in this peaceful village each and all profit by the growing wealth of each and every other, so the great nations of the earth should each and all profit by development of the powers, mental and physical, of each and every other; each and all growing in power for self-direction as each and every other more and more obtains power for controlling and directing the great natural forces; the harmony of all international interests being as perfect and complete as we know to be that of the individuals of which nations are composed.

That such harmony does exist; that trading "warfare," such as has been described, is a grave mistake; and, that its effects on those by whom it is made are as injurious and destructive as they are so well known to be on those against whom it is directed, it is proposed now to show.*

The period of American non-resistance which commenced in 1835, and closed with 1842–3, stands conspicuously out as having been that in which the "warfare" of great British "capitalists" had been productive of changes more frequent and destructive that those of any previous one; the general result on this side of the Atlantic having exhibited itself in so entire a stoppage of the societary circulation as to deprive our people of all power for aiding in restoring that which, in like manner, had elsewhere so nearly disappeared.† How great was the destruction which had then been caused, and how much was at its close the British need for foreign aid, are well exhibited in a passage from a work of high authority given here below. After describing the bankruptcies, the ruin, the poverty, and the wretchedness that had fallen on Bradford, Leeds, and Birmingham, the writer thus continues:—

"Of the vast trade in iron which Wolverhampton formerly carried on with the United States, only one-sixth remained. From injuries sustained in the same quarter, Sheffield had lost more than a fourth of its staple industry; wages had declined some

* Slavery is as injurious to the master as to the man. Recent events, indeed, seem to prove that the injury to the dominant class had been even greater than that inflicted upon the subjected one.

† See note to page 232 for evidence of the total disappearance of American credit at this date.

forty per cent., pauperism was doubled, and in the course of five years no less than £20,000 was expended by four trades alone in the relief of unemployed workmen. Transferring ourselves into the woollen districts of Gloucester, Somerset, and Wilts, we meet the same picture. At Frome, from 1831 to 1841, population had considerably decreased, rents were fifty per cent. lower, one-sixth of the houses were unoccupied, and the only item of increase was the poor-rate. Of Bradford, Stroud, Uley, Wootton, the same tale could be told. Comparing the whole county of Gloucester at the two periods just mentioned, we find a diminution of fifty per cent. in the number of looms employed, and the number of manufacturers who still held their ground was less than the number of those who had failed during that short interval. In Coventry one-third of the population was unemployed; in Spitalfields 8000 looms were idle, and 24,000 persons thrown upon parochial relief; in the whole of the metropolis one thousand letter-press compositors and nine thousand tailors were altogether without work. Other trades throughout the kingdom were in the same condition. To visit the iron works of Scotland, the colliers of Staffordshire, the glovers of Yeovil, the carpet-weavers of Kendal, the glass-blowers of Warrington, the shawl-weavers of Paisley, and the flax-spinners of Dundee, would only be to encounter similar proofs of the entire prostration of industry. In Paisley, for example, no less than thirty failures took place within a few weeks; in less than a year two-thirds of the whole number of manufacturers became insolvent, while one-third of a population which is distinguished, even at the north, for industry and ingenuity, were thrown upon the public for support.

"It was, however, in the manufacturing districts of Lancashire that the vials of wretchedness seemed poured out to their last dregs. It is unnecessary, after the facts we have given, to look at the commercial statistics of the case; we will confine ourselves to a few of their social results. In Bolton, only a third of the people were fully employed, the poor-rate had been tripled in five years, fifteen hundred houses within the borough were unoccupied, and wages had experienced an immense decline. We might infer from these facts alone the condition of the working classes, but we have at hand the surer test of figures. The net earnings of 1003 families averaged only 1*s.* 2*d.* a head per week; more than half the beds in their possession were filled with straw; they had among them 466 blankets, not quite one to every ten persons—while only one-half could boast the humble luxury of a change of linen. At Stockport, Ashton, Oldham, and the other large towns, the picture of misery was but slightly varied. In Wigan, the receipts of 2000 families were only sufficient, if all laid out in bread, to buy each individual 22 ounces a day. The spectacle of distress which meets us when we turn to Manchester is projected on a gigantic scale, and filled up with more harrowing details. At the instance of a number of charitable gentlemen, 12,000 families were brought under visitation, and the mass of destitution which was thus brought to light almost exceeds belief. To buy themselves bread thousands had parted with every stick of furniture and every rag of clothing beyond the merest wants of decency. The value of the property thus pledged by the section of the population just mentioned was probably not less than £28,000. 'It was indeed a touching spectacle,' says the philanthropic gentleman to whom we are indebted for some of these facts, 'to see the care with which the poor creatures brought forth from some concealed part of their scanty dress, or from some hidden corner of their wretched abode, the bundles of tickets which formed their humble title-deeds to articles of personal or household use with which, one after another, they had been obliged to part, and of which they had little chance of ever becoming again possessed.'"*

A constant series of financial earthquakes having resulted in destroying the best of Britain's customers, the British people at large were now discharging the bill of costs for the "warfare" of previous years; "wealthy capitalists" meantime augmenting

* Dunckley. *Charter of the Nations.* London, 1854. This work received the gold medal offered as a prize by the Anti-Corn-Law League, thus receiving that body's fullest endorsement.

their already enormous fortunes by taking for themselves, at their own prices, the works of smaller capitalists who had now been ruined; capital thus acquiring new power over labor, matter over mind, and traffic over modes of thought, always the result of irregularity of the societary movement such as is now exhibited in that of Britain.*

§ 5. In the thirty years that since have passed there have been several occasions on which this terrific story has been more or less repeated, stoppage of motion at the financial centre having been followed by ruin and desolation in all dependent countries, and among the less wealthy masters at home; wretched "proletaires," abroad and at home, meantime perishing as a consequence of constantly increasing competition for the sale of their one commodity, physical or mental effort. Desiring, however, to find the crisis most nearly approaching in its horrors to the one above described, we must look to that of 1866, fresh as it still is in the memories of so many thousands of English men and women who then lost their little alls; and in those of the

* "It is not the dress-maker we consider, but the dress; it is not the butcher whose well-being we care for, but the meat; it is not the grocer whose moral and physical condition is the object, but the grocery; it is not the baker or the bread-eater whose sole satisfaction we seek, but the bread. Nor is it even these goods for the sake of their utility to man, it is the goods as saleable commodities alone. The bread may be adulterated, so that it passes and gets the price of a loaf; it is the same with the butcher's meat, it may rot; with the gown, it may be of counterfeit stuff. But it is the *trade* in the gown, the meat, the grocery, the bread, etc., that is the object of existence; and it is that to which our law-makers look, not the tradesman, the working-man, or the consumer."—*Leader*.

"great capitalists" who then, as always theretofore, had profited of the occasion largely to swell their already prodigious fortunes, and in a correspondent degree to diminish competition for the purchase of human service.* Doing this, we find, not only a similar state of ruin and desolation, but also a permanence of stagnation greatly exceeding that of the terrible period above described, proof thus being furnished that societary disease had become more deeply seated than had been the case at any previous period.†

* A case has been mentioned to the writer in which an eminent manufacturer, as a consequence of repeated crises, has been enabled to become owner of all previously competing works throughout a circuit of many miles.

† "The lamentable depression of trade, and consequent want of employment which have recently prevailed, have now reached a most serious magnitude in many of the larger towns, and most of all in London and its far-spreading suburbs. The intensity of the distress in the metropolitan districts has not been equalled in recent times. And the break down of our Poor-law system, despite all efforts of voluntary associations, has been appalling in its results. Not a week passes without several cases of 'deaths from starvation,' duly attested by the verdict of coroners' inquests, where the medical and other evidence reveals an amount of unaided wretchedness and starvation which one would suppose impossible in a civilized country. Men, women, and children dying from sheer famine in the heart of the wealthiest city in the world!"—*Blackwood's Magazine*, April, 1870; article, "*The State, the Poor, and the Country.*"

Never before had the Government had occasion to utter a cry of distress like that uttered in a circular dispatch addressed to the Governors of British Colonies by Earl Granville, in April, 1870, from which the following is an extract:—

"The distress prevailing among the laboring classes in many parts of the United Kingdom has directed public attention to the question of Emigration as a means of relief. It has been urged on Her Majesty's Government that while there are in this country large numbers of well-conducted and industrious laborers, for whom no employment can be found, there exists in most of the colonies a more extensive demand for labor than

To whom, now, in her distress, could Britain look for help? To any of her dependents? Assuredly not, each and all of these now finding themselves in a condition closely correspondent with that occupied by Americans in 1842. To whom, then, *did* she look? To that American Union for whose destruction throughout the previous half dozen years she had labored with an earnestness not readily to be surpassed. *From* whom was the so much needed aid obtained? From that Union which, happily for England, had five years previously re-entered upon a policy of resistance by means of which a growing interdependence among its people had given the strength required for enabling it not only to look with calmness on the storm then raging throughout the British Islands, but also to take therefrom an amount of merchandise till then without a parallel, paying therefor in the gold that was there so greatly needed.*

the laboring class on the spot can supply. The result of emigration would therefore, it is said, be equally advantageous to the emigrant and the colonies—to the former, by placing him in a position to earn an independence; to the latter by supplying a want that retards their progress and prosperity. Under the circumstances, Her Majesty's Government are anxious to be furnished with your opinion as to the prospects which the colony under your government holds out to emigrants, both of the agricultural and the artisan class."

* Forthwith, on reception of news of the crisis the Treasury vaults were opened, and gold to the amount of twenty or thirty millions sent abroad to aid in sustaining British credit. The "British produce and manufactures" sent in that year to the United States amounted to twenty-eight and a half millions of pounds sterling, exceeding by nine millions, or $45,000,000, the average exports of the four closing years of the non-resistant period, 1857–60. Further than this, all received in 1866 was paid for; whereas, of that received in those other years no inconsiderable

To the aid thus rendered was England then indebted for great alleviation of the troubles under which her people then so severely suffered. But for that they would probably have thrice exceeded those of any previous period. It is indeed scarcely possible to conceive of a state of things more awful than that which would have been presented had the dependence of the Union on foreign traders been as great as that which had existed in 1842 and 1857.

Wholly forgetful of the aid thus rendered; and as wholly unable to appreciate the fact that for it they had been indebted to the resistant policy of 1861; those traders have since spared no expense in the effort for re-establishing here the system under which they themselves had so severely suffered in all the periods in which Britain's great army of non-consuming laborers had proved successful in crushing out the American domestic commerce.

§ 6. The more that matter tends to take upon itself the form of a true pyramid, the greater is its tendency towards stability and permanence. The more, on the contrary, it tends to take that of an inverted one the greater is the danger to all in any manner whatsoever, material or social, therewith connected. In this latter direction it is that British policy tends, and therefore is it that all in any manner thereto subjected so severely suffer by her frequent and rapid changes; those, on the con-

portion went to swell the British account of American bad debts. The bankruptcies of the Union in 1857 were for $299,000,000; whereas, those of 1866 amounted to but $53,000,000.

trary, who refuse to be so subjected, growing steadily in wealth, strength, and power.

Such being the case with her dependents, how is it with herself? Let us inquire.

The basis of a true social pyramid is to be found in a prosperous and intelligent agricultural population. Have the labors of her hundreds of millions of non-consuming slaves tended toward further elevation of the stalwart and intelligent men of earlier date? Have they not, on the contrary, tended to substitute therefor a "proletariat" which, whether in the field, the mine, or the workshop, is becoming daily more and more dependent on its masters; and daily less fitted for entering into competition with the people of other nations for production of commodities demanding exercise of taste or intellect? That such is the fact has been a thousand times admitted; the artistic and mental powers of these "proletaires" declining daily as the grand army of the "great capitalists" grows in numbers and in force. Looking next to those material forces which constitute the base of the industrial pyramid, we find these "proletaires" busily engaged in exhausting the stores of coal and ore; and so compelled from year to year to go to greater depths, thereby incurring greater risks, that already it has become more profitable to look abroad for ores of various kinds than to draw from mines at home; each and every step in this direction rendering more and more helpless the unfortunates who are too poor to seek refuge in other lands whose people resist this pernicious and destructive system.* With each, British society tends more and more to take the form of an inverted pyramid, and hence it is that crises become so steadily more enduring and more destructive, both at home and abroad.

What, then, of the future? For answer to this question the reader needs but to remark, that notwithstanding the wars with which Germany and America have recently been so much afflicted, mind in both is obtaining increased power over matter—labor increased power to negotiate on equal terms with capital; whereas, in the comparatively peaceful Britain the power of capital over labor has in the last decade much increased, the growth of pauperism having kept steady pace with that of the fortunes of "great capitalists" who control and direct the non-consuming hosts.† In both the former the social edifice takes daily more and more the true pyramidal form; that of the latter, on the contrary, becoming from year to year more top-heavy and more dangerous to all around, whether states or people, capitalists or working-men. Let this exhaustive

* Vast quantities of iron ore are now expected to be supplied from Spain at less than the cost of obtaining them at home, giving large employment to low-priced Spanish labor at the further cost of that of Britain. What Chilian labor has already done for Cornish men, that of Spain is now about to do for those of Cumberland.

† "The severance between the rich and the poor is to me an even sadder thing than the wretched state of the labor market. I can fancy a remedy possible for the one, I can foresee no remedy for the other. The gap between them seems widening every day, as trade and land fall into the hands of large capitalists, who absorb all smaller concerns, all smaller holdings." —*Rev. Brooke Lambert.*

policy be continued, and the day will then prove to be not far distant when Britain will be required to take her place among the merely secondary powers of the world; thereby verifying the suggestion of Lord Macaulay here below given, and furnishing proof conclusive that destructive as had been the "warfare" on foreign peoples, it had proved still more destructive to the British nation itself—farmers and laborers, peers and peasants.*

§ 7. For the evils above described where may the remedy now be sought? Such is the question that has for many years been asked, receiving at successive periods widely different answers, but always with the same result, to wit: a daily growing tendency of the toiling millions, whether in the field or the workshop, whether male or female, young or old, in the direction of that "proletariat" at which they are now admitted to have arrived. Half a century since, Catholic emancipation and representative reform were regarded as panaceas for societary disease. Later, the world was assured that the millenium would be close at hand could the corn-

* "I remembered that Adam Smith and Gibbon had told us that there would never again be a destruction of civilization by barbarians; the flood, they said, would no more return to cover the earth. And they seemed to reason justly, for they compared the immense strength of the civilized part of the world with the weakness of that part which remained savage, and asked from whence were to come those Huns and Vandals that were again to destroy civilization? Alas! it did not occur to them that in the very heart of great capitals, in the very neighborhood of splendid palaces, and churches, and theatres, and libraries, and museums, vice, ignorance, and misery might produce a race of Huns fiercer than those who marched under Attila, and Vandals more bent on destruction than those who followed Genseric."

laws but be repealed. Quite recently the same results were to be obtained by means of a much more widely extended suffrage. Still, however, the movement has been in the same direction; pauperism having grown with great rapidity; and governmental difficulties having much increased. Where, then, shall the panacea now be looked for? To the ballot, answers one; his neighbors simultaneously asserting that what is needed is that schools be increased in number; that industrial education be established; that the Church be disestablished; that the Government become the great landlord, the universal rent-collector; that all future increase in the value of land be confiscated to the public use; and so on, the prescriptions being almost as numerous as are the doctors who so confidently believe themselves qualified for treating the various sores which now distress the body politic.

With great respect for the eminent gentlemen to whom the English people stand indebted for such prescriptions, we here suggest for their consideration the ideas, that the obstructions they would thus remove are but the flowers and fruits of a tree whose roots are much diseased; and, that so long as that shall continue to be the case their labors must prove as vain as had been those of the reformers by whom they had been preceded. Seeking to restore the social body to a state of health they need to study the disordered root. That this may advantageously be done we here present some figures drawn from official tables quite recently given to the world by the Treasury Department, as follows:—

Of the exports of British produce and manufactures for the decade 1861–70, there went to the British Possessions in the first of those years £42,-000,000, and in the last £52,000,000; the increase having been less than 25 per cent.

To other foreign countries whose policy has, to a greater or less extent, been in accordance with English teachings, there went in 1861, £41,000,000; and in 1870, £64,000,000; the increase having been 56 per cent. To those countries which have in the past opposed a determined resistance to the monopoly system, there went in 1861, but £42,000,000; whereas the amount in 1870 was £83,000,000; exchanges with those countries having thus almost doubled.*

That the movement above described is still onward, and with accelerated force, is shown in facts just now given to the world, to wit: that the exports to resistant countries had risen in 1871 to £106,000,000, thus exhibiting a further increase of

	1861.	1870.
* Russia	£ 3,041,000	£ 6,991,000
Germany	12,968,000	20,416,000
Netherlands	6,434,000	11,220,000
Belgium	1,925,000	4,481,000
France	8,920,000	11,811,000
U. S. America	9,064,000	28,335,000
	£42,352,000	£83,254,000

The Netherlands in this respect are little else than an outport of Germany. The existing French tariff is more intelligently resistant than that of the United States.

28 per cent.; those to non-resistant ones showing no increase whatsoever. The former have now grown to be 47½ per cent. of the whole, the latter meanwhile declining to 52½ per cent.

At the opening of the decade, commerce with the countries of resistance was little more than a third of the whole amount. In the last year it has been nearly half of the whole.

Comparing now the present with a more distant period, we find that, notwithstanding the gold discoveries of Australia, and the large export thereto of British men and women; notwithstanding, too, the great expenditure on roads in Canada and India; the exports to British colonies have grown so very slowly that the £17,000,000 of 1840 have become but £51,000,000; whereas those to the resistant countries above referred to have grown from £19,000,000 to £106,000,000.

Having carefully studied this exhibit the reader may now, perhaps, be led to the conclusion, that the chief employment of the hundreds of millions of non-consuming slaves who constitute the essential British army has been that of crushing out the power of the world at large to make demand for the labors of millions of men, women, and children now employed in the mills and mines of Britain; and compelled to daily competition with each other for employment, at starvation wages, at the hands of the "wealthy capitalists" to whom those mills and mines belong. Further than this, he may, perhaps be led to ask if the "Science of Exchanges," that has now replaced the humane and Christian-like teachings of Adam Smith, might not more properly be styled the "Science of preventing Exchanges by means of Annihilation everywhere of Power for producing Commodities to be made the Subjects of Exchange"? That he will be so, we feel assured, whensoever he shall have studied the further figures that will now be given, as follows:—

The last decade has been favorable to India to an extent that can scarcely ever again be looked for, the cotton famine having given to its people a market at high prices for a great commodity that previously had been a drug; and yet, the increase of power to compete for purchase of the products of British labor has been less than £3,000,000, or $15,000,000.* Throughout the whole century the force of Britain's great army of non-consumers has been brought to bear on that unfortunate country, yet is its whole power of purchase now but 70 cents per head; that, too, in great measure limited to cotton that had been forced to travel half round the world in search of spindles and looms operated by people so poorly paid that the market for cotton made by the population of the British Islands, rich and poor, male and female, averages but about three

* The cause of this will readily be understood when the reader sees that the whole quantity of India cotton converted into yarn, in 1871, was but 202,000,000 pounds, the equivalent of about 440,000 American bales; the world at large, through Great Britain, thus making on India but six times the demand made on Texas and Alabama by the few mills of the little city of Lowell, with its 40,000 inhabitants mainly engaged in other pursuits.

pounds per head.* Here, as everywhere, the "competition," of which so much is said in Parliament, would seem to have had little other object than that of deciding which of the two could accomplish most in the direction of diminishing the productive force of the other, thereby lessening the power to make exchanges. Let us now suppose the British people to arrive at the conclusions, that the past had been one long mistake; that the world was not meant to be a scene of universal discord; that there really *was* a harmony of international interests; that all would be benefited by the adoption of measures calculated to enable the unfortunate people of India once again to combine together for enabling each and all to find a market for service, physical and mental; that in this manner a beginning should be made in the direction of bringing societary positives and negatives into orderly arrangement; and that there should thus be generated a productive force in some degree approaching that which in so brief a period has been brought about in Germany and Russia; and in others yet more brief in these United States on each and every occasion of resumption of the resistant policy; let us, we say, suppose all these things, and then inquire what might then reasonably be looked for as the results most likely to be obtained.

Were this done, would there not be thus created a demand on Britain for machinery that would make

* See *ante*, p. 257. The American consumption per head is nearly five times as great.

demand for both physical and mental effort greatly superior in its quality to that now required for spinning and weaving the trivial quantity of cotton now converted? Would it not make demand for Englishmen fitted to operate machinery, and to instruct the Hindoos themselves in this necessary work; and would not this tend toward diminution of competition for the sale of British labor? Would British operatives not then consume more Indian rice and cotton, and would not India then make greatly increased demand for the infinitely varied productions of British skill and taste? Such, assuredly, would be the results; society thereafter tending in both countries toward greater steadiness and regularity of movement, with constant diminution of the necessity for maintaining armies, and for crushing out rebellions.*

More than half a century has now elapsed since Mr. Canning boasted of having, as he said, "called a new world into existence;" having freed from Spanish domination the whole of the wonderful region that

* Among the most intelligent and energetic advocates of the existing system was Mr. Wilson, so long editor of the London *Economist*. The day, however, came when he found himself placed in the financial direction of India, and then but little time was needed for satisfying him that, in the absence of a resistant action, Indian labor could not be made productive. To the end that it might so be made, he imposed a duty of ten per cent. on foreign cottons; but the clamor among the officers of Britain's non-consuming army became so great that he was compelled to abandon his poor subjects to the tender mercies of men who were even then rejoicing at having suppressed diversification of employment, and competition for the purchase of labor, "from Smyrna to Samarcand." Since then, the Government has been compelled to heap internal taxes on the heads of poor Hindoos who can find no market for their labor; and with what result has been already shown in the note to page 82, *ante*.

extended northward from Magellan's Straits to the western boundaries of these United States. Throughout all that period the great British army, so often above referred to, has been engaged in trampling out the associative power where it previously had existed, and prevented it from anywhere arising, the result exhibiting itself in the facts, that labor has everywhere been wasted; that ignorant and idle men have been always and everywhere ready for revolution; that mines have everywhere remained unwrought; that agriculture has made no progress; that schools have had little or no existence; that labor has remained unproductive throughout a land abounding in the material required for production of the greatest wealth; and that, as a necessary consequence, the power of an almost continent to pay for the labor of the United Kingdom is now less than two dollars a head for that kingdom's population. Had a different course been pursued; had efforts been made to naturalize there the arts of civilization; had societary positives and negatives been encouraged to come together; it is safe to say that the demand of that continent for products requiring display of taste, and exercise of intellect, would be tenfold greater than that which now exists for those of the wretched operatives who have been so steadily falling to the condition of a mere "proletariat;" indebted, as we are assured, "for being employed at all," to "sacrifices" of their masters in the effort "to gain and keep possession of foreign markets."

Of all the South American States, Brazil is the one whose progress has been least affected by wars or revolutions; and yet so trivial has been the growth of power to purchase the products of British labor that her demands therefor, in 1870, were less than $30,000,000; the increase of the decade having been less than $4,000,000.

With the gold discoveries of Australia her demands rose speedily to $70,000,000. Since then, her population has largely grown, yet does she furnish now a market for less than $50,000,000; that, too, with every reason for believing that if the non-resistant system be maintained it must decline from year to year.

Having studied the figures that have thus been given, the reader may now with advantage compare the wonderful power exercised by Britain with the pitiful results obtained. From the days when Adam Smith cautioned her against conversion of her people into "a nation of shop-keepers," her grand army of non-consuming laborers, now counting by hundreds of millions, has been everywhere engaged in destroying that power for combination in whose absence there can be no economy of human labor; no development of individual faculties; no increase in the productiveness of human effort; no tendency toward orderly arrangement of societary positives and negatives; no increase of power for self-direction; no advance toward civilization; the general result exhibiting itself in the fact, that the few resistant, and therefore advancing, nations of the world promise soon to make demand for the produce of British labor greatly larger than that of all those non-resistant peoples for whose subjugation have been expended almost countless millions, with a waste of human happiness and life, at home and abroad, the like of which the world has never known. Having reflected on these facts, he may perhaps be led to the conclusions, that equally with individuals nations profit by improvement in the condition of their neighbors; and, that the British policy, so long maintained in defiance of the advice of the great father of political economy, has been a mistake so great as to make it doubtful if it may not prove to have been a fatal one.

The engineer who constantly and largely adds fuel to his fire, meanwhile increasing the weights upon his safety valve, prepares thus for seeing his engine, and perhaps his ship, blown to atoms. This, however, is precisely what the British people now are doing, adding daily to the non-consuming army while seeking everywhere to destroy the power either to purchase British products, or to absorb the labor thus deprived of the employment to which it had been accustomed. Happily for them, the resistant nations of Europe do much toward correcting the error that thus is indicated; American resistance co-operating largely by making increased demand not only for the products of labor, but also for the surplus labor itself. *But for this, the explosion would long since have come.* In now endeavoring to bring about a change, Britain is seeking to destroy the friends who, thus far, have done her the largest service.*

§ 8. Thirty years ago we were assured that repeal of the corn-laws would be followed by peace and harmony throughout the world, and the elevation of the laborer wheresoever found. So far, however, have we been from witnessing verification of those agreeable prophecies that the quarter century of "free corn" has been so marked by wars, rebellions, famines, financial and commercial crises, that whig and tory journals now unite in representing the condition of the toiling millions at home as being worse than at any previous period; and, that a "proletariat" now definitively occupies the place which even so late as the days of Adam Smith had been filled by men the like of those who had followed to the field Cromwell, Hampden, and Montrose.

Thirty years since the contributions of those millions toward maintenance of that "warfare" on the labor of the outer world to which, as they are being

* Of all economic phrases, the one now most in fashion is that from which we learn that the laws of *supply* and *demand* are paramount, and are therefore to be held accountable for all the evils above described. The "labor market" being oversupplied, "why," it is asked, "should not that commodity fall as beef and mutton do?" The laborer perishing for want of proper food, "why should he not suffer for the sin committed by his parents in bringing into the world beings for whom no place had been prepared at the table of the great Giver of all good?" To none of these persons does it seem to occur that paralysis in India, Australia, or America, tends to produce paralysis in Britain; that deprivation of power to sell labor in any one country tends, more or less, to produce similar effects in all the countries of the world. To none does it occur to remark that rapidity of the societary circulation anywhere tends, more or less, to cause similar rapidity everywhere.

now assured, they themselves had always been "indebted for being employed at all," but little exceeded £20,000,000=$100,000,000. Now, they are more than twice that sum; consumers of tea, coffee, spices, beer, spirits, and other commodities of which the "proletaires" are chief consumers, furnishing more than £40,000,000 as their contribution toward carrying on a war for reducing the laborers of the world, *themselves included*, to the condition of mere hewers of wood and drawers of water for the benefit of a few thousand persons who control and direct that non-consuming army which grows in number and in force as the British community becomes more pauperized.*

Of the great increase of expenditure thus exhibited, not even a single shilling has been needed in reference to the countries by which this barbarizing system has been opposed; and yet, as has been shown, their power to purchase British labor and its products has more than quintupled in 30 years.† To what then, have those contributions been directed?

* Total expenditures for	1837,	excluding	interest on	the debt,	£21,600,000
" "	1870,	"	"	"	42,000,000

Of this nearly the whole appears to have been paid by articles mainly consumed by those who have labor *to sell*. The contributions of those who need *to purchase* labor appear to do little more than pay interest on debts contracted for maintenance of war upon the general industry of the world.

† Of the exports to British American possessions, and to Mexico, a considerable proportion is intended for smuggling into the United States. So, probably, it is with regard to the resistant countries of Europe. This allowed for, British exports would be very nearly equally divided between the two hundred millions of the world's people who are growing rich by means of resistance, and the nine hundred millions who are being impoverished by the officials of the great non-consuming army of Britain.

To nothing whatsoever but the maintenance of sailors, soldiers, diplomats, officials of all descriptions, engaged in carrying into practical effect the decree that labor was to be everywhere subjected to capital, mind to matter; and in the effort at giving to bankers, brokers, and other traders, all the profit resulting from an import of raw materials to be returned in a finished form to the places whence they had come; the men, women, and children employed in the work of conversion, and taxed to the whole amount required for paying such officials, meantime gradually declining toward that degraded condition for whose indication the word "proletaire" is now so much in use. In the world's history there can be found no case in which the forces of a nation have been so well directed toward destruction of the foundation on which its power had rested, subjugation of labor abroad having been accompanied by similar subjugation of labor at home; matter thus obtaining increased control over mind in all the countries, home and foreign, subjected to the British system.*

* That the reader may more clearly understand how it is that "proletaires" abroad and at home are made to co-operate for their own subjugation, and for maintenance of the power of capital over labor, a few facts derived from Mr. Jenkins's recent work "The Coolie," are here presented, as follows:—

The population of British Guiana is, in round numbers 150,000, a third of whom are coolies who have been "recruited"—in other words, kidnapped—in India, by aid of *official documents* certifying that men can readily earn from 50 cents to $1 per day; the real fact being that their average earnings are less than half the lowest of those sums; those of women and children being low in proportion.

For superintending exchanges between home and colonial laborers the

Thirty years since the military and naval expenditures required for maintaining order among subjects at home, and dependents abroad, were covered by a dozen millions, or $60,000,000. Now they are twice that; and yet, at no time since the days of the Armada has the idea of invasion so seriously occupied the British mind. Then, Britain stood first among the nations of the world. Now, she is

claims of the home government on the products of this little colony are as follows, to wit:—

On 90,000 hogsheads of sugar	£676,000
" 30,000 puncheons of rum	1,769,000
" 15,000 casks of molasses	26,200
	£2,471,200

Equal, in dollars, to 12,356,000; *giving no less than $82 per head of the total population, old and young, rich and poor, male and female, sick and well, as the contribution of these wretched people toward maintenance of officials engaged in carrying on the "warfare" above described on the labor of the world, foreign and domestic.* The larger the tax thus imposed the less is the power of the English proletaire to purchase colonial products, and the lower must be their prices. The less those prices, the less is the colonial laborer's power to purchase the products of English labor; producers and consumers suffering thus alike by reason of the necessity for paying men employed in keeping them asunder. Such is the *free-trade* system now so strongly commended for the use of the world at large.

Absentee proprietorship being almost universal, the direction of the colony is, of course, in the hands of agents who accummulate fortunes and control the local legislature. The governor of these few thousand people has a salary of $25,000 per annum, toward whose payment the wretched coolie contributes by means of a tax on his rice of $5 per ton; the wealthy legislator's coal meantime paying but 36 cents per ton. Working hours vary from 12 to 22, overwork not being generally paid for. Discontented, the poor laborer sometimes rebels; thereby earning months of imprisonment at hard labor. At times he is led to ask the aid of Justice; with little effect, however, beyond that of satisfying himself that the good dinners and fine wines of the rich tend strongly toward closing the eyes and ears of her ministers to the complaints of miserable bondmen like himself. Notwithstanding all this, slavery is, as we are assured, abolished in all the countries under the sway of Britain.

overshadowed by powers which have sought independence by means of measures calculated for establishing domestic interdependence; for diffusing among their several peoples the knowledge required for obtaining control and direction of the great natural forces, and for themselves the power of self-direction. Then, Russia, Prussia, and America, scarcely anywhere found place in the Palmerstonian correspondence that has now been published. Now, as a consequence of having created political and industrial pyramids, they constitute a trio capable of assuming an almost entire direction of the world at large.

Of all the communities the world yet has known there has been none that, as an outpost of Europe, and as freed by insular position from dangers of invasion, has enjoyed advantages equal to those of that British one whose past and present have been here examined. Of all, there is none that so early learned to control the great physical forces of nature. Of all, there is none in which that control has become so great. Of all, therefore, it is the one that has held in its hands the greatest power for evil or for good. That it has not been used in this last direction is very certain, there being no community in the world that has profited of Britain's friendship; no one that has *not* profited when making determined resistance to the monopoly its capitalists have sought to institute; no single one in which the power for self-direction—for freedom of thought, speech, and action—has not grown in the ratio of emancipation from the control that half a century since appeared to have been so well established. Widely different would be now the case had her course been other than is here described; diffusing intelligence and a love of peace, instead of seeking everywhere to prevent advance in civilization. Then, it would have resulted in securing to her troops of admiring friends. Now, she is as friendless to a degree scarcely to be exceeded; and hence the extreme anxiety in reference to "Alabama Claims."

§ 9. "A nation," says a distinguished English writer, "which resists in principle the just social impulses natural to its history and position—which discourages those honorable social emotions with which men regard the proceedings of men—is sure to find, sooner or later, that the forces which she has thus kept back from their regular modes of expansion have found outlets and channels within her own borders less regular, and therefore more perilous and uncertain. Adherence simply to negative precepts [*laissez faire*] seldom obtains in any sphere of policy without being, in a greater or less degree, the mark of all the rest. And it is so here. * * * We fail to set to work with will and indomitable resolution at the task of relieving Ireland from anarchy. We fail to perform, or even to see clearly the pressing necessity of performing, the positive duty of devising some means, and means there must be somewhere in the minds of men, for finally uniting Ireland to ourselves and removing our heaviest reproach in the eyes of Europe.* We are innocent, again, of wishing the poor and ignorant any ill, but there is no sign of a diligent and determined national action to ameliorate their condition and diminish their numbers. And so on throughout all the spheres of government. To that watery self-satisfaction which comes of the discharge of negative duties we are entitled.

---

*Still more is the case with regard to India; and still greater is the danger that there threatens in the not distant future.

* * * An energetic, full-blooded, and generous initiative is no more seen. Under our present set of social conceptions it is forever impossible. The idea of the two great functions of the State is torpid or extinct. The nourishment of a strong and harmonious national life, in the first place; in the second, the maintenance of a wise, unselfish, and upright international life; these are the two ideas at present fatally wanting in English policy. * * * If anybody thinks that we are playing that powerful and beneficent part in our relations with Europe to which our material strength and moral disinterestedness entitle us, or rather which they demand from us, let him reflect that the counsels which Lord Stanley is said to be pressing both at Berlin and Paris count for about as much as if they came from the cabinet of Sweden or of Portugal."—Morley; *Fortnightly Review*, May, 1867.

Forty years since there was in Britain what was called a "reform;" limited, however, to changes of form, leaving the national policy untouched. Other changes in the same direction have since been made; yet others now being called for. Admitting that they be obtained, will they, *can they*, prove more successful than those by which they had been preceded? Assuredly not, if it shall continue to be held that "those who advocate the rights of labor are digging the free-trade grave." Not, if the grand army of non-consuming laborers shall continue to be employed in compelling the poor and weak communities of the world to confine themselves to the work of raising rude produce for distant markets, the proper work of the barbarian and the slave, and of those alone. Not, if the work of her great army shall continue to be that of destroying the power of other states and nations to become competitors for the purchase of British labor. Not, if Britain shall continue to set at defiance, as she now daily does, that great law which teaches that duty to both God and man demands of us to do by others as, under similar circumstances, we should wish them to do by us. Not, if it shall continue to be a cardinal maxim of British policy, that "the end sanctifies the means." Not, if that policy shall continue to be directed toward prevention everywhere, at home and abroad, of that orderly arrangement of societary positives and negatives, producers and consumers, by which alone there can ever be brought about that domestic interdependence which so evidently tends toward maintenance of harmony at home and peace abroad. Not, if it shall continue to be overlooked, that in the social as in the physical world the more rapid the circulation the greater is the force exerted in whatsoever direction it may be most required. Not, if the wonderful power now accumulated in the hands of a few thousand bankers and traders shall continue to be given toward increasing the power of capital over labor, matter over mind; thereby preventing advance of civilization in all the countries subjected to British influence.

§ 10. M. de Tocqueville, writing to Mrs. Grote, speaks as follows:—

"In the eyes of the English, that which is most useful to England is always the cause of justice. The man or the government which serves the interests of England has all sorts of good qualities; he who hurts those interests, all sorts of defects, so that it would seem that the *criterion* of what is right, or noble, or just, is to be found in the degree of favor or opposition to English interests. The same thing occurs to some extent in the judgment of all nations, but it is manifested in England to a degree which astonishes a foreigner. England is often accused on this account of a political machiavellism which, in my opinion, not only does not exist any more, but rather less, than elsewhere."

That this is so none can doubt who have had occasion to observe how little disposed are Englishmen, when abroad, to look at anything through other spectacles than those with which they had left home provided. Further, however, than this, they are generally most unwilling to make themselves familiar with any idea that comes in conflict with their accustomed modes of thought. In proof of this, many facts could readily be adduced; none, however, quite so remarkable as that presented in the case of Mr. Sumner's celebrated speech, discussed by all England, yet read by none; no single British journal having ventured on its reproduction. Commenting on this trait of the English character, and replying to an assertion of Mr. Helps as to "the safety of holding exceptional opinions," a writer in the Contemporary Review* asserts that, greatly lauded as had been Mr. Mill's work "On Liberty," no newspaper "would dare to fly in the face of Providence" by reproducing certain of its expressions in regard to Mormonism and the "peculiar institution" of the lately Confederated States. Further even than this, he says that "*so* safe is it to hold exceptional opinion in this coun-

* Holbeach, Article, *The State and Scientific Morality*. Number for April, 1872.

try, that if Mr. Mill had dared to utter at a public meeting that particular protest of his, neither his years, nor his achievements, nor his disinterested career, nor his special detestation of the 'peculiar institution,' would have saved him from being mobbed, to the danger of his limbs or his life; and that in six days it would have been generally believed in England that he had been in the habit of retiring to Avignon every year expressly for immoral purposes." Recent proceedings within and without the walls of Parliament seem, certainly, to prove that the view thus presented has something better than mere "assumptions" on which to stand.

Such being the case, it can scarcely here be hoped that they now, or at any future date, will find themselves prepared to enter carefully on consideration of the great fact, that they control the operations of hundreds of millions of non-consuming laborers, to none of whom does the world stand now indebted for even the slightest movement in the direction of advancing civilization, whether abroad or at home.

On whom now rests the responsibility for the disturbed condition of the world; for a growth of material at the cost of mental power among hundreds of millions of the world's people; for a growth of capital at the cost of labor so clearly obvious among those millions; for an arrest of civilization everywhere? Assuredly, on those bankers, brokers, traders, and manufacturers who control a power so wonderful for good, if rightly used; so infinitely promotive of evil when used as thus far has been the case with that at their command.

Russia, Germany, and the American Union, seek to bring about an orderly arrangement of the positives and negatives of which their societies are composed; and with every stage of progress the social edifice tends more and more to take that form which secures the greatest strength, stability, and permanence. Britain, on the contrary, seeks everywhere to prevent such arrangement from coming into existence; and at every stage of progress her own edifice tends more and more to take upon itself a form similar to that of defunct societies of the past.*

* "It is dawning on the public mind," says a journalist of the day, "that the growing of corn is a waste of time, land, labor, and capital;" "that it is the manufacture of meat that keeps English agriculture alive;" that, "this must be made the prime object;" and, "that all agricultural operations must be made subservient to it."—The Scottish Highlands have been converted into sheep walks and deer parks, their former occupants having been sent to seek for refuge in Glasgow wynds or Canadian wilds. Ireland is being converted into a great pasture field, preparation therefor having been made by repeated famines and enforced emigration. England is now, as we are told, to follow suit, cattle cultivation having become more profitable than that of corn. With each and every step thus far made in that direction pauperism and vagrancy have grown; capital has obtained more and more control over labor; matter over mind. So must it be in all the future, the societary edifice becoming from hour to hour more and more top-heavy, and the day of its downfall coming more and more near to hand. Never until now has it been supposed that a permanent society could be established on a basis of sheep and cattle, shepherds, deer stalkers, and cattle drivers.

CHAPTER X.

MIND AND MORALS.

§ 1. THE early man, wheresoever found, has been nature's slave. Unable to compel the earth to labor in his service, he is seen to have been everywhere dependent on his power to appropriate such of her products as she may have volunteered to place at his command. At times, the supplies thus furnished exceeding his demands, he has gorged himself to repletion, leaving then to perish what remained unconsumed. At others, they have been short, and then he has suffered from want, even when not perishing of famine. From hour to hour the question has been as to what he *could* do, and not of what he *would;* power for self-direction having thus far not attained to even a shadow of existence. Matter reigns supreme, whether in his relations with the earth on the one hand, or with his fellow men and women on the other; the only law then recognized being that of mere brute force, and the weaker portions of the race, infant or aged, male or female, having no rights that the strong of body need respect. The "fittest"—*i. e.*, those whose physical forces are greatest—now almost alone survive the strife for life; this, too, at a moment when millions upon millions of acres, capable of affording nourishment to tens of millions, are wandered over by mere thousands of wretched beings who have yet to acquire such development of mental force as is required for enabling them to combine together for any purpose beyond that of trapping birds or beasts; or of plundering, even where not murdering, others who have been more fortunate in the chase, or more provident in reference to its products.*

Passing now onward, we find men gradually increasing in numbers and in the power to combine together for waging that war with nature by whose result it is to be determined whether they are to re-

* Mr. Malthus exhibits the strife for life as growing with increase of numbers and consequent increase of power to co-operate together for compelling the physical forces to labor in man's service. Following in his footsteps, Mr. Darwin gives us a "survival of the fittest," and a trampling out of the weak, as necessary consequences of inability of the earth to meet the large demands upon her of an increasing population. In the natural course of things, directly the reverse of this *should* be the case, the strife for life being greatest when a thousand acres scarcely furnish the supplies required by a single individual; and least, when a single well-cultivated acre can be made to furnish more than all the food he needs; greatest, when men are least able to combine together for obtaining power over the natural forces, and least when combination has enabled them to control the wonderful powers of steam, and to exchange ideas on the instant with other men from whom they are separated by broad oceans and almost pathless continents. That so it *is*, is proved by the fact, that man is daily rising in the scale of being in those countries whose population grows most rapidly, to wit: Russia, Germany, and these United States; as steadily declining in all those countries of the East in which population decreases with correspondent decline of the associative power. Where, however, may we look to find the "fittest?" In Ajax, representative of mere brute force and of the early man? Or, in the wise Ulysses, representative of mental force, and of the present man? In this last most certainly: yet is it in the wealthiest societies—in those exercising the largest power for controlling the natural forces—there will be found, as we are assured, the most conclusive proof of the truth of the Malthusian and Darwinian laws. As has been already said, modern theories find little support in social phenomena, when these last are carefully analyzed.

main her slaves, or to become her masters. By slow degrees they acquire power to compel her to furnish food in return to labor applied to cultivation, and now the weaker portions of the family are enabled to contribute to its support, the stronger continuing to follow the chase. At once the former, male or female, young or old, becoming less and less burthens to be carried, acquire a value in the eyes of the latter that before they had not possessed; and thus, as necessary consequence of a growing power of mind over matter, the first step toward EQUALITY is made.* Passing further, other natural forces are now pressed into man's service; the canoe, susceptible of being managed by weaker hands, enabling him to control the powers of water and of wind. At another step, the ox and the horse are reduced to service, lessening the need for mere muscular force, and making that new demand for the powers of the physically weak by means of which they are to be brought more nearly on a level with the strong and active. Numbers still increasing, we meet the village community, in which each man has a house wherein to shelter his wife and children while uniting with his neighbors in cultivation of their common land; inter-dependence thus growing at

* "The only school of manners," says a recent English writer whose name the author now fails to recollect, "is equality; equality, in which no sense of the defects in the political constitution of the United States, or of the evils which beset a vast commercial community and one annually flooded by a torrent of half-civilized immigration, no manifestations of anti-British feeling, however disagreeable to one whose heart is with England, can prevent a fair observer from recognizing the true element of social morality and social happiness to all, but especially to the rich."

each and every stage of progress toward that control of the natural forces which tends to lessen his dependence on nature's merely voluntary action, and more and more enables him to exercise a power for self-direction.*

As mind thus grows in power for the control of matter societary positives and negatives are brought more and more nearly together; kindly feelings become stimulated into action; the husband clings more closely to the wife; the parent feels more and more responsibility for proper care of the little beings by whom he is surrounded; the master becomes more careful of his servant; he himself, meantime, more and more acquiring that feeling of SELF-RESPECT which, while forbidding that he should truckle to the strong, prompts him to hold out a helping hand to others who, being poor and weak, stand in need of aid from those who influence the

* "When the Germanic tribes first advanced from the life of wandering shepherds to dwelling in more settled habitations, they divided the land upon which they settled among the communities of which they were composed, but reserved a superfluous portion as the common possession of the whole tribe. * * * Of the portions of land allotted to the separate communities, a part in each was divided off on which to build dwellings. To each house a smaller piece of land was attached, large enough for a courtyard, a garden, and a bit of pasture, on which the flocks took refuge in case of need, all of which, together with the house, was inclosed by a hedge. The dwelling-places of a community were generally together, and all surrounded by a village hedge. These inclosed dwelling-places were the only strictly private property of the Germanic landowner, over which he had unlimited control. He had only the use of the rest of the land in common with the other householders of the district."—Nasse. *Village Communities*, in the *Contemporary Review*, May, 1872.

movements of the community of which they are component parts.*

At each successive triumph of mental force, from the distaff to the power-loom and the telegraph, inter-dependence grows; at each, there is increased substitution of the fingers and the eyes, the skill and taste, of the weak woman for the muscular force that thus far had been required; at each, the strong man becomes more and more dependent for his comfort and his ease on the wife he has chosen as his life's companion; at each, as steam is substituted for the human arm, his own labors are lightened; the demand for service becomes more regular; service becomes more and more productive; the strong and the weak are enabled more and more to come together on terms of strict equality, with constant growth in all of that feeling of HOPE which stimulates to exertion; truth, honesty, and loyalty come to be held in higher esteem; the real MAN—the being made in the image of his Creator, and capable of acquiring power for self-direction—stands more fully out, prompt on one hand to assert his rights, and on the other, to recognize the fact that there are duties to be performed toward those around him, however humble their condition, and however little they may be capable of self-defence.

* "Natural affections and instincts are the most beautiful of the Almighty's works; but like other beautiful works of His, they must be reared and fostered; or it is as natural that they should be wholly obscured, and that new feelings should take their place, as it is that the sweetest productions of the earth, left untended, should be choked by weeds and briers."—*Dickens.*

The tendency toward equality is thus in the direct ratio of the growth of power in mind to control mere brute matter; that itself growing as the societary positives and negatives are more and more brought into orderly arrangement, and as the interdependence of the various parts becomes more and more complete. The more that tendency, the more rapid is the development of that self-respect—or moral feeling—which forbids our doing to others that which, under similar circumstances, we should *not* desire them to do by us.*

§ 2. Of all the nations of whose history we have

* Mr. Herbert Spencer assumes the existence of a "moral sense" that is "at work universally;" then making of it the foundation on which to raise a sociological structure. (*See Social Statics*, London, 1851, pp. 23, 25.) Further reflection, however, might perhaps satisfy him that its development into vigorous and active life is as much a consequence of sound social action, as is that of a plant a consequence of sound agricultural action. Desiring to understand how results such as he has described have been, or are being, brought about, we need to commence with that "positive knowledge of the uncultured" which, as he assures his readers, "constitutes the basis of all true science." (*See* note to p. 34, *ante.*)

Reasoning downward, metaphysicians have been led to assume the endowment of each and every member of the human race, however ignorant and helpless, with a power of will (see p. 105, *ante*) and an intuitive perception of reciprocal rights and duties, of neither of which, beyond the merest germs, can any trace be found in miserable beings, past or present, all of whose energies have been, or are, required to be given to the search for food. Reasoning upward, from facts to principles, we find a self-directing force, and a self-respect, coming gradually into existence and growing side by side—aiding and aided by each other; the process closely resembling that by means of which male and female plants concur in the work of reproduction.

Of the "utilitarian" doctrine, now somewhat in vogue, little need here be said; it being but fit associate of a *science* by means of which the world is being taught that buying cheaply and selling dearly are, and ought to be, the chief aims and ends of man's existence.

any record, that of England is the one whose movements have been most freed from outward interference; and, as a consequence, that one which may most advantageously here be studied. Of the eight centuries that have elapsed since the Norman Conquest, there have been no less than six (1066–1660), throughout which the tendency was uniformly toward giving to mind increased control over matter; toward equality among men; and toward increased development of that feeling which prompts to respecting other's rights while demanding like respect for those of which we ourselves claim the exercise. Directly the reverse of this was the picture presented across the Channel, the freemen of an earlier period having been there replaced by a proletariat whose members had no rights which those above them were required to respect; and whose eldest sons were regarded as more noble than the rest, the presumption being that they were of noble birth and might properly claim to be descendants of their lords and masters. As a consequence of this, rebellion, in 1358, gave to the world all the horrors of the *Jacquerie*, but left the starving wretches more enslaved than they had been before. But little later (1381), came the Wat Tyler outbreak of England, and its suppression; followed, however, by a grant of the laborer's demands which, though silent, proved so effectual that at the close of the century the small freeholders, and probably the tenants, had become "such important personages in the social order," that they were held fitted for exercise of large political rights soon after embodied in an election statute.*

Thirty years later, sons of such men, self-reliant and self-respecting, fought at Agincourt, "representatives of a nation of heavy archers and spearmen;" divided by no artificial lines from those above them, and therefore constituting, says Macaulay, a "democracy the most aristocratic," standing side by side with an "aristocracy the most democratic" that the world had ever known.† Moving on in the same direction, we find the wars of the Roses to have had little other effect than that of promoting the circulation upward of men of low condition to take the place of those above them who had lost their fortunes and their lives on fields of battle. Tewksbury and Towton, Barnet and Bosworth, witnessed the gathering together, and the subsequent dispersion, of considerable bodies of men; "and yet," says Macaulay, "at the close of another week the farmer was driving his team, and the squire was flying his hawks over their fields, as if no extraordinary event had interrupted the course of human life."

Throughout that period, which looks so very stormy when studied in histories that record little beyond the doings of kings and nobles, the nation

* Rogers, *History of Agriculture*, vol. i. p. 8. *See* also note to page 235, *ante*.

† "The small freeholder was, in his way, better off than the lord. He was liable to no wardship and its concomitant waste; he was unrestrained in the disposition of his property; in his parental authority, in the selection of occupations for his sons, and the gift of his daughter's hand."—*Ibid.* p. 67

grew steadily in wealth and power, with constant improvement in the material condition of the people at large, and a constant increase, on the part of both poor and rich, of respect for each other's rights.*

§ 3. Manufactures being then but few in number, and field labor constituting the laborer's main dependence for employment, the demand for service was irregular; very many persons being needed at harvest time for whom at other periods little employment could be found.† Suppression of the monasteries now throwing upon the public large numbers who had been accustomed to derive their support from the revenues of the Church, and vagrancy and crime much increasing, resort was had for their repression to the severest and most disgraceful modes of punishment. Wealth and population, however, continued to increase, bringing with them better modes of thought; these latter exhibiting themselves in efforts, continued throughout

* "Comines was one of the most enlightened statesman of his time. He had seen all the richest and most highly civilized parts of the Continent. He had lived in the opulent towns of Flanders, the Manchesters and Liverpools of the fifteenth century. He had visited Florence, recently adorned by the magnificence of Lorenzo, and Venice, not yet humbled by the confederates of Cambray. This eminent man deliberately pronounced England to be the best governed country of which he had any knowledge. Her constitution he emphatically designated as a just and holy thing, which, while it protected the people, really strengthened the hands of a prince who respected it. In no other country, he said, were men so effectually secured from wrong. The calamities produced by our intestine wars seemed to him to be confined to the nobles and the fighting men, and to leave no traces such as he had been accustomed to see elsewhere, no ruined dwellings, no depopulated cities."—*Macaulay.*

† See page 12, *ante.*

the reign of the Virgin Queen, at instituting measures for securing support for the "impotent poor," and employment for those capable of work. The whole at length culminated in the celebrated act known as the 43d Elizabeth; one whose passage furnished proof conclusive that steady growth of the power of mind over matter had brought with it a national feeling of self-respect which now compelled recognition of the fact that those who by reason of disease, of wounds received in their country's service, or of acts of God, had been rendered incapable of self-support, might rightfully look to their more fortunate neighbors for aid; and that to afford it was the bounden duty of these latter.

The peaceful reign of James was one of so great prosperity that the legal rate of interest was reduced from 10 to 8 per cent., to the great advantage of sellers of mental or physical force; mind thus gaining further power over matter. Societary positives and negatives were now assuming a more orderly arrangement, and the demand for service was becoming from year to year more regular, with steadily diminishing tendency toward looking to the public for support; and as steadily increasing disposition on the part of those in power not only to give full effect to the act of Elizabeth, but also so to amend it as to make it more efficient for accomplishment of the good work that had been proposed. While providing thus for bodily needs, much attention was given to suppression of those habits of intemperance which theretofore had so greatly tended toward promoting the growth of pauperism, vagrancy, and crime.

Throughout the five and thirty years which intervened between the death of James and the restoration of the Stuarts (1625 to 1660), there prevailed an activity of life such as never had before been known. Occasionally, and locally, interrupted by military operations, these latter exercised little more influence over the general social movement than had been the case in the wars of the Roses above referred to. Daily more and more did societary positives and negatives tend to take their places by each other's sides, with constant increase of productive power; and with such a growth of wealth that while capital declined in its control over labor to the extent of a reduction of the rate of interest from 8 to 6 per cent., labor so rapidly advanced toward equality with capital that wages, whether by the day or year, nearly doubled in the half century from 1610 to 1660.* As a consequence of this, the poor law question ceased to be agitated; the feeling of self-respect meanwhile so extending itself throughout all portions of society as to enable England to exhibit to the world such an army as is here described:—

"That which chiefly distinguished the army of Cromwell from other armies was the austere morality and the fear of God

* See Nicholls's History of the English Poor Law, vol. i. p. 284. Since that date much richer lands have been brought under cultivation, and machinery has so much improved that agricultural labor has become very many times more productive, yet have money wages been but very slightly changed.

which pervaded all ranks. It is acknowledged by the most zealous Royalists that, in that singular camp, no oath was heard, no drunkenness or gambling was seen, and that, during the long dominion of the soldiery, the property of the peaceful citizen and the honor of woman were held sacred. If outrages were committed they were outrages of a very different kind from those of which a victorious army is generally guilty. No servant girl complained of the rough gallantry of the redcoats. Not an ounce of plate was taken from the shops of the goldsmiths."—*Macaulay.*

When but a little later, at the Restoration, these men came to be disbanded, there was exhibited a spectacle the most remarkable of its kind the world till then had ever known, 50,000 men having quietly returned to the bosom of society in the manner here described:*

"In a few months there remained not a trace indicating that the most formidable army in the world had just been absorbed into the mass of the community. The Royalists themselves confessed that, in every department of honest industry, the discarded warriors prospered beyond other men, that none was charged with any theft or robbery, that none was heard to ask an alms, and that, if a baker, a mason, or a wagoner, attracted notice by his diligence and sobriety, he was in all probability one of Oliver's old soldiers."—*Ibid.*

Such were the men protection against whose ancestors had been so often asked of Parliament by those who so recently had been their lords and masters. The growing tendency toward equality of rights had brought with it a mutuality of respect.

* That like causes tend to produce like effects would seem to be proved by the close resemblance to this presented by the dissolution of American armies, counting almost by millions, in the summer of 1865.

§ 4. Of that "positive knowledge of the uncultured" which constitutes the basis of all true science, there is no single part of more universal acceptance than that which prompts to seek development of physical force by means of steady and careful use. "So universally," says a writer of the day,

> "has this principle been recognized and acted upon, that in every half-civilized community, or under all circumstances which give an unquestioned superiority to bodily strength, we may find evidences of special care to foster and increase it. The 'games' obligatory upon the little Spartans, the exercise of 'gentle youth,' during the age of chivalry, the description given by Mr. Catlin of the early training of the American aborigines, are all instances in point; and all show the recognition, under circumstances widely dissimilar, of the principle that the powers of the human organism are bestowed only on possibility—to be developed by culture, or to dwindle under neglect."*

Than the view thus presented nothing could be more strictly accurate, applicable as it is to all human powers, whether those of the body, the mind, or the heart. What, however, is the process by aid of which it had been provided that development of these latter should be attained? Seeking a reply to this question, the reader needs but to study carefully the brief review that has been above presented. Doing this, he can scarcely fail to see that growth of moral feeling had kept steady pace with that increase of mental force which had been required for bringing the physically weak to a level with the physically strong, thus establishing throughout society that inter-depend-

* *Popular Science Monthly*, June, 1872, p. 130.

ence which constitutes the base of independence and tends to diffuse that feeling of self-respect which prompts to recognizing in others those rights for which we claim respect as being inherent in ourselves. Of all the nations the world yet has seen, there has been none in which that process had been so fully carried out as was the case in England in the period above described; and hence it was that, notwithstanding her limited extent and the almost triviality of her numbers, she so early occupied a distinguished place among the powers of the earth.

Louis X. proclaimed (1315) that Frenchmen should of right be free. But little later, Englishmen strenuously asserted for themselves their right to freedom.* The one proposed to *sell* to wretched proletaires certain paper rights. The others peacefully *took possession* of substantial rights, thus daily more and more approaching to an equality with their recent masters. The societary edifice of the one nation, as a consequence of perpetual wars at home and abroad, daily more and more assumed the form of an inverted pyramid; and hence the demoralization that existed down to the days of the Reign of Terror. That of which the others were the base, comparatively peaceful in its action, took more and more the form of a true pyramid; and hence that development of mind, and that improvement in morals, which exhibited themselves in the community which gave to the world the founders of the great Republic of the West.†

* See page 235, *ante*.

† See page 236, *ante*.

Closing here a chapter of the world's history more worthy of careful study than any other that stands recorded, we now enter upon a brief sketch of the crusade that has since been waged of matter against mind, capital against labor, the initial steps of which are found in the prompt expulsion of thousands of ministers of religion;* in the crowding of gaols with men who differed from the ruling powers in their modes of religious thought; and in the re-establishment of semi-serfage by means of an "Act of Settlement."

CHAPTER XI.

MIND AND MORALS.—(*Continued.*)

§ 1. Of all the gospels, that which stands first in chronological order is the one by which it is provided that "in the sweat of his brow" man "shall eat bread;" that one which has been so well denominated the BLESSED GOSPEL OF WORK; that which imposes a necessity for such exertion of man's various faculties as shall enable him to obtain control of the various natural forces, and for himself a self-directing

* "The dominant party exultingly reminded the sufferers that the Long Parliament, when at the height of power, had turned out a still greater number of Royalist divines. The reproach was but too well founded; but the Long Parliament had at least allowed to the divines whom it ejected a provision sufficient to keep them from starving; and this example the Cavaliers, intoxicated with animosity, had not the justice and humanity to follow."—*Macaulay.*

force fitting him to come before the world a real MAN, free of speech, thought, and action; capable of directing, with advantage to himself and to all around him, the wonderful power to be thus acquired. To the end that this may be fully brought about, it is needed always that he be enabled freely to circulate among his fellow men; exchanging thoughts and services; imparting to others what he knows and acquiring from them ideas that as yet he had not possessed. At every stage of progress in that direction we obtain further proof of the universality of that great law by which it is provided, that the more rapid the circulation the greater must be the force exerted.

Turning now again to England of an early period, we find that so limited had been then the self-directing force that her people were being sold to slavery in Ireland. At a later date, they are found attached to the soil and liable to be sold with, though not without it. At another stage of progress, we see them freely circulating throughout the land, the "industrious poor" seeking employment wherever it might be had;* the "impotent poor" being alone restricted to the parishes on which they had a legal claim for aid. Under that new system on whose consideration we are now about to enter, strangers of lower degree than that made manifest by a contract for paying £10 of yearly rent—four times more than was then usually paid by men of the working classes—might at once be seized upon and re-

* Eden, State of the Poor, vol. i. p. 174.

turned to the places to which they legally belonged; there to accept such wages as employers might be disposed to grant. As a consequence of this stoppage of the societary circulation marriage was much discouraged; bastardy increased with great rapidity; capital grew in its control over labor; and the question as to what should be done with the poor and unemployed, so rarely presenting itself in the records of that previous half century in which labor had doubled in its price, became now more the subject of discussion than it had been at any previous date. From year to year the line dividing the sellers and buyers of labor became more clearly marked, with diminution of self-respect in all; the sovereign becoming pensioner of France; maids of honor obtaining grants of Englishmen to be sold to slavery in the tropical regions of the west; and the laborer becoming more and more chained to the soil on which he had been born, more and more compelled to look to his parish for support.

Following closely on the revolution of 1688 we find Locke attributing the great increase of pauperism since the restoration to the "relaxation of discipline and corruption of manners" which had then commenced; and which, as the reader has seen, had come as necessary consequence of reduction of the toiling millions to a state of semi-serfage. Not discouraged, however, by such results of a system that was giving to capital daily increase of power over labor, to matter power over mind, Parliament now pledged itself to the manufacturing capitalists of

England that it would "discountenance the woollen manufacture of Ireland;" simultaneously therewith prohibiting intercourse between that country and the world at large, except so far as it might be carried on by means of British ships and shops, carriers and traders. Irish labor having thus been placed at the mercy of distant capitalists by whom, as a cardinal principle of their religious faith, it was held that Irishmen had no rights which they themselves were bound to respect, we next find that principle applied to their fellow countrymen beyond the Atlantic, and with such effect as to have brought about, at a later date, a rebellion which, as we know, found its termination in a revolution.

Trade now reigned supreme. Colonies were to be acquired by fair means or by foul, that their unfortunate people might be compelled to contribute three-fourths of the product of their labors toward augmentation of the fortunes of British capitalists.* What were the measures by aid of which they *were* acquired, is shown in a passage from Macaulay, relative to India,† already placed before the reader, and exhibiting a course of action worse even than that of Pizarro and his successors toward the people of Peru, so strongly censured in all English books.‡

What was then the state of morals among the higher classes at home is shown in the facts, that

* See page 198, *ante.*

† See page 240, *ante.*

‡ In 1789, a minute of the Viceroy in Council declared that one-third of the province of Bengal was a "jungle, inhabited only by wild beasts."—*Torrens's Empire in Asia*, London, 1872, p. 77.

while lesser robbers purchased seats in Parliament, and were everywhere welcomed, the greater Clive, loaded with crimes, was rewarded with a peerage; that the wife of Hastings, "captain-general of iniquity," as he was styled by Burke, was "received at court, and with every mark of distinction," by the wife of George III.; that, he himself, despite the evidence furnished of his guilt, was not only acquitted, but congratulated thereon by "nobles, prelates, courtiers, soldiers, India directors, and friends of every sort;" East India proprietors, participants in the plunder that had been obtained, then voting him a large amount of money "for the purchase of Daylesford, the darling object of his boyish dreams, for which he had gone so far afield, and waded so deep in sin and shame."*

What was the character of that Hindoo people which was then being ruined, may be inferred from facts thus given by Mr. Torrens:—

"The Governments of Southern Asia, when we began to meddle in their affairs, were strangers to the system of penal laws, which were then among the cherished institutions of our own and nearly every other European State. While no Catholic in Ireland could inherit freehold, command a regiment, or sit on the judicial bench; while in France the Huguenot weaver was driven into exile beyond sea; and while in Sweden none but Lutherans could sit as jurors; and in Spain no heretic was permitted Christian burial;—Sunis and Sheahs, Mahrattas and Sikhs, competed freely for distinction and profit in almost every city and camp of Hindustan. The tide of war ebbed and flowed as in Christian lands, leaving its desolating traces more or less

* *Torrens's Empire in Asia*, London, 1872, page 182.

deeply marked upon village homesteads or dilapidated towers. But mosque and temple stood unscathed where they had stood before, monuments of architectural taste and piety, unsurpassed for beauty and richness of decoration in any country of the world." * * * "Though the supreme Governments were nominally absolute, there existed in the chieftains, priesthood, courts of justice, the municipal system, and above all, in the tenant-right to land, numerous and powerful barriers in the way of its abuse." * * * "Property was as carefully protected by laws as in Europe, and their infringement sometimes cost a prince his throne or life." p. 107.

Passing now over the terrible chapters of Ireland and the western Indies, abounding as they do in proofs, that "the end" had always been regarded as "sanctioning the means;" that the object sought had been always that of increasing the distance between producers and consumers, positives and negatives, with constant increase in the power of capital for control of labor; that the few were steadily becoming greater, and the many less; we may now look to the state of things among the British toilers themselves, as follows:—

Steam had been then impressed into the service of the capitalist, with steady displacement of the laborers who thus far had been employed. Mineral coal was being applied to the manufacture of iron. The services of wind were being daily more and more rendered available for the propulsion of ships, and the transport of merchandise. The addition, in these and other forms, thus made to the productive power might at the close of the century be counted as having been the equivalent of not less than that of sixty to eighty millions of men; and *ought* to have been marked by steady improvement of the laborer's condition. Unhappily, however, the direction of the social machinery having fallen altogether into the hands of "wealthy capitalists," each and every increase of power had brought with it new regulations having for their object the further subjection of mind to matter, labor to capital;* the result exhibiting itself in the facts, that the miners and salters of North Britain were held as property; that miners and artisans everywhere had so far become subjected to their masters that they could neither freely apply their labors at home nor go abroad; that the settlement laws were being enforced with greater strictness; that crime so much abounded that, notwithstanding a frequency of capital punishment without parallel in any nation claiming to be civilized, the prisons became so crowded as to have produced a necessity for one of larger dimensions at Botany Bay; and that, as the poor became from day to day poorer and less self-dependent, the rich became richer and more luxurious; the gulf dividing masters and men becoming thus daily wider, with daily diminution of self-respect in all.

Such was the state of things when the Rev. Mr. Malthus, minister, as he professed himself to be, of of an all-wise and all-merciful God, gave to the world a theory by means of which he satisfied the rich and powerful that the misery and wretchedness

* See page 27, *ante*.

by which they were everywhere surrounded were necessary results of error in divine laws; that population tended to increase faster than food; that all attempts at alleviating the miseries of the poor would prove to be sad mistakes; that rise in wages could have no effect other than that of stimulating the growth of numbers; that they themselves were free from responsibility for any and all these things; and, that they might, therefore, properly and safely eat, drink, and make merry, while closing their eyes to the fact that the condition of their fellow-men was deteriorating in the direct ratio of their own increased power for controlling the great forces that had been given by his Heavenly Master for man's use and service.

The poor, on the contrary, were advised that the cause of all their trouble was to be found in an excessive tendency toward contraction of the marriage tie and consequent increase of numbers; and that for any improvement of their condition they must look to abstinence from that mode of association which, above all others, tends to stimulate into activity the best feelings of the human heart. Simultaneously, however, with this prescription came further regulations on the part of the chiefs of the great non-consuming army, each and all tending toward annihilation of that feeling of self-respect to which alone could we look for temperance in that direction, or in any other whatsoever.* Faith in the future—HOPE—brings with it prudence in the pre-

* See p. 27, *ante*.

sent. Despair, such as was being then produced, brought with it, as yet it brings, that recklessness of which the reverend gentleman's disciples still so much complain.

Of all evidences of the demoralization that then existed there is none more conclusive than that which is furnished in the prompt acceptance of a doctrine so detestable, and so directly contradicted by all real facts, as is the Malthusian Law of Population.

§ 2. Throughout the present century the story of India has continued nearly as it had commenced, presenting, as it does, a constant series of violations of the most sacred pledges given to native chiefs and princes;* plunder of their widows and children, carried so far even as confiscation of personal ornaments in cases where their money values sufficed as warrant for such proceedings;†

* How a right-minded Englishman, and there have been many such in India, viewed the conduct of his Government in one of the many cases of the kind above described, is shown in the following passage given by Mr. Torrens in the volume above referred to:—

"I have all along said, and ever shall say under all circumstances, and in all societies and places where I may hear it alluded to, that the case of the Amîrs is the most unprincipled and disgraceful that has ever stamped the annals of our Empire in India. No reasoning can, in my opinion, remove the foul stain it has left on our faith and honor; and as I know more than any other man living of previous events and measures connected with that devoted country, I feel that I have a full right to exercise my judgment and express my sentiments on the subject. I cannot use too strong language in expressing my disgust and sorrow."—*Sir Henry Pottinger.*

† "Our historians are never weary of reprobating the sudden and summary decree of Bayonne, in which Napoleon informed the world that in the Peninsula the house of Bourbon had ceased to reign, and in repro-

oppression of the weak wheresoever found;* and "warfare" of "great capitalists" on defenceless native industries that for duration and extent, and for the ruin of which it has been the cause, is wholly without parallel in the annals of the world.† That "half the labor of India goes to waste," we are assured by Mr. Chapman,‡ a most reliable witness, there being no more strenuous advocate of the maintenance, and even extension, of the existing depend-

bating the duress under which an imbecile sovereign was driven into an act of formal abdication. And many severe things have been justly said of the pictures taken from the Escurial, and of the bronze steeds borne away from the Piazza of San Marc. But at least Napoleon cannot be upbraided with stealing or selling the gems and apparel of his victims. It was bad enough to appropriate the sword of Frederick, but Napoleon, unscrupulous though he was, would have been ashamed to make away with rings and necklaces of the Prussian Queen, and then to have put them up to the highest bidder among the brokers of the capital. If vice loses half its hideousness by losing all its grossness, it may likewise be said that public violence becomes more hateful when it is tarnished with the reproach of base cupidity. At the very time when the Queen's Lieutenant-General in Asia was thus playing the freebooter and auctioneer, our Foreign Secretary was addressing to the court of St. Petersburg remonstrances against the sequestration of the revenues of certain Polish noblemen upon suspicion of their complicity in seditious designs. Well might the minister of the Czar scornfully retort: 'Physician, heal thyself.'"—*Torrens*, p. 374.

* "At first the lieutenant of the Queen demands restitution of £990, and an apology, from the governor of a Burmese town; without giving time for fair discussion, he raises the terms of his requisition to £100,000 and an apology from the Burmese Court; and while a temperate letter from the King, offering to negotiate, remains unanswered, he hurls an invading force against his realm, drops all mention of compensation or apology, and seizes an extensive province, with threats of further partition of his dominions if he will not pay the expenses of the war, the world being asked the while to believe that all has been done unwillingly, in self-defence.—*Ibid.* p. 356. Numerous other cases of a similar kind are given by Mr. Torrens.

† See note to p. 202, *ante*.

‡ See note to p. 249, *ante*.

ence of Indian people on British ships and mills; and thus does he exhibit a loss that might alone account for the poverty and wretchedness which now exist. When, however, we come to study the case more carefully, we find that it has not been even half presented, no reference having been made to the waste of mental force which has resulted from an almost total annihilation of that power of association which everywhere else has followed so closely upon the creation of a diversified industry; and to which Britain herself stands to-day indebted for that control of the natural forces which has given to her for every man, woman, and child of the United Kingdom from fifteen to twenty laborers who make no demand for food, raiment, shelter, or education.* As a consequence of this waste of force, material and mental, the whole product of the labor of 120,000,000, if not even 150,000,000, of people, occupying a territory not exceeded in its capabilities by any other in the world, has a money value of but £300,000,000 (Torrens, p. 408), or, at the utmost, $12 per annum per head; and out of this trivial sum, each one is required, on an average, to contribute not less than $2 for payment of in-

* At a mill in the writer's neighborhood ten hours' work gives 33,000 miles of cotton thread, seven tons of coal furnishing all the power required. To do this by hand would require the labor of 70,000 women, or more than half the number of men, women, and children that, as shown by the census, are employed in Philadelphia in her various manufactures, the value of whose product is $400,000,000; *more than one-fourth of the total product of the vast population of British India.* In the one, mind is constantly obtaining new control over matter, labor over capital. In the other the power of capital is constantly on the increase.

terest on a debt contracted by their masters for accomplishment of their own especial purposes; for maintenance of officials, civil and military, now employed in preventing any growth of diversified industry, chief among whom is a Viceroy with an allowance of $250,000 per annum; and for payment in Britain of numerous persons whose performance of similar *service* in the past is recognized as having established claims on the oppressed and plundered Hindoo race.*

Students of Roman history are accustomed to regard proconsular administration as the perfection of all that is discreditable and destructive in the way of government; yet is the little finger of British traders in India more oppressive and more ruinous than were the hands and arms of Verres and Fonteius, as exercised in Sicily and Gaul. That these latter largely robbed the subject peoples is very certain; equally so, however, is it that, unlike to what has so steadily been done in India, they never struck at the sources of production. Happily for the provincials the Senate sought dominion, and not a

* "Nineteen-twentieth of our taxes are annually, monthly, it might almost be said daily, respent among us; while of the revenues of India a large portion is exported hither to furnish us with extra means of comfort and of luxury. The manure is thus continually withdrawn from Eastern fields to enrich the island gardens of the West. It has been variously estimated that, irrespective of interest on debt, six, seven, and even eight millions a year are drawn from India, to be spent by Englishmen either there or at home. The process of exhaustion may be slow, but it is sure. . . . We have laid the people and princes of India under tribute, and after a century of varied experiments, the only limit of exaction seems to be the physical capacity of the yield."—*Torrens*, p. 408.

mere monopoly of trade and manufacture. Nowhere do we find it following up rebellions, thus provoked, by measures so mercilessly vindictive as those given on a former page.* Among its members there were many who had "itching palms," but nowhere does it stand recorded that they had invoked the aid of law for compelling subject nations to deal with them for pins and needles, cloth and iron.† Nowhere does the Government present itself as allied with smugglers for forcing, despite all opposition, supplies of poison on a neighboring and friendly nation, thus making itself from hour to hour more dependent on a trade debasing to its subjects, and destined in the end to prove a cause of utter ruin.

Look where we may in the history of British India, we find no evidence of the existence on the part of masters of that self-respect which might be expected to cause, among their slaves, any feeling other than that servile one which everywhere is manifested; and which is no more natural to the Hindoo than it is to the Japanese or Caucasian races. What the former is, he has been made. What, as a consequence, may be looked for in the future, is thus exhibited by the Viceroy who but now has paid, by aid of the assassin's dagger, for some of the crimes of the Government of which he has been the head:—

"A feeling of discontent and dissatisfaction exists among every class, both European and native, on account of the constant in-

---

* See page 141, *ante*.

† See note to p. 87, *ante*.

crease of taxation which has for years been going on. My belief is that the continuance of that feeling is a political danger, the magnitude of which can hardly be over-estimated; and any sentiment of dissatisfaction which may exist among disbanded soldiers of the native army is as nothing, in comparison with the state of general discontent to which I have referred. . . . We can never depend for a moment on the continuance of general tranquillity; but I believe that the present state of public feeling, as regards taxation, is more likely to lead to disturbance and discontent, and be to us a source of greater danger, than the partial reduction which we propose in the native army can ever occasion. Of the two evils I choose the lesser."—*Lord Mayo.*

§ 3. Eighty years since Lord Macartney was sent to China to sue for further grants of commercial privilege. There arrived, he found a government strong in the affections of a people counting by hundreds of millions, and happy in the enjoyment of peace and comfort to an extent greater than could be found among any similar number on the surface of the globe. To-day, the once happy country is to a great extent a scene of desolation consequent upon repeated wars from abroad that have demoralized the Government; and rebellions at home resulting from the demoralization that had thus been brought about. Among all the transactions of the century, monstrous as have been those of India, those of Britain with China stand out conspicuous as having been most unworthy of any community claiming on one hand the possession of any feeling of self-respect; or on the other, a right to the respect of the world at large. So believing, we refer the reader to the appendix for a brief view of the case as recently presented in one of the most respected of English journals;* here contenting ourselves with presenting a passage from a letter of Lord Elgin, written during his second mission to China, as follows:—

"Can I," he writes to Lady Elgin, "do anything to prevent England from calling down on herself God's curse for brutalities committed on another feeble Oriental race? Or, are all my exertions only to result in the extension of the area over which Englishmen are to exhibit how hollow and superficial are both their civilization and their Christianity?" . . . "The tone of the two or three men connected with mercantile houses in China, whom I find on board, is all for blood and massacre on a great scale. I hope they will be disappointed." . . . "No human power shall induce me to become the oppressor of the feeble."†

"That capital may obtain its proper remuneration," said Mr. Huskisson, "labor must be kept down." So we are now assured by those English colonists of the neighborhood of the Southern Cross, who are so busily engaged in enslaving the defence-

* See Appendix D. The reader will there see that the Chinese Government has been compelled in self-defence to sanction the cultivation of the poppy; and that, as a consequence, there has been so large a diversion of land and labor from the production of food as to threaten famine.

† Letters and Journals of Lord Elgin, London, 1872.

The reader who may desire to become acquainted with the extraordinary extent of the yet latent mineral resources of China, and with the course likely to be pursued in advancing "the common cause of civilized mankind," will do well to study an article on those subjects in the *Quarterly Review*, for April last. Doing this, he will scarcely fail to arrive at the conclusion that the trade which had been "created by force, naked physical force," would still "look to force in some form, latent or expressed, for the result." China is there shown to be very weak, and there is no reason for supposing that self-respect will stand in the way of re-enaction of the drama that has been so well performed in India. Here, as there, the end must be regarded as sanctioning the means.

less people of all the lesser islands; cheap labor being regarded as essential for enabling them to compete in British markets with the products of such labor elsewhere employed.* Look thus where

* See British Quarterly Review, January 1872, article: *Kidnapping in the South Seas.*

"A feeble effort has recently been made in the British Parliament to induce Government to stop the Chinese coolie trade. It failed, for the ostensible reason that the depot from which the victims were shipped was a Portuguese colony, although the parties concerned in the infamous traffic were English, and the majority of the coolies sent to British Guiana. (See page 285, *ante.*) *The Pall Mall Gazette* acknowledges that the pretence of emigration bonds is the merest farce and fraud. It is never intended that the wretches shall be paid or returned to their native country.

"The British conscience was but so lately sensitive with regard to our short comings in the matter of negro slavery that its present obtuseness must be noted, even by Englishmen, as a remarkable case of sudden ossification. Who does not remember the thrill of indignation that ran through all England at the mere mention of American bondage; the angry protests in Parliament; the shudder of horror with which Dickens and the other literary voyagers touched the accursed thing; the acclaim of welcome which greeted Uncle Tom, and the contributions from pounds to pennies which flowed in upon its author?

"Where, however, are they now? In Queensland and British Guiana slavery and the slave traffic exist in as brutalized shapes as in the worst days of negro degradation. Besides this direct participation, 20,000 coolies are annually exported from China by a system which the slightest interference on the part of England could prevent, but this is now refused. 'Who touches British soil, is free,' was the boast but a few years since. Now, British colonies are so many caverns of death; like the lion's den of old, many footsteps go in, but none return.

"*The Pall Mall Gazette* argues on the right side of the question, but with a noticeable lack of appeal to any of the principles of justice and humanity which were held to be all-powerful in reasoning with us. Not a word is said of the rights of the heathen coolie, as one of God's creatures, to life and liberty at the hands of the Christian; there is no picture of the Chinese holding up his fettered arms, crying out, 'Am not I a man and a brother?' In its place, we have a sound, practical exposition of the fact that the Chinese slave trade 'won't pay.' It has jeoparded, we are told, the English position in China, and all its material interests. The flood of emigration has overflowed upon the shores of California, while it obsti-

we may, the system tends in the direction of giving to matter increased control over mind; to capital increased control over labor.

§ 4. Turning now westward, we find that although more than thirty years since the colored people of Jamaica were declared to have been emancipated, so little has British policy tended to the production of real freedom that, until recently, the poor producers could not even so far diversify their employments as to subject their own sugar to the first and simplest processes of refinement. The result exhibits itself in the fact, that but a few years since oppression was followed by an insurrection in whose suppression were perpetrated cruelties of which, said the London *Times*, "it is impossible to speak without shuddering."*

nately turns aside from British and Spanish colonies. 'From the former,' as it continues, 'the Chinese see living men return; hear news of relatives and friends, and know that there are work and pay for more; but from the latter they hear no reports, see no returning emigrant. If they hear at all, it is of ill-usage, suicide, and death.'"—*North American.*

* "It is now certain that scores, and perhaps hundreds, of prisoners were flogged before being hung, and often before being tried. It is certain that some, though it is uncertain how many, were compelled to run the gauntlet, after being flogged, through a crowd of brutal spectators, who were allowed to insult them, or pelt them as they pleased. It is certain that several, at least, were shot or hung without the pretence of a trial, at the caprice of an officer or subordinate. It is certain that Mr. Ramsay, the Provost Marshal, stands charged by a multitude of witnesses, black and white, with excesses for which a parallel must be sought among the infamous eccentricities of Oriental despots. It is certain, at least—for the statement rests on the authority of the resident magistrate at Bath—that he flogged with his own hand fifteen men who had never been sentenced, and were to be sent before the court-martial at Morant Bay. It is probable, moreover, that men were bribed with the hope of life—a hope not always realized—to betray their accomplices; that persons accused of

Passing northward, we come to these United States, so long objects of the bitterest comments on the part of British journalists and statesmen, as claiming to represent the principles of freedom while maintaining in subjection millions of the negro race. The time came, however, when pro-slavery and anti-slavery, matter and mind, met face to face on the field of battle, contending for the mastery; and then, as so well is known, the chiefs of the non-consuming army, directors of capital in its war upon labor, were found almost united on the pro-slavery side; that being, as was then supposed, the direction in which might be found the cheapest cotton, to be used in giving employment to "serfs of the loom" the like of those whose condition has already been placed before the reader.*

§ 5. As has been shown, the British edifice takes from year to year more and more the form of an inverted pyramid, the great agricultural base, held by Adam Smith in so high regard, steadily diminishing in its proportions; the apex steadily enlarging as the chiefs of Britain's great non-consuming army grow in wealth and power. As a natural consequence of this, crises become more frequent and more enduring; societary operations, as a necessary result, throughout resuming more and more that gambling character which characterizes societies of an earlier period, but which tends to disap-

crimes were refused permission to call witnesses in their defence, and that some were executed, the only proof of whose guilt was their being found wounded."—*Times*.

* See pp. 264-266, *ante*.

pear as positives and negatives are enabled to come more and more near together. On each successive occasion the great become greater, and the "proletaires" more numerous and more dependent; their ranks being swelled by constant accessions from those intermediate classes, composed of men of smaller means, who have now been ruined; "too proud to work, although to beg they are not ashamed."* To such men, gambling in some one or other form comes as a necessity, to be followed

* Professor Fawcett in the *Fortnightly Review*, Jan. 1871, says: "It would be difficult to overestimate the acute suffering which was caused to tens of thousands of artisans by the vicious system of speculation fostered by such a firm as Overend and Gurney. One undertaking may be cited as an example. The Millwall Iron Ship Building Company obtained from the great Lombard Street discount house advances exceeding half a million. For a time a large business was carried on, and the company gathered together from different parts of the country many hundreds of artisans. These poor fellows exhausted a considerable portion of their hard-earned savings in removing their families to Millwall. At first everything seemed to flourish; the company, however, gradually became so deeply involved that the discount house, afraid that the nature of its business should be exposed, was compelled to continue the advances. The company was never really solvent; the crash at length came; hundreds of shareholders were ruined; the real offenders were, of course, not punished. But amidst all our sympathy for too-confiding investors, there has scarcely been an attempt made to trace what has become of these artisans, many of whom were attracted from long distances to embark their labor in this unsound undertaking. They have no legal claim for redress; their savings have been sacrificed, but they cannot appear as creditors; they were left helpless and stranded, so completely ruined that they had not the means to return to localities where their labor might be wanted."

The facts thus exhibited correspond precisely with those which have here occurred at the close of each and every period of the non-resistant system. None such have ever occurred when the opposite policy has been pursued. Extraordinary as have been the changes, here and abroad, since the re-adoption in 1861 of the resistant one, there has never been even the slightest approach to financial crisis.

by the frauds and forgeries which now so much abound. Self-respect, as we know, grows as men are more and more enabled to meet on terms of strict equality. It declines as the gulf is widened that divides those who have labor to buy from those who need to sell it.* Throughout Great Britain it widens daily, and hence it is, that men whose connections are such as would warrant hope for better things, are found so ready to lend their names to gambling schemes on condition of being paid there-

* The following passages descriptive of the extremes of society, are from recent numbers of one of the most respectable of English journals: "It is coming rapidly to this—that a first-class leader of society with a first-class fortune, to be 'on a level with his position,' wants, or chooses to think he wants, a house in London, a house on the river, two palaces at least in the country, a shooting-box in the Highlands, a hotel in Paris as costly as his London house, a villa at Como; a floor in Rome, an establishment in Cairo or Constantinople, a yacht, a theatre, and a racing stud, and then thinks that life is as monotonous as it was when 'in his cool hall, with haggard eyes, the Roman noble lay.' "—*Spectator.*

"Children of both sexes and of all ages, from five up to sixteen, are, in fact, sold by the wretched laborers to the gang-masters at so much per head per week, generally, we are bound to add, out of the direst poverty. The ganger having collected his children, takes them away to his job, forcing them to walk, or if needful, to carry each other, for distances, which often involve of themselves great cruelty. Five miles out and five back is thought nothing of, in addition to almost continuous labor for at least ten hours a day. . . . The laborers in many English parishes are coarse enough, but among these poor wretches civilization disappears. . . . The single amusement is obscene talk, which becomes so shocking that the very laborers are revolted, and declare they would sooner turn out of the road than meet the gangs returning. All the offices of nature, say twenty witnesses, are performed in public by both sexes, without the faintest effort at concealment. Boys and girls of all ages bathe together stark naked, and the most infamous actions are boasted of with a shamelessness rarely found among savages."—*Ibid.* Mar. 23.

Splendor on one hand and squalor on the other, have never, in any country, been more strikingly exhibited.

for at the moderate rate of a guinea for each and every hour's or day's attendance. Money must be had, at whatsoever sacrifice of feeling or of honor. More than in any other country has Mammon now become the God at whose altar all are required to worship.

§ 6. The material condition of the toiling millions who now constitute the "proletariat," has been already placed before the reader. How far it tends to produce in them that feeling of self-respect which exhibits itself in propriety of dress and of general deportment, he will decide for himself after reflecting on the few facts that will now be briefly given. The total production of cotton throughout the world cannot vary materially from 4,000,000,000 pounds, the equivalent of more than three and a half pounds per head of the population, old and young, slave or free, rich or poor; from the Hindoo who needs little beyond a cloth around the loins, to northern men who need to be covered almost from top to toe.* Of those thousands of millions but 101 were, on an average of 1868–9, consumed by the 30,000,000 of the population of the British Islands;† giving but about the average of the world, from the barbarian negro of Central Africa to the owner of almost counties of British land. Cleanliness and godliness being close relations, where the one may not be found,

* "No species of raw material is produced more abundantly in China than cotton, and if there is one class of manufacture for which the people have peculiar facilities, and which is more extensively followed than any other, it is that of 'coarse cottons.'"—*Quarterly Review*, April, 1872.

† Hoyle, *Our National Resources*, Chap. IV.

the other will in vain be sought for. "Moral purity," says a recent writer,

"is incompatible with bodily impurity. Moral degradation is indissolubly united with physical squalor. The depression and discomfort of the hovel produce and foster obtuseness of mind, hardness of heart, selfish and sensual indulgence, violence and crime. It is the home that educates the family. It is the distinction and the curse of barbarism that it is without a home; it is the distinction and blessing of civilization that it prepares a home in which Christianity may abide, and guide, and govern."*

The total wool production of the world may be taken at 2,000,000,000 pounds; giving an average of about two pounds per head for its entire population; for the hundreds of millions who never need it, as for those who find it difficult to obtain the quantity required for meeting the vicissitudes of temperature. Among these latter are included the people of the British Islands, whose average consumption of woollens for the years 1866–69 is given at 78,572,000 pounds, or two and three-fifth pounds per head;† being less than the average of the world outside the tropics.

We are thus presented with the extraordinary

* Baker, *The Common Nature of Epidemics.*

"Our laborers' dwellings are a national disgrace."—*Contemporary Review*, March, 1872.

"England, with its wealth, its intelligence, its poor laws, and its enormous charities; Scotland, with its high-sounding religious and educational pretensions; are all alike. . . . No abjectness in any city in Europe sinks to the dismal level of rags and wretchedness observable in the fetid alleys of Edinburgh and Glasgow."—*Chambers's Journal.*

The deaths in London, of starvation, in 1871, were 100 in number.

† Hoyle, *Our National Resources*, chap. iv.

fact, that of the two essential materials of that covering which is required by both decency and comfort, the consumption does not exceed, if indeed it equals, the average of the world from the Digger Indian on one hand, to the London or Paris millionaire on the other; this, too, in face of the fact, that Britain controls a productive force equal in power to that of the population of nearly all the world beside.

§ 7. Self-respect makes demand for temperance in all things, but most especially in the consumption of those fluids which "steal away men's brains" and make them, for the time, almost as irresponsible for their actions as is the tiger or the rattlesnake. How far it is thus exhibited throughout the British Islands is shown by the facts, that the consumption, in 1869, amounted to 930,000,000 gallons; the equivalent of more than thirty gallons for every person, old and young, male and female, of the entire population; and that it had grown to that from 707,000,000 in 1860, the rate of increase in the decade having been more than 30 per cent.*

In the same decade the consumption of cotton had

* CONSUMPTION OF INTOXICATING LIQUORS IN THE UNITED KINGDOM.

	1860. Gallons.	1869. Gallons.	Increase per cent.
Spirits, foreign and domestic . .	26,926,011	30,114,624	11.84
Beer, ale, and porter.	674,170,326	885,004,412	31.27
Wine	6,718,585	14,723,534	119.31
Aggregate	707,814,922	929,842,570	31.37

The population in this period increased 7½ per cent.

fallen 36 per cent.—the average of 1858–9 having been 157,000,000 pounds, against but 101,000,000 for 1868–9.* The average expenditure for liquors in the years 1858–61, was £92,000,000. For those of 1866–69, it was £112,000,000.† In the same period, 1859–69, the value of cotton goods consumed had fallen from £11,443,371 to £8,511,737.‡

Facts like these prove a downward tendency almost unparalleled; finance ministers at home, nevertheless, rejoicing in the increase of revenue, as those of India rejoice in a growing Chinese demoralization manifested in an increased demand for opium, to be followed by a rise of price. Greatly, however, would it shock those statesmen to be told that their policy tended toward increasing barbarism, and not in the direction of an advancing civilization. When they shall have studied the facts given here below, and shall then have compared the poverty and demoralization there exhibited with the power for good, if rightly directed, of the wonderful non-consuming army now controlled by Britain, they must, assuredly, arrive at the conclusion, that in their system there exists some error demanding prompt and careful investigation.§

* Hoyle, chap. iv.

† Ibid., chap. vi.

‡ Ibid., chap. iv.

§ On one side of the Atlantic the toiling millions have become a mere "proletariat." On the other, they are tending daily toward an equality with the capitalist; and are more and more acquiring a feeling of self-respect. That the reader may appreciate the moral results of the two systems, the following figures are submtted for his consideration:—

§ 8. More than any other European country England has sought by dissemination of the Holy Scrip-

CONSUMPTION OF INTOXICATING LIQUORS IN THE UNITED STATES IN THE FISCAL YEAR ENDING JUNE 30, 1871.

	Gallons.
Domestic and foreign spirits	54,489,297
Beer, ale, and porter, foreign and domestic	223,307,156
Wine imported	10,700,000
Aggregate	288,496,453

CONSUMPTION PER CAPITA IN THE UNITED KINGDOM AND IN THE UNITED STATES.

UNITED KINGDOM IN 1869.	Gallons.	UNITED STATES IN 1870–71.	Gallons.
Spirits	0.978	Spirits	1.397
Malt liquors	30.500	Malt liquors	5.726
Wine	0.470	Wine	0.274
Aggregate	31.948	Aggregate	7.397
Population in 1869, 30,000,000		Population in 1871, 39,000,000	

Remarkable as is the difference here exhibited, it tells but little more than half the truth as regards spirits. In England, alcohol used in the arts is deteriorated by being mixed with a certain spirit, after which it passes free of duty and is not included in the returns from which the above table has been made. Here, nothing of the kind being done, all alcohol is included, although nearly half is estimated as being used in manufactures. Allowing for this, the American consumption of spirits is greatly less than a gallon per head.

The British consumption of cotton, as we have seen, but little exceeds 3 pounds per head. The American is 13 and likely soon to reach 20. [Of linen the British consumption is greatly larger than the American one, the average of the years 1866–69 having exceeded 3 pounds per head.] The value of the one is but $42,000,000. That of the other is scarcely less than $300,000,000. In the one, thirty per cent. of those who sign the marriage register are said to make their mark; a fact not to be charged altogether to illiteracy, a clergyman having recently explained that one in five of those who thus sign themselves do so because they are too drunk to write! In the other, nearly all of American birth both read and write. In the one, for every thirty gallons of liquor there is consumed less than *one* pound of coffee. In the other, for every *five* gallons of the one there are

tures, and by missions, to familiarize benighted heathens of the East with that religion whose base is found in the great command, that we do to others as under similar circumstances we would desire them to do by us. That the persons thus employed have been active and earnest in the performance of their duties, is not to be questioned. As little, however, is it to be denied, that their progress has borne a proportion absolutely infinitesimal to the risks that have been so cheerfully incurred, to the labors which so faithfully have been performed. Seeking now the cause of this we can scarcely fail to find it in the fact, that so few have seemed to appreciate the idea that the "blessed gospel of work" lay at the root of all morals; that the decree which had imposed upon man a necessity for obtaining his bread by the sweat of his brow had made it THE DUTY of each and all to facilitate, as far as possible,

consumed *six* pounds of the other. Throughout the recent war the soldiers of the Republic, being allowed no spirits, used coffee everywhere on their weary marches, and found in it their best comforter. It was the remark of an old campaigner, that if a halt of a few minutes were called anywhere the men would at once set to work to make a pot of coffee. In this, the workmen who enlisted in the service merely carried with them the habits of home.

As a consequence of the self-respect thus indicated it is, that an Englishman, writing in *Frazer's Magazine*, is enabled to assure his readers that after "a residence of upwards of 17 years in New York," he "cannot call to mind a single instance of any *native* American citizen appearing at the bar of a police court on the charge of wife beating." Further than this, as he continues, "more intoxicated men, and women too, may be seen in the streets of London in one day than in those of the United States in six months." Contrasting the manners of the toiling millions of the two countries, he says, "the American, however humble in position, has a keen sense of personal dignity: no taste for horse play; and, prompt to resent an impertinence or insult, is equally slow, unprovoked, to offer either.

the application, by all, of labor, whether bodily or mental, to the work; that measures tending to prevent such application tended to the production of crime, and were, therefore, criminal in all by whom they were employed; that all the acts of the nation they represented looked in that direction; and, that the first step toward accomplishment of their benevolent purposes lay in the direction of inducing their own employers forthwith to adopt such a course of policy as would tend to enable the poor unbelievers, with advantage to all, at home or abroad, to avail themselves of the powers that God had given them, and of whose use they had been so long deprived. Had such been their course of action—had they commenced by instilling sound Christianity into the minds of the officers in command of Britain's grand non-consuming army—and had their efforts in that direction been crowned with success—the labors of early Christian missionaries to the East would to-day be so completely overshadowed as scarcely at all to be now held in recollection. As it is, these latter stand most brightly out; and for the reason, that in the days of the Apostle of the Indies it yet remained to be discovered that buying cheaply and selling dearly were the essential aims and ends of life; that for their attainment it was justifiable, if not indeed honorable, so to direct the wonderful force of a non-consuming army counting by hundreds of millions as gradually to annihilate the societary arrangements of other hundreds of millions of poor and defenceless men; that in all cases where submission might be refused it was right and proper to set at defiance the laws of resisting peoples, the smuggler being publicly recognized as the "great reformer of the age;" or that, as a rule, the end might be regarded as sanctioning whatsoever means, foul or fair, might be deemed essential to its attainment.*

Happily for Xavier he lived at a time when the working men of England were becoming from day to day more free, and when growing self-respect was prompting all to the adoption of whatsoever measures might be required for giving practical effect to the fundamental "Gospel;" securing employment for the able-bodied while granting aid to those who by reason of age or infancy, deformity or disease, found themselves compelled to look to their more fortunate fellow-men for supplies of food and raiment.

The movement thus suggested is precisely that which now is needed. The heart of the tree being diseased, it is waste of time to attempt any pruning of the branches. Let then the suffering peoples of the world set themselves to work to prove to British masters—to those especially who now so freely give their time and means to support of measures look-

* "The missionary has lately entered into such close partnership with the trader that the people of the countries they wish to 'open up' must be in doubt whether it is our Bibles or our broadcloth, our cotton or our Christianity that we most desire to force upon them; and the attempt to compel them to accept a spurious Christianity and shoddy manufactures by means of bayonets and cannon is not likely to be permanently successful."—*London Free Press.*

ing to enlightenment of the heathen—that their war upon labor, abroad and at home, is not more unjust than it is impolitic; and, that a proletariat like to that which now exhibits itself throughout the British Islands, must become from day to day less fitted for contending on equal terms with men of other nations in whom the feeling of self-respect is a steadily growing one, as is the case in all those countries which protect their people against the "warfare" that so long and so bitterly has been waged.* In proof of this, let them point to the fact that the name of Morse now travels on telegraph wires throughout the world; that that of the German Bessemer travels in like manner with the steel railroad bar; that the American axe is heard in nearly all the forests of the world; that to an American do the sewing women of the world stand indebted for emancipation from the necessity for re-enacting that terrible drama, one of whose scenes is so well described in Hood's sad "Song of the Shirt:" that the American piano now goes throughout the world; that the latest improvements in many departments of manufacture have travelled eastward from America to England; that the Eng-

* "Great and worthy exertions," says the Rev. Mr. Kingsley in his recent work, "are made every London season for the conversion of the negro and the heathen, and the abolition of their barbarous customs and dances." "It is," he continues, "to be hoped that the negro and the heathen will some day show their gratitude to us, by sending missionaries hither to convert the London season itself, dances and all, and assist it to take the beam out of its own eye in return for having taken the mote out of theirs."

lish locomotive has been perfected here;* closing with a request to the chiefs of the great army that they should furnish answers to the questions: "If all this has been done in the green wood, what will not be done in the dry?" "If a people among whom manufactures but recently had scarcely an existence have already gone so far ahead, what will they do in the half century that stands before us? What at its close are to be the relative positions of the now chief nations of the world, if Russia, Germany, and America shall continue to move onward in the direction of carrying their toiling millions upward toward equality with capitalists, Britain meantime wasting her wonderful powers in a war upon those millions wheresoever found, abroad or at home?"†

Than these, questions of higher importance have

* On a recent public occasion an eminent English engineer, Mr. Fairlie, spoke with his friends and associates as follows, to wit: "You may take your best English locomotive with its maximum train, and the American will go before it; drawing it and its train, and one-half more beside." An American engineer now controls the whole railroad system of India.

† The Emperor of France proposed ten awards of 10,000 francs each or 100,000 francs in the aggregate, to ten different individuals or associations, who, in a series of years, had accomplished the most to secure a state of harmony between employers and their work people, and most successfully advanced the material, intellectual, and moral welfare of the same. A special jury was appointed from the different countries represented in the exhibition, C. C. Perkins, of Boston, representing the United States. Five hundred applications were received from France and other countries on the continent of Europe, from Great Britain, and the United States.

Nine of the awards were given to France, Germany, and other countries in Europe, one to the United States—(the *Pacific Mills*, of Lawrence, Massachusetts)—and none to Britain.

never been submitted to the consideration of any people whatsoever. Let then the men who are so sedulous in their efforts to carry the gospel to men and women of distant countries now turn their attention homeward, giving their labors to an effort at placing themselves in a position to be enabled to point to England as the country that, more than any other, furnished practical proof of the physical, mental, and moral advantages resulting from adoption of the religion of Christ, and they will accomplish more in a single decade than will be accomplished in centuries under the existing system.

§ 9. To the end of enabling them to prove conclusively that worldly advantage marched hand in hand with obedience to that great law which so especially requires the rich and powerful to do by others as, were they weak and poor, they would desire should be done by themselves, let them turn to a file of the *Times* and study carefully its highly instructive admission, that "when the Celt has crossed the Atlantic he begins for the first time in his life to consume the manufactures of this country, and indirectly to contribute to its customs." Turbulent, improvident, and unprofitable, while remaining at home, he becomes almost at once, after landing in America, a peaceful citizen and most profitable customer. Such having been, and such being now, the case, the question naturally arises as to what had been the circumstances under which, and the times at which, American attraction had been greatest, enabling England most largely to profit by transfers of population such as are above described. Seeking a reply thereto we find, as shown in the figures given below, that they have invariably been in periods of resistance to the British system; the reverse presenting itself as regularly in those at which submission has been most complete.*

Such having been the facts, we may now, with some advantage, inquire—why it is that emigrants from the British islands so generally seek the American, and not the Canadian or Australian shores? To this the answer is, that in the first they are efficiently protected against the "warfare" of capital upon labor so actively carried on by the officers of Britain's great non-consuming army; whereas, in the other they are not so protected. Why then should not all the British colonies, and all the Spanish American States, be made as useful as America has been, is, and is likely to be in all the future; absorbing people now unemployed, and thus relieving Britain from her grinding and oppressive taxation for the support of hundreds of thousands, of all ages and sexes, who abroad would be enabled

* From 1825 to 1834, a period of resistance, immigration rose from 10,000 to 63,000.

From 1834 to 1842–43, a period of submission, it remained so nearly stationary that the average of these latter years was but 78,000.

From 1843 to 1848, a resistant period, it rose from 78,000 to 226,000.

From 1848 to 1854, the great California period, it rose to 427,000. Notwithstanding the gold discoveries, the decline from 1854 to 1860–61, a period of submission, was such that the average of these latter years was but 122,000, or little more than half the numbers of a dozen years before.

Throughout the resistant period 1861–70, the figures have risen steadily until from 91,000 in the first, they have become 378,000 in the last.

to purchase and pay for millions of pounds, in value, of commodities of an order greatly higher than that of those now furnished by hospital managers and poor-law guardians? An army of *working* Englishmen, 100,000 in number, employed in introducing machinery of every kind into India, and in teaching Hindoos its proper management, would of themselves make larger demand for the products of British industry than now is made by the 150,000,000 of Hindostan. Further than this, they would speedily treble the productive power of that country, thereby enabling its people not only to purchase largely of British products of the higher order, but also so to increase their contributions for the support of government as to free those of England from all necessity for continuing participants in the crime involved in maintenance of the opium trade; productive, as it has already been, of a demoralization compared with which all the damage to the cause of civilization resulting from the invasions of Alaric and Attila combined, sinks into utter insignificance.* Let them next apply the same idea to Canada, Australia, Spanish America, and ask themselves what would be the effect of an annual demand for hundreds of thousands of men and women capable of instructing those already there in the various

* The rapid resuscitation of France in the last twelve months furnishes proof conclusive of the triviality of damage caused by the soldier, compared with that inflicted by the trader with hundreds of millions of non-consuming laborers at his command. The one limits himself to destruction of the flowers and fruits of the societary tree; whereas the other tears up its roots.

industries, agricultural, mining, chemical, and mechanical, suited to the circumstances in which those countries now are placed? Would it not clear the way at home for thousands and tens of thousands of "proletaires," capable of filling positions higher than those now open to them? Would it not produce a desire for education such as now has no existence? Would it not make large demand for the peculiar faculties of the weaker sex? Would not, at every step, the weak of body find themselves coming more and more to an equality with the lithe and active? Would not men and women more and more be enabled, profitably to themselves and to all around them, to unite together for carrying into effect the great command which requires that the earth become more fully peopled? Would not such a course of action speedily bring to a close that infamous slave-trade now so abounding throughout the South Pacific, and so destructive of all moral feeling among British colonists? Would not every step in these directions be attended with growth of that feeling of self-respect which would induce the practice of temperance in all things, and especially in the consumption of intoxicating liquors? Would not then the Malthusian theory be dismissed to take its place among the thousands of other absurdities by means of which the growth of real civilization has been so much retarded?* Assuredly it would, and as assuredly

* Since the re-adoption by the United States of the resistant policy, the demand made by them on the population of Continental Europe has

would the eyes of those who control the movements of Britain's non-consuming army be opened to the facts, that the course hitherto pursued had been a mistake destined, perhaps, to prove a fatal one; that the results thus far obtained had been those of poverty and demoralization at home and abroad; and, that at every stage of progress their countrymen and themselves had been more and more tending in the direction indicated by Macaulay in the passage already placed before the reader.*

To the end that his anticipations may not be realized it is essential that men of influence begin to appreciate the facts, that the harmony of interests among communities is as complete as is that among individuals of which they are composed; and that failure to respect the rights of the weak, such as is now exhibited throughout the Asiatic world, furnishes proof conclusive of the absence, within themselves, of that feeling of self-respect to which alone can we look for evidence of advancing civilization.†

assumed such large proportions as to have compelled several of the powers to study carefully the measures required for inducing their people to remain at home. No where in Europe was the Malthusian theory more fully accepted than in Germany. (*See ante*, note to p. 187.) No where is its refutation becoming more complete.

* See note to page 273, *ante*.

"Men, habitually starved in mind or in body, are not the stuff out of which to make either good saints or good subjects."—*Freeland.*

† Describing the present unhappy condition of France, the *Athenæum* (London, May 26) has just now told its readers that "centralization with cold palsy at its extremities, and frequent attacks of apoplexy at the head, has been there set up as the only *beau ideal* of government." Describing the present position of England, the same precise words might here be used; with the addition, that the *beau ideal* of trading centralization is as

§ 10. To the "positive knowledge of the uncultured" we are required to look for the foundation of every rational "theory of science," and "of the relations of its parts to each other." So is it everywhere, the base of operations for the development of both mind and morals being found among the mass and not among the few by whom that mass is to so great

much more productive of physical, mental, and moral deterioration, as is the British army which counts by hundreds of millions more powerful for evil than that French one which counts by hundreds of thousands.

Seeking evidence of this, the reader may here advantageously study some facts in regard to Orissa, that scene of perpetually recurring famines in which men perish almost by millions, derived from the new volume (London, 1872) of Hunter's *Annals of Rural Bengal*, as follows:—

Situated directly on the Bay of Bengal, Orissa has been a chief seat of the salt manufacture, but so heavy are the salt duties (*see ante*, note to p. 82) that its peasantry "consume great quantities of fish imperfectly dried in the sun, and more or less rotten. The decomposing mass is stored up in baskets, and sparingly doled out to the household as the only dish they can afford to their monotonous rice diet. . . . The estuaries of the great Orissa delta yield an endless supply of fish; and all that is wanting to give to the people a great additional security against famine is the means by which the fish may be kept for eating throughout the year."

Further than this, the Mahanadi, one of its rivers, is the natural channel through which the rural products of Central India should be sent to the coast to be exchanged, but the salt duty of Bengal and Orissa so greatly exceeds that of Madras, that, as we are here informed, "the peasants of inner India find it cheaper to send their goods by a long and costly land route to the Madras district of Ganjam than to float them down the Mahanadi to Cuttack on the Orissa side of the customs line. . . It is as if we had thrown a wall across one of the finest trade routes in the world. Our salt duty just as effectually blockades the Mahanadi as if we had filled it up with rocks."—This is what is now known as free trade, a trade that imposes measureless restrictions on a domestic commerce that under other circumstances would count by thousands of millions, while refusing to permit the adoption of any measures of protection against that grand army of non-consuming laborers to which India stands indebted for the annihilation of a cotton manufacture whose history, as so well is known, "involved no less than a description of the lives of half the people of Hindostan."

an extent controlled. Charlemagne labored assiduously for the advancement of civilization, but his institutions found no soil in which they might take root and be matured. Watt and Howe, inventors of the steam-engine and the sewing-machine, have done more for the advancement of mankind than has been done by all the sovereigns by whom the mighty emperor has been succeeded. In the brain and the heart of lowly men, wheresoever found, exist the germs of all those qualities, mental and moral, by which man is distinguished from the brute. That they might be developed in all their strength and beauty the thrice-blessed GOSPEL OF WORK was instituted; and it is to those who aid in *its* dissemination that mankind is to be indebted for every advance that may be made in the direction of promoting the establishment of that independence on one hand and inter-dependence on the other, among both individuals and nations, which tends to bring about a reign of peace throughout the earth. The more the tendency in that direction the more are the physically weak and the physically strong brought to stand on a level with each other; each and all becoming from hour to hour more dependent on the kindly feelings of each and every other, as they, each and all, grow in independence and in power; standing before the world as controllers of the great natural forces; capable of perfect self-control; and animated always by a feeling of self-respect.

CHAPTER XII.

OF CIVILIZATION.

§ 1. Among the terms enumerated by Archbishop Whately as standing in need of definition, and as being constantly "used without any more explanation or suspicion of their requiring it, than the words 'triangle' or 'twenty,'" is not embraced that important one which heads this chapter; yet is there none, *wealth* alone excepted, that is more frequently both used and misused. Of the many who have undertaken to furnish civilization's history, in our own and other languages, not one has even essayed to supply a definition of the thing itself that might enable his readers to recognize it whensoever and wheresoever it might be found. Mr. Guizot, it is true, gave to his readers certain fancy sketches by whose aid they were, as he thought, to be enabled to make at the least some approach toward its identification; but that he himself had not attained to any clear idea of the constituents of a real civilization would seem to be proved by the fact that, when desiring to bring before his readers the period when Rome was most rapidly advancing in that direction, he should have selected one at which the small proprietors had almost disappeared from the land; when the soil of Italy had become the property of a few great houses;

when palaces abounded, filled with slaves; when the elder Cato fattened slaves for market; when to propitiate the gods human sacrifices were renewed; when the city population was hourly becoming more dependent on free distribution of the corn of subject provinces; and when gladiatorial games, maintained at the public cost, were more and more required for their amusement; preparation thus being made for the barbarism so speedily thereafter exhibited in the destruction of the great cities of Corinth and Carthage; in the proscriptions of Sylla and Marius; in proconsular tyranny like to that of Verres and Fonteius; and in the almost universal pauperism and demoralization of that people which in earlier and better times had given to the world men and women of whom Cincinnatus and Lucretia might be taken as the types.* Facts like these being accepted as proofs of advancing civilization, in what direction should we look when seeking evidence of its decline? The question is one to which the venerable historian would certainly find it somewhat difficult to make reply.†

* "Take, for example, Rome in the splendid days of the Republic, at the close of the second Punic war; the moment of her greatest virtues, when she was rapidly advancing to the empire of the world—when her social condition was evidently improving."—*Hist. of Civilization,* p. 14.

† That like causes tend to produce like effects, and that history tends constantly to reproduce itself, will be obvious to all who remark the close correspondence of the results at different periods of unceasing "warfare," as exhibited in the Rome of the past and the Britain of the present. As was then the case, the small freeholder has now disappeared from the land, his place being filled by the day-laborer, with "no future but the poorhouse." As then, a proletariat now fills the place that had once been occupied by men like those of Naseby and Marston Moor. As then, the

§ 2. Voluminous as is Mr. Buckle's work, he nowhere finds place for any definition of the thing whose history he seeks to place before his readers. In lieu thereof they are told that progress is greatly dependent on the question as to whether men eat rice as in India; potatoes, as in Ireland; maize, as in Mexico; bananas, as in the countries further south; or meat, as in Northern Europe. The reward of labor, as they are told, is always low in hot climates where vegetable food abounds; always, on the contrary, high in those colder climates where animal food is a necessity of life;* these assertions being made in face of the facts, that close on his right and left stood two little countries, Belgium and Ireland, the one ranking among the most prosperous of Europe, the other meanwhile exhibiting famine as almost the normal condition of Irish existence; just as is now the case with those unfortunate Hindoos who, as has been shown, habitually eat putrid fish because of a tax on salt so heavy as to preclude them from availing themselves of its services for preservation of the animal food with which their rivers so much abound.†

space between the higher and lower orders of society is now a constantly widening one. The facts of the earlier and later periods of *civilization* above referred to are one and the same, with little exception other than this: that considerable portions of the contributions of subject Provinces and States were then applied to maintenance of games by which the Roman people could be amused; whereas, no part of the contributions of the poor Hindoo, none of the profits of the opium trade or salt monopoly, is applied to the amusement, and little to the instruction, of those of Britain.

* History of Civilization, vol. i. pp. 46, 47.

† See *ante*, note to page 342.

Of all European countries there is none that more strenuously than Belgium has resisted the tyranny of the British system, and hence it is that civilization has there so steadily advanced. Of all the countries of the world there are none that equally with India and Ireland have been compelled to blind submission, and hence it is that, widely separated as they are, and widely different as are their climates and their national characteristics, the facts presented are of so close resemblance; the Irishman selling his pig because too poor to eat it, and the Hindoo allowing his fish to run to waste because too poor to pay the tax on salt.*

Turning his eyes westward, and back to the days of Cortes, Mr. Buckle might have seen maize-eating Mexicans cultivating the land, living in towns, and fabricating cloth; the meat-eaters of northern prairies meanwhile being driven by actual want to frequent robbery and murder of their more prosperous and civilized southern neighbors.†

Elsewhere, at the moment of writing, he might have seen Pennsylvania and Virginia standing side by side, perfectly agreed in the consumption of both animal and vegetable food; but differing as did the poles in reference to the reward of labor. The one had been consistent in its efforts at bringing together societary positives and negatives, and

* See *ante*, note to page 342.

† Mr. Buckle's theory having made it necessary to place Indian corn, or maize, among the products of hot climates, he seeks to restrict its cultivation within the limits of 40° north latitude; doing this in face of the fact that the chief seat of its cultivation on this continent is north of 38°.

had, therefore, grown in force. The other had been equally consistent in its efforts at keeping them asunder, and hence the weakness that has since been manifested.

Most of all important, however, in our author's eyes was that "general aspect of nature" which, as he assures his readers, "produces its principal results by exciting the imagination, and by suggesting those innumerable superstitions which are the great obstacles to advancing knowledge."* On the fanciful basis thus established he erects his edifice; then exhibiting it in huge volumes abounding in expressions of opinion on the part of himself and others, but presenting for consideration no single one of the important facts in reference to the English movement that have been here submitted. Those of his readers who seek for information relative to the "theological basis of predestination, and the metaphysical basis of free will"† may perhaps be gratified; but widely different will be the case with such as desire to know how it had been that Saxon churls had freed their necks from the degrading collar; that their descendants, self-reliant and self-respecting, had been enabled to do battle for their rights at Worcester; that the chain of serfdom had so soon thereafter been fitted to the ankles of those very men by means of an Act of Settlement; or why it is, that a "proletariat" clamoring for protection against its masters now fills the place once occupied by men against whom

* Ibid., p. 29. † Ibid., p. 10.

those masters had so frequently sought to be protected. To such inquiries our author will prove to be a guide so dumb as not to furnish even a word in answer to any questions having reference to that "blessed gospel of work" which constitutes the foundation on which alone anywhere the grand edifice of civilization can be erected.

Reasoning always downward, Mr. Buckle looks for the causes of change in improved modes of thought. Had he pursued a contrary course he might perhaps have been led to the conclusion, that the societary tree, like all other trees, grows from the roots upward; that modes of thought are but its flowers and fruits; and that any attempt at study of these latter to the exclusion of the former must result in the failure that his ponderous, and already almost forgotten, work has proved to be. It is to the "positive knowledge of the uncultured," and not to the disquisitions of metaphysicians, that we need first to turn when seeking to understand the development of those beneficial influences which may properly be characterized as indications of a real civilization.

§ 3. Mr. Mill assures his readers—

First, of the existence of an all-controlling law, in virtue of which the return to agricultural labor tends to diminish in its relation to population.* Were that different "nearly all the phenomena of the production and distribution of wealth would," as they are told, "be other than they are."

* Principles, vol. i. p. 221.

Second, of "another agency" that is in habitual antagonism to that all-pervading law, and which he characterizes by the term "progress of civilization."*

Third, that under that head are included improved methods of cultivation, better modes of transportation, in short, "every possible improvement of the arts of production" resulting from increased subjection of the forces of nature to man's use and service.†

The great "law" here enunciated tends, as the reader will readily perceive, necessarily to increased inequality of conditions. The counteracting "agency" tends, as we are assured, toward correction of this, and toward equality of condition. At another stage of the process, however, we learn that while this antagonistic "agency" has "enabled an increased number of manufacturers and others to make fortunes," it has done nothing for the working man; civilization having failed "to lighten the day's toil of any human being," and "drudgery and imprisonment" being the sole reward thus far reaped by those who have need to sell their service, whether physical or mental.‡

Admitting the accuracy of the views thus presented, we now reach the remarkable fact, that discoveries, which have placed under British control an army of 500,000,000 non-consuming slaves, have not only *not* tended toward counteraction of the injurious tendencies of Mr. Mill's great

* Ibid., p. 228. † Ibid., p. 232. ‡ Ibid., p. 232.

law of diminished returns to labor; but that, on the contrary, they have combined with it for increasing the power of masters for the control of mind, capital for the control of labor; thus carrying the nation forward in the direction of proletairism and barbarism, and not in that of freedom and civilization.

Of what, however, does this last really consist? Let us inquire.

§ 4. Of all animals, the early man is the most helpless, each and every other coming forth from nature's womb fully armed with the powers needed for their support and preservation. Directly the reverse of this, he not only needs to be clothed, fed, and sheltered during a protracted infancy, but also to have developed within himself the germs of those faculties by whose aid alone can he be enabled to command the services of even that simplest of the great natural forces which furnishes the heat required for so changing the raw produce of the earth as to fit it for man's consumption. How wretched must have been his condition we may to some extent imagine after studying that of the now existing dirt-eaters of the western continent, and bushmen of the eastern one.* How almost infinitely worse than even this it must at very remote periods have been, is being proved by geologists who are

* "The savages of New Holland never help each other even in the most simple operations; and their condition is hardly superior, it some respects it is inferior, to that of the wild animals that they now and then catch."—Mill, *Principles*, vol. i. p. 145.

now so steadily penetrating into the facts of that primitive life when cultivation had not even yet commenced; when men dwelt in caves and gladly sucked marrow from the bones of animals they had been enabled to overcome. In a state of things like this, the one law recognized is that of "every man for himself," allowing who will to "take the hindmost;" *i. e.*, the infant and the aged, the tender woman and the yet more tender child. That under such circumstances the race should have been at all preserved seems so nearly miraculous as to merit, at the hands of gentlemen who discourse with the world upon the "Descent of Man," an amount of consideration far greater than it has yet obtained. Sufficient for the present purpose, however, it is, that SELF-LOVE and the desire for SELF-GRATIFICATION are shown to be, and to have been, the essential characteristics of savage, as of barbarian, life.

Passing onward, we find that as with increase of numbers, and increased ability to combine together, societary positives and negatives are brought to somewhat orderly arrangement, with constant growth of power for direction and self-direction, man becomes more self-reliant and self-respecting—more capable of commanding respect for rights inherent in himself, more and more self compelled to do by others as he would they should do by him.

Selfishness and self-respect, antipodes of each other, are the essential characteristics of barbarism on the one hand, and of civilization on the other.

§ 5. The gradual development, throughout the

centuries which intervened between the Norman Conquest and the Restoration, of the feeling of self-respect has been already placed before the reader. What has been the tendency in that direction, whether individual or national, in those which have elapsed since the restoration of semi-serfage, and since the time when England struck down the woollen manufacture of Ireland, is shown in the fact, that from that hour to the present this latter has been but a mere instrument to be managed by the former, wholly without reference to the feelings or the interests of the Irish people.* Turning to India, and leaving entirely aside the discreditable proceedings of the last century so well described by Macaulay,† we are struck at once with the annihilation of a great manufacture that had, more or less, given employment to the hundred millions of its people; the work of destruction having been accomplished by means of measures so oppressive as to make it cause of wonder that there could exist any community of the world capable of their adoption.‡ Looking further, we see a salt manufacture ruined by oppressive taxation; coal, lime, and ores waiting to be mined; a people susceptible of the highest

* A slight exception to this is found in the period from 1782 to the passage of the Act of Union, in 1800: that one in which the legislative independence of Ireland was recognized, and throughout which there existed protection to Irish manufactures. Of it Lord Clare, then Chancellor of Ireland, spoke, in 1798, as follows:—

"No nation on the habitable globe advanced in cultivation, in commerce, in agriculture, so rapidly in the same period." Of the accuracy of the view thus presented, it would be easy to furnish most conclusive evidence.

† See *ante*, page 240.

‡ See *ante*, note to page 202.

cultivation, and numbering 150,000,000, nine-tenths of whose powers, physical and mental, are so utterly wasted that the average annual product of labor and capital combined is less, per head, than the fortnightly wages of an ordinary factory girl in these United States.* Turning next to the ruling powers of that unfortunate country, we find that, as a consequence of the annihilation of domestic commerce that has thus been brought about, so pressing have been, and are, their needs, and so small the productive force of the great Hindoo population, that the whole British people, by their government, have been made parties to acts of oppression in regard to those of China the like of which the pages of history furnish no record whatsoever.†

Passing now to other countries, we find them to have been subjected to a systematic "warfare," having for its object the prevention of that diversity of employment which gives value to labor and land; of that orderly arrangement of positives and negatives in whose absence there can arise no power for self-direction, no self-respect, no societary force.‡

* See *ante*, p. 318.

† See *ante*, p. 322, and also Appendix D.

‡ The following passage from an official document has been already placed before the reader, but its importance in reference to the views here presented seems to warrant its reproduction.

"The laboring classes generally in the manufacturing districts of the kingdom, and especially in the iron and coal districts, are very little aware of the extent to which they are often indebted for their being employed at all to the immense losses which their employers voluntarily incur in bad times, in order to destroy foreign competition, and to gain and keep possession of foreign markets. Authentic instances are well known of employers having in such times carried on their works at a loss amounting

An eminent English agriculturist has just now told his readers that "it is precisely because British farmers have their customers—the British manufacturers—almost at their doors, and that other corn-producing countries have not such manufacturers, that British agriculture is rich and thriving."* That such is the fact is not to be questioned. Would it not then be advantageous to other "corn-producing countries" to obtain manufacturers? Assuredly, it would. Why do they not? Seeking a reply to this question, let the reader study carefully the terrible "warfare" just above described as being maintained by men who control hundreds of millions of non-consuming laborers, and then determine for himself if a course of proceeding that is now causing a waste of four-fifths of the physical and mental forces of so many hundred millions of people is to be regarded as favorable to the growth of civilization or to that of barbarism.†

in the aggregate to £300,000 or £400,000 in the course of three or four years. If the efforts of those who encourage the combinations to restrict the amount of labor and to produce strikes were to be successful for any length of time, the great accumulations of capital could no longer be made which enable a few of the most wealthy capitalists to overwhelm all foreign competition in times of great depression, and thus to clear the way for the whole trade to step in when prices revive, and to carry a great business *before foreign capital can again accumulate* to such an extent as to be able to establish a competition in prices with any chance of success. *The large capitals of this country are the great instruments of warfare against the competing capitals of foreign countries*, and are *the most essential instruments now remaining by which our manufacturing supremacy can be maintained;* the other elements—cheap labor, abundance of raw materials, means of communication, and skilled labor—being rapidly in process of being equalized."

* Mechi, *How to Farm Profitably*.

† See *Appendix* E.

In those English days when self-respect was daily more and more manifesting itself, and when the word "proletaire" had not been even thought of in connection with the language, Shakespeare taught his countrymen that however "excellent" it might be to "have a giant's strength," it was "tyrannous to use it like a giant"—a lesson that their descendants, controlling a force greater than that of all mankind in Shakespeare's time, have long since totally forgotten. It had not then been taught that to buy cheaply and sell dearly was the chief end and aim of man.

§ 6. That the England of the period preceding the Restoration and that one which since has followed—the England which struck the collars from Saxon necks and that which rivetted the chains around English ankles—have been, and are, two widely different bodies, must, to the reader, now be clearly obvious. How the two were transplanted to the western shores of the Atlantic, and how they are now there represented, will next be shown, as follows:—

The Mayflower (1620) brought with her a spirit of freedom which promptly manifested itself in the establishment of local self-government; in town meetings and in public schools; but *not* in the recognition of the right of every man to worship God according to the dictates of his individual conscience. But few years later, however (1637), Roger Williams, in Rhode Island, set the example of perfect religious freedom, as further south was almost simultaneously done by Lord Baltimore in his Province of Maryland. To New York it was brought by descendants of men who had fought for liberty of conscience under the guidance and direction of William of Orange; Penn following suit thereto in 1680; each and all of these thus giving to the world conclusive evidence of the existence of that self-respect which requires of us that we grant to others that perfect freedom of thought in reference to spiritual matters that we claim to have respected in ourselves. By slow degrees the common school conquered religious prejudice in Massachusetts, thereafter making its way south and west until it had at length become the accepted doctrine throughout the whole country north of Mason and Dixon's line,* and of the Ohio, that, for the general establishment of that feeling which prompts to recognize in others all those rights for which in ourselves we claim respect, each and all the members of the community, poor and rich, male and female, should be placed on a common level so far as regarded facilities for acquiring the primary elements of knowledge. The poor boy, thus prepared for a start in life, becoming rich, next manifests his gratitude by appropriating a part of his means to further extension of that magnificent system to which he feels himself to have been so much indebted; and hence the liberality that in this respect is now exhibited throughout the Northern States.†

* An imaginary line dividing the free and slave States.

† Many years since Captain Lyell, the eminent geologist, expressed

Directly the reverse of this, Virginia, type of all the Southern States, was settled by men representing a London Company composed of noblemen and gentlemen, soldiers, traders and manufacturers; bringing with them a church establishment, tithes, and religious intolerance; a landed aristocracy with its laws of entail and primogeniture; poor whites in abundance, but no middle class; no towns or town-meetings; no common schools. Differing thus in both their composition and their modes of thought, they, of course, differed in their modes of employment; Northern men seeking, so far as was then permitted, to establish diversity of pursuits and thus to create a market for the products of the field; Southern men, on the contrary, exhausting the soil of their large plantations in raising tobacco for a distant market controlled by masters by whom they themselves were prohibited from converting food and wool into hats, food and crude iron into nails or spikes.*

himself as having been greatly struck by the number of donations and bequests to charitable and educational institutions. Since his time, however, the increase in both has been so great that where they then represented tens of thousands of dollars, they now count by millions; and with each successive year their growth is probably thrice that of the population requiring to be instructed. Contrasting this remarkable feature of American life with the corresponding one among his own fellow-citizens, Mr. Mill speaks as follows :—

"In England whoever leaves anything beyond trifling legacies for public or beneficent objects when he has any near relatives living, does so at the risk of being declared insane by a jury after his death; or, at the least, of having the property wasted in a chancery suit to set aside the will."—*Principles*, vol. i. p. 283.

* See *ante*, pp. 27, 198.

As early as the arrival of the Mayflower in Massachusetts, cargoes of negro slaves had been received in Virginia, and thenceforward human animals, black and white, became regarded as chattels liable to be bought and sold in open market. Forty years later, that same class to which this latter had stood indebted for its distinctive characteristics, gave to their countrymen at home an "Act of Settlement" re-establishing a state of semi-serfage.* Thenceforward, mother and daughter travelled side by side together, the Virginia planter gradually becoming a mere trader engaged in raising slaves for exportation; the officers of Britain's great non-consuming army meanwhile paving the way for adoption of the foul word "proletaire" as one "greatly needed" for indication of that vast proportion of the British people who must sell their labor, physical or mental, if they would have food for their children or themselves.

Throughout all this period the tendencies of those Americans who believed in public schools, and in the gradual elevation of man, were in the

* "Surely it is a great imprisonment, if not slavery, to a poor family to be under such restraint by law, that they must always live in one place whether they have friends, kindred, employment, or not, or however they might mend their condition by removing, and all because they had the ill luck to be born or to have served or resided a certain time there. Such persons, if they had spirits, have no encouragement to aspire to a better condition, since, being born poor and in a place which gives no means to be otherwise, they are not allowed to go and search it elsewhere, and if they find it they are not permitted to entertain it. Then their spirits sink, and they fall into a sottish way of living, depend on the parish, who must, however wretchedly, maintain them."—Hon. Roger North, quoted by Nicholls, *History of English Poor Law*, vol. i. p. 300.

direction of resistance to that monopoly system which was being maintained by aid of the destructive measures above described; Virginia and the South, on the contrary, gradually becoming more and more submissive to the distant masters.* Step by step the two became more widely separated, the North travelling steadily forward in the direction of regarding all men as equal before the law; the South as steadily pressing on toward full belief in the idea that the inferior race had "no rights which white men were required to respect;" until at length it came to be there asserted, that the highest evidence of civilization was to be found in the establishment of the right of capital to own labor, and to buy and sell the laborer with or without his wife and children.

Differing thus widely, the day at length arrived on which the great question was to be settled by force of arms. On which side, then, did the officers of Britain's great non-consuming army then place themselves? On that of common schools and the equal rights of man; or on that of crass ignorance and the right to treat the laborer as a mere chattel liable to be bought and sold? On that of civiliza-

* In the earlier and better days of Virginia, *i. e.*, before her chief employment had become that of raising slaves for market, her Washington, Jefferson, Madison, Monroe, and others among the most eminent of her people, were energetic advocates of the resistant policy, seeing clearly that political independence and industrial dependence could not coexist. These men, and others like them, had sought before the Revolution the passage of laws prohibiting the import of slaves, but they had been defeated by a government that was then busily engaged in enacting laws providing for the enslavement of artisans at home. See *ante*, p. 27.

tion, or that of barbarism? Where *could* they place themselves, seeing that all home tendencies were then in the direction of the establishment of a "proletariat" as the normal condition of that class which had given to the world a Shakspeare, a Bunyan, and a Burns; a Watt, a Stevenson, and an Arkwright? On that of barbarism assuredly, and there at once *were* they found.*

§ 7. The more orderly the arrangement of societary positives and negatives, and the more intimate the relations of producers and consumers, the greater becomes the economy of physical and mental

* The reader may now readily understand why it is that between Americans of the free States and the now dominant portion of the English people there exists, on either side, so little of that kindly feeling which should prevail throughout the world. So far as the former claim descent from England, they represent the country of Hampden and Milton, and *not* that of Charles II. and his successors. So far as they are Scottish, or Scotch-Irish, they more or less represent the men who so severely suffered at the hands of Lauderdale and Claverhouse. So far as they are Irish they represent the only nation on record that, in effect, has perished in a time of profound peace. So far as, together, they are Americans, they have, throughout the past and present centuries, been constant sufferers under that "warfare" which has had for its object that of compelling the sale of food and raw materials at low prices, and the purchase of cloth and iron at high ones. Seeking for evidence as to how they otherwise have been made to suffer, he may now advantageously turn to the note at page 201. Of all arts, the one in which Britain is most deficient is that of conciliating friendship, whether that of her own provincial subjects, or that of independent nations. Why the fact is so, will be seen on turning to a passage from a letter of M. De Tocqueville given at page 290.

Contrasting his countrymen and the Spaniards at Manila, in this respect, Lord Elgin tells us that these latter "are not separated from each other by that impassable barrier of mutual contempt, suspicion, and antipathy which alienates us from the unhappy natives in those lands where we settle ourselves among inferior orders of men."—*Letters and Journals*, p. 379.

force; the larger is the production; the more instant becomes the COMMERCE; and the more thorough the development of that feeling of self-respect which prompts to actions tending to bring into full activity the best feelings of the human heart. The less, on the contrary, that order, and the greater the separation of positives and negatives, the greater is the waste of labor, the smaller the production, and the more is the tendency toward increase of the power of that TRADING CLASS the end and aim of whose lives are those of buying cheaply and selling dearly; of disposing at will not only of the produce of the land, but also of the laborer himself, to the sweat of whose brow that production had been due. At each and every stage of progress in this direction master and slave become more widely separated, and the former is more and more led to think of the latter as a mere machine bound to obey his orders, and liable to be punished at his own discretion for any failure so to do.* Just as self-

* How injurious is the moral effect of a course of policy tending toward converting the toiling millions into bands of mere "proletaires," is thus exhibited by an eminent German manufacturer quoted by Mr. Mill:—

"Whilst in respect to the work to which the English workmen have been specially trained they are the most skilful, they are in conduct the most disorderly, debauched, and unruly, and least respectable and trustworthy of any nation whatsoever whom we have employed; and in saying this, I express the experience of every manufacturer on the Continent to whom I have spoken, and especially of the English manufacturers, who make the loudest complaints. * * * When the uneducated English workmen are released from the bonds of iron discipline in which they have been restrained by their employers in England, and are treated with the urbanity and friendly feeling which the more educated workmen on

respect grows at every stage in the direction of placing the physically weak on a level with the physically strong, so does the necessity for self-indulgence grow with every movement toward increasing inequality, whether between the sexes, or between those who are rich and strong and those who, being poor, are little capable of self-defence.

That so it is in England would seem to be proved by the fact that in no country claiming to be held as civilized does the feeling of *kindliness* less than there enter into the relations of buyers and sellers of service, whether mental or physical. That in none is the feeling of contempt for the toiling masses more freely expressed is very certain; and yet, among those millions there are thousands who, under other and more favorable circumstances, would probably shine before the world with a light far brighter than that of those who now speak of them in terms more contemptuous than are used in any other part of Europe.* How that same feeling exhibits itself in the East was thus described in Parliament some years since by the now Earl Russell:—

the continent expect and receive from their employers, they, the English workmen, completely lose their balance: they do not understand their position, and after a certain time become totally unmanageable and useless. This result of observation," says Mr. Mill, "is borne out by experience in England itself. As soon as any idea of equality enters the mind of an uneducated English workingman, his head is turned by it. When he ceases to be servile, he becomes insolent."—*Principles*, vol. i. p. 136.

* The reader may accept, as specimens, the "mob;" the "rabble;" the "great unwashed;" and now the "proletariat;" terms most generally used to indicate any gathering of the "lower orders" of what is claimed to be the most wealthy and most civilized country of the world.

"That very morning he had received a long letter from Sir F. Bruce, lamenting the insolence and disregard for Chinese customs and feelings, which were exhibited by Englishmen in that country. He lamented their want of courtesy, and improper behavior to the Chinese, whom they regarded as an inferior race. He (Earl Russell) was afraid the same was the case in Japan. But conduct of that kind was not exhibited to the Chinese and Japanese alone; for he found, in a book recently published, that the same kind of conduct was practised towards the Indian race."*

Of all tyrants, the trader, whether in men or things, is the most relentless—the most implacable in cases of disobedience. Of this, no better evidence need be desired than that exhibited in the treatment of Northern prisoners in Georgian and Virginian prisons, as compared with that granted to Southern captives at the North. Seeking elsewhere the parallels of these phenomena, the reader may now with advantage study the vindictive character of the closing measures of the recent Indian and West Indian rebellions;† the sacking of great cities and

* Full confirmation of the view thus presented is furnished in Lady Duff Gordon's charming volume, as is shown in the following extracts:—

"What chokes me is to hear Englishmen talk of the stick as being the only way to manage Arabs."—*Letters from Egypt*, p. 105.

"It is really heart-breaking to see *what* we are sending to India now. The mail days are dreaded. We never know when some brutal outrage may excite 'Mussulman fanaticism.' They try their hands on the Arabs in order to be in good train for insulting the Hindoos."—*Ibid.*, p. 309.

Confirming all this, Lord Elgin tells his readers, that he had seldom in the East "heard a sentence which was reconcilable with the hypothesis that Christianity had come into the world. Detestation, contempt, ferocity, and vengeance," as he continues, "whether Chinamen or Indians be the object."—*Letters and Journals*, p. 199.

† See *ante*, notes to pp. 141, 324.

the distribution of "loot" among the men in chief command; the bombardment of Canton and the destruction of the wonderful Summer Palace at Pekin; the execution and expulsion of recent Irish rebels; then remarking the great fact, that, of the millions of persons more or less engaged in the recent Southern rebellion, not one has, since the war was closed, suffered in property, limb, or life; nor are there more than half a dozen scores who are, at this moment, not as free to exercise every political right as they had been in the days when slavery ruled triumphant throughout the land. Conscious strength, magnanimity, and civilization have here thus marched hand in hand together, and to an extent wholly without parallel in the world's history.

The more the reader shall study the views above presented, the more must he become convinced that nations grow in self-respect as positives and negatives are brought into closer relation with each and every other, and as they themselves grow in strength; declining therein as producers and consumers become more widely separated, and they themselves become more subjected to the trading power.

§ 8. "To prohibit a great people," said Adam Smith, "from making all they can of every part of their own produce, or from employing their stock and industry in the way they judge most advantageous to themselves, is a manifest violation of the most sacred rights of humanity." Further than this, he showed most clearly that the policy thus denounced tended in the direction of creating a "nation of mere shopkeepers," and that the results, whether as regarded individuals or the nation at large, must prove in the end most disastrous; making, as it must, the whole societary body more and more liable to injury from causes occurring in distant lands, and over which it could exercise no control whatsoever. Most firm was he in his belief that the road to independence, at home or abroad, was to be found in the establishment of that interdependence among the members of a community by means of which a market should be made on or near the land for its products; the domestic commerce thus created tending to bring into activity all the best feelings of the human heart. He was no mere trader, nor had he learned to believe that the science whose foundation was then being laid was so soon to become limited to the questions of "material wealth alone," and as how to buy in the cheapest market, and sell in the dearest one; those which, above all others, tend to produce the narrowness which is the chief characteristic of most of that now given to the world as economic science. Greatly lauded was his work, but so entirely did it fail to carry to its readers conviction of its truth that from that hour to the present, as has been shown, Britain has been so earnestly engaged in warring against labor that, while her own capitalists have reaped large profits from the great discoveries of the almost century which since has passed, no advantage has thence resulted to that great working

British world in whose future, as so well is known, the immortal author of the *Wealth of Nations* both felt and expressed so warm an interest.

That the few were becoming greater, and the many more and more enslaved, became from day to day more clearly obvious, until at length, twenty years later, Mr. Malthus undertook the task of conciliating the blindest selfishness with an enlightened self-respect; to that end assuring capital that all the privations, all the suffering, of the laboring multitude were consequent upon an error of his own Divine Master; provision having been made for a geometrical increase in the number of human beings and for only an arithmetical increase in the supply of commodities required for their use. This all important law, as he assured them, was absolute, and any attempt at interference with its action, whether by exercise of charity or liberality, must prove a mere absurdity, productive of evil and not of good. Here was a great discovery. Need we wonder that capital gladly clutched it, feeling thereafter that it might, most piously, eat, drink, and hoard up money, while closing its eyes and its ears to the fact that the more its growth, and the greater its power, the greater became the tendency toward that "proletariat" at which the laboring masses seem now to have arrived? Assuredly not! Of all contrivances for crushing out all Christian feeling, and for developing self-worship, that the world yet has seen, there has been none entitled to claim so high a rank as that which has been, and yet daily is, assigned to the Malthusian *Law of Population.*

Passing on, we find Mr. Ricardo assuring his readers that the "natural rate of wages is just that price which is necessary to enable the laborers, one with another, to subsist and perpetuate their race, without either increase or diminution;" not, however, explaining why he himself, who never labored, should be entitled to claim any higher "rate" than that he thus established for the class which had given to the world men like Shakspeare and Luther, Guttenberg and Franklin, Arkwright and Watt.

In like manner, the planter assures himself that the "natural rate of wages" is just so much "hog and hominy," or rice and molasses, as will enable the laborer, and the laborer's wife, to perform their daily work in the field and to perpetuate their race. Being mere chattels why should they, or those others of whom Mr. Ricardo speaks, ask for more? In what, however, are his claims superior to those of Uncle Tom, or little Topsy?

Next came Mr. M'Culloch, bringing balm to be applied to the tortured feelings of great landholders, in form of an assurance that absenteeism should be regarded as a blessing rather than a curse; and that they might, with perfectly clear consciences, continue to subject tens or hundreds of thousands of "proletaires" to the "tender mercies" of agents whose duty it had been made to extract from labor and land all that could be extorted out of either, the proceeds to be then applied to the support of singers, actors, and dancers abroad; their own poor dependents meanwhile starving at home for want of power to sell their labor. We have here a great step toward conciliation of self-indulgence, the characteristic of barbarism, with self-respect, that of civilization; and how admirably it has done its work is proved by the coolness with which capital regards the famines and desolations of Ireland; the sheep-walks and deer-parks of Scotland; the approaching universality of cattle farming in England; and the fact that English agricultural labor has before it no future but that of the poorhouse.

§ 9. Thus far the tendency of the great *scientific* discoveries above described had been only that of misleading the public mind in reference to facts occurring within the bosoms of societary bodies, leaving to a later day their application to the relations of the world at large. For this the time has now arrived; that extension of the Malthusian doctrine which exhibits itself in "survival of the fittest," and consequent crushing out of those least "fitted" for life's contest, having already come to be regarded as being as applicable to communities whose numbers count by hundreds of millions, as it originally had been to towns and villages whose numbers were limited to tens or hundreds of thousands.

Being weak, why should not the Hindoo or Chinese race now give place to the powerful Caucasian one? Suffering as the former do, may not the reason therefor be found in the fact, that nature is thus providing place for the "fitter" race by whom they are to be succeeded? So, as we are told, it must assuredly be, the whole earth having been intended for that superior race which, for all the centuries that have elapsed since the days of Vasco de Gama, has been engaged in plundering and murdering those less instructed people who make their homes on the borders of the Indian Ocean, and in the lands of the South Pacific.*

Throughout that long period, the traders of *civilized* Europe, Portuguese and Spaniards, Dutch, French, and English, have been engaged in making

* Commenting upon the *scientific* issues thus presented, an eminent English naturalist invites attention to the fact that the brain of the savage is much in excess of his present needs, following this up by the question:—

"Does this not read to us another and a greater lesson? Does it not tell us, that the savage has organs of mind which require development by education and civilization? Can any language be plainer than that shown by the brain of the savage? Does it not show that these beings are not to be slain and exterminated because they are savage? Ay, plainer, I say, than language can describe, or eloquence illustrate, does this grand biological fact tell us that the savage has the means given him by his Creator, by which the blessings of education can evolve within him the thoughts, the feelings, the actions, the responsibilities, and the hopes of civilization." —Bree, *Fallacies of Darwinism*, p. 267.

What is the process by means of which *civilization* is now being carried among such people may be seen by turning to the exhibit as made, p. 323.

The community toward which *civilization* is now directing its most earnest efforts is that Japanese one recently described by Lord Elgin, in the words that follow:—

"A perfectly paternal government; a perfectly filial people; a community entirely self-supporting; peace within and without; no want; no ill-will between classes. This is what I find in Japan in the year 1858, after one hundred years excluding foreigners. Twenty years hence, what will be the contrast?"—*Letters and Journals*, p. 271.

Seeking an answer to this question, the reader may now, with advantage, review the facts here above given in regard to India and China.

of those vast territories, homes as they are of more than half the human race, a scene of horrors such as elsewhere find no parallel whatsoever. Throughout, everything has been done to destroy that power of association and combination in whose absence there can be obtained no increased control of the great natural forces, no growth in that power for self-direction so essential to development of the feeling of self-respect; and now, when oppression is being carried to a point that till now had never even been imagined, *science* most happily steps in to give countenance to immoralities the like of which the world has never known; assuring us of a great law in virtue of which the fittest, *i. e.*, *the strongest*, are to inherit the kingdom of the earth to the exclusion of gentler races which *practise* virtues that are *taught* in Christian edifices whose founders to so great an extent find in buying cheaply and selling dearly the one end and aim of life.* For all these barbarizing doctrines the world stands indebted to English teachers; but, happily, *not* to those of that earlier England in which the Saxon churl was freed from the degrading collar, thus enabling his descendants to stand as freemen on the fields of Agincourt and Marston Moor. On the contrary, to *that* England it is that it stands indebted for the present existence of a nation numbering forty millions, that has been engaged in an almost unceasing effort at resistance of the British "warfare" above described; one that in all international relations has

* See *ante*, p. 312, and note to page 239.

manifested an obedience to the great law of Christianity such as is without parallel in history;* and that now, as a consequence of that obedience, may claim to stand as equal with any community of the world, whether considered in regard to the intelligence of its people, or the material wealth at their command.

§ 10. Civilization consists in that self-respect which comes as necessary consequence of growing power to command the great natural forces; and which manifests itself in respecting in others, whether individuals or nations, those rights whose exercise we claim as inherent in ourselves. Barbarism exhibits itself in that self-indulgence, on the part of those who are strong and rich, whose effects, throughout all those portions of the world subjected to the control of Britain's great non-consuming army, now manifest themselves in growing tendency toward the establishment of serfage as the condition of the toiling millions; and whose best apologists are found in men who teach that in quiet submission to the orders of that army's chieftains is to be found the panacea for all human ills.†

* The single exception to this is found in the treatment that the Red Men of the west have so often met at *Christian* hands. Of this, much has been due to the fact, that the non-resistant policy has so greatly tended toward exhaustion of the soil, with steadily growing necessity for seizing on new and more distant lands.

† "Nothing is more adverse to the tranquillity of a statesman (says the author of an éloge on the administration of Colbert), than a spirit of moderation; because it condemns him to perpetual observation, shows him every moment the insufficiency of his wisdom, and leaves him the melancholy sense of his own imperfection; while, under the shelter of a

CHAPTER XIII.

OF SCIENTIFIC RELATIONS.

THROUGHOUT nature, the power of combination is in the direct ratio of the individualization of the several parts. The more perfect it becomes, the more rapid is the circulation and the greater the force exerted. So precisely is it with man. The more societary positives and negatives are brought together, and the more his power of association, the greater is the tendency toward development of his various faculties; the greater becomes his control of the forces of nature, and the more perfect his own power for self-direction; mental force thus more and more obtaining control over that which is material, the labors of the present over the accumulations of the past. The physically weak, and the physically strong, whether male or female, youthful or aged, tend

few general principles, a systematical politician enjoys a perpetual calm. By the help of one alone, that of a perfect liberty of trade, he would govern the world, and would leave human affairs to arrange themselves at pleasure, under the operation of the prejudices and the self-interests of individuals. If these run counter to each other, he gives himself no anxiety about the consequence; he insists that the result cannot be judged of till after a century or two shall have elapsed. If his contemporaries, in consequence of the disorder into which he has thrown public affairs, are scrupulous about submitting quietly to the experiment, he accuses them of impatience. They alone, and not he, are to blame for what they have suffered; and the principle continues to be inculcated with the same zeal and the same confidence as before."—*Quoted by* WAKEFIELD: *Preface to Wealth of Nations.*

more and more to meet on terms of strict equality; the circulation increasing in its rapidity at each and every step in that direction, with daily growth of that feeling of confidence which prompts to maintenance of our own rights when these are threatened to be invaded; and of that self-respect which demands compliance with the divine decree by which we are required to do to all others as, under like circumstances, we should desire to have them do by ourselves.

Such are the relations of physical, social, mental, and moral science.*

CHAPTER XIV.

DEFINITIONS.

A TRUE definition is one that embraces all which should be included while excluding all that should not. Those here given, as it is believed, fulfil these conditions.

* "That the scientific method of inquiry is inadequate, and inapplicable to the higher study of man, is a widely prevalent notion, and one which seems, to a great extent, to be shared alike by the ignorant and the educated. Holding the crude idea that science pertains only to the material world, they denounce all attempts to make human nature a subject of strict scientific inquiry, as an intrusion into an illegitimate sphere. Maintaining that man's position is supreme and exceptional, they insist that he is only to be comprehended, if at all, in some partial, peculiar and transcendental way. In entire consistence with this hypothesis is the prevailing practice; for those who, by their function as teachers, preachers, and lawgivers, profess to have that knowledge of man which best qualifies for

Utility is the measure of man's power over nature.

Value is the measure of nature's power over man; of the resistance she offers to the gratification of his desires. Its extent is limited within the cost of reproduction.

Wealth consists in the power of man to command the always gratuitous service of nature—in the sum of the utilities developed.

Production consists in directing those forces to man's service.

Capital is the instrument by help of which the work is done, whether existing in the form of land, ships, wagons, houses, mental or physical force.

Trade consists in the performance of exchanges *for* other persons, being the instrument used by—

Commerce, which consists in the exchange of services, products, or ideas, *by* men, and *with* their fellow-men.

As the power of association grows, utilities increase, while values decline.

As the value of commodities declines, that of man rises, with increase in the development of individuality, and in the security of property and of person.

directing him in all relations, are, as a class, confessedly ignorant of science. There are some, however, and happily their number is increasing, who hold that this idea is profoundly erroneous; that the very term 'human nature' indicates man's place in that universal order which it is the proper office of science to explore; and they accordingly maintain that it is only as 'the servant and interpreter of nature' that he can rise to anything like a true understanding of himself."—Youmans, *Lecture on the Scientific Study of Human Nature.*

As person and property become more secure, men and capital tend to become more fixed, and a smaller proportion of both remains in the floating state.

As men and capital become fixed, and the powers of nature are more and more developed, local centres increase in number and importance, with daily tendency toward establishment of the same beautiful system by means of which the harmony of the universe is maintained.

As local centres thus increase in number and attraction, societary positives and negatives are brought to more intimate association, each with every other; each and every stage of progress in this direction being attended with diminution of necessity for the trader's services, increase in the power of production, in the growth of capital, and in the rapidity of its circulation—with corresponding increase of commerce.

Competition may be for the SALE of human force, physical or mental, or its products; or, it may be for the PURCHASE of each and all of these. The first increases as societary positives and negatives become more widely separated; as labor becomes less productive and more controlled by capital; and as matter thus obtains power over mind. The second grows as positives and negatives are brought into more intimate connection each with every other; as labor becomes more productive, and as the laborer of the present grows in power as compared with the accumulations of the past; mind thus obtaining increased control over matter. In the one case the tendency is in the direction of inequality of condition, growing selfishness and *barbarism*, and daily diminished societary force. In the other it is toward equality of condition, growing self-respect, *civilization*, and daily growing societary force.

The British system looks to annihilation of competition for purchase of labor or its products elsewhere than in Britain. The resistant one looks to production of such competition throughout the world. Hence it is, that while the former tends everywhere toward subjection of mind to matter, and toward the subjugation of labor to capital, the latter tends equally toward perfect freedom of thought, speech, and action among all mankind.

APPENDIX.

THE LAW OF DISTRIBUTION.

§ 1. CAPITAL, the instrument by means of which man acquires power over the forces of nature, is a result of the accumulated mental and physical efforts of the past. The fibre of the wood which Crusoe required for his bow had been at all times equally capable of rendering service; but without an exercise of mental effort the bow would have remained unmade. Once made, its value was great, having been obtained at the cost of serious labor; its utility was, however, small, for it was capable of little work.

Friday had no canoe. Had he desired to borrow that of Crusoe, the latter might have said: "Fish abound at a little distance from the shore. Without the help of my machine you will scarcely obtain food enough for yourself; whereas with it you will, in little time, take enough to supply us both. Give me three-fourths of all you take, and the remainder shall be your own."

Hard as this might seem, Friday would have accepted the offer, profiting of Crusoe's capital though paying dearly for its use. Reflecting, however, that if he can become owner of a boat he will then retain the entire product, he next makes terms with Crusoe for the use of his knife, and by its aid succeeds in making one. Both being now capitalists their conditions have much approximated, notwithstanding the advances that Crusoe may himself have made. At first his wealth stood at 10, while that of Friday was at 0. The former has now reached 40, but the latter has attained to 10. Tendency toward equality is thus the certain result of that growth of wealth by means of which man is enabled to substitute mental for merely physical force. Every increase in his power over nature is but the preparation for greater progress in the same direction; here as everywhere, it being the first step which is the most costly yet the least productive. Look where we may, we find man passing from the weaker to the more powerful instruments of production; the poor settler using wood in the production of iron, though surrounded by mineral coal capable of performing thrice the service at a cost of half the labor. The more the capability of rendering service the greater is the resistance to be overcome, whether we desire to command the aid of things or of men. The laws of nature are thus, as we see, of universal truth.

§ 2. The bow and the canoe enabling Friday to economize his time, he gives his leisure to construction of a knife and a sail—all now combining to give him power to construct a house; the quantity of labor required for *reproducing* and increasing capital diminishing with every stage of progress. The first stone knife had been the fruit of far more effort than is now required for making one of bronze, and yet the latter is by very far the more efficient instrument. The axe of stone has now no value, though its services had at first been held as equal to three-fourths of those of the man who used it. The still more efficient axes of iron and steel coming into use, the bronze axe, in turn, declines in value. Mind obtaining command over matter the great natural forces become centred in man, who now discards the earlier instruments; preserving specimens only as curious evidences of the inferiority of his predecessors.

Measuring himself against his products, man attributes to himself every increase of utility in the materials by which he is everywhere surrounded. The greater that utility the higher is his own value, and the less that of the things he needs. The cost of reproduction steadily declining, he himself as steadily rises, every reduction in the value of existing capital being so much added to the value of the MAN.

§ 3. Little as was the work that could be done with the axe of stone, its value to the owner was very great; and the man to whom he lent it might, therefore, profitably pay largely for its use. The latter, cutting with it more wood in a day than without it he could have done in a month, though paying three-fourths of his product finds his wages largely increased, large as is the *proportion* claimed by its proprietor, his neighbor capitalist.

The bronze axe being next obtained and proving far more useful, its owner, being asked to grant its use, is required to recollect that not only has the productiveness of labor greatly *increased*, but the quantity required to be given for its reproduction has greatly *decreased*. He therefore demands but two-thirds of the product of the far more useful instrument. The distribution now may thus be stated:—

	Total product.	Laborer's share.	Capitalist's share.
Axe of stone . . .	4	1	3
Axe of bronze. . .	8	2.66	5.33

The reward of labor has more than doubled; being an *increased proportion* of an increased quantity. The capitalist's share has not quite doubled, he receiving a *diminished proportion* of the same increased quantity. The position of the laborer, which had been at first as 1 to 3, is now as 1 to 2, with great increase of power to become himself a capitalist.

The axe of iron coming next, the cost of reproduction again diminishes, while labor again increases in its proportion as compared with capital. The new instrument cuts twice as much as had done that of bronze, yet is its owner compelled to be content with claiming half the product. The new distribution will be as follows:—

	Total.	Laborer.	Capitalist.
Axe of stone	4	1	3
Axe of bronze	8	2.66	5.33
Axe of iron	16	8	8

The axe of steel now coming, the product is again doubled, with further diminution in the cost of reproduction; and now the capitalist must content himself with a less proportion, the distribution being as follows:—

	Total.	Laborer.	Capitalist.
Axe of steel	32	19.20	12.80

The laborer's share has increased; and, the product having largely increased, the augmentation of his quantity is very great. That of the capitalist has diminished in proportion; but, the product having so much increased, *this reduction of proportion has been accompanied by large increase of quantity*, both thus profiting by the improvements that have been effected.

Such is the great law governing the distribution of labor's products. Of all recorded in the book of science it is perhaps the most beautiful, being that one in virtue of which there is established a perfect harmony of real and true interests among the various classes of mankind. Still further, it establishes the fact that, however great may have been the oppressions of the many at the hands of the few, however large the accumulations resulting from exercise of the power of appropriation, however striking the existing distinctions among men, all that is required for establishing everywhere perfect equality before the law, and for promoting a general equality of social condition, is the pursuit of a system tending to establish in the highest degree the power of association and the development of individuality; thereby maintaining peace and promoting the growth of wealth and population both at home and abroad.

B.

OF THE OCCUPATION OF THE EARTH.

§ 1. The first American settlers of English race established themselves on the barren soil of Massachusetts, founding the colony of Plymouth. The continent was before them, but they had to take what, with their small means, they could command. Other settlements were formed at Newport and New Haven, and thence they may be traced following always the course of the rivers, but taking the higher lands and leaving the clearing of timber and the draining of swamps to their successors. The most productive New England soils are those reclaimed within the last half century.

In New York the process has been the same. The unproductive soil of Manhattan Island, and the higher lands of the opposite shore, claimed early attention, while richer lands, close at hand, remain even yet uncultivated. Thence we trace the settlers along the Hudson to the Valley of the Mohawk, where they established themselves near the head of the stream on lands requiring but little of either clearing or drainage. Geneva, and other towns and villages now seen in the rich western lands of the State, scarcely existed sixty years since; while the high lands bordering on Pennsylvania were early settled; those on Coshocton Creek having been described as very valuable because of "their total exemption from all periodical disorders, particularly fever and ague."

In New Jersey we see the Quakers occupying the high lands towards the heads of rivers, or selecting along the Delaware the light soils that bear the pine, while avoiding the heavier ones on the opposite shore of Pennsylvania, and neglecting altogether rich lands that still remain covered with the finest timber. Passing through sandy districts of the State we find hundreds of little clearings long since abandoned, attesting the character of the land that men cultivate when population is small, and land is most abundant

On the sandy soil of Delaware, the Swedes settled Lewistown and Christiana; and in the now decaying little towns of Elkton and Charlestown, near the head of the Chesapeake Bay, we find evidence of the poverty of the soils first occupied, when fine meadow lands, now the richest farms in the State, were wholly worthless.

Penn follows the Swedes, first selecting the high lands on the Delaware, about twelve miles north of the site of his future city, but afterwards taking the tongue of land near the confluence of that river and the Schuylkill. Thence we find population extending northwest along the ridge running north and between the rivers, where miles of early settlements still remain. On the maps of a somewhat later period, the fertile lands near the river, almost to the head of tide water, are shown as held in large tracts and yet uncleared, while those more elevated are divided into little farms. Further on, cultivation almost leaves the river bank, but at a distance therefrom we find farms that have now been cultivated for more than a hundred years. The old road, made to suit the early settlers, is seen winding about as if in search of hills to cross; the new roads keeping near the stream, on the low lands which have but recently been subjected to cultivation. Crossing the mountains, we see near their tops the habitations of early settlers, who selected the land of that pine whose knots afforded a substitute for candles they were too poor to purchase. Beyond, we find, in the valley of the Susquehanna, meadow lands, still uncleared, and covered with heavy timber. Everywhere, we find cultivation to have commenced on the hillsides, and gradually to have descended, the valleys becoming more cleared of timber, and meadows and cattle appearing, the most certain signs of increasing wealth and population. Passing west, at the foot of the Muncy hills, we find fine limestone land, whole tracts of which were exchanged for a jug of whiskey, or a dollar. Taking a bird's eye view of the country, we trace the courses of the little streams by the timber standing on their banks, conspicuous among the cleared, but elevated, lands that are everywhere around. Crossing the ridge of the Allegheny to the headwaters of the Ohio, we see a scattered population occupying the higher lands; but as we descend, those near the river become cleared, until at length we find ourselves at Pittsburg, in the midst of a dense population actively employed in bringing into connection the coal, the limestone, and the iron ore, with a view to preparation of the machinery required for enabling the farmer to plough more deeply, and to drain the fertile lands of the river bottoms.

The early settlers of the West uniformly selected the higher lands, avoiding the valleys of streams on account of the fevers which even now sweep off so many emigrants. Seeking a dry place for his dwelling, the settler always selected the ridges, as affording a facility for obtaining speedily some small crop; the same reason which prevented him from attempting artificial drainage in reference to his house, operating with equal force in regard to the land required for cultivation.

In Wisconsin the traveller finds the first white settler placed on the highest land, known by the title of "The Blue Mound;" and he follows the early roads along ridges upon which are found the villages of the primitive settlers; occasionally crossing a "wet prairie," the richest land of the State, and always the terror of the early emigrant.

Arrived at the confluence of the Ohio and the Mississippi, we find only the poor wood-cutter who risks his health while providing wood for the numerous steamers which pass the place. For hundreds of miles we pass through fertile lands clothed with the heaviest timber, as yet of no value for cultivation, for the reason that the air around is filled with gases that are destructive of both health and life.

Descending further, we meet population and wealth ascending the Mississippi, from the shores of the Gulf of Mexico. Embankments, or *levées*, keep out the river, and the finest plantations are seen on land corresponding with the uncultivated region left behind, while to seek the habitations of the early settlers we must leave the river bank and ascend the hills. If, instead of descending the Mississippi, we ascend the Missouri, the Kentucky, the Tennessee, or the Red River, we find, invariably, that the more dense the population, and the greater the mass of wealth, the more are the rich soils cultivated; that as population diminishes with our approach to the head-waters, and land becomes more abundant, cultivation recedes from the river bank, and the undrained meadow and timber lands become more abundant—scattered inhabitants obtaining from the superficial soils a scanty return to labor, with little power to command the necessaries and comforts of life.

In Texas we see the town of Austin, the seat of the first American settlement, to have been placed high up on the Colorado, millions of acres of the finest lands having been passed over as incapable of paying the cost of simple appropriation. In the Spanish colony of Bexar, we see further illustration of the same universal fact, that colonization tends always toward the head-waters of the rivers.

So, too, in the Southern Atlantic States. The richest lands of North Carolina still remain undrained, while men waste labor on those which yield but three to five bushels of wheat per acre. South Carolina, Georgia, Alabama, and Florida, have millions of acres of the finest lands unoccupied and waiting the growth of population to yield immense returns to labor.

The facts are everywhere the same: for the same reason that

the settler builds himself a log-house, to provide shelter till he can have one of stone, he begins cultivation where he can raise some small crop. Whenever settlements have been attempted on rich lands they have either failed, or their progress has been very slow indeed. We see this in the repeated failures of the French colonies of Louisiana and Cayenne, compared with the steady growth of those formed in the region of the St. Lawrence; and in the slow progress of the colonies planted on the rich lands of Virginia and Carolina, as compared with that of those begun on the sterile New England soils. The former cannot compensate men working for themselves, and hence it is that we find the richer colonists purchasing negroes and compelling them to perform the work, while the free laborer seeks the light sandy lands of North Carolina. No man, left to himself, will begin the work of cultivation on the rich soils, because it is from them that the return is then the least; and it is upon them that the condition of the laborer is worst, when the work is undertaken in advance of the habit of association that comes with the growth of wealth and population. The settler on the high lands obtained, at least, food; had he attempted to drain the rich soils of the Dismal Swamp he would have starved, as did those who had sought to occupy the fertile island of Roanoke.

§ 2. Passing now into Mexico, we find further illustration of the universality of this law of occupation. Near the mouth of the river, but at some distance from its bank, is Matamoras, a city of recent date. Passing upward, through rich lands in a state of nature, he reaches the mouth of the San Juan, ascending which he finds himself in a somewhat populous country, with Monterey for its capital. Northward, on the high land of Chihuahua, he sees cultivation keeping away from the river banks; while westward from Monterey, through Saltillo, his road lies over sandy plains which yet are occupied. Arriving in Potosi, he finds himself in a country in which failure of the periodical rains is followed by famine and death; yet downwards towards the coast, he sees a magnificent territory, watered by numerous rivers, in which cotton and indigo grow spontaneously, and which could supply the world with sugar; but there he sees no signs of population. The land is uncleared, for those who should undertake the work, with the present means of the country, would either starve, or perish by reason of the fevers that there so much prevail.

Passing on, he sees Zacatecas, high and dry, like Potosi, yet cultivated. Tlascala, once the seat of a wealthy people, occupies the high lands whence descend little streams flowing to both the Atlantic and the Pacific Oceans. The valley of

Mexico, in the time of Cortez, supported forty cities; but population has declined, and the remaining people have retired to the high lands around to cultivate the poorer soils from which the single city that yet remains derives its supplies of food. Fertile land is superabundant, but the people fly from it; whereas, according to Mr. Ricardo, it should be the first appropriated.

Passing southward, the fertile lands of Tabasco are seen almost unoccupied; but in Yucatan, a region in which water is a luxury, we find a prosperous population, near neighbors to the better soils of Honduras, still a wilderness affording subsistence to but a few miserable logwood and mahogany cutters.

In the Caribbean Sea we find the litle rocky islands of Monserret, Nevis, St. Lucia, St. Vincent, and others, cultivated throughout; the rich soil of Trinidad remaining even yet almost in a state of nature, and the fertile Porto Rico but now beginning to be subjected to cultivation.

Looking now southward, we see, in Costa Rica, and in Nicaragua, lands of incomparable fertility totally unoccupied, Indian villages meantime abounding on the mountain slopes.

Further south, are seen the cities of Santa Fé and Quito, centres of population, where men cluster together on high and dry lands leaving the valley of the Orinoco unoccupied; the same facts being here exhibited, which, on a smaller scale, have been shown to exist in Pennsylvania. The only civilized people of the days of Pizarro, occupied Peru, the rapid course of whose little streams prevented the formation of marshes where decaying vegetable matter might give richness to the soil.

On the east is Brazil, watered by the largest rivers in the world, and capable of yielding in untold abundance all the products of the tropics, and with the precious metals lying near the surface; but yet a wilderness. Having no elevated table lands, it affords no eligible site for European colonists. On the steep slope of Chili, we find a people advancing in population and wealth, the fertile valley of the La Plata remaining plunged in barbarism.

§ 3. Crossing the ocean, and landing in the south of England, the traveller finds himself in a country where the streams are short and the valleys limited; and, consequently, fitted for early cultivation. There, Cæsar found the only people of the island who had made any progress in the art of tillage, the more inland tribes living on the spoils of the chase, or on the milk yielded by their flocks. In the barren Cornwall he sees marks of cultivation of great and unknown antiquity; and in a part thereof now seldom visited are found the ruins of Tintagel, the castle in which King Arthur held his court. He finds the seats of early cultivation in the sites of rotten boroughs, or in those parts of the kingdom where men who can neither read nor write still live in mud-built cottages, and receive but six or eight shillings for a week of labor. He sees the palace of the Norman kings at Winchester, and not in the valley of the Thames; while in South Lancashire, with its rich fields of waving grain, he finds the country whose morasses had nearly swallowed up the army of the conquering Norman on his return from devastating the North; and which daunted the antiquary, Camden, so late as the age of James I. Asking for the lands most recently reduced to cultivation, he will be shown the fens of Lincoln and Cambridgeshire, now yielding the best crops of England; but which were without any money value until the steam-engine had been brought to aid the labors of the agricultulist.

To find the seats of the earliest cultivation in Scotland he must visit remote districts, now abandoned to a few black cattle; the newest soils being found in the Lothians, or on the banks of the Tweed, but recently inhabited by barbarians whose chief pleasure was found in plundering expeditions into England—the forests and swamps of the days of Mary and Elizabeth presenting the finest farms of Scotland. We find the poorest people in the Western Isles, or in the Orkneys, once deemed so valuable as to be received by the King of Norway in pledge for repayment of a sum of money far greater than would now purchase the fee-simple of the land.

§ 4. In France, in the days of Cæsar, we see the most powerful tribes seated on the flanks of the Alps, and the centres of trade in the rich cities of Bibracte, Vienne, and Noviodunum; the now fertile Belgica presenting but a single place of note, and that at the passage of the Somme, where now stands Amiens. Amongst the Alps themselves, the Helvetii had a dozen cities and nearly four hundred villages. Seeking the cities of the days of Philip Augustus, Chalons, St. Quentin, Soissons, Rheims, Troyes, Nancy, Orleans, Bourges, Dijon, Vienne, Nismes, Toulouse, or Cahors, this last once the centre of the banking operations of France, we find them far towards the heads of the streams on which they stand, or on the high ground between the rivers. The centres of power at a later period are found in the wild Brittany, where wolves even yet abound; in Dijon, on the flank of the Alps; in Auvergne, but recently "a secret and safe asylum of crime;" in the Limousin, which gave to the Church so many popes that the Limousin cardinals almost dictated the proceedings of the Conclave; or on the slopes of the Cevennes, where literature and art flourished when the richer soils, vast tracts of which even yet remain undrained, were wholly waste.

In Belgium we find the poor Luxemburg and Limburg to have been cultivated from a remote period; the fertile Flanders remaining until the seventeenth century an impenetrable desert. Even till the thirteenth century, the forest of Soignies covered the site of Brussels, and the fertile Brabant was almost uncultivated; while in the now almost abandoned *Campine* of Antwerp were found the ancient cities of Gheel and Heerenthal, and the castle of Westerloo, one of the oldest in Belgium, whose ditches even yet supply their visitors with implements of war dating back to Roman days. In the time of Cæsar, Maestricht was known only as the place of passage of the Maes, as the Broecksel of a later period, now Brussels, was but the passage of the Senne.

In Holland, we see a miserable people, living on islands of sand and subsisting chiefly on fish, whose poverty exempted them from the grinding taxation of Rome. Slowly they increased in numbers and in wealth. Chief among the provinces was the narrow and barren Hauptland, which gave its name to the entire region. Unable to obtain food by means of agriculture, the Dutch sought it in the direction of manufactures and trade; but with the growth of population and wealth came the clearing of woods and draining of marshes, and we see them then becoming the richest nation of Europe.

§ 5. Further north, we find a people whose ancestors, passing from the neighborhood of the Don through the plains of Northern Germany, selected the barren mountains of Scandinavia as the land best suited to their then condition. Everywhere throughout this country the marks of early cultivation are found on high and poor lands long since abandoned. To such an extent is this the case, that it has afforded countenance to the belief that this must have been the seat of the great "Northern Hive" by which Southern Europe was supposed to have been overrun. The facts, however, are but a repetition of those described in regard to North and South America, England, Scotland, France, and Belgium, and which recur again in Russia, where, as an English traveller tells his readers, "we see the poorest soil selected for cultivation, while the richest remains neglected in its close vicinity."

Germany, in the country watered by the Danube and its tributaries, exhibits a population abounding at the heads of streams, but diminishing as we descend that great river until, on reaching the richest lands, we find them to be entirely unoccupied. In Hungary "the Puzta," the cradle of Hungarian nationality, presents to view a wide plain consisting of wave-like sand hills; while beyond the Theiss rich lands abound, destitute of human life.

In Italy, a numerous population occupied the highlands of Cisalpine Gaul when the rich soils of Venetia were yet unoccupied. Southward, along the flanks of the Appenines, we find a gradually increasing population, and towns whose age may almost be inferred from their situation. The Samnite hills were peopled, Etruria occupied, and Veii and Alba built, before Romulus gathered together his adventurers on the banks of the Tiber.

In Greece, we meet the same universal fact. On the hills of Arcadia were settlements which long preceded those of the lands of Elis watered by the Alpheus; and the meagre soil of Attica was early occupied, while the fat Bœotia followed slowly in the rear. On the hill-tops, in various quarters, the sites of deserted cities presented in the historical times of Greece evidences of long previous occupation. On the short slope of eastern Argolis, early abandoned, are found the ruins of the palace of Agamemnon; and north of the Gulf of Corinth, we see the Phocians, Locrians, and Ætolians clustered on the high and poor lands, while the rich plains of Thessaly and Thrace remained destitute of population.

The mountainous Crete, likewise, was occupied from a period when the Delta of the Nile was a wilderness. Ascending that river, cultivation becomes at each step more ancient, until we reach Thebes, the first great city of Egypt. With the growth of population and wealth, Memphis became the capital, the Delta not having been reclaimed until a still later period.

Along the north of Africa, the most civilized portion of the people are seen clustering on the slopes of Mount Atlas; and farther south, the capital of Abyssinia is found at an elevation of eight thousand feet above the sea, while lands of the greatest fertility remain entirely uncultivated.

§ 6. In the Pacific Ocean we find innumerable islands whose lower lands are unoccupied, their richness rendering them fatal to life; while population clusters round the hills. The valleys of Australia are inhabited by tribes the lowest of the human race; while on the little high-pointed islands around are found a superior race, with houses, cultivation, and manufactures.* In the dominions of the King of Candy, in Ceylon, the people show the same aversion to the low and rich lands as is felt by those of Mexico and Java. Entering India by Cape Comorin,

* Professor Hearne, of Melbourne College, in his *Plutology*, recognizes the accuracy of these views as to the order of Australian occupation.

and following the range of high lands, we find the cities of Seringapatam, Poonah, and Ahmednugger, while below, near the coast, are the recent European cities of Madras, Calcutta, and Bombay. The Indus rolls its course through hundreds of miles almost without a settlement on its banks; the higher country, right and left, presenting a numerous population. The rich Delta of the Ganges is unoccupied, but far towards the head of the river we meet Delhi, the capital of India while the government yet remained in the hands of native sovereigns. Here, as everywhere, man avoids the rich soils that need drainage, and raises his food on the higher lands which drain themselves; and here, as always where the superficial soil alone is cultivated, the return to labor is small; and hence it is that we find the Hindoo working for a rupee or two per month, sufficient only to give him a handful of rice per day, and to purchase a rag of cotton cloth with which to shield his nakedness. The most fertile soils exist in unlimited quantity close to that which the laborer scratches with a stick for want of a spade, gathering his harvest with his hands for want of a reaping-hook, and carrying home on his shoulders the miserable crop for want of a horse and cart.

Passing northward, by Caboul and Affghanistan, leaving to the left that Persia, whose dry and barren soil has been for ages cultivated, we find amongst the Himalayas the villages placed on slopes which yield but scanty crops of millet, maize, and buckwheat. Here we have the cradle of the human race, and may trace hence the course of successive tribes passing toward more productive soils; sometimes stopping to cultivate such hilly lands as can be made to yield a small supply of food; then crossing the sea to place themselves on little peaked islands like those of the Ægean, so early cultivated. Some of these tribes reach the Mediterranean, where civilization is first found, and soonest lost under successive waves of emigration: others, passing further west, enter Italy, France, and Spain, while still others reach the British Isles. After a few centuries of rest, we find them crossing the Atlantic, and ascending the slope of the Alleghany, preparatory to the ascent and passage of the great range which divides the waters of the Pacific from those of the Atlantic. In all cases we see the pioneers seizing on the clear dry land of the steep hill-side, thence, as population increases, descending towards the rich lands of the river bottom; or penetrating to the lower soils, combining the upper clay or sand with the lower marl or lime, and thus compounding a soil capable of yielding large returns to labor. Everywhere, with increased power of union, man exercises increased power over land.

Everywhere, as new soils are brought into activity, we find more rapid increase of population, producing increased tendency to combination of exertion, by aid of which the powers of men are often fifty-fold increased, enabling them to provide better for their immediate wants, while accumulating the machinery needed for bringing to light the vast treasures of nature. Everywhere, we find that with increasing population the supply of food becomes more abundant and regular, clothing and shelter are obtained with greater ease, famine and pestilence tend to pass away, health becomes more general, life more prolonged, and man more happy and more free.

In regard to all human wants, except the single one of food, such is admitted to be the case. It is seen that with the growth of population and wealth men obtain water, iron, coal, and clothing, and the use of houses, ships, and roads, in return for diminished labor. It is not doubted that the gigantic works by means of which rivers are carried through our cities enable men to obtain water at smaller cost then when each man took a bucket and helped himself on the river bank. It is seen that the shaft which it took years to sink supplies fuel at far less cost of labor than had been required when the settler carried home scraps of half-decomposed timber, for want of an axe with which to cut the already fallen log ; that the gristmill does the work of thousands of human arms ; and that the gigantic factory supplies cloth more cheaply than has done the little loom ; but it is denied that so it is in reference to the supply of food. In regard to everything else, man begins with the worst machinery, and proceeds upward to the best ; but in regard to land, and that alone, he begins, according to Mr. Ricardo, with the best and proceeds downward toward the worst ; and with every stage of progress finds a decreasing return to labor, threatening starvation, and admonishing him against raising children to aid him in his age, lest, like the people of India, or of the Pacific Isles, they should bury him alive or expose him on the river bank, that they might divide among themselves his modicum of food.

How far this is so the reader will now determine for himself. All the other laws of nature are universally true ; and he may now agree with us that there is but *one* law for food, light, clothing, and fuel—that man, in all cases, commences with poor machinery and proceeds onward to the better ; being thus enabled with the growth of wealth, population, and the power of association, to obtain with constantly diminishing labor an increased supply of all the necessaries, conveniences, comforts, and luxuries of life.

Whenever population and wealth, and the consequent power of combination, are permitted to *increase*, there arises a tendency toward abandonment of the poor lands first cultivated, as is proved by the experience of England, Scotland, Sweden, and some of our Northern States. Whenever, on the contrary, these *decline*, it is the rich soils that are abandoned, men flying to the poorer ones to obtain the means of subsistence. With every step in the former direction, there is an increase in the value of man as compared with the commodities required for his use, accompanied by a growing facility of accumulation; whereas, with every movement in the latter one, he becomes more and more the slave of his fellow-man, with constant increase in the value of commodities, and as constant decline in his own.

C.

STATISTICAL FACTS ILLUSTRATING THE WORKING OF THE RESISTANT AND NON-RESISTANT POLICIES IN THE UNITED STATES.

THE decade of 1850–60, was one of quiet submission to the British system, and of somewhat quiet preparation, on the part of the advocates of non-resistance, for the great rebellion. In that period POPULATION increased 35 per cent., having grown from 23,200,000 to 31,450,000. Of this, no inconsiderable portion was the result of attractive gold discoveries in the now Pacific States. Of the decade that followed, nearly half was given to a war that greatly affected the growth of numbers; and as a consequence, the ratio of increase was but 23½ per cent.; giving 38½ millions as the population of 1870.

The non-resistant decade commenced with an IMMIGRATION of 310,000. By 1860 it had fallen to 153,000. In 1870, under the resistant policy, it had grown to 373,000. That of 1872 promises to be nearly half a million, with a money value of $500,000,000.

The WEALTH of the country, by the census of 1850, *corrected*, slaves excluded, was probably $8,000,000,000.* In 1860 it had but reached $14,000,000,000. In 1870 it was $30,000,000,000; the increase in the decade having been greatly more than the

* "The increase of property from 1850 to 1860, according to the estimates of the census, was from $6,174,000,000 to $14,183,000,000, or 129 per cent. Much of this large increase, however, is known to have been due to more accurate methods of enumeration, and to the inclusion of many

accumulations of the centuries since the "Mayflower's" arrival. To this may now be added, an increase in the value of human service representing a capital nearly equal to that exhibited in the growth of material capital in the same decade.

FOREIGN COMMERCE.

Domestic exports, gold included.	Imports retained for consumption.
1850, $137,000,000	$163,000,000
1860, 373,000,000	335,000,000
1870, 513,000,000	513,000,000

Customs, Revenue.—1850, $40,000,000; 1860, $53,000,000; 1870, $206,000,000.

PUBLIC DEBT, created in the last three years of the non-resistant period, $70,000,000; extinguished in the last three of the resistant one, $300,000,000.

RAILROADS, miles of, in 1850, 7000; in 1860, 31,000; in 1871, 62,000.

In 1860 the money value of railroad property averaged less than half its cost. Now, it is probably considerably more than cost; and yet, the amount that has been applied within the last decade toward increasing the efficiency of the various works is perhaps as great as their original cost had been.

IRON PRODUCTION, 1847–8,* 800,000 tons; 1858–60, average, 820,000; 1870, 1,900,000.

IRON CONSUMPTION, of foreign and domestic products, 1847–8, 900,000 tons; 1858–60, 1,200,000; 1870, 2,500,000.

WOOL PRODUCTION, 1850, 52,000,000 pounds; 1860, 60,000,000; 1871, 171,000,000.

WOOL CONSUMPTION, foreign and domestic manufacture, 1850, 87,000,000 pounds; 1860, 125,000,000; 1870–71, 266,000,000.

COTTON CONSUMPTION, 1847–48, 540,000 bales; 1858–60, 666,000; 1871, 1,154,000.

MANUFACTURES, 1850, $1,019,000,000;† 1860, $1,885,000,000; 1870, $4,306,000,000.

elements previously left unnoticed. A careful review made at the request of the Secretary, by the Commissioner, * * resulted in the conclusion that the then rate of increase was about 65 per cent.; * * or certainly not in excess of 80 per cent."—*Report of Commissioner Wells*, 1869, p. 11.

* This was the closing year of the resistant policy, the tariff of 1846 having gone into effect at the opening of 1847.

† For the reasons above given in reference to the *wealth* of the country, this is probably considerably below the truth. It was a first attempt at obtaining such information and much was overlooked. The figures might, perhaps, be more correct if made to read $1,200,000,000.

Coffee Consumption, 1850, 130,000,000 pounds; 1860, 182,000,000; 1871, 312,000,000.

Tea Consumption, 1850, 27,000,000 pounds; 1860, 26,000,000; 1871, 45,000,000.

Sugar Consumption, 1850, 606,000,000 pounds; 1860, 930,000,000; 1870, 1,469,000,000.

Orchard Fruits; production, 1850, $8,000,000; 1860, $20,000,000; 1870, $47,000,000.

Saving Fund Deposits.—In the closing year of the non-resistant decade (1860), the deposits in the four New England States, Maine, New Hampshire, Massachusetts, and Rhode Island, and the two cities of Philadelphia and Newark, amounted to but $66,000,000. In the following year they were still less. Seven years later (1868), they amounted to $153,000,000. In New York, in 1860, the depositors numbered 300,000, and the amount at their credit was $67,000,000. Eight years later, the former had grown to 537,000, and the latter to $151,000,000.

As here is shown the only important advance made in the first of these decades, that of submission, was in the foreign trade, and in railroad construction for carrying raw produce to the ports, and finished commodities back to the farmer and the planter. Unprofitable to the country at large, this latter proved to the capitalist most disastrous, ruin having been the result of the major part of the work thus performed. Of manufactures, allowance having been made for the census errors of 1850, the growth had been but little in excess of that of population. In regard to all other of the figures we have the great fact, that in no case, of sugar and wool alone excepted, had consumption kept pace with the growth of numbers. Nevertheless, to this decade it was that the country had stood indebted for the marvellous increase of the gold supply by which the world at large had been so greatly stirred.

What, under these circumstances, was the condition of the working man, may be inferred from the fact that, despite the gold attractions of the Pacific States, immigration had fallen in 1860 to less than half the figures of 1850.

Turning now to the remarkable decade which so recently has closed, distinguished on one hand as it has been by terrific waste of both property and life; and on the other by a perseverance in the resistant policy such as the country before had never known; we find that while population has less than one-fourth increased, the customs' revenue has almost quadrupled; the growth of manufactures having meantime been greatly more than had been their total amount at the opening of the war. So, too, as the reader sees, has it been with regard to the *consumption* of nearly all the commodities that have been here referred to.

More than all remarkable, however, are the facts, that so great has been the demand for human service, and so abundant its reward, that immigration has already almost thrice increased; and that it promises now to grow with more rapidity than it has done at any period we have ever known.

The difference between the two periods consists in this: that in the first, positives and negatives were daily becoming more widely separated, with constant diminution in the rapidity of circulation and in the societary force; whereas, in the other they have been coming daily more and more near together with constant increase in the economy of human effort, and as constant growth in the rapidity of the circulation and in the manifestation of societary force. Throughout the one, self respect so rapidly decreased that slavery was allowed daily to grow in power. Throughout the other, self respect has grown with steady growth as the equal rights of all have been more and more acknowledged.

D.

[From the *Fortnightly Review*, London, September, 1871.]

THE OPIUM TRADE.

Mr. Gladstone, in speaking of the opium war with China, once remarked that "justice was on the side of the Pagan." Never was this more true than at the present time, when a Pagan government, in spite of domestic anarchy, of the paralyzing influence of official corruption, and of the perpetual menace of foreign intervention, yet nobly endeavors to exert what remains of its shattered authority on the side of virtue and the good order of the State. On the other hand, I know of nothing more ignoble than the heartless indifference with which the failure of these patriotic efforts is regarded by so-called civilized nations, or the immoral cynicism with which English statesmen not only excuse but justify our share in entailing the greatest of calamities on one-third of the human race. If it were possible for us to escape from the responsibility which must ever attach itself to the authors of the first Chinese War; if we could prove that in forcing the legalization of the opium trade by the treaty of Tientsin we yielded to iron necessity; if, moreover, we could demonstrate that our duty to India compelled us to prefer the temporary exigencies of revenue to the lasting interests of morality—it would still be incumbent on us to face the fact that our position is at once shameful and humiliating. But when we know that the direct responsibility of every act that has led to the degradation and rapid decline of the Chinese Empire lies at our own door, and that the policy which has borne these evil fruits is still being, in a great measure, carried out by the concurrent action of Anglo-Indian administrators and British statesmen, the ignominy demands some fortitude for us to bear it. We, however, do bear it; and, at the same time, lose no opportunity of ministering to our self-love by pretending that wherever English commerce extends, or English influence penetrates, both confer untold benefits upon the less-favored nations of the world.

A few historical facts will show how entirely Great Britain is answerable for the desolating effects of the opium trade in China. Before the East India Company executed the project of embarking in the trade, the only opium exported into China was conveyed thither by the Portuguese from Turkey. The annual supply did not exceed 200 chests, and it was used strictly for medicinal purposes. In 1773, the company first engaged in the traffic, but for many years the Chinese regarded it with so little favor that it proved very unprofitable. The Company, in fact, had to create the appetite, which has since given the extraordinary stimulus to the demand for the drug which we see existing in our own day. The Chinese Government, from the outset, exhibited a resolute determination to restrain its subjects either from carrying on the trade, or from becoming personally addicted to the use of opium. The severest penalties were imposed by law, and, in many instances, actually enforced. The punishment of the bamboo and the pillory not sufficing to curb the appetite of the opium-smoker, far severer punishments—including that of death—were added. The persistence of the Celestials in resisting the encroachments of the East India Company was only equalled by the perseverance with which the latter prosecuted its designs. A government monopoly in the drug was established. Large districts of fertile territory were confiscated to the cultivation of the poppy, and the ryots were openly coerced into growing it. The finest and swiftest vessels were employed to convey the prepared drug from India to China. How "the foreign devils"—and surely the phrase is not altogether misapplied—violated the laws of the empire is graphically described by Heu Naetze, Vice-President of the Sacrificial Court at Pekin:—

"At Canton," he says, "there are brokers of the drug, who are called melters; these pay the price of the drug into the hands of the resident foreigners, who give them orders for the delivery of the opium from the receiving-ships. There are carrying-boats plying up and down the river, and these are vulgarly termed 'fast-crabs' and 'scrambling-dragons.' They are well-armed with guns and other weapons, and are manned with some scores of desperadoes, who ply their oars as if they were wings to fly with. All the custom house and military posts which they pass are largely bribed; if they happen to encounter any of the armed cruising-boats, they are so audacious as to resist, and slaughter and carnage ensue."

The war of 1839 was the natural outcome of these lawless proceedings. The authorities at Canton, in the exercise of a strict right, required the British merchants to send away the "receiving-ships;" but these persons would neither send away the ships nor deliver up the opium. Commissioner Lin then ordered the merchants to be imprisoned until the opium was surrendered—a measure which had the effect of placing the whole of the drug then in Chinese waters, amounting to 20,000 chests, in his possession. Even in the light of the tragical events which ensued one may be excused for exulting in the moral courage which the Chinese Commissioner displayed. He might have retained the opium, to be given up under pressure; or he might, as easily, have confiscated it, reserving to himself, according to Eastern fashion, a lion's share of the plunder. Instead of adopting either of these courses he caused the entire stock—the estimated value of which was three millions sterling—to be thrown into the sea, and thus gave to the world an example of thoroughness in dealing with a great abuse which, fatal though it proved to China, may not be without its use hereafter. In this way originated the opium war, the parent of all the succeeding wars with China—a struggle in which British grape-shot mowed down the Celestials like grass, and our men-of-war made equally short work of the Chinese junks. We compelled the Chinese to sue for peace, and to pay an indemnity of upwards of four millions sterling; but there was one thing which they stubbornly refused to do—they would not legalize the trade to which all their misfortunes were due. It was pointed out to the Emperor that if he insisted on declaring the trade contraband, smuggling would still go on; whereas if he consented to impose an import duty on the opium, he might derive therefrom a revenue of £1,200,000 a year. His answer merits the attention of those Indian administrators who argue that they ought not to give up the traffic because of the princely revenue it yields. "It is true," he said, "I cannot prevent the introduction of the flowing poison; gain-seeking and corrupt men will, for profit and sensuality, defeat my wishes, but nothing will induce me to derive a revenue from the vice and misery of my people." It needed two other wars, as well as the moral impression produced by the sack of the Summer Palace and the fall of Pekin, to break down what some people are disposed to regard as the stupid prejudices of the Chinese against the legalization of the noxious drug.

Lord Elgin's treaty apparently placed the trade upon a secure footing. At last the ban of Celestial law was withdrawn from it, and opium was enabled to take its place side by side with the products of Lancashire looms and Birmingham workshops. The opium smuggler was transformed into an opium merchant. No pirate could have been made more respectable if the Admiralty, besides condoning his past offences, had appointed him to the commission of one of Her Majesty's ships. As for the Imperial Government, nothing could have been more opportune than the legalization of a trade for the prosecution of which, on the political extinction of the East India Company, it necessarily became largely responsible. That Government was enabled to cultivate opium under the Indian monopoly, and even to extend the area of cultivation as the now lawful appetites of the Chinese were enlarged, without any further apprehension from prohibitory laws, which the sword had cut in twain, and which, indeed, Lord Elgin's treaty had formally abrogated. There was, however, one fly in the pot of ointment. The Chinese, from eating opium in ever-increasing quantities (for since the year 1800 the exports from India have multiplied nearly forty-fold), have taken to cultivating it on a large scale. I have the authority of a gentleman who recently made a journey of more than three thousand miles in the west of China, traversing the provinces of Hoo-pih, Sze-chuen, and Shen-se, "and found nearly everywhere evidence of extensive cultivation." This home cultivation has all grown up during the last twenty years. It has already driven out the opium which formerly enriched Burmah at the expense of Western China Chinese opium has two qualities which render it a formidable competitor to the Indian poppy. It only costs half the price, and is not nearly so deleterious. It therefore seems probable that while the rich epicure will still consume the foreign article, the poorer slaves of the vice will be content with wasting their substance on the drug of native growth and manufacture.

The Imperial edicts prohibiting the cultivation of the poppy in the provinces of the empire are still unrepealed, but for the present they remain a dead letter. What adequate motive can the Emperor and his council have for enforcing these edicts so long as they are not permitted to deal with the foreign trade? The money expended on opium, if spent in the country, would not be so absolutely unproductive as if it were all sent abroad in exchange for the Indian drug. On the other hand, the Chinese Government is naturally alarmed at the extent to which the good lands of the empire are being used up by the cultivation of the poppy. China is an excessively poor and overcrowded country, and cannot afford to give to opium land which ought to yield food for the people. Choo-Tsun, a statesman who lived long enough to foresee, but not long enough actually to witness, the downfall of the empire, many years ago put this pertinent question: "If all the rich and fertile ground be used for planting the poppy, and if the people, hoping for a large profit therefrom, madly engage in its cultivation, where will flax and the mulberry-tree be cultivated, or wheat and rye be planted?" Two years ago the answer to this inquiry was virtually given by one of the censors at Pekin, who, in a memorial to the throne, complained that there had been "a great scarcity of food in Shensi and Kiangsu, where the opium-farming mostly prevails," and that "the laborers give their strength and time to the poppy, while wheat and millet are neglected."

Last year the Under-Secretary for India was somewhat despondent at the falling off in the opium revenue. This session his tone is more hopeful. The revenue has revived, and the prophets of evil—who were, however, chiefly connected with the Indian Department—stand rebuked. It is not impossible that the new-born confidence may be as premature as the recent depression. It is true that Mr. Grant Duff plumes himself on "the excellent" quality of Indian opium. It is indeed so "excellent" that it destroys the Chinese more quickly than the homemade drug; and if the object be to decimate China, or to multiply the number of sensual imbeciles and paupers, no one can deny that this end is likely to be attained. But unfortunately for the prospects of Indian opium, Mr. D. B. Robertson, her Majesty's Consul at Canton, has lately discovered a marked improvement in the quality of native opium which is now, he says, equal to Malwa—a tribute calculated to induce Mr. Grant Duff to look well to his laurels. M. Huc, who published his "Chinese Empire" sixteen years ago, anticipated this very state of things, and, indeed predicted that when the Chinese made at home all the opium necessary for their own consumption, "British India would experience a terrible blow—one that might possibly even be felt in the British metropolis." In allusion to the increasing use of laudanum in our manufacturing towns, the learned French traveller even speculated upon the possibility of England one day sending to China for the means of gratifying the depraved tastes of her own people. Those who have read Dr. Bridge's remarks on the prevalence of this evil in our northern towns, will hardly regard M. Huc's idea as so fanciful as to be absurd.

In the debate on Sir Wilfrid Lawson's motion, the Under-

Secretary endeavored to produce the impression that the evils of opium-smoking and opium-eating had been enormously exaggerated. Mr. Gladstone, in a more cautious temper, argued that the question was an open one; and by resorting to what I must call a species of casuistry, gave just offence to many of his supporters, who thought that he, at any rate, would not fail to recognize the value of those moral considerations to which the originators of the discussion had appealed. The time has gone by for impeaching the facts upon which the exceptional enormity of the traffic is based. In China, from the Emperor and his chief officers down to the native painter who, after the manner of Hogarth, has depicted the successive stages of the opium-smoker's progress from prosperity to ruin, there has been but one testimony as to the frightful injury which the use of opium is inflicting on the people. It may consist with official ideas of expediency to represent the assailants of the trade as drawing upon their imaginations for their facts, but it must not be forgotten that there is the strongest official evidence in support of even the extreme views which found expression in the speeches of the minority in the House of Commons. A select committee of that House is not a bad witness in such a case, and the select committee which sat in 1840, reported that "the demoralizing results of the opium trade are incontestable and inseparable from its existence;" while the East India Company, in a notable access of candor, declared that "were it possible to prevent the use of the drug altogether, except strictly for the purpose of medicine, we would gladly do it in compassion to mankind." A sentence like this conclusively reveals the existence of those mortal perturbations which secretly disturb the equanimity of even the most confirmed offenders against public morality. Similarly the slaveholders of the Southern States would sometimes admit that their "peculiar institution" was an evil of colossal magnitude, although, like the East India Company, they never sufficiently turned from their evil ways to resist the temptation to extend the system of which they professed to be unwilling supporters.

The opium trade has vitiated the whole of our relations with the Chinese Empire. That trade simply embodies in its most odious form the pretended right of the strong to ride rough-shod over the weak. The mob who, in driving a missionary out of a Chinese city, taunted him with hypocrisy in coming to teach them virtue when his countrymen "had burned their palace, killed their emperor, and sold poison to their people," may have been as brutal and unreasoning as mobs of the lowest class generally are, but it would be absurd to deny that their shout had in it a painful element of truth. The horrible spirit of fanaticism which resulted in the recent massacre at Tientsin merited a severe example of retributive justice; but it should, nevertheless, be remembered that during the last few years the French have dragooned the Chinese Government into making concessions which were eminently calculated to inflame the passions of an ignorant populace. To mention only one fact—the French Government has compelled the Chinese to restore to the Jesuits property which, although granted to them two centuries back, was confiscated at the time of the Christian persecution a hundred and fifty years ago. An observant Englishman, writing to me from China, says that "the right of beating Chinese servants is openly claimed by the English masters, and our consular agents shrink from restraining this violence by proper severity." If the European, intoxicated with the pride of race, behaves in this lawless manner to his Chinese dependants, is it surprising that the latter should avail themselves of the first opportunity to retaliate? Professor Pumpelly of Harvard University, in his work "Across America and Asia," relates an incident which, if he did not speak with the authority of an eye-witness, one would be disposed to read with incredulity. After remarking that to the average foreigner "the teeming population around him is simply a swarm of chattering animals useful as producers of tea and consumers of opium," he says:—

"A steamboat which had been undergoing repairs made a trial trip, crowded with most of the leading foreigners of Shanghai, all, like myself, invited for a pleasure excursion up the Wusung River. As we were steaming at full speed we saw some distance ahead of us a large scow, loaded so heavily with bricks as to be almost unmanageable by the oars of four Chinamen who were propelling it. They saw the steamer coming, and knowing well how narrow was the channel, worked with all their force to get out of it and let the boat pass. As we all stood watching the slow motion of the scow, which we were rapidly approaching, I listened every instant for the order to stop the engine. The unwieldy craft still occupied half the channel, the coolies straining every muscle to increase her slow motion, and uttering cries which evidently begged for a few instants' grace. There was yet time to avoid collision, when the pilot called out, 'Shall I stop her, sir?' 'No,' cried the captain, 'go ahead.' There was no help for it. Horrified at hearing this cold-blooded order, I waited breathlessly for the crash, which soon came. The scow, striking under the port bow, veered around lengthwise, and was almost instantly under the paddles. A shriek, a shock, and a staggering motion of our boat, and we were again steaming up the channel. Going to the stern I could see but one of the four Chinamen, and he was motionless in the water. Among the faces of the foreigners on the crowded decks there were few traces of the feelings which every newcomer must experience after witnessing such a scene. The officers of the boat looked coolly over the side to see whether the bow and paddles had suffered any damage, and such remarks as were made on the occurrence were certainly not in favor of the victims."

This being the temper of many of the Europeans in China, it is impossible that we can regard the future of our relations with that empire with a feeling of confidence or of hope, unless indeed we believe that a day will come when the British public will insist upon conferring on the Chinese a community of rights as well as of duties. If that day should ever dawn the doom of the opium traffic—let its abolition cost Great Britain what it may—will be sealed. Indian financiers, ignoring the dictum of the Dutch Commissioners, who, in 1830, declared that "no consideration of pecuniary advantage ought to weigh with a European Government in allowing the use of opium," appear to think that in preferring revenue to morality they are clearly performing their duty to India. English statesmen, who are or should be something more than the guardians of the State money-bag, may well be excused if they think of the honor of their country and of her moral influence, which has been so rudely shaken by the selfish and aggressive character of her policy in the East. The silk and tea which we export from China render her the benefactress of the world. The opium which we introduce into the Flowery Kingdom is of a value nearly equal to the two commodities with which she enriches the commerce and the homes of the civilized world. To suppress the opium traffic, now that its roots have struck so widely and so deeply, may appear to be a Quixotic enterprise; but, at all events, there can be no just reason why the Indian Government should not be divorced from its present indefensible connection with the cultivation, manufacture, and sale of the poison, or why the Chinese Government should not be at liberty to prohibit or to restrict its importation into the empire in such manner as it may consider practicable.

In the debate of last session Mr. Grant Duff based his defence of the Bengal monopoly mainly on two grounds: first, that a revenue of seven or eight millions could not be sacrificed without gross injustice to the people of India; and, secondly, that the evils of opium smoking had been enormously exaggerated. Upon the second point I might have heaped authority on authority—Ossa upon Pelion; but enough has been said to show that the Chinese themselves entertain a very different opinion from that expressed by the Under-Secretary, and also that the Indian Government itself formerly held language which it is impossible to reconcile with the new theory of the comparative harmlessness of the drug. With regard to the question of revenue, while I cannot admit that the moral argument is affected by considerations of this nature, it must yet be admitted that, if the Indian Government were to retire from the monopoly and to substitute for it a system of export duty, the nation itself would be relieved from that direct complicity with the traffic which appears to me especially odious and indefensible. Sir William Muir, the Lieutenant-Governor of the Northwest Provinces, strongly advocates the abolition of the Government monopoly ; and he does so, partly because he believes it would greatly tend to diminish the spirit of gambling which, he says, "has ruined many a firm in Western India," and also because he is of opinion that "the change would relieve the British Government from the odious imputation of pandering to the vice of China by over-stimulating production, over-stocking the markets, and flooding China with the drug, in order to raise a wider and more secure revenue to itself." Nor does Sir W. Muir stand alone in urging these views. Mr. George Campbell, late Chief-Commissioner of Oude and now Lieutenant-Governor of Bengal, in speaking at the Newcastle Social Science Congress, declared himself in favor of abolishing the monopoly and of limiting the export from India; the Chinese Government, on its side, undertaking to do all in its power to restrict the use of the drug among its own subjects. The major question is one which comes properly under the purview of Mr. Fewcett's India Committee, which will render a service to the empire if it takes into serious consideration the present fluctuating and unstable character of the opium revenue. I so far agree with Mr. Campbell, that I believe our statesmen could not do themselves or their country more honor than by giving the Chinese Government to understand, that if it really desires to abate this great evil it would meet with every encouragement at our hands, and that no financial considerations on our part would be allowed to stand in the way of restricting or abolishing the use of the drug in the Celestial dominions.

F. W. CHESSON.

NOTE.—Since this article was written, the Indian Finance Committee has held numerous sittings. When the Blue Book reporting its proceedings is published, the reader will find in the evidence of Sir Rutherford Alcock, Dr. George Smith, of Calcutta, and the Rev. Dr. Wilson, of Bombay, ample corroboration of the statements I have made.

E.

EFFECTS OF AN EXCLUSIVE AGRICULTURE.

THE exhaustive character of the system by means of which so large a proportion of the world's population is compelled to limit itself to the barbarizing work of raising raw produce for distant markets, is well exhibited in a paragraph from a journal of the day descriptive of the state and prospects of the great COFFEE TRADE, as follows:—

"Since the emancipation of the negroes in Jamaica, where formerly large crops were gathered, coffee culture has almost entirely ceased. Cuba has changed from coffee to sugar, though that island has exported as high as fifteen thousand tons per annum. The production in the French colonies has almost ceased, amounting to less than two hundred tons per annum. St. Domingo's production, in consequence of the disorganized condition of public affairs there, is also yearly decreasing. Porto Rico yields gradually less every year, while the plantations of Surinam, Berbice, and Demerara have not been worked for several years. Venezuela maintains about an average crop, but cannot be counted on for any portion of the increase necessary to meet an increased demand. Maracaibo produced twenty-five hundred tons in 1867, and may be counted upon for something near that figure constantly. Trinidad orchards are worn out and abandoned. Coro and Curacoa produce an insignificant quantity. It was at one time supposed that Costa Rica would become a large exporter of coffee, but the scarcity of capital and hands has reduced the quantity expected from that quarter very much. Brazil has unquestionably reached her maximum production, and will not average more than two millions of bags per year, during any decade of ten years, with the probability of falling below that figure, owing to the edicts of emancipation promulgated there recently. In Ceylon there is some increase probably. The production of Manila is steadily, though slowly, on the decline. In Hindostan English energy and capital are employed in planting hundreds of new orchards, but the result is in the future. In Java and Sumatra the cultivation depends upon the forced labor of the inhabitants, who are not allowed to participate in the profits; hence the supply has reached its maximum, and it is maintained at its present height with the greatest difficulty. In Liberia a number of coffee orchards have been planted, and a source of new supply, of more or less extent, will in time come into being. In the mean time consumption increases at the rate of twenty per cent. in this country, and ten per cent. counting the civilized nations of the world ; and higher prices and adulteration seem almost certain to follow."

Throughout the whole century there has been an unceasing effort at crushing out the COTTON MANUFACTURE of India, and thus compelling export of the raw wool to Britain; and yet the whole consumption, in this latter, of India cotton, in 1871, was but 202,000,000 pounds. Nevertheless, as the highest British authorities assure us—

"The soil of India is one of the richest in the world; its productions are of the most various and most exchangeable kind; and several of its tribes show remarkable capacity for both industry and war. Altogether, the resources of this country are immense."—Greg. *Political Problems.* Quoted in *Contemporary Review*, July, 1872, p. 230.

Notwithstanding all its advantages, the total product of capital and labor, by its 150,000,000 of people, is stated at $1,500,000,000, or $10 per head. See *ante*, p. 318.

Strongly contrasting with this are the facts in regard to the French SUGAR TRADE here given, as follows:—

	Francs.	Equal to about
CANE SUGAR IMPORTED.		
1862	40,311,000	$8,060,000
1872	22,928,800	4,600,000
RAW BEET EXPORTED.		
1862	1,826,000	365,000
1872	23,298,000	4,660,000
REFINED EXPORTED.		
1862	11,632,000	2,326,000
1872	36,994,000	7,400,000

A judicious system of protection has thus, as we see, not only enabled France to supply all her own needs in regard to this important commodity, but also to contribute largely to the supply of other countries.

It is safe to say that under a system of perfect protection to American and Indian industries, like to that which in France has been given to the beet root culture, the cotton production of the two countries would be now treble what it is; enabling their people to consume thrice more largely of the products of European skill and taste than they do of the inferior manufactures with which they are now supplied.

F.

THE PROLETARIAT.

THE general adoption by English writers of the word "proletaire" as indicating the man who lives by the labor of his hands, and the danger that the bad example may be elsewhere followed, seem to make it proper here to show how essentially different are the conditions of the "proletariat" of the past, and that of the present, as this latter is now exhibited in Britain herself, and in her dependencies. That it is which it is proposed here to do, as follows:—

The Roman Census and the Assessment Roll were one and the same. Therein, the proletaire figured as a citizen of the lowest class, paying revenue to the state only by means of begetting children for its service.* That he was, *on that score*, considered a valuable member of the community, is a fact which exhibits itself in works of the chief writers on the Roman law. The time had yet to come when, under the trading dispensation, man was to be regarded, and treated, as "a drug," and population as "a nuisance;" yet is it doubtful if, in the long period that has since elapsed, there has been any material, if indeed any, increase in the numbers of mankind.†

Looking now to the "proletaire" of that chief of the British possessions, India, we find him to have been so entirely deprived of power for combining with his fellow men, that of the physical and mental power with which he has been endowed by far the larger portion is absolutely wasted. As a consequence of this, production is so insignificant that the government, although sole rent-receiver, finds itself wholly unable to meet the demands upon it except by aid of taxation on one hand, and monopoly on another, destructive beyond anything that is elsewhere known.‡ Still unable to cover the constantly recurring deficit, it has now

* "*Proletarius*, according to a division of the people by Servius Tullius, a citizen of the lowest class, who served the state, not with his property, but only with his children."—ANDREWS's *Latin-English Lexicon.*

† The Western Continent seems then to have been far more fully peopled than it is at present. Such, too, was the case with Africa, with Eastern Europe, and with Western, Central, and Northern Asia. The increase in Southern and Eastern Asia, and in Western Europe, may have sufficed to make amends for diminution elsewhere, but that it cannot have done much more than this is very certain; Mr. Malthus's remedies for the disease of over population, war, pestilence, and famine, having throughout the whole period been in most active operation.

‡ See pages 82, 318, 343, *ante.*

been found necessary to introduce that latest invention of the trading school of economists, an income tax, whose very idea as applied to a country in which the total product of labor and capital is but about $10 per head, seems pre-eminently ridiculous.* What is its operation is well exhibited in a pamphlet just now published, from which the following is an extract:—

"Many days ago, we wrote, a poor man was assessed in the Koomaikhalle Subdivision at 6 rupees ($3). Not able to pay it, 'the judge' fined him 12 rupees ($6), and in default he was sentenced to twelve days' imprisonment. His property was sold and realized Rs. 12. The amount then demanded was raised to Rs. 15, and the man was again apprehended for the remaining Rs. 3. The judge again mulcted him in double the amount and for Rs. 6 instead of Rs. 3. He was sentenced to twelve days' imprisonment with hard labor. If his property could realize no more than Rs. 12, it is clear that he ought not under the law to have been assessed. This man supported his family by his daily labor; he is now imprisoned, and what have they to look to? The Mahommedan rulers took away property by force; Biswanath Baboo was a noted robber. But these afflicted the rich, not the poor. Our government says, the tax only affects those who have property, but here we cannot walk on the streets for the crying of the poor."†

Ground to the earth by taxation while practically prohibited from making any profitable use of time or mind, the unfortunate "proletaire" sells himself to slavery in the Mauritus, or in Guiana, in which latter he may now be studied, as follows:—

Turning to page 285, *ante*, the reader will see in that colony a population of 150,000, unprovided with any but the rudest machinery of production, paying to those who stand between them and their customers a direct tax of *eighty-two dollars per head.* Add to this, the abounding indirect taxes paid on the long and tedious road by which their products need to travel in search of consumers, and it will be seen that the process of to-day is but a repetition of that pursued in the days when Joshua Gee rejoiced in the idea, that of the product of colonial labor three-fourths centred in the hands of British merchants.‡ So far as regards the question of population, it is, too, little other than a reproduction of the state of things so long exhibited throughout those British West Indian Islands which at the day of emancipation exhibited little more than one slave for every three who had been imported; leaving wholly out of view the vast numbers of children that must have been there produced and murdered, under a system at which the pagan Roman would have shuddered.

* See page 343, *ante*.

† "Why was Lord Mayo assassinated?" By J. Wilson, editor of the *Indian Daily News*. London, 1872. See page 320, *ante*, for the views of Lord Mayo himself, in reference to this oppressive system of taxation.

‡ See page 195, *ante*.

Looking now to Britain herself, we see fleets, armies, and other govermental machinery, on the largest scale, requiring for their maintenance $350,000,000 per annum, but little of which is paid by any but those who must sell their services, physical or mental, if they would provide for their families or themselves. Of this vast sum a very large proportion is paid by direct taxation of commodities mainly consumed by the mere laboring class. Another is taken by means of stamps, and of those other devices which attend so large a portion of the exchanges between the laborer who has produced, and the laborer who needs to consume, the tea, the coffee, the rum, and the sugar of distant lands. The income tax bears with equal force on the man whose unremitting labor enables him to earn a few hundreds a year, and his neighbor who has realized property yielding the same amount. If the former owns the house in which he needs to live it is taxed to its entire value; whereas, his neighbor's ornamental park, embracing hundreds of acres, is scarcely taxed at all. Suffering under a system of taxation that throws upon laboring men, great and small, nearly the whole burthen of a system that is maintained for the exclusive advantage of "great capitalists" engaged in merciless "warfare" on the laborers of the world; and that thus in every manner, at home and abroad, diminishes their power to make demand for British labor; the complaining "proletaire" receives for answer, that population is so superabundant as to have become "a nuisance;" that man is "a drug;" that the laws of supply and demand apply equally to cattle and to men; and that, if he *will* marry, and *will* have children, he has no right to a seat at the table of the Giver of all good, none having been there provided for poor creatures like himself.

The Orissa "proletaire" dies of famine because unable to pay the tax on salt required for preservation of his fish; the Indian viceroy meantime receiving $250,000 a year. The Bengalese, his neighbor, driven to seek refuge in Guiana, works sixteen to twenty hours per day for a mere pittance of wages, the governor of this little colony meanwhile receiving $25,000 a year. The female "proletaire" of Liverpool makes, as we are told, six pairs of pantaloons for a shilling; the wretched den in which she lives, and for which she pays a rent, constituting part of the property of a millionaire who holds high rank among the merchant princes of the earth. The system is thus the same, look at it where we may; all these poor wretches being required to compete with each other for their own destruction.

That the "proletaire" of ancient times was a being widely different from the one here presented for consideration, will to the reader now be clearly obvious: the one having been so valued for his services in begetting children as to have freed him from taxation; the other, on the contrary, while forced to bear nearly all the burthens of the state, being condemned to celibacy to the end that he may not add to the pauperism and vagrancy to which so discreditable a system has already given birth.

The difference in the tendencies of the Roman and the British systems exhibits itself most clearly in the fact, that Ireland alone requires for maintenance of peace among its "proletaires," more troops, and, as a consequence, more taxation, than were required within the provinces of the Roman Empire; extending as this latter did from the Atlantic to and beyond the Valley of the Euphrates, and from the Cataracts of the Nile to the Irish and Baltic Seas. The whole armed forced, military and naval, under Tiberius, scarcely exceeded 170,000 men; and of these so nearly the whole were required for guarding the frontiers that the troops stationed in Italy, Spain, France, Belgium, and Germany within the Rhine, were but 10,000 in number.* Happily for the people there was then no war of capital against labor like to that which now exists; and it is as a consequence of this, that between the central power and the subject peoples there then existed none of the hostile feeling here described by one of the chief philosophers of the age as existing throughout the European Continent, in reference to the English people and their government:—

"The Indian mutiny and the Crimean war show the little sympathy for England abroad. * * * I venture to affirm that the whole Continent, though it detested the cruelties of your enemies, did not wish you to triumph. Much of this is, without doubt, to be attributed to the evil passions which make men always desire the fall of the prosperous and the strong. But much belongs to a less dishonorable cause—to the conviction of all nations that England considers them only with reference to her own greatness; that she has less sympathy than any other modern nation; that she never notices what passes among foreigners, what they think, feel, suffer, or do, but with relation to the use which England can make of their actions, their sufferings, their feelings, or their thoughts; and that when she seems to care most for them, she really cares only for herself. All this is exaggerated, but not without truth.—De Tocqueville, *Correspondence and Conversations with N. W. Senior*, London, 1872.

The tendency toward internal disturbance, foreign war and hatred, oppressive taxation, and the establishment of a proletariat, exists everywhere in the ratio of submission to the British

* For full information on this head, see the works of M. de Champagny —"*Les Cæsars*" and "*Les Antonines;*" or the review thereof in the *British Quarterly Review*, for July, 1871. The sum total of the imperial revenue is there shown to have been but $80,000,000; or little more than two-thirds of what is now required for military and naval expenses incident to the "warfare," on the labor of the world above described.

system. In all countries that effectually resist it, the reverse of this occurs; man then growing daily in his power for self-direction, and in his self-respect. Seeking evidence to this effect the reader needs but to co,mpare the American growth of the decade which closed in 1860 with that of the one that has been now completed.* That obtained, he will scarcely be led to agree with *Quarterly Reviewers* that the incorporation of the word "proletaire" into the English language is a necessity here, however it may elsewhere be required. The more carefully he shall study the facts, the more must he be led to the conclusion, that all that is needed for makiag it a "much needed" part of the languages of the world at large, is quiet submission to a system which looks to limiting all other nations to the one pursuit of raising raw products to be converted in distant markets that are controlled by traders who find in buying cheaply and selling dearly the one end and aim of human, and even of Christian, life.

As this sheet is passing through the press the receipt of the *Fortnightly Review* for the current month, September, 1872, enables the author to place before his readers important facts, by aid of which they will be enabled to determine for themselves how far recent English movements in reference to *skilled labor* have been in the direction of giving to mind increased power over matter; or, on the contrary, toward increasing the power of capital over labor, and thus reducing working men to the condition indicated by the now so frequent use of the word "proletaire."

The work reviewed on this occasion,† is one that is entitled to the highest credit, its author having, says the reviewer,

"collected the cardinal facts about industry, work, and wages, from a source which is almost inaccessible to the world, the books, the agents, and the subordinate staff of an employer of the first order, whose experience of industry was on the whole wider than that of any one else in our age. And all this," as he continues, "is worked out in a practical spirit, with perfect candor. In a word, we may say that this is almost the first time that capital has ever honestly laid its budget on the table."

At the works thus referred to, the men employed numbered 600, embracing all the departments, 13 in number, of a great machine shop. Of these, in the period from 1854 to 1869, when the world was being inundated by the products of Californian and

* See Appendix C.

† *Work and Wages*, by Thomas Brassey, M.P. London, 1872.

Australian mines, there were 3 whose wages remained perfectly stationary, 4 who gained, and 6 who lost; the general result having been reduction of wages to the extent of a shilling (24 cents) per day, for each and every of these 600 men.

By the official tables of the Royal Yard at Sheerness, it is shown that in the 20 years ending in 1869 there had been an increase of wages averaging one penny, or two cents, per day.

From 1859 to 1869, the average rate of wages in the locomotive shops of the kingdom had advanced little more than one-half of one per cent.

At the great Millville Iron Works the average rate from 1851 to 1869 had remained almost unchanged; the general result, however, having been that of a very slight decline. Commenting on this latter statement, the reviewer speaks as follows:—

"It is a curious comment on the industrious mendacity which so often obscures labor questions, thus to find the real truth about the wages of London shipwrights. It will," as he continues, "be remembered that about 1867 and 1868 the newspapers were filled with lamentations over those extortionate demands under which we were told the trade was being driven from England. It now turns out, on the authority of a manager of one of the largest London works, that the wages of shipwrights in the Thames have never risen since 1851, and that they fell between 1865–1869 from 42–48, to 39–42; and in 1869 again fell to 36–39; showing a maximum fall between 1865 and 1869 of 9*s.* upon 48*s.*, which is not far short of 20 per cent."

We have thus the great facts, that although the foreign trade had more than doubled; although investments in railroads had grown from 88 to 530 millions; although taxable incomes had enormously increased; although luxury had attained a height that before had been unimagined; the average money value of skilled labor had declined; rents, beef, mutton, pork, and cheese having, meantime, on an average almost a third increased. How entirely is all this in accordance with Mr. Huskisson's declaration to the effect that "wages must be kept down, to the end that capital may obtain proper remuneration," will be now obvious to the reader. That it might do so, the laborer, skilled or unskilled, has been, and is being, ground between the upper and the nether mill-stone.

In face of facts like these, and in face of the daily widening gulf that divides the few from the many, it is, that advocates of the existing system have the hardihood to assure the latter that "for being employed at all," they are indebted to the "sacrifices" of the former;* others meanwhile assuring advocates of labor's rights that they are "digging the free-trade grave;" con-

* See p. 183, *ante.*

servative *Quarterly Reviewers* joining in the chorus, asking of the "proletaires" to determine for themselves whence their wages are to come if the employers cease to be able to underwork the world as in times past they so generally have done.*

Directly the reverse of all this, as here is shown, wages have in the same period so largely advanced in France, Belgium, Prussia, Wurtemberg, and even in those parts of British India which now profit of railroad intercourse, that in many of the cases mentioned they have fully doubled; while in others that increase has been 40 per cent., when not even more.

The facts thus exhibited as occurring in the free-trade England, and in the protected nations of continental Europe, are in precise accordance with those here observed in periods of submission to the British system, and of resistance thereto such as now exists. In the one, there has always been large competition for the *sale* of labor, and the laborer has tended in the direction of becoming a mere "proletaire." In the other, the competition has been for the *purchase* of labor, and the laborer has daily more and more acquired power for self-direction.†

Note to Appendix B.

The results of personal observation by an accomplished English traveller, in reference to the occupation and cultivation of the earth, are so entirely confirmatory of those which have above been given, that the author deems it well here to submit them for the reader's consideration, as follows:—

"The soil about the Fox, the Buller, the Okitski, and other west coast rivers on which gold is found, is a black mould of extraordinary depth and richness; but in New Zealand, as in America, the poor lands are first occupied by the settlers, because the fat soils will pay for clearing only when there is already a considerable population on the land."—Dilke, *Greater Britain*, London edition, p. 333.

---

* See p. 257, *ante*.

† See pp. 204 to 208, *ante*.

INDEX.

CATALOGUE

OF

PRACTICAL AND SCIENTIFIC BOOKS,

PUBLISHED BY

HENRY CAREY BAIRD,

INDUSTRIAL PUBLISHER,

No. 406 WALNUT STREET,

PHILADELPHIA.

☞ Any of the Books comprised in this Catalogue will be sent by mail, free of postage, at the publication price.

☞ My New and Enlarged Catalogue, 95 pages 8vo., with full descriptions of Books, will be sent, free of postage, to any one who will favor me with his address.

ARMENGAUD, AMOUROUX, AND JOHNSON.—THE PRACTICAL DRAUGHTSMAN'S BOOK OF INDUSTRIAL DESIGN, AND MACHINIST'S AND ENGINEER'S DRAWING COMPANION: Forming a complete course of Mechanical Engineering and Architectural Drawing. From the French of M. Armengaud the elder, Prof. of Design in the Conservatoire of Arts and Industry, Paris, and MM. Armengaud the younger and Amouroux, Civil Engineers. Rewritten and arranged, with additional matter and plates, selections from and examples of the most useful and generally employed mechanism of the day. By William Johnson, Assoc. Inst. C. E., Editor of "The Practical Mechanic's Journal." Illustrated by 50 folio steel plates and 50 wood-cuts. A new edition, 4to. . $10 00

ARLOT.—A COMPLETE GUIDE FOR COACH PAINTERS. Translated from the French of M. Arlot, Coach Painter; late Master Painter for eleven years with M. Ehrler, Coach Manufacturer, Paris. With important American additions . . $1 25

ARROWSMITH.—PAPER-HANGER'S COMPANION: A Treatise in which the Practical Operations of the Trade are Systematically laid down: with Copious Directions Preparatory to Papering; Preventives against the Effect of Damp on Walls; the Various Cements and Pastes adapted to the Several Purposes of the Trade; Observations and Directions for the Panelling and Ornamenting of Rooms, &c. By James Arrowsmith. 12mo., cloth $1 25

BAIRD.—THE AMERICAN COTTON SPINNER, AND MANAGER'S AND CARDER'S GUIDE:

A Practical Treatise on Cotton Spinning; giving the Dimensions and Speed of Machinery, Draught and Twist Calculations, etc.; with notices of recent Improvements: together with Rules and Examples for making changes in the sizes and numbers of Roving and Yarn. Compiled from the papers of the late ROBERT H. BAIRD. 12mo. . . . $1 50

BAKER.—LONG-SPAN RAILWAY BRIDGES:

Comprising Investigations of the Comparative Theoretical and Practical Advantages of the various Adopted or Proposed Type Systems of Construction; with numerous Formulæ and Tables. By B. Baker. 12mo. $2 00

BAKEWELL.—A MANUAL OF ELECTRICITY—PRACTICAL AND THEORETICAL:

By F. C. BAKEWELL, Inventor of the Copying Telegraph. Second Edition. Revised and enlarged. Illustrated by numerous engravings. 12mo. Cloth . . . . .

BEANS.—A TREATISE ON RAILROAD CURVES AND THE LOCATION OF RAILROADS:

By E. W. BEANS, C. E. 12mo. . . . $2 00

BLENKARN.—PRACTICAL SPECIFICATIONS OF WORKS EXECUTED IN ARCHITECTURE, CIVIL AND MECHANICAL ENGINEERING, AND IN ROAD MAKING AND SEWERING:

To which are added a series of practically useful Agreements and Reports. By JOHN BLENKARN. Illustrated by fifteen large folding plates. 8vo. $9 00

BLINN.—A PRACTICAL WORKSHOP COMPANION FOR TIN, SHEET-IRON, AND COPPER-PLATE WORKERS:

Containing Rules for Describing various kinds of Patterns used by Tin, Sheet-iron, and Copper-plate Workers; Practical Geometry; Mensuration of Surfaces and Solids; Tables of the Weight of Metals, Lead Pipe, etc.; Tables of Areas and Circumferences of Circles; Japans, Varnishes, Lackers, Cements, Compositions, etc. etc. By LEROY J. BLINN, Master Mechanic. With over One Hundred Illustrations. 12mo. $2 50

BOOTH.—MARBLE WORKER'S MANUAL:

Containing Practical Information respecting Marbles in general, their Cutting, Working, and Polishing; Veneering of Marble; Mosaics; Composition and Use of Artificial Marble, Stuccos, Cements, Receipts, Secrets, etc. etc. Translated from the French by M. L. BOOTH. With an Appendix concerning American Marbles. 12mo., cloth . . $1 50

BOOTH AND MORFIT.—THE ENCYCLOPEDIA OF CHEMISTRY, PRACTICAL AND THEORETICAL:

Embracing its application to the Arts, Metallurgy, Mineralogy, Geology, Medicine, and Pharmacy. By JAMES C. BOOTH, Melter and Refiner in the United States Mint, Professor of Applied Chemistry in the Franklin Institute, etc., assisted by CAMPBELL MORFIT, author of "Chemical Manipulations," etc. Seventh edition. Complete in one volume, royal 8vo., 978 pages, with numerous wood-cuts and other illustrations. $5 00

BOWDITCH.—ANALYSIS, TECHNICAL VALUATION, PURIFICATION, AND USE OF COAL GAS:

By Rev. W. R. BOWDITCH. Illustrated with wood engravings. 8vo. $6 50

BOX.—PRACTICAL HYDRAULICS:

A Series of Rules and Tables for the use of Engineers, etc. By THOMAS BOX. 12mo. $2 50

BUCKMASTER.—THE ELEMENTS OF MECHANICAL PHYSICS:

By J. C. BUCKMASTER, late Student in the Government School of Mines; Certified Teacher of Science by the Department of Science and Art; Examiner in Chemistry and Physics in the Royal College of Preceptors; and late Lecturer in Chemistry and Physics of the Royal Polytechnic Institute. Illustrated with numerous engravings. In one vol. 12mo. . $1 50

BULLOCK.—THE AMERICAN COTTAGE BUILDER:

A Series of Designs, Plans, and Specifications, from $200 to to $20,000 for Homes for the People; together with Warming, Ventilation, Drainage, Painting, and Landscape Gardening. By JOHN BULLOCK, Architect, Civil Engineer, Mechanician, and Editor of "The Rudiments of Architecture and Building," etc. Illustrated by 75 engravings. In one vol. 8vo. $3 50

BULLOCK.—THE RUDIMENTS OF ARCHITECTURE AND BUILDING:

For the use of Architects, Builders, Draughtsmen, Machinists, Engineers, and Mechanics. Edited by JOHN BULLOCK, author of "The American Cottage Builder." Illustrated by 250 engravings. In one volume 8vo. $3 50

BURGH.—PRACTICAL ILLUSTRATIONS OF LAND AND MARINE ENGINES:

Showing in detail the Modern Improvements of High and Low Pressure, Surface Condensation, and Super-heating, together with Land and Marine Boilers. By N. P. BURGH, Engineer. Illustrated by twenty plates, double elephant folio, with text. $21 00

BURGH.—PRACTICAL RULES FOR THE PROPORTIONS OF MODERN ENGINES AND BOILERS FOR LAND AND MARINE PURPOSES.

By N. P. BURGH, Engineer. 12mo. $2 00

BURGH.—THE SLIDE-VALVE PRACTICALLY CONSIDERED:

By N. P. BURGH, author of "A Treatise on Sugar Machinery," "Practical Illustrations of Land and Marine Engines," "A Pocket-Book of Practical Rules for Designing Land and Marine Engines, Boilers," etc. etc. etc. Completely illustrated. 12mo. $2 00

BYRN.—THE COMPLETE PRACTICAL BREWER:

Or, Plain, Accurate, and Thorough Instructions in the Art of Brewing Beer, Ale, Porter, including the Process of making Bavarian Beer, all the Small Beers, such as Root-beer, Ginger-pop, Sarsaparilla-beer, Mead, Spruce beer, etc. etc. Adapted to the use of Public Brewers and Private Families. By M. LA FAYETTE BYRN, M. D. With illustrations. 12mo. $1 25

BYRN.—THE COMPLETE PRACTICAL DISTILLER:

Comprising the most perfect and exact Theoretical and Practical Description of the Art of Distillation and Rectification; including all of the most recent improvements in distilling apparatus; instructions for preparing spirits from the numerous vegetables, fruits, etc.; directions for the distillation and preparation of all kinds of brandies and other spirits, spirituous and other compounds, etc. etc.; all of which is so simplified that it is adapted not only to the use of extensive distillers, but for every farmer, or others who may wish to engage in the art of distilling By M. LA FAYETTE BYRN, M. D. With numerous engravings. In one volume, 12mo. $1 50

BYRNE.—POCKET BOOK FOR RAILROAD AND CIVIL ENGINEERS:

Containing New, Exact, and Concise Methods for Laying out Railroad Curves, Switches, Frog Angles and Crossings; the Staking out of work; Levelling; the Calculation of Cuttings; Embankments; Earth-work, etc. By OLIVER BYRNE. Illustrated, 18mo., full bound $1 75

BYRNE.—THE HANDBOOK FOR THE ARTISAN, MECHANIC, AND ENGINEER:

By OLIVER BYRNE. Illustrated by 185 Wood Engravings. 8vo. $5 00

BYRNE.—THE ESSENTIAL ELEMENTS OF PRACTICAL MECHANICS:

For Engineering Students, based on the Principle of Work. By OLIVER BYRNE. Illustrated by Numerous Wood Engravings, 12mo. $3 63

BYRNE.—THE PRACTICAL METAL-WORKER'S ASSISTANT:

Comprising Metallurgic Chemistry; the Arts of Working all Metals and Alloys; Forging of Iron and Steel; Hardening and Tempering; Melting and Mixing; Casting and Founding; Works in Sheet Metal; the Processes Dependent on the Ductility of the Metals; Soldering; and the most Improved Processes and Tools employed by Metal-Workers. With the Application of the Art of Electro-Metallurgy to Manufacturing Processes; collected from Original Sources, and from the Works of Holtzapffel, Bergeron, Leupold, Plumier, Napier, and others. By OLIVER BYRNE. A New, Revised, and improved Edition, with Additions by John Scoffern, M. B , William Clay, Wm. Fairbairn, F. R. S., and James Napier. With Five Hundred and Ninety-two Engravings; Illustrating every Branch of the Subject. In one volume, 8vo. 652 pages . $7 00

BYRNE.—THE PRACTICAL MODEL CALCULATOR:

For the Engineer, Mechanic, Manufacturer of Engine Work, Naval Architect, Miner, and Millwright. By OLIVER BYRNE. 1 volume, 8vo., nearly 600 pages $4 50

BEMROSE.—MANUAL OF WOOD CARVING: With Practical Illustrations for Learners of the Art, and Original and Selected designs. By WILLIAM BEMROSE, Jr. With an Introduction by LLEWELLYN JEWITT, F. S. A., etc. With 128 Illustrations. 4to., cloth $3 00

BAIRD.—PROTECTION OF HOME LABOR AND HOME PRODUCTIONS NECESSARY TO THE PROSPERITY OF THE AMERICAN FARMER:

By HENRY CAREY BAIRD. 8vo., paper 10

BAIRD.—THE RIGHTS OF AMERICAN PRODUCERS, AND THE WRONGS OF BRITISH FREE TRADE REVENUE REFORM.

By HENRY CAREY BAIRD. (1870) 5

BAIRD.—SOME OF THE FALLACIES OF BRITISH-FREE-TRADE REVENUE-REFORM.

Two Letters to Prof. A. L. Perry, of Williams College, Mass. By HENRY CAREY BAIRD. (1871.) Paper 5

BAIRD.—STANDARD WAGES COMPUTING TABLES:

An Improvement in all former Methods of Computation, so arranged that wages for days, hours, or fractions of hours, at a specified rate per day or hour, may be ascertained at a glance. By T. SPANGLER BAIRD. Oblong folio $5 00

BAUERMAN.—TREATISE ON THE METALLURGY OF IRON.

Illustrated. 12mo. $2 50

BICKNELL'S VILLAGE BUILDER.

55 large plates. 4to. $10 00

BISHOP.—A HISTORY OF AMERICAN MANUFACTURES:

From 1608 to 1866; exhibiting the Origin and Growth of the Principal Mechanic Arts and Manufactures, from the Earliest Colonial Period to the Present Time; By J. LEANDER BISHOP, M. D., EDWARD YOUNG, and EDWIN T. FREEDLEY. Three vols. 8vo., $10 00

BOX.—A PRACTICAL TREATISE ON HEAT AS APPLIED TO THE USEFUL ARTS:

For the use of Engineers, Architects, etc. By THOMAS BOX, author of "Practical Hydraulics." Illustrated by 14 plates, containing 114 figures. 12mo. $4 25

CABINET MAKER'S ALBUM OF FURNITURE:

Comprising a Collection of Designs for the Newest and Most Elegant Styles of Furniture. Illustrated by Forty-eight Large and Beautifully Engraved Plates. In one volume, oblong $5 00

CHAPMAN.—A TREATISE ON ROPE-MAKING:

As practised in private and public Rope-yards, with a Description of the Manufacture, Rules, Tables of Weights, etc., adapted to the Trade; Shipping, Mining, Railways, Builders, etc. By ROBERT CHAPMAN. 24mo. $1 50

CRAIK.—THE PRACTICAL AMERICAN MILLWRIGHT AND MILLER.

Comprising the Elementary Principles of Mechanics, Mechanism, and Motive Power, Hydraulics and Hydraulic Motors, Mill-dams, Saw Mills, Grist Mills, the Oat Meal Mill, the Barley Mill, Wool Carding, and Cloth Fulling and Dressing, Wind Mills, Steam Power, &c. By DAVID CRAIK, Millwright. Illustrated by numerous wood engravings, and five folding plates. 1 vol. 8vo. $5 00

CAMPIN.—A PRACTICAL TREATISE ON MECHANICAL ENGINEERING:

Comprising Metallurgy, Moulding, Casting, Forging, Tools, Workshop Machinery, Mechanical Manipulation, Manufacture of Steam-engines, etc. etc. With an Appendix on the Analysis of Iron and Iron Ores. By FRANCIS CAMPIN, C. E. To which are added, Observations on the Construction of Steam Boilers, and Remarks upon Furnaces used for Smoke Prevention; with a Chapter on Explosions. By R. Armstrong, C. E., and John Bourne. Rules for Calculating the Change Wheels for Screws on a Turning Lathe, and for a Wheel-cutting Machine. By J. LA NICCA. Management of Steel, including Forging, Hardening, Tempering, Annealing, Shrinking, and Expansion. And the Case-hardening of Iron. By G. EDE. 8vo. Illustrated with 29 plates and 100 wood engravings. $6 00

CAMPIN.—THE PRACTICE OF HAND-TURNING IN WOOD, IVORY, SHELL, ETC.:

With Instructions for Turning such works in Metal as may be required in the Practice of Turning Wood, Ivory, etc. Also an Appendix on Ornamental Turning. By FRANCIS CAMPIN, with Numerous Illustrations, 12mo., cloth . . $3 00

CAPRON DE DOLE.—DUSSAUCE.—BLUES AND CARMINES OF INDIGO.

A Practical Treatise on the Fabrication of every Commercial Product derived from Indigo. By FELICIEN CAPRON DE DOLE Translated, with important additions, by Professor H. DUSSAUCE. 12mo.

CAREY.—THE WORKS OF HENRY C. CAREY:

CONTRACTION OR EXPANSION? REPUDIATION OR RESUMPTION? Letters to Hon. Hugh McCulloch. 8vo. 38

FINANCIAL CRISES, their Causes and Effects. 8vo. paper 25

HARMONY OF INTERESTS; Agricultural, Manufacturing, and Commercial. 8vo., paper $1 00
Do. do. cloth $1 50

LETTERS TO THE PRESIDENT OF THE UNITED STATES. Paper $1 00

MANUAL OF SOCIAL SCIENCE. Condensed from Carey's "Principles of Social Science." By KATE MCKEAN. 1 vol. 12mo. $2 25

MISCELLANEOUS WORKS: comprising "Harmony of Interests," "Money," "Letters to the President," "French and American Tariffs," "Financial Crises," "The Way to Outdo England without Fighting Her," "Resources of the Union," "The Public Debt," "Contraction or Expansion," "Review of the Decade 1857—'67," "Reconstruction," etc. etc. 1 vol. 8vo., cloth $4 50

MONEY: A LECTURE before the N. Y. Geographical and Statistical Society. 8vo., paper 25

PAST, PRESENT, AND FUTURE. 8vo. $2 50

PRINCIPLES OF SOCIAL SCIENCE. 3 volumes 8vo., cloth $10 00

REVIEW OF THE DECADE 1857—'67. 8vo., paper 50

RECONSTRUCTION: INDUSTRIAL, FINANCIAL, AND POLITICAL. Letters to the Hon. Henry Wilson, U. S. S. 8vo. paper 50

THE PUBLIC DEBT, LOCAL AND NATIONAL. How to provide for its discharge while lessening the burden of Taxation. Letter to David A. Wells, Esq., U. S. Revenue Commission. 8vo., paper 25

THE RESOURCES OF THE UNION. A Lecture read, Dec. 1865, before the American Geographical and Statistical Society, N. Y., and before the American Association for the Advancement of Social Science, Boston 50

THE SLAVE TRADE, DOMESTIC AND FOREIGN; Why it Exists, and How it may be Extinguished. 12mo., cloth $1 50

LETTERS ON INTERNATIONAL COPYRIGHT. (1867.) Paper 50

REVIEW OF THE FARMERS' QUESTION. (1870.) Paper 25

RESUMPTION! HOW IT MAY PROFITABLY BE BROUGHT AROUT. (1869.) 8vo., paper 50

REVIEW OF THE REPORT OF HON. D. A. WELLS, Special Commissioner of the Revenue. (1869.) 8vo., paper 50

SHALL WE HAVE PEACE? Peace Financial and Peace Political. Letters to the President Elect. (1868.) 8vo., paper 50

THE FINANCE MINISTER AND THE CURRENCY, AND THE PUBLIC DEBT. (1868.) 8vo., paper . . 50

THE WAY TO OUTDO ENGLAND WITHOUT FIGHTING HER. Letters to Hon. Schuyler Colfax. (1865.) 8vo., paper $1 00

WEALTH! OF WHAT DOES IT CONSIST? (1870.) Paper 25

CAMUS.—A TREATISE ON THE TEETH OF WHEELS:

Demonstrating the best forms which can be given to them for the purposes of Machinery, such as Mill-work and Clock-work. Translated from the French of M. CAMUS. By JOHN I. HAWKINS. Illustrated by 40 plates. 8vo. $3 00

COXE.—MINING LEGISLATION.

A paper read before the Am. Social Science Association. By ECKLEY B. COXE. Paper 20

COLBURN.—THE GAS-WORKS OF LONDON:

Comprising a sketch of the Gas-works of the city, Process of Manufacture, Quantity Produced, Cost, Profit, etc. By ZERAH COLBURN. 8vo., cloth 75

COLBURN.—THE LOCOMOTIVE ENGINE:

Including a Description of its Structure, Rules for Estimating its Capabilities, and Practical Observations on its Construction and Management. By ZERAH COLBURN. Illustrated. A new edition. 12mo. $1 25

COLBURN AND MAW.—THE WATER-WORKS OF LONDON:

Together with a Series of Articles on various other Waterworks. By ZERAH COLBURN and W. MAW. Reprinted from "Engineering." In one volume, 8vo. . . $4 00

DAGUERREOTYPIST AND PHOTOGRAPHER'S COMPANION:

12mo., cloth $1 25

DIRCKS.—PERPETUAL MOTION:

Or Search for Self-Motive Power during the 17th, 18th, and 19th centuries. Illustrated from various authentic sources in Papers, Essays, Letters, Paragraphs, and numerous Patent Specifications, with an Introductory Essay by HENRY DIRCKS, C. E. Illustrated by numerous engravings of machines. 12mo., cloth $3 50

DIXON.—THE PRACTICAL MILLWRIGHT'S AND ENGINEER'S GUIDE:

Or Tables for Finding the Diameter and Power of Cogwheels; Diameter, Weight, and Power of Shafts; Diameter and Strength of Bolts, etc. etc. By THOMAS DIXON. 12mo., cloth. $1 50

DUNCAN.—PRACTICAL SURVEYOR'S GUIDE:

Containing the necessary information to make any person, of common capacity, a finished land surveyor without the aid of a teacher. By ANDREW DUNCAN. Illustrated. 12mo., cloth. $1 25

DUSSAUCE.—A NEW AND COMPLETE TREATISE ON THE ARTS OF TANNING, CURRYING, AND LEATHER DRESSING:

Comprising all the Discoveries and Improvements made in France, Great Britain, and the United States. Edited from Notes and Documents of Messrs. Sallerou, Grouvelle, Duval, Dessables, Labarraque, Payen, René, De Fontenelle, Malapeyre, etc. etc. By Prof. H. DUSSAUCE, Chemist. Illustrated by 212 wood engravings. 8vo. $10 00

DUSSAUCE—A GENERAL TREATISE ON THE MANUFACTURE OF SOAP, THEORETICAL AND PRACTICAL:

Comprising the Chemistry of the Art, a Description of all the Raw Materials and their Uses. Directions for the Establishment of a Soap Factory, with the necessary Apparatus, Instructions in the Manufacture of every variety of Soap, the Assay and Determination of the Value of Alkalies, Fatty Substances, Soaps, etc. etc. By PROFESSOR H. DUSSAUCE. With an Appendix, containing Extracts from the Reports of the International Jury on Soaps, as exhibited in the Paris Universal Exposition, 1867, numerous Tables, etc etc. Illustrated by engravings. In one volume 8vo. of over 800 pages $10 00

DUSSAUCE.—PRACTICAL TREATISE ON THE FABRICATION OF MATCHES, GUN COTTON, AND FULMINATING POWDERS.

By Professor H. DUSSAUCE. 12mo. $3 00

DUSSAUCE.—A PRACTICAL GUIDE FOR THE PERFUMER:
Being a New Treatise on Perfumery the most favorable to the Beauty without being injurious to the Health, comprising a Description of the substances used in Perfumery, the Formulæ of more than one thousand Preparations, such as Cosmetics, Perfumed Oils, Tooth Powders, Waters, Extracts, Tinctures, Infusions, Vinaigres, Essential Oils, Pastels, Creams, Soaps, and many new Hygienic Products not hitherto described. Edited from Notes and Documents of Messrs. Debay, Lunel, etc. With additions by Professor H. DUSSAUCE, Chemist. 12mo. $3 00

DUSSAUCE.—A GENERAL TREATISE ON THE MANUFACTURE OF VINEGAR, THEORETICAL AND PRACTICAL.
Comprising the various methods, by the slow and the quick processes, with Alcohol, Wine, Grain, Cider, and Molasses, as well as the Fabrication of Wood Vinegar, etc. By Prof. H. DUSSAUCE. 12mo. $5 00

DUPLAIS.—A COMPLETE TREATISE ON THE DISTILLATION AND MANUFACTURE OF ALCOHOLIC LIQUORS:
From the French of M. DUPLAIS. Translated and Edited by M. MCKENNIE, M D. Illustrated by numerous large plates and wood engravings of the best apparatus calculated for producing the finest products. In one vol. royal 8vo. $10 00

☞ This is a treatise of the highest scientific merit and of the greatest practical value, surpassing in these respects, as well as in the variety of its contents, any similar volume in the English language.

DE GRAFF.—THE GEOMETRICAL STAIR-BUILDERS' GUIDE:
Being a Plain Practical System of Hand-Railing, embracing all its necessary Details, and Geometrically Illustrated by 22 Steel Engravings; together with the use of the most approved principles of Practical Geometry. By SIMON DE GRAFF, Architect. 4to. $5 00

DYER AND COLOR-MAKER'S COMPANION:
Containing upwards of two hundred Receipts for making Colors, on the most approved principles, for all the various styles and fabrics now in existence; with the Scouring Process, and plain Directions for Preparing, Washing-off, and Finishing the Goods. In one vol. 12mo. $1 25

EASTON.—A PRACTICAL TREATISE ON STREET OR HORSE-POWER RAILWAYS:

Their Location, Construction, and Management; with General Plans and Rules for their Organization and Operation; together with Examinations as to their Comparative Advantages over the Omnibus System, and Inquiries as to their Value for Investment; including Copies of Municipal Ordinances relating thereto. By ALEXANDER EASTON, C. E. Illustrated by 23 plates, 8vo., cloth $2 00

FORSYTH.—BOOK OF DESIGNS FOR HEAD-STONES, MURAL, AND OTHER MONUMENTS:

Containing 78 Elaborate and Exquisite Designs. By FORSYTH. 4to., cloth $5 00

*** This volume, for the beauty and variety of its designs, has never been surpassed by any publication of the kind, and should be in the hands of every marble-worker who does fine monumental work.

FAIRBAIRN.—THE PRINCIPLES OF MECHANISM AND MACHINERY OF TRANSMISSION:

Comprising the Principles of Mechanism, Wheels, and Pulleys, Strength and Proportions of Shafts, Couplings of Shafts, and Engaging and Disengaging Gear. By WILLIAM FAIRBAIRN, Esq., C. E., LL. D., F. R. S., F. G. S., Corresponding Member of the National Institute of France, and of the Royal Academy of Turin; Chevalier of the Legion of Honor, etc. etc. Beautifully illustrated by over 150 wood-cuts. In one volume 12mo. $2 50

FAIRBAIRN.—PRIME-MOVERS:

Comprising the Accumulation of Water-power; the Construction of Water-wheels and Turbines; the Properties of Steam; the Varieties of Steam-engines and Boilers and Wind-mills. By WILLIAM FAIRBAIRN, C. E , LL. D., F. R. S., F. G. S. Author of "Principles of Mechanism and the Machinery of Transmission." With Numerous Illustrations. In one volume. (In press.)

GILBART.—A PRACTICAL TREATISE ON BANKING:

By JAMES WILLIAM GILBART. To which is added: THE NATIONAL BANK ACT AS NOW IN FORCE. 8vo. . . . $4 50

GESNER.—A PRACTICAL TREATISE ON COAL, PETROLEUM, AND OTHER DISTILLED OILS.

By ABRAHAM GESNER, M. D., F. G. S. Second edition, revised and enlarged. By GEORGE WELTDEN GESNER, Consulting Chemist and Engineer. Illustrated. 8vo. . . . $3 50

GOTHIC ALBUM FOR CABINET MAKERS:
Comprising a Collection of Designs for Gothic Furniture. Illustrated by twenty-three large and beautifully engraved plates. Oblong $3 00

GRANT.—BEET-ROOT SUGAR AND CULTIVATION OF THE BEET:
By E. B. GRANT. 12mo. $1 25

GREGORY.—MATHEMATICS FOR PRACTICAL MEN:
Adapted to the Pursuits of Surveyors, Architects, Mechanics, and Civil Engineers. By OLINTHUS GREGORY. 8vo., plates, cloth $3 00

GRISWOLD.—RAILROAD ENGINEER'S POCKET COMPANION.
Comprising Rules for Calculating Deflection Distances and Angles, Tangential Distances and Angles, and all Necessary Tables for Engineers; also the art of Levelling from Preliminary Survey to the Construction of Railroads, intended Expressly for the Young Engineer, together with Numerous Valuable Rules and Examples. By W. GRISWOLD. 12mo., tucks. $1 75

GUETTIER.—METALLIC ALLOYS:
Being a Practical Guide to their Chemical and Physical Properties, their Preparation, Composition, and Uses. Translated from the French of A. GUETTIER, Engineer and Director of Founderies, author of "La Fouderie en France," etc. etc. By A. A. FESQUET, Chemist and Engineer. In one volume, 12mo. $3 00

HATS AND FELTING:
A Practical Treatise on their Manufacture. By a Practical Hatter. Illustrated by Drawings of Machinery, &c., 8vo. $1 25

HAY.—THE INTERIOR DECORATOR:
The Laws of Harmonious Coloring adapted to Interior Decorations: with a Practical Treatise on House-Painting. By D. R. HAY, House-Painter and Decorator. Illustrated by a Diagram of the Primary, Secondary, and Tertiary Colors. 12mo. $2 25

HUGHES.—AMERICAN MILLER AND MILLWRIGHT'S ASSISTANT:
By WM. CARTER HUGHES. A new edition. In one volume, 12mo. $1 50

HUNT.—THE PRACTICE OF PHOTOGRAPHY.

By Robert Hunt, Vice-President of the Photographic Society, London. With numerous illustrations. 12mo., cloth . 75

HURST.—A HAND-BOOK FOR ARCHITECTURAL SURVEYORS:

Comprising Formulæ useful in Designing Builders' work, Table of Weights, of the materials used in Building, Memoranda connected with Builders' work, Mensuration, the Practice of Builders' Measurement, Contracts of Labor, Valuation of Property, Summary of the Practice in Dilapidation, etc. etc. By J. F. Hurst, C. E. 2d edition, pocket-book form, full bound $2 50

JERVIS.—RAILWAY PROPERTY:

A Treatise on the Construction and Management of Railways; designed to afford useful knowledge, in the popular style, to the holders of this class of property; as well as Railway Managers, Officers, and Agents. By John B. Jervis, late Chief Engineer of the Hudson River Railroad, Croton Aqueduct, &c. One vol. 12mo., cloth $2 00

JOHNSON.—A REPORT TO THE NAVY DEPARTMENT OF THE UNITED STATES ON AMERICAN COALS:

Applicable to Steam Navigation and to other purposes. By Walter R. Johnson. With numerous illustrations. 607 pp. 8vo., ... $10 00

JOHNSTON.—INSTRUCTIONS FOR THE ANALYSIS OF SOILS, LIMESTONES, AND MANURES.

By J. W. F. Johnston. 12mo. 35

KEENE.—A HAND-BOOK OF PRACTICAL GAUGING,

For the Use of Beginners, to which is added a Chapter on Distillation, describing the process in operation at the Custom House for ascertaining the strength of wines. By James B. Keene, of H. M. Customs. 8vo. . . . $1 25

KENTISH.—A TREATISE ON A BOX OF INSTRUMENTS,

And the Slide Rule; with the Theory of Trigonometry and Logarithms, including Practical Geometry, Surveying, Measuring of Timber, Cask and Malt Gauging, Heights, and Distances. By THOMAS KENTISH. In one volume. 12mo. . . $1 25

KOBELL.—ERNI.—MINERALOGY SIMPLIFIED:

A short method of Determining and Classifying Minerals, by means of simple Chemical Experiments in the Wet Way. Translated from the last German Edition of F. VON KOBELL, with an Introduction to Blowpipe Analysis and other additions. By HENRI ERNI, M. D., Chief Chemist, Department of Agriculture, author of "Coal Oil and Petroleum." In one volume. 12mo. $2 50

LANDRIN.—A TREATISE ON STEEL:

Comprising its Theory, Metallurgy, Properties, Practical Working, and Use. By M. H. C. LANDRIN, Jr., Civil Engineer. Translated from the French, with Notes, by A. A. FESQUET, Chemist and Engineer. With an Appendix on the Bessemer and the Martin Processes for Manufacturing Steel, from the Report of ABRAM S. HEWITT, United States Commissioner to the Universal Exposition, Paris, 1867. 12mo. . . $3 00

LARKIN.—THE PRACTICAL BRASS AND IRON FOUNDER'S GUIDE.

A Concise Treatise on Brass Founding, Moulding, the Metals and their Alloys, etc.; to which are added Recent Improvements in the Manufacture of Iron, Steel by the Bessemer Process, etc. etc. By JAMES LARKIN, late Conductor of the Brass Foundry Department in Reany, Neafie & Co.'s Penn Works, Philadelphia. Fifth edition, revised, with extensive Additions. In one volume. 12mo. $2 25

LEAVITT.—FACTS ABOUT PEAT AS AN ARTICLE OF FUEL:
With Remarks upon its Origin and Composition, the Localities in which it is found, the Methods of Preparation and Manufacture, and the various Uses to which it is applicable; together with many other matters of Practical and Scientific Interest. To which is added a chapter on the Utilization of Coal Dust with Peat for the Production of an Excellent Fuel at Moderate Cost, especially adapted for Steam Service. By H. T. LEAVITT. Third edition. 12mo. . . . $1 75

LEROUX.—A PRACTICAL TREATISE ON THE MANUFACTURE OF WORSTEDS AND CARDED YARNS:
Translated from the French of CHARLES LEROUX, Mechanical Engineer, and Superintendent of a Spinning Mill. By Dr. H. PAINE, and A. A. FESQUET. Illustrated by 12 large plates. In one volume 8vo. $5 00

LESLIE (MISS).—COMPLETE COOKERY:
Directions for Cookery in its Various Branches. By MISS LESLIE. 60th edition. Thoroughly revised, with the addition of New Receipts. In 1 vol. 12mo., cloth . . $1 50

LESLIE (MISS). LADIES' HOUSE BOOK:
a Manual of Domestic Economy. 20th revised edition. 12mo., cloth $1 25

LESLIE (MISS).—TWO HUNDRED RECEIPTS IN FRENCH COOKERY.
12mo. 50

LIEBER.—ASSAYER'S GUIDE:
Or, Practical Directions to Assayers, Miners, and Smelters, for the Tests and Assays, by Heat and by Wet Processes, for the Ores of all the principal Metals, of Gold and Silver Coins and Alloys, and of Coal, etc. By OSCAR M. LIEBER. 12mo., cloth $1 25

LOVE.—THE ART OF DYEING, CLEANING, SCOURING, AND FINISHING:
On the most approved English and French methods; being Practical Instructions in Dyeing Silks, Woollens, and Cottons, Feathers, Chips, Straw, etc.; Scouring and Cleaning Bed and Window Curtains, Carpets, Rugs, etc.; French and English Cleaning, etc. By THOMAS LOVE. Second American Edition, to which are added General Instructions for the Use of Aniline Colors. 8vo. 5 00

MAIN AND BROWN.—QUESTIONS ON SUBJECTS CONNECTED WITH THE MARINE STEAM-ENGINE:

And Examination Papers; with Hints for their Solution. By THOMAS J. MAIN, Professor of Mathematics, Royal Naval College, and THOMAS BROWN, Chief Engineer, R. N. 12mo., cloth $1 50

MAIN AND BROWN.—THE INDICATOR AND DYNAMOMETER:

With their Practical Applications to the Steam-Engine. By THOMAS J. MAIN, M. A. F. R., Ass't Prof. Royal Naval College, Portsmouth, and THOMAS BROWN, Assoc. Inst. C. E., Chief Engineer, R. N., attached to the R. N. College. Illustrated. From the Fourth London Edition. 8vo. $1 50

MAIN AND BROWN.—THE MARINE STEAM-ENGINE.

By THOMAS J. MAIN, F. R. Ass't S. Mathematical Professor at Royal Naval College, and THOMAS BROWN, Assoc. Inst. C. E. Chief Engineer, R. N. Attached to the Royal Naval College. Authors of "Questions Connected with the Marine Steam-Engine," and the "Indicator and Dynamometer." With numerous Illustrations. In one volume 8vo. $5 00

MARTIN.—SCREW-CUTTING TABLES, FOR THE USE OF MECHANICAL ENGINEERS:

Showing the Proper Arrangement of Wheels for Cutting the Threads of Screws of any required Pitch; with a Table for Making the Universal Gas-Pipe Thread and Taps. By W. A. MARTIN, Engineer. 8vo. 50

MILES—A PLAIN TREATISE ON HORSE-SHOEING.

With Illustrations. By WILLIAM MILES, author of "The Horse's Foot"

MOLESWORTH.—POCKET-BOOK OF USEFUL FORMULÆ AND MEMORANDA FOR CIVIL AND MECHANICAL ENGINEERS.

By GUILFORD L. MOLESWORTH, Member of the Institution of Civil Engineers, Chief Resident Engineer of the Ceylon Railway. Second American from the Tenth London Edition. In one volume, full bound in pocket-book form $2 00

MOORE.—THE INVENTOR'S GUIDE:

Patent Office and Patent Laws: or, a Guide to Inventors, and a Book of Reference for Judges, Lawyers, Magistrates, and others. By J G. MOORE. 12mo., cloth $1 25

NAPIER.—A MANUAL OF ELECTRO-METALLURGY:

Including the Application of the Art to Manufacturing Processes. By JAMES NAPIER. Fourth American, from the Fourth London edition, revised and enlarged. Illustrated by engravings. In one volume, 8vo. $2 00

NAPIER.—A SYSTEM OF CHEMISTRY APPLIED TO DYEING:
By JAMES NAPIER, F. C. S. A New and Thoroughly Revised Edition, completely brought up to the present state of the Science, including the Chemistry of Coal Tar Colors. By A. A. FESQUET, Chemist and Engineer. With an Appendix on Dyeing and Calico Printing, as shown at the Paris Universal Exposition of 1867, from the Reports of the International Jury, etc. Illustrated. In one volume 8vo., 400 pages $5 00

NEWBERY.—GLEANINGS FROM ORNAMENTAL ART OF EVERY STYLE;
Drawn from Examples in the British, South Kensington, Indian, Crystal Palace, and other Museums, the Exhibitions of 1851 and 1862, and the best English and Foreign works. In a series of one hundred exquisitely drawn Plates, containing many hundred examples. By ROBERT NEWBERY. 4to. $15 00

NICHOLSON.—A MANUAL OF THE ART OF BOOK-BINDING:
Containing full instructions in the different Branches of Forwarding, Gilding, and Finishing. Also, the Art of Marbling Book-edges and Paper. By JAMES B. NICHOLSON. Illustrated. 12mo. cloth $2 25

NORRIS.—A HAND-BOOK FOR LOCOMOTIVE ENGINEERS AND MACHINISTS:
Comprising the Proportions and Calculations for Constructing Locomotives; Manner of Setting Valves; Tables of Squares, Cubes, Areas, etc. etc. By SEPTIMUS NORRIS, Civil and Mechanical Engineer. New edition. Illustrated, 12mo., cloth
$2 00

NYSTROM.—ON TECHNOLOGICAL EDUCATION AND THE CONSTRUCTION OF SHIPS AND SCREW PROPELLERS:
For Naval and Marine Engineers. By JOHN W. NYSTROM, late Acting Chief Engineer U. S. N. Second edition, revised with additional matter. Illustrated by seven engravings. 12mo.
$2 50

O'NEILL.—A DICTIONARY OF DYEING AND CALICO PRINTING:
Containing a brief account of all the Substances and Processes in use in the Art of Dyeing and Printing Textile Fabrics: with Practical Receipts and Scientific Information. By CHARLES O'NEILL, Analytical Chemist; Fellow of the Chemical Society of London; Member of the Literary and Philosophical Society of Manchester; Author of "Chemistry of Calico Printing and Dyeing." To which is added An Essay on Coal Tar Colors and their Application to

Dyeing and Calico Printing. By A. A. FESQUET, Chemist and Engineer. With an Appendix on Dyeing and Calico Printing, as shown at the Exposition of 1867, from the Reports of the International Jury, etc. In one volume 8vo., 491 pages . . $6 00

OSBORN.—THE METALLURGY OF IRON AND STEEL:

Theoretical and Practical: In all its Branches; With Special Reference to American Materials and Processes. By H. S. OSBORN, LL. D., Professor of Mining and Metallurgy in Lafayette College, Easton, Pa. Illustrated by 230 Engravings on Wood, and 6 Folding Plates. 8vo., 972 pages $10 00

OSBORN.—AMERICAN MINES AND MINING:

Theoretically and Practically Considered. By Prof. H. S. OSBORN, Illustrated by numerous engravings. 8vo. (*In preparation.*)

PAINTER, GILDER, AND VARNISHER'S COMPANION:

Containing Rules and Regulations in everything relating to the Arts of Painting, Gilding, Varnishing, and Glass Staining, with numerous useful and valuable Receipts; Tests for the Detection of Adulterations in Oils and Colors, and a statement of the Diseases and Accidents to which Painters, Gilders, and Varnishers are particularly liable, with the simplest methods of Prevention and Remedy. With Directions for Graining, Marbling, Sign Writing, and Gilding on Glass. To which are added COMPLETE INSTRUCTIONS FOR COACH PAINTING AND VARNISHING. 12mo., cloth, $1 50

PALLETT.—THE MILLER'S, MILLWRIGHT'S, AND ENGINEER'S GUIDE.

By HENRY PALLETT. Illustrated. In one vol. 12mo. . $3 00

PERKINS.—GAS AND VENTILATION.

Practical Treatise on Gas and Ventilation. With Special Relation to Illuminating, Heating, and Cooking by Gas. Including Scientific Helps to Engineer-students and others. With illustrated Diagrams. By E. E. PERKINS. 12mo., cloth . . . $1 25

PERKINS AND STOWE.—A NEW GUIDE TO THE SHEET-IRON AND BOILER PLATE ROLLER:

Containing a Series of Tables showing the Weight of Slabs and Piles to Produce Boiler Plates, and of the Weight of Piles and the Sizes of Bars to Produce Sheet-iron; the Thickness of the Bar Gauge in Decimals, the Weight per foot, and the Thickness on the Bar or Wire Gauge of the fractional parts of an inch; the Weight per sheet, and the Thickness on the Wire Gauge of Sheet-iron of various dimensions to weigh 112 lbs. per bundle; and the conversion of Short Weight into Long Weight, and Long Weight into Short. Estimated and collected by G. H. PERKINS and J. G. STOWE $2 50

PHILLIPS AND DARLINGTON.—RECORDS OF MINING AND METALLURGY:

Or, Facts and Memoranda for the use of the Mine Agent and Smelter. By J. Arthur Phillips, Mining Engineer, Graduate of the Imperial School of Mines, France, etc., and John Darlington. Illustrated by numerous engravings. In one vol. 12mo. . $2 00

PRADAL, MALEPEYRE, AND DUSSAUCE.—A COMPLETE TREATISE ON PERFUMERY:

Containing notices of the Raw Material used in the Art, and the Best Formulæ. According to the most approved Methods followed in France, England, and the United States. By M. P. Pradal, Perfumer-Chemist, and M. F. Malepeyre. Translated from the French, with extensive additions, by Prof. H. Dussauce. 8vo. $10

PROTEAUX.—PRACTICAL GUIDE FOR THE MANUFACTURE OF PAPER AND BOARDS.

By A. Proteaux, Civil Engineer, and Graduate of the School of Arts and Manufactures, Director of Thiers's Paper Mill, 'Puy-de-Dômé. With additions, by L. S. Le Normand. Translated from the French, with Notes, by Horatio Paine, A. B., M. D. To which is added a Chapter on the Manufacture of Paper from Wood in the United States, by Henry T. Brown, of the "American Artisan." Illustrated by six plates, containing Drawings of Raw Materials, Machinery, Plans of Paper-Mills, etc. etc. 8vo. $5 00

REGNAULT.—ELEMENTS OF CHEMISTRY.

By M. V. Regnault. Translated from the French by T. Forrest Benton, M. D., and edited, with notes, by James C. Booth, Melter and Refiner U. S. Mint, and Wm. L. Faber, Metallurgist and Mining Engineer. Illustrated by nearly 700 wood engravings. Comprising nearly 1500 pages. In two vols. 8vo., cloth $10 00

REID.—A PRACTICAL TREATISE ON THE MANUFACTURE OF PORTLAND CEMENT:

By Henry Reid, C. E. To which is added a Translation of M. A. Lipowitz's Work, describing a new method adopted in Germany of Manufacturing that Cement. By W. F. Reid. Illustrated by plates and wood engravings. 8vo. $7 00

RIFFAULT, VERGNAUD, AND TOUSSAINT.—A PRACTICAL TREATISE ON THE MANUFACTURE OF COLORS FOR PAINTING:

Containing the best Formulæ and the Processes the Newest and in most General Use. By MM. Riffault, Vergnaud, and Toussaint. Revised and Edited by M. F. Malepeyre and Dr. Emil Winckler. Illustrated by Engravings. In one vol. 8vo. (*In preparation.*)

RIFFAULT, VERGNAUD, AND TOUSSAINT.—A PRACTICAL TREATISE ON THE MANUFACTURE OF VARNISHES:

By MM. RIFFAULT, VERGNAUD, and TOUSSAINT. Revised and Edited by M. F. MALEPEYRE and Dr. EMIL WINCKLER. Illustrated. In one vol. 8vo. (*In preparation.*)

SHUNK.—A PRACTICAL TREATISE ON RAILWAY CURVES AND LOCATION, FOR YOUNG ENGINEERS.

By WM. F. SHUNK, Civil Engineer. 12mo., tucks . . $2 00

SMEATON.—BUILDER'S POCKET COMPANION:

Containing the Elements of Building, Surveying, and Architecture; with Practical Rules and Instructions connected with the subject. By A. C. SMEATON, Civil Engineer, etc. In one volume, 12mo. $1 50

SMITH.—THE DYER'S INSTRUCTOR:

Comprising Practical Instructions in the Art of Dyeing Silk, Cotton, Wool, and Worsted, and Woollen Goods: containing nearly 800 Receipts. To which is added a Treatise on the Art of Padding; and the Printing of Silk Warps, Skeins, and Handkerchiefs, and the various Mordants and Colors for the different styles of such work. By DAVID SMITH, Pattern Dyer, 12mo., cloth $3 00

SMITH.—THE PRACTICAL DYER'S GUIDE:

Comprising Practical Instructions in the Dyeing of Shot Cobourgs, Silk Striped Orleans, Colored Orleans from Black Warps, ditto from White Warps, Colored Cobourgs from White Warps, Merinos, Yarns, Woollen Cloths, etc. Containing nearly 300 Receipts, to most of which a Dyed Pattern is annexed. Also, a Treatise on the Art of Padding. By DAVID SMITH. In one vol. 8vo. $25 00

SHAW.—CIVIL ARCHITECTURE:

Being a Complete Theoretical and Practical System of Building, containing the Fundamental Principles of the Art. By EDWARD SHAW, Architect. To which is added a Treatise on Gothic Architecture, &c. By THOMAS W. SILLOWAY and GEORGE M. HARDING, Architects. The whole illustrated by 102 quarto plates finely engraved on copper. Eleventh Edition. 4to. Cloth. $10 00

SLOAN.—AMERICAN HOUSES:

A variety of Original Designs for Rural Buildings. Illustrated by 26 colored Engravings, with Descriptive References. By SAMUEL SLOAN, Architect, author of the "Model Architect," etc. etc. 8vo. $2 50

SCHINZ.—RESEARCHES ON THE ACTION OF THE BLAST-FURNACE.

By CHAS. SCHINZ. Seven plates. 12mo. $4 25

SMITH.—PARKS AND PLEASURE GROUNDS:

Or, Practical Notes on Country Residences, Villas, Public Parks, and Gardens. By CHARLES H. J. SMITH, Landscape Gardener and Garden Architect, etc. etc. 12mo. $2 25

STOKES.—CABINET-MAKER'S AND UPHOLSTERER'S COMPANION:

Comprising the Rudiments and Principles of Cabinet-making and Upholstery, with Familiar Instructions, Illustrated by Examples for attaining a Proficiency in the Art of Drawing, as applicable to Cabinet-work; The Processes of Veneering, Inlaying, and Buhl-work; the Art of Dyeing and Staining Wood, Bone, Tortoise Shell, etc. Directions for Lackering, Japanning, and Varnishing; to make French Polish; to prepare the Best Glues, Cements, and Compositions, and a number of Receipts, particularly for workmen generally. By J. STOKES. In one vol. 12mo. With illustrations $1 25

STRENGTH AND OTHER PROPERTIES OF METALS.

Reports of Experiments on the Strength and other Properties of Metals for Cannon. With a Description of the Machines for Testing Metals, and of the Classification of Cannon in service. By Officers of the Ordnance Department U. S. Army. By authority of the Secretary of War. Illustrated by 25 large steel plates. In 1 vol. quarto $10 00

SULLIVAN.—PROTECTION TO NATIVE INDUSTRY.

By Sir EDWARD SULLIVAN, Baronet. (1870.) 8vo. . $1 50

TABLES SHOWING THE WEIGHT OF ROUND, SQUARE, AND FLAT BAR IRON, STEEL, ETC.

By Measurement. Cloth 63

TAYLOR.—STATISTICS OF COAL:

Including Mineral Bituminous Substances employed in Arts and Manufactures; with their Geographical, Geological, and Commercial Distribution and amount of Production and Consumption on the American Continent. With Incidental Statistics of the Iron Manufacture. By R. C. TAYLOR. Second edition, revised by S. S. HALDEMAN. Illustrated by five Maps and many wood engravings. 8vo., cloth $6 00

TEMPLETON.—THE PRACTICAL EXAMINATOR ON STEAM AND THE STEAM-ENGINE:

With Instructive References relative thereto, for the Use of Engineers, Students, and others. By WM. TEMPLETON, Engineer 12mo. $1 25

THOMAS.—THE MODERN PRACTICE OF PHOTOGRAPHY.
By R. W. THOMAS, F. C. S. 8vo., cloth 75

THOMSON.—FREIGHT CHARGES CALCULATOR.
By ANDREW THOMSON, Freight Agent $1 25

TURNING: SPECIMENS OF FANCY TURNING EXECUTED ON THE HAND OR FOOT LATHE:
With Geometric, Oval, and Eccentric Chucks, and Elliptical Cutting Frame. By an Amateur. Illustrated by 30 exquisite Photographs. 4to. $3 00

TURNER'S (THE) COMPANION:
Containing Instructions in Concentric, Elliptic, and Eccentric Turning; also various Plates of Chucks, Tools, and Instruments; and Directions for using the Eccentric Cutter, Drill, Vertical Cutter, and Circular Rest; with Patterns and Instructions for working them. A new edition in 1 vol. 12mo. $1 50

URBIN—BRULL.—A PRACTICAL GUIDE FOR PUDDLING IRON AND STEEL.
By ED. URBIN, Engineer of Arts and Manufactures. A Prize Essay read before the Association of Engineers, Graduate of the School of Mines, of Liege, Belgium, at the Meeting of 1865–6. To which is added a COMPARISON OF THE RESISTING PROPERTIES OF IRON AND STEEL. By A. BRULL. Translated from the French by A. A. FESQUET, Chemist and Engineer. In one volume, 8vo. $1 00

VOGDES.—THE ARCHITECT'S AND BUILDER'S POCKET COMPANION AND PRICE BOOK.
By F. W. VOGDES, Architect. Illustrated. Full bound in pocket-book form. $2 00
In book form, 18mo., muslin 1 50

WARN.—THE SHEET METAL WORKER'S INSTRUCTOR, FOR ZINC, SHEET-IRON, COPPER AND TIN PLATE WORKERS, &c.
By REUBEN HENRY WARN, Practical Tin Plate Worker. Illustrated by 32 plates and 37 wood engravings. 8vo. . . $3 00

WATSON.—A MANUAL OF THE HAND-LATHE.
By EGBERT P. WATSON, Late of the "Scientific American," Author of "Modern Practice of American Machinists and Engineers," In one volume, 12mo. $1 50

WATSON.—THE MODERN PRACTICE OF AMERICAN MACHINISTS AND ENGINEERS:

Including the Construction, Application, and Use of Drills, Lathe Tools, Cutters for Boring Cylinders, and Hollow Work Generally, with the most Economical Speed of the same, the Results verified by Actual Practice at the Lathe, the Vice, and on the Floor. Together with Workshop management, Economy of Manufacture, the Steam-Engine, Boilers, Gears, Belting, etc. etc. By EGBERT P. WATSON, late of the "Scientific American." Illustrated by eighty-six engravings. 12mo. $2 50

WATSON.—THE THEORY AND PRACTICE OF THE ART OF WEAVING BY HAND AND POWER:

With Calculations and Tables for the use of those connected with the Trade. By JOHN WATSON, Manufacturer and Practical Machine Maker. Illustrated by large drawings of the best Power-Looms. 8vo. $10 00

WEATHERLY.—TREATISE ON THE ART OF BOILING SUGAR, CRYSTALLIZING, LOZENGE-MAKING, COMFITS, GUM GOODS,

And other processes for Confectionery, &c. In which are explained, in an easy and familiar manner, the various Methods of Manufacturing every description of Raw and Refined Sugar Goods, as sold by Confectioners and others . . . $2 00

WILL.—TABLES FOR QUALITATIVE CHEMICAL ANALYSIS.

By Prof. HEINRICH WILL, of Giessen, Germany. Seventh edition. Translated by CHARLES F. HIMES, Ph. D., Professor of Natural Science, Dickinson College, Carlisle, Pa. . . $1 25

WILLIAMS.—ON HEAT AND STEAM:

Embracing New Views of Vaporization, Condensation, and Expansion. By CHARLES WYE WILLIAMS, A. I. C. E. Illustrated. 8vo. $3 50

WORSSAM.—ON MECHANICAL SAWS:

From the Transactions of the Society of Engineers, 1867. By S. W. WORSSAM, Jr. Illustrated by 18 large folding plates. 8vo. $5 00

WÖHLER.—A HAND-BOOK OF MINERAL ANALYSIS.

By F. WÖHLER. Edited by H. B. NASON, Professor of Chemistry, Rensselaer Institute, Troy, N. Y. With numerous Illustrations. 12mo. $3 00

www.ingramcontent.com/pod-product-compliance
Lightning Source LLC
LaVergne TN
LVHW020922110826
845150LV00004B/736

* 9 7 8 1 4 2 5 5 5 4 8 7 3 *